D1416138

Kriegies, Caterpillars and Lucky Bastards

Other books by Robinson Typographics

Munster: The Way it Was

By Ian Hawkins

The Munster raid of 10 October 1943 examined in detail.

Vampire Squadron

The Saga of the 44th Fighter Squadron

by William H. Starke

They fought the war in the South Pacific from Pearl Harbor to victory.

The Saga of '54 — and More

By Charles Arthur Hair

The story of the 310th Bomb Group in their B-25s in North Africa.

Kriegies, Caterpillars and Lucky Bastards

by Glenn A. Stephens

Published by

Robinson Typographics
Anaheim, California

Copyright © 1987 by Glenn A. Stephens

All rights reserved. No part of this book may be used or reproduced
in any manner whatsoever without written permission except in the
case of brief quotations embodied in critical articles and reviews.

Library of Congress Catalog Card Number: 87-050302
ISBN Number: Regular Edition: 0-918837-05-7
Deluxe Edition: 0-918837-06-5

Printed in the United States of America
Robinson Typographics
1614 South Clementine Street
Anaheim, California 92802

Dedication

In the attack on Europe by Allied air power, almost 2,700,000 tons of bombs were dropped, more than 1,440,000 bomber sorties and 2,680,000 fighter sorties were flown. The number of combat planes reached a peak of some 28,000 and at the maximum 1,300,000 men were in combat commands. The number of men lost in air action was 79,265 Americans and 79,281 British. More than 18,000 American and 22,000 British planes were lost or damaged beyond repair.

Allied air power was decisive in the war in Western Europe. Hindsight inevitably suggests that it might have been employed differently or better in some respects. Nevertheless, it was decisive. In the air, its victory was complete. At sea, its contribution, combined with naval power, brought an end to the enemy's greatest naval threat — the U-boat; on land, it helped turn the tide overwhelmingly in favor of Allied ground forces. Its power and superiority made possible the success of the invasion. It brought the economy which sustained the enemy's armed forces to virtual collapse, although the full effects of this collapse had not reached the enemy's front lines when they were overrun by Allied forces. It brought home to the German people the full impact of modern war with all its horror and suffering. Its imprint on the German nation will be lasting.

(U.S. Strategic Bombing Survey)

This book is gratefully dedicated to the airmen and ground crew who participated in that great struggle some of whose stories are presented in this book.

With a prayer that their sacrifices will be remembered and keep my son EM1C Brian P. Stephens (US Navy) and my grandson, (born March 6, 1986) Brandon Ewalikokalikoonalani Stephens from going through the same kind of horror for their country, but that man will soon decide to live together in peace, not send their youth to die in senseless war.

The personal reminiscences of individuals included in the text of this book are those of the people to whom they are attributed, and, as nearly as possible, are in those persons own words. The author and the publisher, while grateful to those contributors, cannot accept responsibility for the content of, or opinions expressed in the individual stories. They are the creations of their authors.

Acknowledgment

This book has been a work that at times I did not think I would ever complete, however, I felt it would have been a disservice not to finish for those brave and loyal men who gave of their time and memories. There are many more stories to be written down for posterity. The airmen gave of themselves in dark flak and fighter filled skies of Europe and relived that period for me. I consider them all to be heroes.

I would like to give credit to my wife, Lorraine, for her patience throughout the years when I left her alone while I wrote and researched for this book, for the proofreading she did, and for the typing she helped me with.

To Lauri (Mekelberg) Lockwood, for the hundreds of mistake-free pages of manuscript she typed for me.

To my niece, Cherie Richman, for a difficult task of deciphering and typing many of my handwritten transcripts.

To Dave Jehu, who made photograph copies for me.

To Ms. Margaret B. Livesay of the 1361st Audiovisual Squadron, AAVS (MAC), Arlington, Virginia, for fullfilling the many requests for photography, both in person and by mail.

To the good people at the Defense Audiovisual Agency, Washington, D.C. who also researched photographs for me.

To Mr. Gerrie J. Zwanenburg, MBE., Identification and Recovery Officer, Royal Netherland Air Force. For information and maps that spot the crash site of *Blizen Betsy* as well as the fate of the crew. Also for searching for the crash site of *No Excuse* Bob Maddox B-17 that crashed after the 2/10/44 raid to Brunswick.

To Mr. & Mrs. Leslie (Margaret) Moran for putting me in touch with Mr. Jimmy Walker, the last surviving member of the Sunderland Life Boat, who with his dear wife have volunteered over 90 years service to that Service.

Mrs. Moran also made it possible for me to meet Mr. Bob Rutter, the grandson of Ron Rutter one of the original lifeboat crew on the rescue of the Nagorka crew, 9/16/43.

To Mr. Bob Reay, Secretary, Sunderland Life Boat, who brought the records of the rescue mission, but which I was unable to view.

To the Harbor Master at Seahouses, who took me on a tour of the Life Boat house and held a light so I could take a photo of the Tally Board which lists the rescue of one aeroplane.

To Mrs. John Baxter Douglas for her hospitality and information on the events of 9/16/43, and for introducing me to Mr. John Cooney, the son-in-law of Mr. & Mrs. Douglas. He at this time is operator of the lighthouse on Farne Island where the Nagorka crew landed in their dinghy.

To Ed Hutzinger, secretary of the 388th Bomb Group Association for his help in locating addresses and vital information.

To Joe Vieira, 303rd Bomb Group Association secretary and to all the dedicated members of that organization.

Last but not least to all my friends, my daughter, Linda, and my son, Brian, who continued to encourage me to finish "the book" even though I was a U.S. Navy veteran infected with a respect and love for flying.

Respectfully,

Glenn A. Stephens

Preface

The United States was plunged into World War II by the Japanese attack on Pearl Harbor December 7, 1941. Twelve unarmed B-17 E bombers arrived in the middle of the attack, low on fuel after a nine-hour flight from Hamilton Air Base in California, they landed wherever they could find a spot. Heavy bombers from this day until the day of victory would play a major role in the destruction of the axis powers ability to wage war.

The decision was made to win the war in Europe first, then concentrate on the Japanese in the Pacific. To do this, a plan was made to select the most strategic targets for the bombers to hit in precision daylight raids. Until we had sufficient bombers to carry out this objective, our bombers hit targets close to the French coast.

Between 17 August 1942 when 12 B-17s bombed the marshalling yards at Rouen and Sotteville, and 30 December 1942 when 77 aircraft attacked the U-boat pens at Lorient, 1,547 sorties were flown. Targets were: marshalling yards, 4; airfields, 15; shipyards, 4; industrial aviation targets, 3; U-boat pens and bases, 1.

On 14 May 1943 Operation "Pointblank" was approved by the combined Chiefs of Staff. To quote in part: "The mission was the progressive destruction and dislocation of the German military, industrial and economic system, and undermining the morale of the German people to a point where their capacity for formal resistance is fatally weakened."

The principal objectives: A study by operations analysts consisting of eminent United States experts concluded that destruction of 60 targets would impair and might paralyze the Western Axis war effort. British and US experts agreed to this and selected six systems, comprising seventy six precision targets, within the tactical radius of the RAF and USAAF. Destruction was directed against three major elements of the German Military machine; its submarine fleet, its Air Force, and its ground force, and certain industries vital to their support. The 6 systems were:

Submarine construction yards and bases
German aircraft industry
Ball bearings
Oil
Synthetic rubber and tires
Military transport vehicles

The Germans, recognizing the vulnerability of their vital industries, were rapidly increasing the strength of their fighter defenses. The German fighter strength in western Europe was being augmented. *If the growth of the German fighter strength was not arrested quickly, it could have become literally impossible to carry out the destruction planned and thus to create the conditions necessary for ultimate decisive action by our combined forces on the Continent.*

This objective was carried out by the gunners in the B-24s and B-17s as well as the escorting P-51 and P-51 fighters. German fighter losses claimed in January 1944 were 1,115; in February, 1,118; and in March, 1,217. The losses in planes were accompanied by losses in experienced pilots. By the spring of 1944 opposition of the Luftwaffe had ceased to be effective.

This book is the story of many young men who went about implementing the "Pointblank" Offensive. Follow them through the flak and fighter-filled skies over Magdeberg, Vienna, Nis, Hanau, Bremen, and Paris just to name a few. Always working as a team, ready to make any sacrifice for a crewmate. These narratives are in their own words as they lived them and recorded them in a log book or diary. Many were so very young: O.A. "Jack" Farrar was just 19 as second pilot and was first pilot at 20 and he had a 43-year-old top turret gunner that had to get a waiver for each mission: he flew 51 missions in Jack's B-17 in both the 8th and 15th Air Force.

With a start of 12 B-17s in August 1942 to 1,200 plane raids in 1945 there are men who flew them all. "Pete" Norman went to Rouen in 1942, and to Wilhelmshaven. Billy Bittle went into Berlin and dropped food to the Dutch in May of 1945, including some fresh oranges. When you have read the book I am sure you will have a better understanding of what these men went through both those who flew, and those who waited. Nothing takes the place of being there. But, hopefully, this book will take you as close as the written word can.

Table of Contents

Bibliography

100th Bomb Group *Contrails,* Contrails Publishing, Inc., 1947.
The Story Of The 390th Bomb Group, 1947.
The Impact Of Air Power, D. Van Nostrand Co., Inc., 1959.
Hostages Of Colditz, Preager Publishers, New York.
Fortress For Freedom, Newsphoto Publishing Co., San Angelo, Texas.

A Flight Crew's Journey to War
Narrator: Lt. Raymond Baier

In 1942 the vast power of United States manufacturing facilities began to turn out materials for war. At the same time military training schools of all types were training men and women to fill critical positions in planes, ships, tanks, companies, all which were important to the war effort no matter how insignificant the job seemed, it was important and necessary.

The Monday after the Pearl Harbor attack, the recruiting offices all over the country were filled with eager young men ready to go to war for a country unique with the idea that freedom was our most precious gift. And that this freedom must be protected at any cost. The same feelings were felt at this time as were present in 1320 when the Scottish Council drew up the Declaration of Arbroath proclaiming their desire to be free. The declaration ended with the words: "We fight not for glory nor for wealth nor for honor, but for that freedom which no good man surrenders but with his life." This was why America went to war. These are the stories of some of those men.

Thousands flocked to join, the training centers filled to overflowing to the point that many were forced to wait to get into schools and training centers. This situation was to continue throughout the war, but this was to be a large plus for the men who went overseas as they were not rushed pell-mell in and out of schools and into battle ill trained. Training was the best we had at the time, only actual hands-on battle experience would give them the real training they needed to survive, training not available in the States.

The Army Air Corps was going all out to get planes to the fighting fronts around the globe. As the pilots, navigators, and bombardiers graduated they were united with a well-trained enlisted crew of men to become a well-oiled working machine when they got their new B-17 or B-24. There were other crews and other bombers of twin engine type, but we will be dealing with Bomb Group (H). The low level heroes in the twins are worthy of a book of their own.

The air war in Europe in early spring and summer of 1943 was

1

heating up as we sent more and more planes on missions and we experienced more and more casualties. More often than not, when a heavy bomber went down the crew became prisoners of war; or worse, became war dead. A few evaded. To fill these losses, a constant stream of planes and crews from our Arnenal of Democracy poured across the Atlantic. In these earlier ferry trips some crews became "original" crews of the many Bomber Groups just being formed, others like Ray Baier were replacement crews.

Being "original" to these young warriers of the air was something to be proud of, especially when they had a few missions under their belt. In talking to veterans at reunions this forty plus years later, they proudly say they "were one of the original crew." Not many made it through under those circumstances. These men were the ones who flew the planes over that became a new Bomb Group. Few hold this distinction. Most were replacement crews that lost their new planes as soon as they got to Bovington.

Lt. Raymond Baier was one of the replacement crews and had written a detailed log of his time in training and the missions he flew with the 92nd Bomb Group. In his words, this is his story as he wrote it in July, 1943 to his wife Elizabeth. You can at once feel the joy, the frustration of waiting, of wanting to talk to a loved one and not being able to do it, the boredom of just waiting for something to happen. Lt. Baier had begun his career in the Air Corps as an enlisted man in 1939 working in Supply. His log begins with his frustrating times after his pilot training. His log:

I remember I kissed you as the bus moved out about 12:30 a.m. on Friday July 16th. I called you later on Friday before your train left. I know you would like to know what I've been doing but now I can't write freely anymore, but this is a continuous log that no censor can look at.

The wing tip on my B-17 that was damaged here at Kearny was at last repaired, baggage loaded, a full load of gas aboard; and Saturday about 10 a.m. we started the engines and slowly taxied out to runway N13. We checked the engines as usual and then left Kearney, Nebraska — that Chamber of Horrors. We circled that place just once and then took a heading to Fort Wayne, Indiana. We ran into some weather and dropped as low as 300 feet off the ground. It's very flat there, and we arrived at Ft. Wayne without incident. We took on an illegal passenger here, a young G.I. trying to get back East because of a death in the family. We bent regulations considerable and took him along, after signing him on the manifest and issuing him a parachute.

2

After refueling we left for Syracuse, New York, having been told that combat planes were not supposed to fly after dark in the U.S. and that if we could not make Bangor we should land at Syracuse. We flew low over the navigators home town and continued on toward Syracuse. After consulting the radio facility chart, the navigators map, it was obvious that we should proceed to the cone of silence of the Syracuse radio network, turn due south and the airport should be just off the right of the south leg of the beam. We did this and after flying for several minutes began to wonder where this airport was. We knew where we were, because we had the beam turned on throughout the entire flight. Everyone in the ship was looking for it, suddenly a small airport came into view just ahead off the right wing. We circled to the left once and I said to the co-pilot, Lt. Harold Toombs, "Lets give the tower a buzz and get landing instructions."

"Tower from Army 595, tower from Army 595, circling field from left, request landing instructions, over to you."

"Army 595 from Syracuse control, Army 595 from Syracuse control, land runway 28, runway 28, wind velocity 6 miles per hour."

"Army 595 to tower, roger."

Again we circled the field; we could see a runway 27 in big yellow letters but there was no runway 28, so I called the tower a second time telling them we could not see any runway marked 28. I said to Toombs "Thats a strange looking Army base." He replied, "There's a ship down there with a star on the wing and they told us this base was built in the woods, and very well camouflaged, so I guess this is it." "Okay landing check list, we'll give it a whirl."

We came over the woods, missing the tree tops by a matter of feet and got in as close as we could to the end of the runway. At that we had to use the entire runway to get stopped. We turned about and taxied into the line only to find we had landed at the municipal airport which had been built for light airplanes. A handful of civilians greeted us and the fire department met us. We killed the engines and Toombs and I went into the control tower and checked a more up-to-date map. The tower told us that they have a stray B-17 land there every week. We were treated very courteously and a glance at the map in their operations showed us where our mistake had been. The Army field had not been on any of our maps and it lay on the east leg of the Syracuse beam, hardly a half dozen miles from where we were. They phoned the Army field and obtained clearance for us to take off. We concluded that the tower operator at the Army base should have realized when he gave us landing instructions and didn't see us that we were circling the Municipal airport. The fact that we told him that we could not see his runway 28 should in itself have been the tipoff. This premature landing had aided in our getting the passenger off our hands that we had taken aboard at Ft. Wayne, the enlisted man on emergency leave. We got off to the Army base by giving

3

the ship full flaps halfway down the runway. A check with weather told us we would not be able to continue until the next day around noon. The enlisted men were given passes and went into Syracuse for one last chance to call home before they were overseas.

After lunch the next day we all gathered at the plane and the crew chief had pre-flighted it in the morning and noticed number 3 engine was throwing oil. We got a mechanic to look at it and found the oil pump ready to fall off, he tightened it and pronounced it good. We again checked the weather, and it was to be clear over Bangor so we got clearance and made an uneventful trip. Arriving over the field I saw countless B-17s parked everywhere. After landing, a jeep met us and we were told to follow it. As soon as we parked, an A.T.C. officer asked if we had any mechanical problems and we mentioned our radio was not as it should be. We checked in and did all the paperwork, immunization records, dog tags, clothing and equipment records etc., assigned quarters — passes were denied. As I had served at this base earlier in Air Corps Supply, I knew many people, military and civilian, who were still here. I spent the evening in the club with three stenographers from Air Corps Supply. We talked over old times and who was where and who was left. They all wanted a ride in a B-17, which I said if it was at all possible I would do.

I saw Louise and Josie Sunday night and the next day I saw everyone and took them for a ride at 5 p.m. After that, we went to Penobscot Exchange for dinner. Gee, I was missing you!! After we left the hotel we went to see the "D"s. Daddy "D" is really failing. At midnight we ended up in the Pilots Grill for coffee and then I went back to "prison." Fran knew the Major so I got a pass.

On Tuesday they got us up early and we were supposed to get off for Newfoundland. Due to some repair holdups on a window (radio hatch) I didn't take off until noon. Louise and Ellen Drummy saw me off and I buzzed the Air Corps Supply on take off. Once again Bangor treated me just wonderfully. We made Gander in Newfoundland in just three and a half hours and then all time ceased to exist. Dan is here but is on pass and unless he hurries back I'll miss him. Tom Wingate and Lt. Strikle are here and numerous others that used to be in Bangor. We got here July 20 on a Thursday and today is Friday the 23rd and still here. We've rechecked the ship and are waiting weather. Tomorrow if we don't leave I'll tell you all about Newfoundland. They call it Newfooyland. I guess this log or diary will be my closest companion until we are reunited. If ever I find a way to send these pages back to the States to you I will. *(He didn't).*

Every day we are scheduled for briefing at 3 p.m. Briefing was cancelled every day until Saturday July 24th. Each day the weather wasn't exactly suitable. We didn't have enough tail winds to help us across. For four days we waited. Two crew members (E.M.) had to stay with the ship each night.

4

While at Bangor I named the ship, you know what, I hardly have to say, "E", of course, I had it painted on, just beneath the Pilot's window. It was a free hand E not a printed one. I was proud of it, I could reach down from the pilot's window and give it a pat. I saw much of Tom Wingate and Strickle while at Gander but Dan was on a 5-day pass. He left on the 20th when I left Bangor and wasn't due back until the 25th. Oh yes, another bit of bad news, I had a bottle of scotch stolen from me our last night in Kearney. I replaced the bottle in Syracuse. I saw much of Gander through Wingate who, by the way, is only a T/Sgt. yet. He was a S/Sgt. when we were in Bangor together. There is no town near Gander, only the air base. If the food at the mess doesn't appeal to you, you simply await the next meal as there is no place to get a hamburger. Each morning I slept late, say to 11 or 12 noon, then check with operations to see when and if we were leaving. The big hop was ahead. After the first couple of cancellations the tension wore off. As I had expected, it became just another hop. We knew we were going across the so-called southern route, meaning straight to Scotland. The northern route is via Iceland and emergency fields on the Greenland coast then down to Scotland. Our trip as planned gave us a 1950 mile overwater flight. Everything was readied. Sgt. Sack, Engineer and top turret gunner, checked all engines, actually looked at fuel pumps and strainers. The "E" was ready to GO!

At last on the 24th the notice was posted. Weather briefing at 3 p.m. Greenwich time, which was 1½ hours ahead so at the conclusion of the briefing which was at 3:30 p.m., Gander time, we set our watches at 5 p.m. Each ship was called off and given its time to take-off. Ships were to leave at 3 minute intervals. Altogether there were 55 B-17s and 1 B-24. The B-24 was to lead. The "E" was number 7 due to take off at 1918 (7:18 p.m.). Our weather briefing was complete.

We could expect a tail wind between 20 and 30 mph all the way. Also we could expect two weather fronts with rain. I might say now that the forecast was extremely accurate. The trip was to take 12 hours with a 150 mile an hour speed. Our destination was Prestwick, Scotland, across Northern Ireland. We had 15 hours of gasoline and untried navigators.

At 1900 we all gathered under a wing and ate some ice cream that I got through Wingate. All was ready, we climbed aboard and at 1910 I started engines and 1915 began to taxi toward our runway. We had 2700 gallons of gas and 60,000 pounds to get into the air. Quite a load, 30 tons. My left outboard propeller narrowly missed a field boundary light, which stood a good four feet off the ground but that was the only near mishap we had. (Julian Brown later hit the same one!) Then at 1930, just 12 minutes behind schedule, the tower cleared us for take-off. I said to Toombs. "Ready to go?" and he replied, "OK, let her go!" I gave the "E" a pat, closed the window, switched on the generators and began easing the throttles forward. We

5

were off! Gee that ship wanted to fly. I circled slightly to the left and picked up Dougherty's course. In five minutes we were over our last tip of rocky Newfoundland with the grey Atlantic before us. There were some icebergs below and clouds southeast of course. Sunset came rather quickly and with it an undercast appeared. An undercast is a solid sheet of clouds beneath you, an overcast is one above you. The sun hung on the horizon for a brief moment, a huge red ball seemingly at rest before taking a great plunge. I thought as I looked back at it, "That's our last sunset in the new world for many months to come," then twilight. The threatening skylight skipped by swiftly, then darkness. The stars came out overhead, dusk was behind us and to the southward, heavy clouds seemed to gradually curve around in front of us a long, long way ahead.

I had instructed Sgt. Donald J. Sack, the engineer, to check our gas supply every half hour for the first two hours and every hour thereafter. The boys, five of them, including Sgt. E. R. Newton, tail gunner; Sgt. John I. Johnson, waist gunner; Sgt. Vaughn Bowers, waist gunner; Lt. Fred Dougherty, navigator; Lt. Bennett, Bombardier (replaced later by Lt. William Munro), were in the nose. Dougherty was working while the others played blackjack. I was glad so many were in the nose, better distribution of weight and assisted in holding down our gas consumption. Normal operation requires slightly less than 50 gallons of gas per engine per hour, 200 gallons per hour for flight. By 8 p.m. we had burned about 150 gallons. That would mean 300 per hour but that included take-off. At 8:30 we had dropped to 125 and by 9 pm just over 100. At 9:30 I told Sack to make an hourly check thereafter. We were then burning 200 gallons per hour which would give us a nice reserve.

At the 10:30 gas check we noticed the air speed had picked up to nearly 160 mph, so we reduced our throttle settings, slowing down to 150. As the ship became lighter through the consumption of gas, the engines would require less fuel to maintain our planned average speed of 150 mph.

All hands were wearing their Mae Wests. I went aft to the radio room, talked to Sgts. George Rinko, the radio operator, and James Geibell, right waist gunner and assistant radioman. We had a cigarette and split one of Bennett's cokes (stolen). Until nightfall we had one ship about 25 miles off our right and ahead. We had been catching up on him and the last we saw he was directly off our wing. Either he or we were slightly off course, I figured we were right.

I took my binoculars and went back to the tail gunners perch but could not see anything — too dark. There were 55 heavy bombers within minutes of each other somewhere over this stretch of ocean. As I went back through the radio room, the radio operator told me he had picked up a garbled report of some ship in trouble, but he couldn't understand whether the ship was returning to Gander or was being forced down. I asked him to let us know if he heard anything further. He said he would and said he was receiving

Gander control very clearly.

At 2300 hours we finally had our sandwiches along with some lemonade and tomato juice (the juice had been stolen by the bombardier). At midnight we suddenly were engulfed by hard heavy rain which lasted about a half an hour. Toombs had been doing the flying but when the rain hit I took over. At 0100 we made a close check on gas. At 0230 we again checked closely and then decided we had a huge margin so I advanced the speed from the 160 it had crept up to, to 185. I used a power setting of 31 inches at 2100 rpm, we really scooted. I asked Fred Dougherty what our E.T.A. would be into Prestwick. He said that if we maintained 160 mph speed we should arrive between 0700 and 0730, so I had increased it. At 0330 I asked Fred for another celestial fix at our new speed and he came back that we had covered 210 miles the last hour. We asked for a new E.T.A. based on the new ground speed and he replied, "Before 0700."

Dawn came about 0400, I was in the radio room stealing a cat nap when I heard voices saying "Ireland." I went forward and turned on the Prestwick beam. The first signal we got was the on-course hum. When you are to the right of the beam you get a coded "A" and to the left a coded "N". Fred had navigated the entire ocean without radio assistance and because the automatic pilot was inoperative we had flown the ship manually, even the enlisted men had been at the controls, and we were exactly on course. We congratulated Fred and laughed that he was able to do such a good job in spite of the lack of training in this phase. This actually was his first cross country flight since his cadet training at Monroe, Louisiana.

Rapidly the dawn of July 25th broadened into full light and we noted the undercast was slightly broken with some holes in it. Through one of these holes we saw the first green pasture land of Ireland. We began to let down from 9000 feet hoping to get a better view of the Emerald Isle. Many minutes went by and our altitude faded to 1500 feet. The next hole revealed pasture land and small lakes, then we broke through the last veil of clouds which had formed this undercast. Without warning we passed over the Irish east coast and were over the Irish Sea. The radio operator had contacted the Prestwick control and identified us to them. Suddenly the engineer, who had been standing between the pilot seats said "Look," and pointed off to the right. There arose that 1200 foot pinnacle of rock we had been warned about at the briefing back at Gander. Fred had the location of this rock on his chart so we knew just where we were. He told the radio operator our exact E.T.A. and this was radioed to Prestwick control. In return we were given weather conditions at the airdrome. We passed near a fighter strip and soon saw some B-24s and large British bombers so we circled once and came in for a landing (hot and rough). Our landing time was 0625: just 9 hours and 55 minutes. We taxied to our parking spot, the first ship in. It was well after 0700 before the second ship landed and from then on a steady stream kept

7

everyone busy.

My biggest jolt came when I was told I would lose the "E". Yes, old 230595 was being taken away from us. We had been assured that we would keep the ship we flew overseas, but everyone except permanent crews lost their ships.

All through the 2nd Air Force training we were told we would be given a new airplane to take to combat. This would be ours to fly in combat. They had impressed this on us at Kearney when the ships had been assigned to us. Once again we started getting kicked around. We never saw 595 again. We were told to remove our baggage and a truck would come and pick us and it up and take us to a hanger. The non-breakable stuff we just salvoed out of the bomb bay, the other breakables we handed down. We all had sensed that we might lose some of our belongings. We were first to load up and hoped we would be able to keep track of our stuff. We had sidearms, carbines, navigational gear, personal gear, parachutes, bedrolls, tent roll, gas mask, etc. We were directed to a dirty WWI age hanger to stow our stuff, then to another building for de-briefing. There I had to turn over the secret document file, maps and secret orders, as well as keys to the ship. Again I made an effort to find out why we were losing 595. The officer in charge looked blank for a moment and then said, "Didn't they tell you back there that all ships coming in from the states had to be modified and you could not keep your ship? This has been going on since the 8th Air Force first came over here." There was nothing more to say. I went into another room where I received a receipt for one airplane.

Again we loaded onto a truck that would take us to the mansion. It was a short trip, but we had a chance to see some of the Scottish countryside. The country was rolling and green with stone fences, cattle, hogs and barnyards. It looked a lot like New England with the small fields and abundant shade trees. We had a problem with our driver driving down the narrow roads on the "wrong" side, but he had been at this for some fourteen months and it was old hat to him.

The approach to the mansion was lined with shrubs, and a green carpet of grass seemed to stretch endlessly. The beauty of it was very restful. We marveled at this Yank drivers ability to wind down the narrow road on the wrong side. There was great activity as we drove up, trucks, staff cars and jeeps coming and going.

We were told lunch would be served at noon and where we should eat, where we could wash up, and where we could change our American money for British. Crews were arriving regularly, gathered in bunches talking about the flight over, but most of the conversation was on the confiscation of our ships. Before lunch we went up to exchange for some British money. They had run out. We could not send a cable because we had no British money and we could not buy anything because we had no ration cards, so we returned to the mansion. It was just in time for lunch, which turned out to be quite good. Our crew name was paged and we were told our gear had been brought over from the hangar, so we went to pick it up and sure enough we found some of it was already missing. As we could do nothing else and could not leave, the crews spread out over the grass, sleeping. At four o'clock word was passed for each crew to take its baggage to a station in a town about ten miles away. Six of us managed the baggage and the other four maintained their siesta. On our return we found that we all would depart about seven from the station. So, back again we went to the station, but we did not board until nine. We made a tour of the town and found our way to the Red Cross club where we had a cold plate dinner. Then back to the train, which came in on schedule. The conductor pulled the shades for blackout purposes. This brought home the realization that we were in a war zone. A poker game soon began and wagering went on heavily even though using the British notes the bettor had no real idea how much it was worth. One gunner did come out some three hundred dollars ahead by covering five pound notes with one of smaller value, but of similar look and size. Most of us went to sleep and had to be awakened when we got to Bovington, 20 miles north of London.

We unloaded our baggage and rode to the Combat Crew Replacement Center located at Bovington. We were only replacement crews so we were at the bottom of the pile again. I signed papers until I almost got writers cramp. We were given quarters, signed pay vouchers and per diem. The school will last about two weeks. The picture became very clear that while we knew our jobs as individuals we knew nothing of tactics or strategy or military flying. We began to resent the chart system we had trained by back in the 2nd Air Force. Some of us had never flown formation at altitude enough to be proficient. School would begin July 30 and we were told London was off limits. The gunners went to the Wash for further training, we were to attend lectures by instructors who were combat veterans. These lectures would cover security, aircraft identification, radio procedures, air traffic rules in the United Kingdom, combat films, formation strategy and ditching procedure as well as items of general interest.

The A. A. F. and the R. A. F. are doing remarkably good work. The A. A. F. equipped and trained for daylight missions, while the R. A. F. hits the continent by night. During the London blitz when the Germans attempted mass daylight raids their tremendous losses produced a school of thought which relegated the bombing plane to night operations. The British, profiting by the German defeat during the blitz, devoted their energies toward building a night bomber fleet. The innovation of high altitude formation flying, the Norden bombsight, and the heavy defensive fire power of our heavy bombers achieved success in daylight raiding whereas the Germans had failed and the British never attempted it.

9

During our second week the first crews that began school were already preparing to leave for their combat units. Today is August 7th and each of us knew that soon he would be leaving here for his permanent outfit. When we first moved into this barracks (Nissen hut) there had been just eight of us, J. T. Brown and his three officers,, and the four officers of my crew. That left three empty bunks — we were to see a lot of empty bunks before our tours came to an end. On this occasion three more officers moved in a few days later, as others would do in the future. None of us had been in aircraft since we'd landed at Prestwick and this was beginning to wear on us.

On Monday August 9, 1943 our work was complete at Bovington and we were to pack and be ready to go to our new assignments. Some outfits were universally condemned and the record was produced to prove it. Everyone was interested in the record of losses of the outfit he was assigned to. At headquarters we saw the assignment sheet and through a stroke of luck the three crews in our barracks were going to the same bomb group. Its combat record was good, their losses low. This was the 92nd Bomb Group.

The next day at noon we were on a truck with our gear headed for our permanent station. Arriving, we were asked if two of us would like to stay together as there were two vacancies in the third squadron, J. T. Brown and I decided to stick together. J. T. returned to the truck to tell our enlisted men what the situation was and they were driven to the E. M. quarters where they were within walking distance of the mess, we were five miles up the road.

As we turned into the area where our quarters were we could see this small village of 30 or 40 people. There was a mansion house after which the village was named (Stukley Hall?). The manor house was now occupied by Captains and Majors. Officers of higher rank occupied even more pretentious quarters nearer the flying field. After appraising the situation, J. T. promptly dubbed them, the House of Lords and the House of Commons. We were quartered in some tar paper shacks.

Just seconds after getting our gear unloaded the truck's horn began tooting, this was the last call for dinner and we all ran out and grabbed onto the tail gate and got in as best we could, then off we roared to the mess hall. The food was so much better than what we had had at Bovington. Here they must have had some cooks. We were strangers, no one knew us and we knew no one. The club room was filled with officers, many of whom wore ribbons, and as far as we could see, 2nd Lts. were scarce. Our gold bars signified better than anything else that we were new crews. After eating, we went out to the truck so we would not have to make a 5 mile walk back to our hut. After we had arranged some of our things like we wanted them, one of the older officers came over and inquired of us where we had come from and we replied, "Oh, from the Second Air Force and Bovington." He said, "Yeah, I figured as much. Did you learn anything back there?" I said, "Well, not too much, but that school at Bovington isn't too bad. It is too bad the 2nd Air Force doesn't have some instructors with combat experience." He replied, "Well, they might have some day if we all don't go down."

The day after this conversation, August 12, 1943 the 92nd had gone to Gelsenkirchen and lost three ships. Two of these were officers from Ray Baier's barracks. Already they were having empty bunks. Ray mentioned a scene that took place in the squad room where the two empty bunks stood. Lt. Tucker, a pilot, walked up to "The Goats" bunk (the goat is Lt. Doolan) and asked where the goat kept his money so they could get a money order and send it home. There was a general effort made to give the cigars and other perishables away, which no one wanted. During this time of packing and disposing, it was mentioned that if they did not pack all his things to send home the KIWIs would get it. The KIWI is a ground officer. A couple stories were told of Lt. Doolan. On one occasion a congressional delegation was inspecting the 92nd and Doolan was standing at attention under his planes wing. One congressman stopped to inspect his ship and introduced himself. "I'm Congressman so and so from Kansas," to which Doolan replied right back, "Glad to meet you, I'm Doolan from Ohio!" Lt. Doolan had been forced to ditch in the Channel last week. Now he was more than likely a POW. This brought up a conversation about "The Flak Widow." This lady lives in Peterborough and had dated six flying officers of the 92nd Bomb Group. All six have been victims of flak. The Goat was number seven and now he is gone too. An officer in another group actually asked her not to date any of the flying officers in his group. It is said that everytime she sees the B-17s flying she cries.

Just a few days later Lt. Raymond Baier went on his first mission, to Flushing, Belgium. It was a short three hour and twenty-five minute trip with some flak and no injuries. He did see "Hepcat" once again. This was Lt. Al Rumman's original plane. When Ray Baier had painted "E" on his ship, Al had painted *Hepcat* on his. As said before, these ships had been taken away from them at Prestwick, but old *Hepcat* did not make the mission. On the take-off run the wheels collapsed and that was the end of *Hepcat*. Luckily there were no injuries though a prop came off and went into the plane just behind the pilots seat.

We will later pick up Lt. Baier's log on August 17, 1943.

Date: 17 July 1943
Target: **Amsterdam, Holland**
Group: **388th Bomb Group**

Mission 1 for the newly organized 388th Bomb Group was to be Amsterdam. The target was an aircraft factory, July 17, 1943.

For this first mission 20 a/c were airborne by 0626 hours. Colonel David was the Group Leader with Major Satterwhite as Deputy Leader. The Group and Wing formation was accomplished and the briefed route was followed with only a slight deviation at the IP. Two Groups were involved, the 388th and the 385th, with the 388th as lead.

Three a/c aborted. Lt. Eccleston in a/c 42-30193, as he had to feather #3 engine due to high oil pressure and temperature; Lt. Cox in a/c 42-5906 turned back at 0740 hours at Great Ashfield with a broken oxygen line; Lt. Pickard in a/c 42-30202 returned at 0745 hours because of poor radio communications. The 21st a/c scheduled, Lt. Bernard blew a tire on take-off.

Bombing results on the assigned target — an aircraft factory in Amsterdam — were poor. Cloud coverage was 7/10th in the target area which made it difficult to pick up the target. Bombing was from 22,000 feet and the bombs landed in a congested business center. Of the 17 a/c over the target, 15 dropped all of their bombs. Lt. Swift in a/c 42-5900 dropped only six as he had a malfunction in the rack and brought the other four back. Lt. Bailey in a/c 42-30207 returned with all of his bombs as he could not identify the target.

No fighter opposition was encountered with only two enemy aircraft seen. Flak was not severe with meager flak at Ijmuiden on the route in and moderate flak at the target.

All aircraft from this Group returned to base by 1019 hours.

12

Once we became airborne we formed up and settled in our old position, "Coffin Corner." Low plane, low corner, low squadron, low group. We were flying ship #793. The target was the tire and rubber plant located at Hannover, Germany. Just after we crossed the enemy coast we were met by a group of ten Me 109 German Fighter Planes, who started hitting us, but we suffered only slight damage. They left us when we got near the target. When we approached the IP we picked up a new group of enemy fighter planes and flak. The enemy fighters came up through their own flak to attack us. We now were confronted with FW 190s making head on attacks as well as the flak, but we were able to take some evasive actions to help the fighter attacks, but we were receiving some damage anyway.

With near constant fighter attacks all the gunners were firing as the fighter positions were called out. While we were not able to knock any of the fighters down, neither was our squadron suffering any fatalities planewise. As we came in on the bomb run the Bombardier took over the control of the plane by flying it with the bomb sight. All planes broke formation and spread out so as not to interfere with each other during the bomb drop. This is the time which seems to be an eternity as the planes have to fly a straight course as the bombardiers line up the plane for the drop with the bomb sight. No evasive action to evade the fighter planes or flak. Just sit there and plod along while they zero in on us and you wait and hope. We made a good drop and a good strike.

As soon as we made our bomb drop, Captain Belser, our pilot, said over the intercom, "Let's get out of here." We made a right turn and were hit by a heavy area of flak. The nose of our plane was blown off by a sudden burst of flak. The plane staggered from the sudden intake of air into her hull, but the pilot and co-pilot kept her under control. We were lucky that no fires occurred. A few minutes later a flak shell exploded above and a little to the right. The top of the turret exploded. A piece of flak an inch square ricocheted around inside the turret and hit the top turret operator on the first finger of his right hand which was wrapped around the control grips of the gun turret, severing his first finger at the second joint and leaving the finger in the nearly-severed finger of his glove. The piece of flak then bounced off and burned through his clothing and lodged next to the skin of his chest, searing a spot on his chest bone as it cooled off.

We tried to keep up with our group but we were in trouble. Engines three

13

and four had been hit and lost their oil. The pilot couldn't feather the props because of lack of oil pressure. The pilot had to overwork the other two engines to try to keep up and we were falling behind. A cripple is what the enemy planes look for. The enemy planes must have been running low on fuel because they finally broke off their attack, all except one. He was determined to get us. He kept coming at us from the front and just as he would start to fire our pilot would drop the nose of our plane and slip to the left, which would raise the tail of our plane and he was tearing our plane to pieces. A 20mm cannon shell sheared off two feet of the right wing. He blew a hole in the dorsal fin large enough to hold a kitchen range. All of the rudder was blown away save a section two feet long at the top. The elevators were blown away by flak except for a few pieces. The top of the tail gunner's position was blown away and the tail gunner's position was riddled with flak and bullet holes. How he escaped being mortally wounded or killed is beyond imagination. Also the right waist gun position and right side of the plane was riddled with flak and sieved with bullet holes. The bottom of the plane was also riddled with flak. We were falling behind and losing altitude. It began to look doubtful if we would make it to the coast or not. The navigator and bombardier were freezing because of the nose being gone. The pilot and co-pilot had frostbit hands and flew the plane for a time with their elbows until we were down to a lower altitude and warmer temperature. After the mission Captain Belser said that one more hit and we would have had to bail out. The plane couldn't take any more punishment.

Luckily before we reached the enemy coast a group of our own fighter escort planes met us and escorted us far enough toward base that we were safe. Before we reached base we lost the third engine. It burned out. We had lost altitude to the point where we couldn't fly the pattern to land. The hydraulic system was shot out, we had no brakes, one tire was blown out, most of the instruments didn't work and the plane was vibrating all over. All the way back we feared it would split open and pieces flew off all the way home. We had to crank the landing gear down by hand. Captain Belser elected to try to land with one tire blown out and no brakes rather than risk fire and explosion with a belly landing.

We had landing priority as we had a wounded man aboard, only one engine and an almost demolished airplane. We all braced ourselves for a rough landing. Captain Belser and Lt. Jones, our co-pilot, came in on the runway as far back to the end as possible to take advantage of all the runway they could. The blown-out tire was on the left side. They brought the plane in with the left wing as high as they dared, without the right wing tip dragging on the runway and brought her in on the right wheel. A "One Wheeler" landing. As she rolled down the runway #793 settled slowly down on both wheels. The flat tire slowed the plane down and as it slowed down Captain Belser and Lt. Jones managed to keep it on the runway until #793

14

was going slow enough to steer it out on the grass where it came to a stop. We had an almost perfect landing with no brakes, one flat tire, one engine and practically no steering surfaces on the plane.

Even as we came to a stop the ambulance was there to take Sgt. Spangeberg to the hospital. Before we could get out of the plane the engineering officer was in the plane. He hurried to the cockpit, picked up the log book and across the page we had used that day he wrote the word, "Condemned." Captain Belser looked up and in his Texas drawl he said, "If you will fix her up, we'll fly her again!" The engineering officer shook his head and said, "Captain, there isn't enough of her left, but she will give her remaining parts to the other planes so they can keep flying, so she will in a way, fly again."

After we all had gotten out of the plane, the tail gunner and I, Sgt. Mac McDaniel, stood off at the right rear side of the plane and looked #793 over. The tail gunner was shaking like a leaf and his knees were knocking. He looked at the tail gunner's position and at the top of it, blown off and how it was riddled with flak and machine gun bullets and where all the tail section was missing and in a voice that shook, Sgt. Barton said, "I didn't know it was that bad! How did we make it?" I looked at my own position and looked at all the bullet and flak holes and the floor was riddled too and I thought the same thing.

I went back in the plane and into the top turret compartment. I looked down and saw Sgt. Spangenberg's glove lying on the floor. I picked it up. His finger was still in it. I walked back to my position, picked up a screwdriver, went outside and buried the glove and finger beneath the sod.

As we prepared to leave I took one long last look at #793. I am reminded of a great proud eagle as it lay on the ground, crumpled, broken and dead from the hunter's gun, but nothing could take away her strong, proud look. No. 793 too was broken, torn and would never fly again, but she had taken everything the enemy could throw at her and flown her heart out. By her strength, the skill of two of the best pilots who ever flew, a dedicated crew and the grace of God, we came home.

It was time to go to debriefing and eat. It had been a long day.

Date: 26 July 1943
Target: Hannover, Germany
Narrator: Lt. Henry J. Nagorka
Group: 388th Bomb Group

1st Lt. Henry J. Nagorka, pilot, 388th Bomb Group, 560th Squadron, flew fourteen missions from July 17, 1943 to October 9, 1943. This short three month period was to take him and his crew from East Anglia as far south as Africa, and as far east as Gydnia, Poland. In this time Lt. H. J. "Nick" Nagorka used up four B-17s.

His first plane was named *Iza Angel* in honor of his girl friend, whose name was Izabella, (the Polish version of Isabelle), and who a nurse — an angel of mercy. *Iza Angel* was to be lost on the fourth mission, the July 26, 1943 mission to Hannover, the site of the Continental Gummi Werke, a major synthetic rubber factory.

Lt. Francis Tierney, navigator, stated, "The Germans did everything they could to keep us out of Hannover, but once we were there and bombed, they did not want any of us to get out. It was, overall, a bad raid for us."

"Nick" recalls the mission: "I was leader of the low squadron, with Lt. Horn and Lt. Melville on my wings, It was the longest air fight we experienced during our whole tour of duty — lasting over an half a hour of intense battle action in the air. This was dramatically unusual. Most air fights are of just a few minutes duration."

The official mission summary follows and provides only the very minimum of facts. The bravery and the great courage shown by the men who manned these "Flying Fortresses" is not described in official accounts. However, the heroism under fire of the crew of *Iza Angel,* as well as all the flight personnel of the 8th Air Force, can never be too deeply inscribed upon the glorious records of dedication and sacrifice for God and country.

Twenty-one ships of the 388th Bomb Group took off between 0745 and 0754 hours. The group formed up in the air and proceeded to the rendezvous point. After considerable difficulty identifying each other, the wing formation was assembled and it proceeded on course.

Four planes aborted over the North Sea. Lt. Kelley in #205 turned back at 0901 with low oil pressure on #2 engine; Lt. Eccleston in #193 turned back at

1015 because of prop runaway on #1 engine, but while making his way back alone, Eccleston was attacked by an Me. 110 which made four passes before breaking off; Lt. Mohr in #203 turned back at 1056 after feathering #1 engine. The course was followed as briefed but with slight deviation.

As the formation crossed the Frisian Islands, it was picked up by enemy fighters. Thereafter our group was subjected to continual fighter attack the entire route in and out again, and not breaking off until we were 20 minutes back out over the North Sea. Flak was relatively meager until the Initial Point was reached. Lt. Denton's ship was hit on this leg of the route. Over the target and on the way back to the rally point the flak was extremely intense and accurate. Lt. Horn's ship went down over the target.

Weather to the target was clear and visibility unlimited, and the fifteen remaining ships dropped directly on the target. The strike photos show an excellent pattern enveloping the mean point of impact of the factory buildings to the north of the goods warehouse.

On the route back three more ships were lost (Lt. Porter's crew were picked up by Air-Sea Rescue — all are safe.) Ten planes returned to base landing between 1456 and 1517. Lt. Beecham's ship was landed by the Co-Pilot at Faultham. Lt. Bliss' ship was landed by the Co-Pilot at RAF Saltby. Wounded in Action:

P   2nd Lt. Chas. C. Bliss
P   2nd Lt. William Beecham
TT   T/Sgt. Jewell W. Delamar

P	1st Lt. J.R. Denton	KIA	RO	T/Sgt. F.A. Glose	POW
CP	F/O N.E. Fair	KIA	BT	S/Sgt. E.J. Cordts	KIA
N	2nd Lt. W.B. Davis	POW	RW	S/Sgt. I.K. Walter	POW
B	2nd Lt. E.A. Basham	POW	LW	S/Sgt. T.H. Kennedy	KIA
TT	T/Sgt. R.C. Hayman	POW	TG	S/Sgt. C.T. Scott	KIA

Lt. Denton in a/c 42-30225 *Mister Yank* was hit by two bursts of flak at Aurisk on the way to the target hitting the left wing and a few seconds later the right wing and N3 engine caught fire. The plane exploded.

P	2nd Lt. E.P. Horn	KIA	RO	S/Sgt. E.L. Hobbs	POW
CP	2nd Lt. D.W. Wetherbee	KIA	BT	S/Sgt. F.W. Whittaker	POW
N	2nd Lt. I.S. Cohen	KIA	RW	S/Sgt. H.H. Hoffman	POW
B	2nd Lt. R.G. Bailey	POW	LW	S/Sgt. S.W. DeGeorgio	POW
TT	T/Sgt. R.E. Baker	POW	TG	S/Sgt. O.W. Deckard	KIA

Lt. Horn in a/c 42-30224, was hit over the target and N 3 engine was on fire when he left the formation. He was then hit by enemy fighters and the plane exploded.

P	2nd Lt. A.M. Bobbitt	POW	RO	T/Sgt. J.L. Duncan	KIA
CP	2nd Lt. P.P. McCahill	POW	BT	S/Sgt. P.E. Warren	KIA
N	2nd Lt. L.W. Wiegman	POW	RW	S/Sgt. J. Langley	KIA
B	2nd Lt. G.L. Amos	KIA	LW	S/Sgt. L.R. Hopewell	KIA
TT	T/Sgt. R. Clabourne	POW	TG	S/Sgt. W.J. Hart	POW

Lt. Bobbit in a/c 42-30198, was hit by fighters and went down on the return route. When Lt. Wiegman hit the ground, he was picked up by German civilians and taken to a beer hall. Knowing that his escape kit would have German Marks in it, he ordered beer for everyone a couple of times. Then as he was about to pay for it a couple of German soldiers entered and to his surprise his escape kit had French Francs in it. One of the Germans had to pay for the beer as he was taken prisoner.

P	2nd Lt. J.B. Gunn	POW	RO	T/Sgt. E.T. Switzer	KIA
CP	2nd Lt. J.C. Brown	POW	BT	S/Sgt. D.H. Babcock	POW
N	2nd Lt. H.E. VanAnda	POW	RW	S/Sgt. F.L. Guardino	POW
B	2nd Lt. E.E. Baca	POW	LW	S/Sgt. J.D. Reese	POW
TT	T/Sgt. D.E. Fuller	KIA	TG	S/Sgt. E.L. Bleeden	POW

Lt. Gunn in a/c 42-30189 *LaChiquita*, bombed the target and was lost on the return route. They went down in the North Sea and were picked up by German Air Sea Rescue. The radioman drowned in the North Sea and the engineer died later in a German hospital. The captured enlisted men were in Stalag 17-B.

Weaver, Tyre C. was captured this day but not listed in the 388th Bomb Group. He was wounded and his left arm had to be amputated.

Lt. Nagorka recalls:

This was an intense air fight and it went on and on. We took a beating, but laid our bombs on the target so effectively that smoke from the burning plant reached up to 22,000 feet. We got a lot of flak over the target and the Germans were even lobbing shells at us from aircraft. This, with the attacks from single engine fighters, kept us busy trying to stay tucked in to the other planes for protection. A series of flak bursts right under our wing nearly skinned the wing. It ripped holes in the wing and sheets of metal — the skin of the wing — were hanging down.

The Germans would make passes at everybody as they came through the formations. They observed closely to see whose formation flying was the poorest; this was the indication that these were the greenest flyers or the least experienced.

That day we had problems in our group. As a matter of fact one pilot nearly caused a mid-air collision with another of our planes. All kinds of things happened to us that day. The Germans, seeing this, began to concentrate on us after making passes at other groups.

They came from all directions. I do not know how many fighters were attacking us, but I would judge there were several squadrons. Attacks would come quite quickly and frequently from all directions. Everybody was firing all the time. All my gunners were firing at incoming and departing fighters; Sgt. Jack Harris from the tail, Claud 'Whitey' Whitehead from the right waist position, his opposite Ed Christenson, while Ed Keisler in the top turret kept a steady fire of 50 caliber bullets streaming at the enemy, while ball turret gunner Sgt. Robert Blankenburg kept his turret whirling to face the fighters as they were called in by the crew, the pilots and Ed Keisler.

Fortunately we came through that without a single injury, but the ship was full of holes. And when we landed, everyone walked away. It was a ticklish job landing. We didn't know whether the wheels would hold up or if the tires were flat due to bullet holes, etc., but the landing went smoothly. As I pulled into our tarmack, my poor crew chief took one look at *Iza Angel* and put his hands on his head. He thought he would have to repair the plane, but that was the end of *Iza Angel*. She was cannibalized for parts and became a hangar queen.

The 92nd Bomb Group had its heroes that day also. *Ruthie II*, piloted by 1st Lt. Robert L. Campbell, was hit in a frontal attack by a 20mm shell and a .303 caliber bullet came in the co-pilot's window angling toward the pilot, severely wounding him in the head. He slumped over the control column. Flying officer John C. Morgan, the co-pilot, had to use extreme force to wrestle control of the plane from his grasp. He called on the intercom for help, but got no answer. He chose to continue on the mission as the other bombers would offer the protection of their guns during fighter attacks. Also, he reasoned, he had a load of bombs to deliver to Hannover.

S/Sgt. T.C. Weaver was hit by the same burst of flak and his left arm was severed at the shoulder. He slumped to the floor near the navigator, 2nd Lt. Keith Koske, who gave him aid, but decided to get him out of the plane as his arm was gone too close to the shoulder to put on a tourniquet. Koske got Weaver's chute on, but it began to open when Weaver inadvertantly pulled the cord. Since only the small pilot chute came out, Koske tucked it under Weaver's good arm and out he went over Germany. Lt. Koske expected Weaver to get medical attention when he reached the ground.

Sgt. Dean Sommers, a ball turret gunner in a neighboring ship of the 92nd Bomb Group, tells what it looked like from his position ... "Our crew was wondering what was wrong with that pilot. The escape hatch was gone; his flying was so erratic — up and back. The crew did not hear anything on the intercom. Co-pilot Morgan's ship was in a different squadron, but he had dropped out when it was hit and he pulled up and flew off our right wing for quite a little while. We didn't know what happened until we got back to the base."

"As for the gunner, Sgt. Weaver, I met him in P.O.W. camp later after I got shot down. His story was that no one threw him out. He couldn't get out quick enough!He said he got picked up right after he landed."

When all crews had been accounted for, this crew had been shot down and recovered by Air-Sea Rescue, North Sea: B-17 42-30209 561st Squadron.

P	2nd Lt. Al D. Porter	TT	T/Sgt. John H. Moffit
C-P	2nd Lt. Hal Thompson	BT	S/Sgt. Ralph Mallicote
N	2nd Lt. Henry Rowland	WG	S/Sgt. Ross Miller
B	2nd Lt. Vernon Adams	WG	S/Sgt. Morris Malamed
RO	T/S John R. Ash	TG	S/Sgt. Ken Schroeder

```
                          Chamberlain——Bernard
                               P 234

                          Gunn        Bobbitt
                          U 189       R 208

                               Denton
                               J 225

                          Miller      Pfieffer
                          W 349       H 213

          Nagorka                                        Bailey
          H 214                                          T 207

   Melville      Horn                              Swift        Penn
   F 201         G 212                             Q 900        P 291

          Mohr                                           Porter
          G 203                                          U 209

   Beecham       Beeby                             Eccleston    Kelley
   R 217         A 293                             R 193        S 205

                               Wick
                               A 284

                          Bliss       Rodgers
                          T 177       E 906
```

Tour Summary - 1943
Narrator: Earl C. Hurd
Group: 93rd Bomb Group, 329th Squadron

Lt. Earl C. Hurd, Pilot, 93rd Bomb Group, 329th Squadron went into Ploesti in the first wave of Liberators on August 1, 1943. Lt. Hurd's story starts with his entry into the Air Corps:

I went in the Air Corps in January of 1942 to Bakersfield from Omaha, then to Santa Maria primary. Funny thing happened there, there was a submarine alert and we were still in civilian clothes, we are all given a loaded rifle and sent out on the beach to patrol. I had never used a gun before, never went hunting 'till I was 35 or so. Here I was in civilian clothes patrolling a beach looking for a submarine. Never found any.

Soloed in a Stearman in two to fifteen minutes then went to Lemoore, California for basic. I got married there and went on to Victorville to 2-engine school. Just six months later on July 20, 1942, I got my wings and commission. They called us all in and said that everyone who had 200 hours total time and night and instrument check were going to McDill Field in Florida to go into B-25s and B-26s. After three days there we were just beginning to like it, but in those days you could pick up a paper and it would tell of a B-25 or B-26 taking off from McDill and plunck! Down it would go. Something was wrong and they'd go in the drink. Everyone was sceptical about this so they transferred us down to Ft. Myers to a B-24 Group. We were there a month and left for overseas. Sixteen of us extra co-pilots went over on the Queen Elizabeth. Two squadrons of the 93rd Group flew nonstop from Gander, Newfoundland to Prestwick, Scotland. We arrived on September 15.

Things got pretty rough that fall and winter since we did not have much in the way of fighter escort, so they told us if we flew 25 combat missions we would return to the zone of the interior and never have to face the enemy in combat again. They kind of got away from that, but did let us off combat with 25 missions. The thing was, we wanted to get in as many missions as we could so we could go home. We tried to fly as many as we could and would go to other squadrons to see if any co-pilots were missing. We even did this when we were in Africa, borrowing an airplane when our plane was out of commission because the missions over Italy were a lot easier than out of England.

When we got to England we were the first B-24 Group, there were three B-17 Groups at the time. The English people would invite us over for Sunday dinner, and we would find out that they had used their whole month's ration coupons for meat to give us that Sunday dinner. For a while we worked a deal with the mess hall for some extra stuff for them. But after awhile there were more Americans than English and the Americans got to be so unbearable that we started to have some friction. But they treated us very well and I liked them and still do.

We pulled our first mission on October 9, we were part of a diversion and I think all we did was ruin some tulips in Holland some place. We extra co-pilots would go around after a mission to other squadrons to see if any co-pilots were missing so we could get on a crew. On this first mission I was Julian Harvey's co-pilot and we had General Hughes along. Julian Harvey said to the General, "All due respect General, but my co-pilot sits in that seat," (pointing to the right hand seat.) So the General stood behind my seat. The Fortresses got all the publicity but we were there, too, and as a matter of fact, General Hughes got the Silver Star for that mission.

Those Generals were not in condition for that kind of flying. General Timberlake was an ex-fighter pilot and at the time was just 32. He did not like the 25,000 foot missions, he liked the low ones, those were the most dangerous. He was not allowed to go on the Ploesti mission. But he was a combat pilot. Most of them were not, they would go on the missions not to get medals, but to see what should be done.

Clark Gable got hell for going on 5 missions to get an air medal when he was 40.

I was co-pilot to Julian Harvey for thirteen missions and he taught me how to fly a B-24. I had a total time of 210 hours flying. I had never been above 15,000 feet in any aircraft. I had never used oxygen in an aircraft and had never flown formation in a B-24. He was a natural pilot and could lay off for weeks and come right back in and do a great job of flying. He was a handsome man with manners and had been a model and was really a lady's man, never had any problems getting a date. He did have a problem with one of his lady friends back in the states, got married to her by proxy and he never dated again after that. He wanted that child he had sired to have a name and he respected the girl enough to marry her and he quit running around.

Julian Harvey was a strict disciplinarian, he would say, "Get that wing up there, get it up there!" We took off in the #1 spot in the right wing on this first mission, he made me fly formation looking across, which is hard to do, then he flew over the target and then he made me fly back. Julian Harvey taught me how to fly a B-24.

I still had less than 300 hours when I got my own plane and crew, but we learned fast. Some time before I got my own ship, a British Lysander was brought in to our base and we were to use it to tow targets a couple of times. Charlie Weiss was our ordinance officer. We got checked out in the plane and after two hours time had to fly it. Charlie said, "I'll fly with you." I said,

"Sure, get in back." Well, there was no seat belt back there, just a tripod type thing to attach a gun or camera to, so he held on to that. This Lysander had flaps and slots so you could fly it as slow as 60 miles an hour. I took off and we got up to about three hundred feet and the propeller came off. One thing they had told us when checking us out, "When they crash they burn." I was not familiar with the plane and just started on the left hand side of the instrument panel and turned everything off. There was a plowed field straight ahead of us and we landed in that. The landing gear stayed where we lit and we slid on in — no damage — the plane didn't burn. Charlie banged his knee up a little. They came out and got us and we went back to the base.

The next morning Colonel Timberlake, Col. "Ted" as it was in those days, our Group Commander, called me in to his office. I thought, "Here's where I get it." But he said, "Congratulations for landing that plane without a prop, we are going to put you in for a medal." And they did, but it was for a purple heart for the skill I'd shown in landing a disabled airplane. Of course, by the time it went to the 8th Air Force and came back it was the wrong medal. We were already in combat so they forgot all about it, but I was almost the first decorated guy in the Group. Charlie took some pictures of the crash.

The winter of 1942-'43, three of our squadrons went to Africa. The 329th, my squadron, stayed behind to learn the new British deal called a "Gee" Box where you could bomb in cloudy weather and do night bombing more accurately. You could bomb targets that you could not see. It worked on the principle that there were two points that the "Gee" box would line up on so the navigator could keep track of the position, by the time lag in the signals received from the two transmitters.

While we were training for this we went down to one of the British Lancaster bases, and we trained with the British for a couple of weeks for night missions. I also went on one night leaflet mission to France with the British. My gosh! It scared me to death. We would go over in the daytime and you would see the flak coming up, and that was scary. Fighters coming in did not seem to bother me but then at night the night fighters came in and you would see these tracers coming in and it seemed like there were hundreds of them. And only every ten or so were tracers, you would see a tenth of what was really coming at you. The antiaircraft came up and instead of a black puff of smoke it was like the fourth of July and coming right at you — scared me to death. I was just willing to let the English do the night missions, and we do the daylight missions. The deal never came off for us so we left Bungay.

We had several missions to Brest, France and the sub pens. The submarines were holding up the shipment of the supplies we needed to wage war against the Germans so we had to try and eliminate them. We went over to drop bombs. Spitfires were to join us and escort us to the target. We get to the coast, no spitfires, so we go over the target and drop our bombs. As we were coming out here comes a whole bunch of planes. Well this is only our second or third mission, and every gun in the outfit opens up on them. One Spitfire pilot rolled his plane on its side to show the British roundel and the distinctive wing. I don't know how many bullet holes he got in that wing. This was a late afternoon mission and the bad part of it was that we had to land at their base after the mission.

These Spitfire pilots were not British, but Polish, Czechoslovakian and other non-British. They had lost their homes and families and all they wanted to do was kill Germans. Most of them did not speak English, but had come over and joined the RAF and were good pilots. They made up this group and we have to land at their base after we had been shooting at them. Col. "Ted" had to take several bottles of Scotch over to their commanding officer so we could get off the base alive. From then on 'till next spring, we didn't have any fighter escort.

One of the roughest missions I had was one just across the channel, two and a half hours total time. We went over to get a German ship coming up the channel, between England and France. We put up a maximum effort to go bomb it, and we had fighter escort that day. The escort was getting the devil beat out of it because the Germans were really protecting this ship. We had Spitfires flying under us for protection.

A mission into Germany was too far to keep radio contact with the escort, so they couldn't let them go in with us at that time. Also, the fuel limitation had a lot to do with it too.

P-47s and P-51s were most often used for escort, there were some P-38s, but they were used more in the Pacific. When we got the P-51s, they could go wherever they wanted to — they were really an airplane. I never flew one but did fly a P-47. When I had finished my missions and was attached to Headquarters of the 2nd Bombardment Division, they brought in a couple of war-weary P-47s for us to fly. General Timberlake and I decided to fly those P-47s, I read six pages of the Tech orders and he didn't read any of them. I knew how to start it. I got mine started and took off. General Timberlake had to have the crew chief start his. When I got up I had a red light come on indicating that I did not have my tail wheel locked. If I landed with the tail wheel unlocked I'd ground loop the thing. I finally found a button on the "wheel up" thing that you had to push to lock the tail wheel. By the time I got the wheel locked, here was General Timberlake flying off my wing. He used to be a fighter pilot, he was hunting and pecking and finally he settled in a grove. Now I thought, we aren't allowed to buzz, but when you've got a Brigadier General on your wing, that ought to be the time. So I buzzed hell out of everything I could find and went back and landed. General "Ted" said, "Earl you shouldn't buzz." That's all I heard of it.

We'd see those P-47 pilots and ask them, "What do you do about the gasoline smell?" "Put on your oxygen mask!" "What about all that noise and vibration?" "Turn on your radio — loud."

I always liked to do stunts in them. We would use our P-47s to monitor the formations for the missions. When we were all done with that, I'd do some stunts, power dives, etc., but I never did open one up, they were too fast for me. I had flown B-24s too long. Getting a little ahead of the story but we did have fun with those P47s.

I did about twelve missions with Julian Harvey as his copilot and then one morning a fellow named Leon Packer from Boise, Idaho came by and asked me to go on a mission as his copilot.

Leon was a real nice guy and had been Airdrome Officer at Fort Myers at night. One night a plane had an accident so he cleared the field, jumped in his jeep and got about to the end of the runway and here comes a plane landing without any lights, without radio. It just got stopped by the time it got to Packer, the props were still turning and the outside prop broke the finger Leon had on the steering wheel and clipped him on the back of the head, so he was a little shaky after that.

He knew a lot about flying and was experienced. They had already had the briefing and the mission was to Brest, France. Well, I'd been to Breast a couple of times already — pretty easy missions. We went on this mission and lost the supercharger on #3 engine. We were supposed to hit the target and turn left and we could not stay up with the formation so we had to drop down a bit and cut inside. There were only about six or eight enemy planes in the area and they jumped us. They hit the #3 engine again and it started to run away and wouldn't feather, then we proceeded to get pretty badly shot up. We had lost our radio so I got up, left my parachute on the seat, and went back to the bomb bay. Our doors were still open as we had dropped our bombs. I reached over the bay to shut off the gas to the #3 engine. When it stopped after running out of gas it feathered. As I got back to the cockpit, Packer was just finishing feathering the other three engines, so I reached up and unfeathered them and said, "For crying out loud we can make it back."

Parke Davis the bombardier, would dress up in a freshly cleaned full uniform before every mission and say, "Achtung! I'll be the best dressed prisoner in Germany." He had seen me get out of my seat, Packer had called "Bail out!" Some heard him and some didn't. Davis tried to get out the wheel cover for the front wheel but only one opened so the navigator kicked him out and we never heard from Davis again. We were over the water at the time so I suppose he drowned.

I climbed back into the co-pilot seat, the navigator decided to stay with the plane, and Packer was pretty ashamed about that time. I took control of the plane and dove down as close to the water as I could get. The last enemy plane made an attack from below and behind when we were as close to the water as we could get. The top turret man got this enemy plane just as he

25

was coming over. We were badly shot up — hydraulics, everything. The navigator got us to Lands End. I worked it up to about 1,000 feet and I told Packer he had better let me pump the flaps down because there was a big hole out there by the flaps on the right side and they might not work. We discussed this for a minute or two, finally he let me put them down as far as they would go, about a third. We pumped the landing gear down and he took over, as he was the Captain of the ship, and I was a Second Lieutenant then. At Lands End they had eight or ten barriers to keep the water out, Packer undershot. There we were, one engine out, the flap on the bad engine side would not go down any further, he could not pull it up any more so we sheared off one landing gear on the last barrier. One of our enlisted gunners had not gotten a scratch during the airfight but got a broken ankle on the landing. The next morning they sent a B-17 to pick us up — that was the worst part of it.

George Brown, at this time, was our Commanding Officer for the 329th. I did not know that he had called in all the other crew members and talked to them. I liked Packer and would not say anything against him. I did say that "Julian Harvey is the only guy on this base I'll fly co-pilot for." He talked to the other guys. They gave me my first DFC for that. And they have me my own plane and crew.

I had a total of 290 hours when I got my own plane and crew. My co-pilot was Joe Clements and how he got to be my co-pilot is a story. He was an experienced pilot as were most of them, and had been in the Air Corps for a while. Joe had to abort from a mission, I believe the problem was a bad supercharger, anyhow, he saw an RAF pilot come by and bail out in the Channel. In the Atlantic in the winter you could live just a few minutes at the most. Joe circled and flew low and slow and tried to drop one of their life rafts, of which they had two, but this one got tangled up in his tail surfaces on that side so he went around and dropped the other and it hit inflated. They waited until he got in the life raft. They had called Air-Sea Rescue. Joe came home and they took his plane away from him for jeopardizing a plane and the lives of ten men to save one man. They made him my co-pilot. Two or three weeks later he got a commendation from the British through our Air Corps for saving that British pilot. Our outfit punished him and the British gave him a commendation.

I got *Tarfu,* which had been badly shot up, and half the crew. I also got half a crew of another that had been shot up. They didn't know if *Tarfu* would be safe to fly or not so we spent a couple weeks just flying it around England.

Our bombardier, T.C. Dick, a real nice guy had been badly shot up when Major Cowart had the plane before me. The plane also had a special bomb sight on it. T.C. Dick had a very bad gash on his leg from a 20mm shell on the last mission and whenever he'd see a FW190 he'd freeze. He was in the hospital and was getting better and he had heard the doctor talking, "Well, we had better send "Dicker" back to the 8th Replacement Depot." But all of us knew about that depot for that was where the people went that were just coming into the Groups for placement. Dicker thought, "I might get assigned to the 44th Group or one of the others that are getting shot up worse than we are." So he said, "Send me back to my old Group." The doctors thought, "There's a hero." So they sent him back to the 93rd. What we didn't know was that the 8th Replacement Depot was also where they send you to ship you back to the states.

So every mission I would ask Dicker if he wanted to fly today and he'd say, "Yes," because the only way to get back to the States was to get in the missions, 25 of them. And that is what we were trying to do.

When we came back from Ploesti and I had finished my 25 missions, I was sent to the 409th Squadron and made Operations Officer. Dicker would try like hell to go on missions but just couldn't. He tried but just could not do it. Then I got sent up to 2nd Bomb Wing and got him transferred home.

In the first week of May 1943, we began to do a lot of low level flying in England, and low level flying in a B-24 is silly.

Tarfu to Ploesti

We went down to Africa in June of 1943. There were two Groups there already, having gone down the year before to bomb Tokyo, but General Doolittle beat them to it. They tried a mission to Ploesti that was was not too successful. They stayed down there and flew missions.

When we got down to Africa we started to do the low level formation flying. We did have problems with dust and maintenance. We were a long way from any place, we were 18 miles from Benghazi. We practiced flying six abreast coming up to a dummy target, things like that. We flew a few missions to Italy before the Ploesti raid.

We were briefed two weeks before the mission, the pilots, co-pilots, navigators, and bombardiers. There were two initial points — one was five minutes after the first one, and the second one was the main one — both looked very much alike. That is where our trouble started.

Everything had been going great. August 1st was on a Sunday. They wanted to bomb while everyone was in church so they could see what we were doing. We were going to take them by surprise.*

The day of the mission was a quiet day, no wind, dust all over everything. It held up the take-offs. Some planes would take off down the runway and just come back down — plop. It happened not only in our Group but others

*LUFTWAFFE cryptanalysis's greatest achievement was the decipherment of the Allied signal concerning the great attack on the Ploesti oil fields, August 1, 1943. The antiaircraft batteries were given sufficient warning to greet the American bombers with such a withering fire that 53 of the bombers were shot down. (Kahn, David, *The Codebreakers*, Macmillan, NY, 1967.)

too.

With a B-24 we were always overloaded on a mission. It had a red line, it seemed to me, of 64,000 pounds, something like that. We'd load them so the tail wouldn't drag, then it would fly. On this mission we carried two bomb bay tanks and so we had only two bomb bays to carry the bombs in. We had four one-thousand pound chemically-fused bombs.

The take-off, assembly and everything was late because of the dust problems in take-off. Our maintenance was the best you could put out, but how could you carry supplies for that many planes so far from home? Dust got in the engines, etc. When we were just south of Greece, one plane peeled off and went down in the sea. (Lt. Brian Flavelle in *Wingo Wango*.) Julius Harvey, a real good friend of mine, who had taught me to really fly the B-24, had to abort because an engine froze up. We went on and were to rendez-vous with the other groups. We got to the mountains going over into Yugoslavia and we had to go up to 14,000 feet and when we did there were clouds up there. When we came out of the clouds there were just two groups. The group ahead was from the Middle East, the 376th Group led by K.K. Compton. He continued to climb straight up and so Colonel Baker signaled us to climb right up through the cloud. Anyhow, when we came out there we were, just two groups. We made a big 360, never saw the other groups and so we went on toward Ploesti.

We got up to the first Initial Point and the lead navigator turned West at this first I.P., five minutes too soon. You could just sense Col. Baker, who was our C.O., trying to decide to do it right or to follow the other group. We were on radio silence and as he was shot down and killed, we will never know just what he was thinking, but he made the turn with some of the other group. K.K. Compton went on toward Bucharest.

At briefing we had been told that defenses of Ploesti had been set up for an attack from the south, so we were supposed to go in from West to East. We had ended up straight south of the target. We could see the smudge pots, they knew we were coming! General Ent and Colonel Compton went on toward Bucharest, but Colonel Baker was not going to come this far and not hit the target. We went in six abreast.

My navigator, Lt. James R. Steeg, knew where we were and that the lead plane had made a wrong turn.

I was in the first wave of six. They had said the Germans couldn't get their antiaircraft guns to bear on us flying that close to the ground. We took tops off shrubs, had grass stains on our antenna. There were farmers out in the fields shooting at us with shotguns, rifles, and whatever else they had.

Our gunners were briefed not to shoot at balloons and they had balloons flying pretty low too. If you hit a tight cable you had a chance of breaking it, a slack cable would do the damage. As might be expected, I hit a balloon cable and it took off a deicer boot. My co-pilot, Joe Clements, who was actually a

28

more experienced pilot that I was, was a nut about guns but never had a chance to use one. Joe had a submachine stuck out the window shooting back at the farmers. I reached over and tapped him and said, "For God's sake, Joe, be ready to take over when they get me." I didn't have any doubt, we were flying so close to the ground. I had to pull up to clear trees and bushes, things like that.

We were going over the wrong target from the wrong way, the south. I imagine Colonel Baker thought we had better hit what we could and as we were over a target (Columbia Aquila) we had better hit some refineries. We pulled up and dropped our bombs, hit the refineries, tank farms and whatever was in the way. We pasted Target White Five pretty good. Colonel Baker's plane was hit when we got to the target and moved over one plane. I slid under him and he pulled off to the side and got up to maybe 300 feet high. One chute came out and started to open but never did get open before it hit the ground. Of course, this was one plane I knew no one got out of because I saw it. There were three planes left of the first six. George Brown (later four star General and Joint Chiefs of Staff in Washington, D.C.), was flying in his old plane with Raymond Walker, who had been his copilot and was the pilot of the plane, *Queenie* I believe was the name of it, and of course, Walt Stewart in *Utah Man*. We formed up on George Brown right after we got out. We did hit some refineries and as we came out, here came the other three groups from the right I.P.

Some of our bombs went off early, some went later, but some were going off when the other groups came in to bomb and the smoke and flame was making it hard for them to see the targets. Our losses were heavy but we got over and beyond the target and then the fighters came after us and we shot up some of them. All during the fight my gunners were working over anybody on the ground that was shooting at us as well as any flak batteries they could see. The mission lasted about 30 minutes. Farmers were shooting at us before we even got to the defenses. When we got within the refinery defenses, I don't suppose it lasted ten minutes, but it seemed like an eternity.

I did come home alone, though, we were in no condition to fly formation or even try to as we were so shot up. We were thinking about gas conservation, how much we had lost, how much we had left. We made no effort to fly formation with anybody. At this point the only other one that I knew who had got out of Ploesti of the six of us that went in on the first wave was Walt Stewart in *Utah Man*.

We had been taking flak hits and one of then got us right in the toilet. This would have been bad enough, but most of the crew were suffering from dysentery. I had two engineers on my plane, but one had dysentery so bad he had to stay home and his replacement was Sgt. Thomas D. Gilbert from New York.

It was funny in some respects now when you look back on it, but not at that time. When the fighters left us, I went back to check on things in the plane. The right waist gunner was staring at his fifty caliber gun barrel, I looked at it and could hardly believe what I saw. About three inches from the end of the barrel it was bent at right angles and at that point it had a bullet hole in it. You would swear it was impossible. Roy Davis could not use his gun any more. The other gunner, Tom Gilbert had been hit in the butt from below, not a bad wound but a painful one. This was his first combat mission.

Some of our control cables had been shot out but luckily they were for the auto-pilot so I could fly all right. Our oxygen system had been shot out and all we had was three walk-around bottles. A twenty millimeter shell had come up through one of our bomb bay tanks and we did not know how much fuel we had lost from that tank. We used up that tank first, some had leaked out and it had sealed itself up again. But we did have enough fuel to make it back to the base.

We had to climb to 18,000 feet to go over the mountains so I had the crew all lay down while I used the oxygen to fly the plane over the mountains, and when we came down the other side we were all right again. Some were not so lucky. I saw two planes that were flying higher than us go into some clouds and neither one of them came out. They had collided and all were killed except three enlisted gunners from 1st Lt. Victor E. Olliffe's, *Let 'er Rip.* They were Sgts. Clifford E. Koen, Harold Murray, and Eugene Engdahl.

When we got back we had been airborne for 13H hours and there were not many planes getting back. Some landed at other bases and, of course, some never did get back. I helped Sgt. Gilbert out of *Tarfu* and was asked if all the missions were this bad and I replied that some were really rough, but then I truthfully replied that indeed this had been my roughest so far of the 22 I had flown.

Tarfu was so badly shot up they wanted to salvage it out for parts because we were short of parts. My plane was a B-24D and I thought they flew a lot better than the new ones — the H and K models. "Well," I said, "Now wait a minute, we've got a Norden bombsight in our plane that was donated by the workers at the Norden Bombsight Co. They took up a collection and they donated this bombsight to the 8th Air Force. Now we have to send in a report periodically to the Air Force and they in turn send it back to the States about this bomb sight. So we had better save this plane." They let me fly the plane over to Deversoir by the Suez Canal, and it was fixed up and we got it back in time to fly it back home.

While my plane was at Deversoir I flew Ray Walker's plane, *Queenie,* that had taken he and Col. George Brown to and from Ploesti. I flew a mission in it to Foggia, Italy and we were dropping 100 pound fragmentation bombs because we did not want to ruin the field as we were planning on taking it over and using it. I was flying my own crew off Walt Stewart's wing. Walt Stewart had been a Mormon missionary in England before the war, he had borrowed my long coat to visit the King and Queen and the Princess, so my coat got to meet them. Walt's a real nice guy, anyhow, we go over Foggia and Walt could not drop his bombs. I dropped mine OK, but his would not drop. He made a big 360, came back and finally dropped his bombs. I stayed right on his wing, then he speeded up to catch up with the group. When I pushed my supercharger I did not get any more speed, I just got red lines on my engines, so I had to throttle back. We could see the other group off to our right. We were the far left group. Off to the right, the group was being attacked by fighters. Then eight or ten fighters came in from the left. As we were trailing the other groups, the fighters flew right along with us, off a ways. We could see them recoil when they would shoot. We did not know what the deal was. They had some kind of missle deal they would shoot out of their planes. Because of the weight they could not carry machine guns. The missles would explode off by the groups ahead but were not accurate. My top turret man, Sgt. Gerrard E. Sullivan, shot down the lead one, so the fighters moved over to the other side of us. My right waist gunner was a duck hunter and he began to shoot them down from the rear and he got five of them before they gave up and left. These were Macchi 200's, I believe. If they would have had machine guns we would have been sitting ducks for them.

At de-briefing when we got back to the base we were asked a lot of questions about this and this was the first deal of this sort that had been reported. The Germans had developed their first air-to-air rockets to use in bomber interception.

When we got back to England we were told that anyone caught flying below 1,000 feet would be court martialed, but a little town of Bungay, England, got a real buzz job. They had exceeded their quota of war bonds in England by the largest percentage of anybody. So three guys out of our group were picked to fly a low level formation in B24s over Bungay. Julian Harvey flew the right wing, Charlie Merrill flew lead and I flew left wing. We put on a low level exhibition and that was really fun. I really enjoyed that, because I admired Charlie Merrill and Julian Harvey as two of the best pilots I had flown with in 1942 and 1943.

Back in Africa we had found some English communication lads who had been there for a long time. There were four or five of them and they had to scrounge around for everything. They had little to keep body and soul together. We got acquainted with them and they ate with us for some time.

The first time I went to London after getting back from Ploesti, I looked up the sister of one of those English lads, Lance Corporal Baker. When I went to London I went with Doc Toomey and we would go to the movies in the daytime and a play at night which would end about 9:30. I went to see Baker's sister and she asked if we had any plans for the night and I said,

"No". She asked us for dinner. She wanted to call out to Baker's wife and his folks — so we did this. We got out to this pub and had a big dinner and everything. I was showing them some pictures I had of Baker and telling about him. As the mail situation was really bad they had not had much news from him. We visited and drank most of the night — had a great time.

The actual damage at Ploesti was minimal, but it did illustrate the fact that it could be done, which was an encouragement to the Bomb Groups. It was very upsetting to the Germans and encouraging to the Allies that Ploesti could be bombed. Later when the 15th Air Force worked out of Foggia, Ploesti was pretty well taken care of, but always heavily defended. It was a full year of bombing before it was neutralized.

The Ploesti raid could have been made from Russia in three hours flying time, but they would not let us base there.

After my 25 missions were in, I got my second DFC and the Silver Star for the Ploesti mission and a transfer to the 409th as Operations Officer. Shortly, I went over to the 2nd Combat Bomb Wing with General Timberlake. He was the youngest Brigadier General — made it when he was 33 years old. I was one of the Assistant Operational Officers. There were sixteen of us. We ate and slept together in the same building. We each put so much money into a pot each month. We had a cook who was a professional cook and a baker that had been a professional. The cook would buy stuff on the black market and we lived like kings. But all I could think of was getting home. I had just gotten married a few months before I went overseas.

The other Assistant Combat Wing Operations Officer and I would alternate working up the missions for the Groups. There were 3, then 4, and then 5. The one that didn't work up the mission would go down to the Lead Group briefing. We also trained new Groups as they came in and we'd alternate.

I went down to this one Group and I would talk to the whole Group's pilots, co-pilots, bombardiers, and navigators and gunners. Then we would split up. Pilots talked to pilots and navigators to navigators etc. When I came back, General Ted said, "How do your boys look?" I said, "They've got a lot of experience." there was one long tall drink of water that looked familiar as the devil and he was asking real intelligent questions. I can't place where I've seen him before. General Ted said, "Was it Jimmy Stewart?" "Sure."

James Stewart was a Captain at the time — a Squadron Commander. They'd put him in for Major after he got there and he had turned it down until the enlisted men he had put in for promotion got their promotion, then he took his. He was a real capable fellow.

The Squadron Commanders would take turns giving briefings. And we were concerned about Major Stewart and we timed him. We thought he might take too much time to do the briefing. He wasn't any slower than anybody else, and he didn't have to repeat things. He spoke so plainly and articulately that he got through the briefings the same time as everybody else.

I remember one time when he was leading the Division. He'd gone over the target, Wilemshaven, obscured by clouds, made a 360, went over the target again, still clouds, all the time flak and enemy planes. He went around again and the third time the clouds broke and they dumped and he did a good job on the target. He got back and was telling us about it and he said, "There weren't too many fighters but the !*)N†‡¢(Flak!

I worked on timing and details for sending the bombers over just before the invasion of France. Then I got a chance to take a promotion and stay over or come home so I came home.

When we got home from a mission we had a good place to sleep. It wasn't the best, but it was good and we could get cleaned up. It was warm, and we could get something to eat. It wasn't like the poor devils in the front lines.

PLOESTI

by T/Sgt. Deloros R. Brumagin (44th)

There was training in the desert,
There were Twenty-Fours galore;
And flying o'er the sand dunes,
Had sometimes proved a bore.

Now we had a practice target,
Built to scale and bombed for fun;
But we knew the day was coming,
When we'd use it on the "Hun".

We'd been assigned a target,
PLOESTI, was the name.
General Brereton was commanding
The raid that came to fame.

He called his Group Commanders,
All the leaders for the "Day";
And with words that's since made
    History,
So proudly did he say:

"It's the most important mission,
Any force has been assigned;
And with quick, complete destruction,
A Victory we will find.

They need that oil so badly,
The problem here is clear;
We'll bomb it from existence,
Though the price we pay is dear.

This task will be accomplished,
With an 'On the deck' attack;
With every Lib around Benghazi,
That'll fly to there and back."

The night before the mission,
The Chaplins' blessings gave;
And the message made things
    brighter,
For the soul that God can save.

It was early in the morning,
August First was then the date;
Every man and plane was ready,
Just to shake the hand of fate.

The sun was shining brightly,
As we flew across the Med;
With the words of General Brereton,
Still droning through each head.

The minutes grew to hours,
And we crossed the mountains high;
Where the Yugoslav Guerillas
Were watching us go by.

Then we streaked across the valley,
Rousing peaceful Peasants there;
And the roaring of the engines,
Seemed like thunder cracked the air.

There was Rumania's golden wheat
    fields
But their beauty soon was lost;
With oil wells in the distance,
And "Blue Danube" as we crossed.

That creek will be remembered,
The loveliest in the land;
But we used it for a landmark,
To know the target was at hand.

Then every heart was heavy,
Every eye was open wide,
As we asked the Lord, Our Maker,
To be our strength and guide.

Our minds' eyes saw a picture,
Of loved ones we hold dear,
God placed it there to aid us
Through all our strife and fear.

In the distance was the target,
And to us a gruesome sight,
We lost our thoughts of reverence,
In preparing for the flight.

We could see the flaming debris,
Some group had marked it so;
By mistake they'd left their bombs
    there,
Why? No man will ever know.

The time bombs were exploding,
And oil fires raging high;
We could see "their" guns ablazin'
It was us to do or die.

Our leader knew his duty,
Disregarding fear and life;
With no sign of hesitation
Led his "Boys" through fire and strife.

We saw many things distinctly,
As swiftly on we flew,
We saw the German gunners,
We could see then dying too.

The battle was a nightmare,
Unreal in every thought;
But we needn't be reminded,
How fiercely it was fought.

Of the tempest o'er the target,
No man alive can tell,
There was shooting, burning, dying,
It was sure a living Hell!

Though the action lasted seconds,
It was a lifetime to us all,
As we watched the big guns blasting,
And our planes and comrades fall.

As the target flew behind us,
And through the thickest of the fight;
Every plane of ours was damaged,
And their holes a ghastly sight.

There were many started homeward,
But failing to return,
They had crashed up in the
    mountains,
And were left up there to burn.

Some fell out with engine trouble,
To the "Cause" their lives they gave;
Then their fuel had been exhausted,
And crashed beneath the waves.

There were several airmen wounded,
But their will surpassed the cost,
'Cause they knew they had the
    vengeance
For the blood that they had lost.

Now in tribute to those heroes,
Who died but not in vain,
Their deeds will be remembered,
Though forgotten be their names.

They had answered duty bravely,
Yes! Every loving Mothers' son;
We thank God for all our airmen,
And the victory that they won.

33

Date: 1 August 1943
Target: Ploesti, Roumania
Narrator: Raymond A. Wolf, Jr.

S/Sgt. Raymond A. Wolf, Jr. did not man his top turret guns on the Ploesti Mission, though he was an excellent engineer and top turret gunner. He tells about it in his story. He had already flown several missions that had been traumatic air battles.

Raymond Wolf enlisted in the Army Air Corps in August of 1941 and was sent to Aircraft Mechanic School at Chanute Field, Illinois. His first assignment was with the 97th Bomb Group at Sarasota-Bradeton, Florida as an aircraft mechanic.

Sgt. Wolf relates his pre-Ploesti experiences and how he got from the B-17s of the 97th Group to the B-24s of the 93rd Bomb:

On June 4, 1942 I left the states on the Queen Mary bound for England. The ground crews and some of the flight crews arrived some weeks before the B-17s arrived from the states.

When the flight crews were being assigned to planes of the 97th Bomb Group one of the flight engineers refused to fly combat duty for some reason or another, so I volunteered to take his place. We flew a number of missions to France including the first one to Rouen. The Group also flew support for the Dieppe landings and we went into Abbieville/Drucat airdrome, the home field of the famed "Yellow-nosed Messerschmits," often called "The Abbieville kids."

"One day a B-24 flew in with a Major Cowart as the pilot (Major William Cowart, Jr.). The next day our crew was assigned to him and his plane *Tarfu*. This plane was equipeed with highly sophisticated radio equipment and the crew was assigned to the 93rd Bomb Group. Our crew was told we would not be flying regular missions with the Group. The explanation was that Headquarters in London had a huge wall map of Europe and the mission was to fly solo under dense cloud cover and London would keep track of us. They were to send signals when to correct our course and instructions when to drop bombs on various cities. We never dropped any bombs. The missions were aborted. Just a couple of missions were attempted. The crew was reassured each time that a meteorologist would verify dense cloud cover to Germany and back, but every mission, even before reaching the target, we ran out of cloud cover. We took flak and could see fighters taking off and we would race back under the protection of clouds before the fighters attained altitude.

Since this was experimental equipment we had, we were not allowed to take *Tarfu* on regular missions. Occasionally our crew borrowed a plane from a crew on leave and flew that one on a mission. One such mission was with a small group of planes to Rouen, France. Our group was attacked by an estimated 75 German fighters and there were heavy losses on this mission. Our crew had borrowed *Thar She Blows* and we lost #3 and #4 engines and could not maintain altitude. Bombardier Lt. Dick was severly wounded in the leg and could not bail out. All the crew elected to stay with the plane.

Our pilot made a crash landing on a field outside of London and the plane was a complete loss, but we had no injuries due to the crash. Shortly after this incident, the experimental missions with *Tarfu* were abandoned and the special equipment removed. We then participated in the regular bombing missions of the 93rd Bomb Group. Several months later Major Cowart was reassigned as Squadron Commander of a B-17 group.

Major Cowart's replacement was 1st Lt. Earl Hurd, and at this time I was promoted to T/Sgt. This brings me to the Ploesti mission.

In the spring of 1943 our 93rd Bomb Group started those intensive low level flying exercises. We left England and arrived at a base in Libya, about 23 miles from Benghazi. We continued practicing low level flying.

July 31, 1943 the enlisted men were told we were to bomb the Ploesti oil refineries in Romania. We were briefed in detail about the targets, and the importance of doing a good job of bombing.

I remember the evening before the raid, Captain Hurd went out to the plane for a last check on the engines and found that #2 engine was malfunctioning. We talked about this and he sid he would get a replacement engine before the mission. I don't know how he did it, but sure enough he did. The crew chief and I worked most of the night installing the new engine. Normally a new engine was flight tested for eight hours before it is accepted for combat flight, but this was not a normal situation.

Shortly after take off, flying low over the Mediterranean, I saw one plane ahead of us, all four engines had quit. It dove straight down into the water! This may have been the first casualty of Ploesti. In my opinion this was due to the flight engineers mistake. In all probability he was switching from main tanks to auxiliary tanks and it was extremely important to open fuel cocks on the lines running to transfer pumps and wait a minute before turning on the fuel pumps. I think what happened is, he turned the fuel pump on first and got an airlock, cutting off fuel to all four engines.

While crossing the Mediterranean, Captain Hurd told me to switch to the auxiliary bomb bay tank. We would use this fuel on the way to Ploesti. This turned out to be a wise decision because we took a 20mm shell in one of these tanks. If we had not used these tanks we would not have had enough fuel to return to our base. We proceeded to Ploesti. On this raid Captain Hurd (he was a 1stLieutenant, but Captain of our plane) told me that I would not be manning my guns, but that I should stand between him and the co-pilot, Lt. Clements, in the cockpit.

Arriving at Ploesti, the 93rd, under the command of Colonel Addison Baker, veered off from the leading group. They had taken a wrong turn and were headed for Bucharest. Colonel Baker realized this and had our group turn and head for the oil fields.

Going into Ploesti, Colonel Baker was in front of us and I saw his plane take several hits and burst into flames, and finally fly into a building. Our regular radio operator, T/Sgt. Sullivan had chosen to go with Colonel Baker that day. All of the crew were killed. I saw many planes go down and oil storage tanks exploding. We were attacked by fighters before we reached the target and also after we left the refinery area.

I remember thinking, how can any of our planes survive this intense ground fire at point blank range, and if any manage to come off the target they would be so battered we would all be easy prey and be finished off by German and Romanian fighter squadrons. I felt our plane jerk, we had hit a barrage balloon cable with our left wing, the balloon cable snapped and then I heard a thud behind me. I looked down and saw where an artillery shell had severed the catwalk between our two auxiliary gas tanks. The shell had gone through the top of the plane and never exploded! Probably fired in such haste the fuse had not been set. The plane had lost a lot of structural stability. I was not hooked up to the intercom system so I yelled to Captain Hurd to tell Lt. Dick to find a target fast and unload the bombs, "Lets get the hell out of here!"

As soon as we got our bombs dropped and after we left the target area, which seemed to be a long time but was only a few minutes, I went back to check on the crew. When I got to the rear of the plane I discovered three gunners had been hit. The right waist gunner, Sgt. Davis, was bleeding from his face, the front of his machine gun had been blown off. The left waist gunner, if I remember correctly, Sgt. Gilbert, was bleeding in the hand and butt. This was his first mission, he had never fired a shot and was in a state of shock, just staring blankly. I administered first aid to the two gunners, then checked on the tail gunner, Sgt. Demas, who was hit in the back with a piece of shrapnel. I tried to remove it and couldn't budge it. Strange but this was the only raid on which I ever carried a tool kit. I got a pair of pliers from the kit and pulled the protruding shrapnel from Sgt. Demas back and put on some sulfa and a bandage.

Next I started to examine our plane, *Tarfu*, for damage. It was not hard to find our first hit, we had a direct hit in the toilet. We also had a damaged control cable. I got a roll of wire from the tool kit and proceeded to repair the damaged cable. About this time Captain Hurd came back and sat down on the floor facing me and said, "Sgt. Wolf, what do you think? Should we head for Turkey or try to make it back to the base?" I thought for several

36

moments and said, " Lets head home." Captain Hurd then left to talk to the injured gunners and returned to the cockpit, making the decision to try for Libya. After finishing repairing the control cable I again checked on the injured men, then went forward to the cockpit and took my position between Captain Hurd and Lt. Clements, the co-pilot. Captain Hurd turned to me and said, "Sgt. Wolf we're putting you in for the Silver Star." I requested that he not do this. Many times during the past years I have regretted this.

We did make it back to base alright and the day after, the crew chief drained off our remaining gas and found we had just five more minutes of fuel left in our tanks.

Thar She Blows did not become a total loss, but was repaired and went on to fly the Ploesti mission, survived that and many other missions before becoming a formation assembly ship for the 458th Bomb Group at Horsham Saint-Faith. As a matter of fact the 93rd Bomb Group supplied many war weary B-24Ds for formation assembly ships. It is also worthy to note that Major Cowart recommended Sgt. Wolf for flying cadet in March 1943. But nothing more was heard of it until September of 1943, and by this time the toils of war had decimated Sgt. Wolf and he could not pass the physical.

Date: 17 August 1943
Target: Schweinfurt, Germany
Narrators: Raymond Baier, and Marshall McDaniel

August 17,1943 was the first anniversary of the U.S. Air Corps operations against Fortress Europe. The 8th Bomber Command prepared 376 B-17s for this raid on the ball bearing plant at Schweinfurt and on the Messerschmitt aircraft factory at Regensburg, both deep in Germany. What an anniversary! Just a year ago the 8th flew that first mission to Rouen, France (twelve B-17s flying 56 miles to target). Now 376 Fortresses were to fly 500 miles into Germany. Never had they prepared for so rough a mission. At Alconbury, Station 102, the 92nd Bomb Group crews were aroused at 0100 for a 0600 take off.

Lt. Raymond Baier, pilot, wrote a very detailed account of his mission soon after the Schweinfurt mission:

I had slept the afternoon of Monday, the 16th, and had a hard time in getting to sleep that night. About 10 p.m. Julian Brown was called to the phone and told he too was alerted. He wasn't on the first alert order. At 0105 Tuesday, the orderly came in and awoke us. The truck would leave for the mess hall at 0145 — we ate at 0215 — briefing at 0330. I continued to doze until 0135 then rushed to brush my teeth and wash. We had fried eggs for breakfast — I had three. Then to the flying line. Harvy, the assistant operations officer, wasn't going, so we knew it would be a rough one. Finally at 0400 the briefing began. Julian met Captain Sergeant and I was introduced. Sergeant was the pilot of 835. I was reading a pocket type magazine and on the back were four cartoons. One was good so I showed it around and we all got a laugh. The cartoon had two ground officers (Kiwi), one with an arm in a sling and the other chap saying sympathetically, "Too bad, your briefcase arm, too!" Julian told Sergeant about a couple of minor ommissions his crew had been guilty of — interphone, etc. Then into the inner-sanctum of the Briefing Room. All eyes went straight to the huge map of Europe where a string is always stretched from our base in England to the objective. This morning it seemed that string would reach around the world! It went to Schweinfurt, almost to the Swiss border. This was the first time we knew where we were going. I turned to Willie and said, "Well, pretty rough, but it could be worse." Briefing consists of target and weather information with photographs and the type of and amount of opposition

38

that can be expected, also taxi instructions. Stations time was 0605, taxi at 0630 and take off at 0640. Then the first postponement came — the first of many, so we finally went in to get something to eat. I met Slim Turner just before we had a sandwich and talked for a few minutes. Not long, because a Colonel and a Lt. Colonel were talking to him and I didn't want to take up too much of his time. I didn't get him a sandwich for the same reason. Finally the weather broke and we took off at 1220. The hop lasted six hours and 25 minutes.

In 1943 the U.S. Air Corps was still growing. The German Luftwaffe had already reached its peak. Our boys taking their battle folders knew it. By the time flight crews had turned in their personal stuff it was well understood the projected double-header would bring on a large scale and costly air battle. In chapels all over England most of the men turned to their ministers, rabbis, and priests for comfort and encouragement, assurance for the rough hours ahead.

Getting into the trucks to the planes, the aircrews didn't dream that August 17 was to be written into air history, not only because of them, but because there were other soldiers in the skies and on the ground. This was the same day Sicily fell to the Allies, the same day that the R.A.F. bombed Peenemunde (the V-2 rocket plant), the same day that General Kenny's 5th Air Force B-25s destroyed 200 Jap planes at Wewak in eight minutes. This day our double mission involved the deepest penetration ever attempted into Germany, and the largest bomber force to be dispatched to date. The Airmen knew that as they went further into Germany the bombers would hurt her more, but they also knew they would have to pay a higher price for admission. And now the last briefing as the pilots rechecked the details of the mission with their crews. Individuals no longer existed. They were now a ten man team, and on team work would depend the success of the mission and perhaps their lives.

S/Sgt. Marshall McDaniel, assistant radio operator and right waist gunner, 306th Bomb Group, 368th Bomb Squadron, would fly with the First Division in the first task force. He had fifteen missions to his credit, one of which was the epic air battle of July 26 when the 8th went to Hannover, fighting their way in and out. Mac had a good idea what to expect on this mission. His left waist gunner did not. Since ground crew spend many more months overseas than those combat crews who managed to beat the odds and become "Lucky Bastards," the left waist gunner had requested flight status, taken gunnery

39

training and was on his first mission.

In taxiing out to the flight line, Mac's plane, a veteran of many missions, developed a mechanical problem and was returned to the tarmack. A new plane was rolled out and readied for this mission of importance. Certain very critical modifications had not been made on this new plane. This was to cause "Mac" to sweat it out later in the mission. Ship number 23586 was clean and fresh, lacking the dirty black oil streaks and smudges of exhaust gases. No flak patches marred its fresh olive drab paint.

Action against Schweinfurt got underway. The Regensburg Task Force had just hit their target. A vast and integral machine of destruction had been set in motion. Behind these modern warriors were weeks of high command planning. Now crewmen took care of routine duties. Ahead lay four hours of rugged action. The guns were to be especially important today. Sgt. Forrest "Pete" Norman, tail gunner who had been shot down in the March 18 mision to Vegasack with the 303rd Bomb Group, spent six months in the hospital recovering from two broken legs. He was back in the tail on this important double mission. Knowing first hand that a smooth operating pair of 50 calibre guns was good insurance of a safe return from Germany, he had his own maintenance procedure. He would take his guns to his barracks and also would polish the shell "feeders" with crocus cloth so the guns would not jam. One other Sergeant gunner, Charlie Capek, used Prestone or Zerex to keep his guns from freezing up.

"Mac" McDaniel had no chance to give his guns any special care. He said, "They told us at briefing we'd have help from short range fighters and 8th Air Force medium bombers. The fighters were to take us half way, the mediums to bomb diversionary targets." But due to the socked in weather at the First division airfields, the diversion was not coordinated. The Schweinfurt planes were still on the ground while the Regensburg groups were under attack near Eupen. The diversion had only left the English coast at 1000. The diversion did help draw approximately thirty-nine German enemy aircraft from the Schweinfurt groups. The double mission had been well planned, but due to weather conditions it was uncoordinated and this cost many bombers and many lives. But some say the destruction that was done was worth the price.

The worst part of the trip would be the period that the bombers would be on their own. Finally, after the few hours delay, 2300 men counted the seconds.

At Thurleigh the new 306th bomber was taxied out to take-off position by pilot Captain Joseph H. Belser. New 42-23586 was to have quite an indoctrination, as was the former ground crewman and now new-graduate of gunnery school, the left waist gunner. 586 was formed up with a composite group behind the 303rd Group, "Hells Angels," from Molesworth.

As every Group had four squadrons, one squadron could be taken from each Group to complete a Composite Combat Wing. Each Wing was formed in the normal three combat boxes, with lead, high and low Groups, then in turn into lead, high and low squadrons. The lead Group would fly it's lead squadron at 25,000, high at 25,100, and the low at 24,750 feet; the lead squadron in the high Group would fly at 26,000, high at 26,100, and low squadron at 25,750 feet; the low Group would have it's lead squadron at 24,000, high at 24,100 and low at 23,750 feet. This formation of 216 aircraft crossed the enemy coast and headed for Schweinfurt.

So far American formations had never been prevented from reaching their objectives once they had responded to the green "take-off" signal. As always each thundering take-off was never a success until nearly 30 tons of bombs, plane and men were lifted from the earth.

The leader of the 2nd Air Task Force, Colonel William Gross, swept a huge circle around the field. Gradually the second and third bombers edged into position. The sky quickly filled with stately Fortresses riding thru space, but as soon as they got into formation over the British field, they were picked up by German radar. Across the Channel the tentacles of the German locator system, having touched the Flying Fortresses now, pin pointed them in space. Luftwaffe experts accurately plotted the American altitude, course and speed, and promptly informed their fighter control. Immediately, at a dozen Nazi airdromes, from as far north as Denmark, German fighter units began to send up everything they had. Their orders — "Intercept and destroy the oncoming Fortresses." The German answer to the increasing Allied bomber Offensive was this, "Stepped up German fighter strength." Waves of opposition screamed off the map of Europe. In spite of the Luftwaffe, allied plotters selected their targets according to Allied Air Force priorities. That is why nearly three hours after the 4th Bomb Wing had bombed the Nazi Messerschmitt aircraft factory at Regensburg the 1st Bomb Wing was on its way to strike Schweinfurt in the face of an already-aroused enemy.

On this day the 92nd Bomb Group dispatched 22 aircraft, its largest total so far, in the first of the famous attacks on the ball bearing plants at Schweinfurt, Germany. The 92nd Group aircraft, led by Major James W. Griffith and Captain Earl A. Shaefer, submitted claims of 17-3-1 and suffered the loss of two planes. Lt. J.D. Stewart's crew was lost to enemy fighters just before the target, Captain Roland Sergeant's crew just after target.

Lt. Raymond Baier continued his mission summary:

We climbed out and formed over the field as usual, then the Group went to Thurleigh and the Wing was formed with the 305th and 306th Bomb Groups. Then it headed over the Channel toward Holland. We saw fighters just after we passed the Dutch coast, but someone said, "P-47s!! - yeah P-47s." The first thing we knew they came in and no one mistook them at closer range because those 20mm shells burst as they went past. They were Me109s and FW190s — in droves! Throughout the raid we had two bad nose attacks and six or eight abreast attacks. Oh yes, our position was the worst imaginable — low Group and low squadron. The fighters would attack from four to eight abreast and try to spray our formation with shells. I can still see them even though it was two months ago! They would climb higher than we were and way out ahead, then turn and come back through, aiming at the lead squadron of the low group in a slanting dive. Their speed no doubt exceeded 400 miles an hour. If they missed the lead squadron then their shells would possibly get the low squadron. As they approached from this head-on attack they would do a half roll and split S out beneath us, then go back of us climbing again for a tail attack position. Sergeant lost one engine on one of these attacks, another due to flak and finally went down under a concentrated fighter attack. They saw most of them bail out. For a period of 45 minutes all you could hear over the interphone was "Fighter 4 o'clock, fighter 7 o'clock, fighter 6 o'clock attacking, fighter 5 o'clock. Attack followed attack and the rear element really caught it — mister, they had it. At 1508 we bombed the target and turned back. Our bomb racks didn't work so we had to salvo them. Meantime we could see feathered props all over the formation. Many B-17s had already gone down (later we learned we lost 36).

The hour between 1600 and 1700 was the longest hour I have ever lived. It was rough! Plenty! While the 1st Wing was going to Schweinfurt the 4th Wing went to Regensburg and from there to Africa. But we had the rougher deal because we had to fight our way back, but they sure caught plenty from enemy fighters. I had met Slim Turner just before take-off and learned that he was leading the Group which I was in. I also learned that there would be no more raids on the Ruhr. The flak wasn't so bad although we did get one hole near the Belgian coast on the way out. But the fighters were persistant and plentiful. Estimates ran as high as 200 enemy fighters. We again lost two ships from my squadron, but 'chutes were seen coming from both of them. Just before target ship 835 lost an engine, due to flak I think. After the target he began to straggle and asked the formation to slow down, which we did, then he couldn't keep up any longer. He called the leader and said he was dropping out — his wheels came down, some 'chutes were seen, and some said the ship exploded before all got out. All of my friend Julian Brown's crew were with him (Captain Sergeant). Julian Brown was to have ridden as co-pilot in #835 but was dropped by the pilot because he wanted a co-pilot with more experience. On the way back nose attacks diminished — we had only one — and tail attacks increased. Flak was heavy off our right as we passed the Ruhr and we saw some more over Belgium. The fighters followed us to the Channel. We found out that when we salvoed our bombs we had hit a railyard and round-house and much rolling stock — so our trip helped the cause after all.

The lead and high squadrons recalled similar action. As we began to run into flak our gunners could feel the entire German Airforce swarming up. Flying in enemy territory was like a goldfish in a bowl, waiting for the attack! Strict radio silence was maintained while trained eyes searched the sky. The Luftwafe struck, unleashing every trick. B-17s suffered the most savage blows since the war began. Me109s, FW190s, Me110s, Ju88s, a few He111s bent to the attack. Although Gerry knocked down twenty bombers out of the sky on their way to Schweinfurt, the remaining bombers never broke formation. Despite the fury of the attack, extending all the way to the target, they pressed on. Our own guns kept burning the enemy out of the sky. Approaching the target from the I.P. was the most critical defensive period. Here we divided into smaller groups sacrificing our defensive fire power to bomb our target more effectively.

The crucial moment, the moment around which the entire mission revolved, now rested in the steady hand of the bombardier. Each bomber was not permitted more evasive action till — BOMBS AWAY!! At this time the formation was most vulnerable to attack — it didn't matter — we had a job to do at Schweinfurt. We had 400 tons of high explosives to deliver. After getting 80 hits on the main ball bearing plants we could defend ourselves again. We started evasive action against flak and fighter attacks. The main and only idea now was to get home! Fast! At landing fields in Britain the word on the sky battle was out, and red flares were expected (wounded aboard). These planes had priority in landing. Many of the Fortresses themselves were crippled, with feathered props, no landing gear, one landing gear, great holes rent in their sides, fire-blackened engine nacelles. One plane was committed to a crash landing. It had no gear; a perfect wheels-up landing was made. The plane was *My Prayer.*

The anniversary battle lost us more men and aircraft in a single day than the 8th Bomber Command had lost in the first six months of operations over Europe. Those who carried the war 500 miles into the enemy's industrial heart knew better than anyone how expensive it was. They had lost sixty bombers and their crews. What happened August 17, 1943 was a testament to American men with modern weapons and a very old idea — fighting for freedom. On this day high altitude bombers engaged in their greatest, and from the point of view of loss, their most disastrous air battle to date. None the less, the end justified the price they paid.

Sgt. Dean Sommers went to Schweinfurt as a ball turret gunner with the 92nd Bomb Group, flying in the 1st Air Task Force in the low Group. Just moments after the cloud cover had dispersed enough to take off, about six-tenths cloud cover, and the co-pilot made the take-off, as often was the case in a mission flight. In this case Lt. Joe Thornton took the plane up and formed up with the 305th and 306th Bomb Groups over the North Sea.

Sgt. Sommers recalls:

We were lead Group or at least our Wing was lead and I do think we were lead Wing. The fighters attacked just past the coast and we had them with us all the way. All the guns were going on our plane as we had attacks from all directions. Mostly from the front. The plane suffered a lot of holes, but nothing serious, some hydraulic lines. The right waist gunner had the cover plate shot right off his 50 caliber gun! We were hit the worst before we got to the target. The fighters came in from the right side. Joe Thornton was the co-pilot on this mission and we all accused him of sitting on the pilot's lap because the 20mm cannon shells and bullets came thru his seat! — clear thru the back of the armor plate and the fragments from that burst of gun fire went on to severely wound the engineer in the legs and back. This attack also did some damage to the tail of the plane and the trim tabs were all shot up. We gave the engineer first aid and we went on to finish this mission. He

44

went to the hospital when we got back from Schweinfurt and was still there when we got shot down later. He never did get back into flying service again. I have no idea what ever happened to him. I can't recall that any of us shot down any enemy aircraft, but when one enemy aircraft is going down and everyone is shooting at him, it is hard to tell, and to me it did not matter who got the credit, what matters is if you get over AND back again.

Sgt. Sommers goes on:

My Prayer came back from Schweinfurt at ground level. The pilot, co-pilot, and top turret gunner brought her in. That engineer was eventually shot down and was in a P.O.W. camp with us. His name was Cherry, least ways that is what they called him in camp. I don't know his real name. I also met Charles Myano. He went out over Schweinfurt, too. that was one bad mission, but I guess for me the worst one was the "milk run" up to Knaben, Norway.

Sgt. Marshall McDaniel also kept a log of his missions and he referred to it just once, and from then on it was as if the action had just happened the day before:

We formed up as lead Group in the 102nd Combat Wing. The 92nd came over from Alconbury to form up with us at Thurleigh. We picked up altitude and test fired our guns. My guns worked for a short test burst. When we reached the coast I looked up from my right waist gun position and saw them — they were waiting for us! There were swarms of them milling around. It looked like a swarm of bees! The Germans had everything that would fly up there to get us: Me109s, Me110s, Me210s, Ju88s, FW190s, He113s, even a He111 or two. We paid a price for that delay we had. We had some flak, too. One hit right under us and just lifted that bomber up! Captain Belser said, "That was a close one." He was a cool head — never got excited. On other missions he would tell the co-pilot, "You fly her, Dub. I want to take some pictures." But when we came off this mission you could tell by his eyes that he was a tired man. We had fighters coming in at us from all directions and nearly all the guns were firing. I say nearly because the waist guns in this new ship had not had the latest modification that made the ammo belts feed steady. The belts were too long and the guns would not pull up the fresh ammo. I could get off a few rounds and they would hang up. We were having a hell of a time. Captain Belser called back on the intercom and asked why those waist guns were not firing at those fighters as they were called in. I answered that we were having some trouble with the guns not feeding. He said, "Well, get them fixed." In gunnery school we had been told what to do in this case, but the other waist gunner got mad and just sat down and said, "To hell with it." I got mad too, but did not sit down. I tore off the 'chutes and held the belt with one hand and fired with the other. I

45

went from one side gun to the other firing those guns, the sweat was pouring off me. It was way below zero in the plane and I was wet with sweat. I never did tell the pilot what the other gunner did on that mission, and maybe I shouldn't now, but he just lost his cool. I'll tell you, though, that is a sight to behold when you are flying along and you look up there and see about twenty fighters queued up, and then here they come — one after another right at you or line abreast with their cowl and wing guns blinking with little lights as the guns fired at you. They would roll under us and give us a look at their belly, which I always suspected had three inches of armor on it. This was my sixteenth mission, the other waist gunner's first. I've seen our 50's bounce right off them. One after another they come at you. On this mission I've never seen so many planes in all my life. The sky was full of planes and pieces of planes, parachutes of white and yellow. The Germans were doing everything they could to get us down. They dropped bombs on us and shot rockets at us. The Air Corps wanted to hit that target and we did, but we paid a price for it. Boy, that scared me! We could handle a few fighters because those B-17s had a lot of fire power when they were all tucked in good. And in some cases you could do some evasive action. We were still making out pretty good, though we were taking some hits. The ball turret gunner, Sgt. Leonard Norman, had lost his oxygen. His guns quit firing and he did not answer the intercom, so Sgt. McDaniel, on two occasions, checked on him with a portable oxygen bottle before they got his hose repaired.

The German fighters had sufficient time to attack the Regensburg force, land, refuel and rearm, then come back up to attack the Schweinfurt Groups in relays. When one Gruppen got low on fuel its place was taken by a fresh Gruppen. B-17s were going down all along the way. Many planes had feathered props and smoking engines. Sgt. McDaniel continues:

We had moderate flak over the target. Our bombardier had a good bomb run and we had good results with our bombs. About 1515 we got to our rally point and headed for home, and it was a repeat of what we had gone thru to drop our bombs on Schweinfurt. About an hour later we were elated to see the contrails of our P-47s, which immediately began to mix it up with the German fighters. At this point I began to think we might make it back from this mission after all. I was still wet with sweat and had a terrific headache and was sore and aching, but alive and all my crewmates were unharmed! The young B17F 23586 landed at Bedford with all engines running, now a real veteran. We would not fly 586 again until December 20.

Sgt. Marshall McDaniel was to become one of the rare members of the "Lucky Bastard Club" for completing twenty-five missions over the skies of Germany at a time when the odds were that a combat airman would only complete six missions before going down. "Mac" began his combat flying in early May 1943 and finished up in November of 1943. During this time period the German Luftwaffe could and did put up the cream of its fighter force at a time when the 8th Air Force was just building up its fighter Group strength. "Mac" summed up this mission in these words:

I would say it was the most huge and maximum effort we ever put out. I never saw so many dogfights; our fighters were in the thick of it trying to protect us as long as their fuel would last. The Germans had a little plane that resembled the English Spitfire. They used a ruse that we'd never seen. A German fighter would chase this look-alike spitfire right through our formation; at a distance we would think he was chasing a Spitfire so we would hold our fire in order to avoid hitting the mock Spitfire. This would allow them to get almost on top of us and then they would cut loose on us with their guns.

It was a blood-chilling sight to see our B-17s and fighters being blown to pieces on every side by the Germans. Every time one blew up, it meant ten or more of our boys were destroyed. With all that, the dog fighting and the haze, it was like a kaleidescope in front of our eyes. We were all exhausted physically and mentally when we got back, but we had accomplished our goal and I am glad to be able to say how proud I am to have been a part of a group of real men who did their job and risked their lives and never whined or complained. But I am more proud of the ones who didn't make it back and paid the maximum price for their country.

Date: 17 August 1943
Target: Regensburg, Germany

Mission Summary

A teletype to the 100th Bomb Group in August 1943 stated: "Regensburg is the most important target to be attacked by any aircraft to date. The production is estimated at 200 ME-109 aircraft per month, or approximately 25 to 30 per cent of Germany's entire single engine production. There has been a remarkable increase in production within the last year of this particular type of aircraft. There has been an increase of 120 per cent as compared to two per cent for other types of single engine fighters.

"This plant is the second largest of its kind in Europe, the largest being at Weiner Neustadt, which was attacked by the 9th Air Force on 14 August, and it is estimated that 72 per cent of the increase which has occurred in the operational strength on the western front has been derived from this plant alone.

"It is estimated that the complete destruction of the plant will entail a nine months' delay in production and that immediate results will be felt in operational strength within one and a half to two months."

A second teletype came from Colonel Curtis LeMay, the air leader of the mission, and the man who was later to head the B-29 force in the Mariana Islands. It came from North Africa the day after the raid.

"Mission flown as planned. Fighter support poor. Wing under constant attack from Antwerp to thirty minutes after leaving target. Objective believed to be totally destroyed. Detailed report impossible at this time. Airplanes have landed at a number of fields other than those scheduled due to battle damage and gas shortage."

Between those two teletypes passed a drama that was never exceeded in Air Force annals. It was the first attempt at a shuttle mission; it was the deepest penetration to date, and together with the raid to Schweinfurt, was a challenge to the Luftwaffe to fight it out plane for plane.

The Forts of the 100th Bomb Group plowed across the German sky, paying a high price, but extracting a price in return. To quote from "Contrails" the History of the 100th:

"It seemed that the Hundredth was bearing the brunt of the entire strength of the German Air Force. It was extremely difficult, well nigh impossible to estimate in distance, time or place where ships were going down."

Maj. Gale "Buck" Cleven's low squadron was hard hit. Lt. Hummel's ship was seen exploding near Bad Mergerheim. Lt. Braley left the formation with fire streaking from Number One engine. Lt. Claytor left the Group sinking rapidly. Cleven and Lt. Scott continued, flanked by Lt. DeMarco and Lt. Hollenback in a shrunken three ship formation. Hollenback's ship had sustained a hit in the bomb bay and had jettisoned the load, but limped in faltering step with the others. Cleven's ship was a flying sieve. Cannon fire had exploded much of the electrical system, wounding T/Sgt. J. Parks, the top turret gunner. Another 20mm shell got the radio compartment, killing the operator, T/Sgt. N. Smith. The gun installations in the nose were shelled away and Bombardier N. Norman wounded. Hydraulic fluid spouted into the cockpit as the system was smashed, and another projectile severed rudder cables. Number Three engine was knocked out and caught fire.

It did not seem possible that the plane could continue at all, much less reach the target, bomb the plant and keep on going toward the Alps, throught the Brenner Pass, over the Mediterranean to North Africa. This survey of a seemingly impossible situation did not take into consideration the personal traits and characteristics of Cleven. He had every justification for giving the bail out signal. The crew prepared to abandon ship. There was nothing else to do, but Cleven did it. As the co-pilot pleaded with him to give the order for the exodus, Cleven countered by blistering a few choice phrases into the intercom. They did the trick; their effect was instantaneous, and the aircraft continued its harried way to the target.

Col. Beirne Lay, flying as observer with Lt. Murphy, later recorded his impressions of Regensburg and Cleven in a widely read article, "I Saw Regensburg Die."

The situation did not ease. ME 109s swept in armed with rockets. Air-to-air bombing was attempted by Junkers 88s. The lead squadron lost two ships. Captain R. Knox left the formation near Aachen. Lt. Biddick left near Frankfurt with the cockpit on fire. The aircraft disintegrated.

In the high squadron, Lt. Shotland broke from the formation near Nurenberg with the ship's left wing in flames. The plane was under attack by three fighters that buzzed hungrily about, stinging and thrusting until the weary ship became one huge flame and exploded. Lt. Oakes drew away with a wounded ship before the aircraft reached the target area. Later, reports were to place him as landing safely in Switzerland.

The remaining planes approached the target area. The pressure eased somewhat as the Initial Point was reached. Bandits still patrolled the skies, but their attacks had slackened. Visibility was clear, and the target waited in the sunlight as the planes turned into the bomb run at 17,000 feet.

Bombardier Lt. Douglas released, and the group followed suit. The 250-pound incendiaries showered down in fiery profusion upon the primary home of the Nazi single-seater aircraft, and the entire target area lifted in flames. Stately columns of smoke rose from the clustered buildings, and the men of the group watched the destruction with a satisfaction too deep for verbal expression. Later, the Intelligence reports were to state that..... "Bombing results were excellent....." Now, the planes swung wide and headed for the Alps.

The remainder of the journey was uneventful...if you call sporadic attacks, some flak, planes ditching, fuel tanks emptying and Lt. Van Noy heading for Switzerland with Number Four engine on fire uneventful.

However, compared to the tempestuous swathe cut through Germany against the most violent opposition in the history of aerial warfare, these were minor misfortunes and subject to discount. The Division, led by Col. Curtis LeMay, pointed for the Mediterranean.

It was after 1800 hours when the remaining airborne aircraft of the Hundredth circled in the sultry air of Africa and hit the drome, raising clouds of dust and coming to rest in the desert.

Some, like Van Noy, had been forced to ditch into the sea. Some had crashed on the beaches. The planes had been in the air more than eleven hours. Only twelve out of the starting twenty-two landed at the briefed bases. The Luftwaffe had lost forty-nine aircraft to the Hundredth, with eleven probably destroyed and an additional ten damaged.

It had been a momentous day, during which almost thirty percent

50

of German single-engine fighter production had been destroyed. Ninety men of the Hundredth were listed as missing in action.

Others more fortunate slept on the soil of Africa and marveled at their good fortune.

Months later, the entire Division received a Presidential Citation:

WAR DEPARTMENT
Washington 25, D.C. 1 May 1944

GENERAL ORDERS)
   NO. 36
EXTRACT

XIII BATTLE HONORS.-2. As authorized by Executive Order No. 9396 (Sec. 1, Bull. 22 WD, 1943) Superseding Executive Order No 9075 (Sec. III, Bull. 11, WD, 1942) the following unit is cited by the War Department under provisions of the section IV, Circulate 333, War Department, 1943, in the name of the President of the United States as public evidence of deserved honor and distinction:

The 3rd Bombardment Division (H) (then the 4th Bombardment Wing (H) is cited for outstanding performance of duty in action against the enemy on 17 August 1943. This unprecedented attack against one of Germany's most important aircraft factories was the first shuttle mission performed in this theatre of operations and entailed the longest flight over strongly defended enemy territory yet accomplished at that date. For 4H hours the formation was subjected to persistent, savage assualts by large forces of enemy fighters. During this bitterly contested aerial battle 140 German fighter aircraft were definitely destroyed and many more damaged. Despite desperate attempts by the enemy to scatter the bombers, the group of the 3rd Bombardment Division (H) maintained a tight, defensive formation and, coordinating as a perfectly balanced team, fought their way to the assigned target at Regensburg. Though weary after gruelling combat the bombardiers released their bombs accurately on the target and wrought vast destruction on an aircraft factory of vital importance to the enemy's war effort. The high degree of success achieved is directly attributable to the extraordinary heroism, skill, and devotion to duty displayed by the members of this unit. Their actions on this occasion uphold the highest traditions of the Armed Forces of the United States.

By order of the Secretary of War:

OFFICIAL:

ROBERT N. DUNLOP,
   Brigadier General,
     Acting The Adjutant General.

G.C. MARSHALL,
   Chief of Staff.

With Regensburg, the Hundredth scaled the heights of glory, heights which once attained, were held with all the tenacity and purpose of men who had made it their life work to preach the destruction of a way of life with which there could be no compromise. The average American airmen, if indeed, there was any average, was not a politically conscious person. The science of airmanship was paramount, the dialectics of the various ideologies involved were of secondary importance. The issues were clear-cut. It was them or us, and they were the bastards. There was no hint of the boyish face lifted into the sky of an automobile ad, sighing and saying: "This is what I'm fighting for...the right to drive my 1947 Super-Eight Podunk..."

The issues were at once simpler, yet paradoxically more complex. The men were told what to do, and executed their orders in a more than exemplary manner. Yet, although the preparations and movements involved were almost mechanical, the action usually focused to a point where it became a question of one type of team against another type in the struggle for survival.

There were of course men who were afraid. That covered the great majority. Fear is only dangerous when it acts as a deterrent to action. The actions of the Hundredth were etched deep into the bowels of Hitler Europe, and they were the actions of free men who fought to perpetuate their heritage.

The words of Col. Alkire were brought back to the minds of many men:

"...and I have every confidence that your conduct will not only gain great glory for the Old Century Group, but will prove I wasn't such a bad leader after all..."

Captain Frank Gregory, Bombardier of the 100th Bomb Group went to Schweinfurt on one of the later missions with the Group. He had this to say about Schweinfurt and Regensburg:

Any time we made those deep penetrations into Germany they were quite obnoxious about it, because they could read the handwriting on the wallpaper — that if we got their factories, etc., they were not going to be able to put out many products. So they would put up everything in the world to prevent it. Later on they began to let the marshalling yards go and the oil, etc., but we found out later that they had brand new airplanes sitting on the ground because they had no petrol for them. They were just sitting there in the revetments.

They really made an effort to make sure we didn't get into Regensburg. It was so far down there. I did not go on that Regensburg mission, but it was a mess. When the bombers did get there (Africa) they were not ready for them; they could not take care of them. There again they were running out of fuel by the time they'd crossed the Mediterranean and got there. They knew how far those B-17s would fly, but you get a change of wind or something and your fuel consumption is going to change, particularly when you have adverse conditions on the way. Do some maneuvering along the way; can't hold the same course you were holding before; everybody in trouble. By the time they get there, they're out of ammunition, gasoline and everything else. They have wounded and are pushing to get there.

Those are the ones that are tough and the Regensburg and Schweinfurt raids were just that. The Schweinfurt groups had to fight their way in and out, and the Regensburg groups had to try to stay in the air 'till they got to Africa.

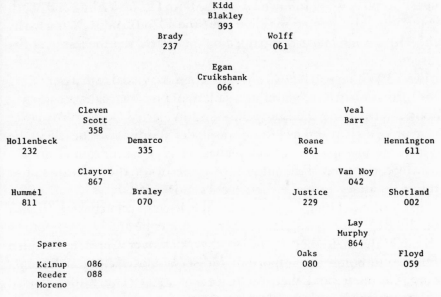

The 100th Bomb Group formation, 17 August 1943; Regensburg, Germany.

Exactly 146 planes left England 17 August 1943 headed for Regensburg, Germany. Of this number 127 attacked the target and 24 were lost.

An olive drab B-17 with the name *Iza Angel II* proudly lettered on its nose was one of these planes. Lt. Henry "Nick" Nagorka was the pilot. He was with the 403rd Combat Wing flying with the 388th Bomb Group in the low group position. The 96th led with Gen. Curtis LeMay in the lead plane. The 390th flew in the high position. The 401st Combat Wing followed with the 94th Group leading and 385th completing the formation. Then came the 402nd Combat Wing led by the 95th Group and accompanied by the 100th, and the last over the target.

The 390th dispatched 20 aircraft. There was a delay in assembling the formation over England, and gallons of precious fuel were wasted. Soon after passing the European coast an alerted German Air Force rose up to do battle. The Group was under steady attack nearly to the Alps, meeting upwards of 100 planes. They attacked from all angles, usually coming out of the sun, and using decoys on the opposite side of the main attack to make their tactics more effective.

390th Bomb Group Captain Gerald F. Richter piloted *Rick-O-Shay* on the Regensburg mission. For many hours he and his crew fought through the hell they found in the skies over German occupied Europe, to bomb the important Messerschmitt factory at Regensburg, Germany, and then for fifteen hours afterward they tended their wounded, and searched for comrades who were lost in the northern costal hills of Africa.

First came the fighters, in swarms! Silver fighters and sky-blue fighters, fighters with black crosses and yellow spinners, fighters with hell-for-leather Luftwaffe veterans at the controls. "Fighters until you couldn't count them any more," said Richter. "Ganging up on us by the tens and twenties, and moving in with their wings sparkling red. It was fighters all the way over the target, and then we got in a six-minute bomb run without interference."

"We circled Regensburg after the bombing," Lt. Ted Archeluta, bombardier, reported, "and the smoke had pillared up to nearly ten thousand feet. It was a sweet piece of bombing."

The fighters were waiting for the bombers as they came out of the target area, and in a running fight to the Alps saw the *Rick-O-Shay* battling desperately. "There were Me-109s and FW-190s," Richter reported, "but the Me-109s were the toughest. We had no protection from the tail. A twenty mm shell exploded in front of the tail gunner and ripped up his arms and chest pretty badly. The waist gunner kept him alive."

"The flak wasn't bad, just big black cloud over the target when I looked back," Archeluta declared. "It was the fighers that kept us worried — the 109's lined up and made rolling attacks through the formation, cork-screwing away at the end."

"The *Rick-O-Shay* crossed the Alps with its oxygen system shot out, and several times Richter almost lost consciousness at the controls. Lt. Winfred W. Alfred, co-pilot, reported: "We were so groggy most of the time that we hardly knew what we were doing."

The formation headed out over the Mediterranean, bound for Bon, Tunisia. Gas became the problem then. Not a pilot in the group was sure he could make Africa, and several plane commanders knew they could not. "One by one they started slipping out of formation, headed down to the water. I saw three splash in before I realized that we'd have to go too," Richter declared. "The crew threw everything over board to lighten the plane. Guns, tools, ammunition, helmets, camera and anything else they could tear loose went over the side before we settled down to ditch."

Richter was watching the waves looking for a trough to set the ship in when Alfred spotted the African coast straight ahead. "I pulled up the nose, prayed a little, and gunned the engines," said Richter. "The funny part is that we made it, landing on a dry lake bottom. We turned to taxi off the the side and engines quit — out of gas."

"There were Arabs all over the place, grinning, friendly and strong-smelling," Alfred continued. "They told us about ships cracked-up in the hills nearby. I got a few of the men together and we started out to find them."

"While Rich was getting things organized for the trip to Bon, we were having plenty of trouble with our search mission," Alfred recounted. "It was only five miles up to the hills where the planes were supposed to be, but we hadn't counted on the jungle underbrush, and it took us more than five hours to make it. When we finally made it, we discovered that they weren't our ships. What we found were the charred remains of a Wellington and a Mitchell that must have collided. There were human bones strewn around, and a couple of letters with names on them. There were lion tracks all over the place, and we decided to get the hell out of there in a hurry. There was no path through the underbrush, and we didn't have the slightest idea of our direction. We were so tired that we just fell down on the ground. I don't know how much later it was, but I heard an Arab some distance away yelling 'Comrade!' I yelled back 'Mohammed!' and kept calling until I saw him break out of the brush. We were never more glad to see anyone."

It was nearly a week before Richter and his crew and other crews of the Group were assembled at Bon in shape for the return trip to England, which completed the first shuttle bombing operation of the war. Less than half the ships had been accounted for. We had lost a couple over Germany. One had landed in Switzerland, and another was seen headed for Spain, and two had ditched in the Mediterranean. Later we learned the rest of the planes had landed at intervals up to fifty miles along the African coast, and that the two crews which had ditched had been rescued. For the men of *Rick-O-Shay* the mission had been their first — their baptism by fire.

Iza Angel II made it thru the fight to Regensburg and did drop their bombs on the target. Just after coming off the target the fighters began to swarm in on the bombers. Lt. Nagorka describes what happened:

One of the 109s dove at us from the left side and gave us a burst of 20mm stuff. One of the shells came through the side of the ship right next to me, barely touched my knuckle, went down thru the instrument panel, severed cables and some of the instruments, went on down to the Bombardier's compartment, took off Tierney's right hand, bounced on the armor plate and richocheted over to bruise the foot of the Bombardier. Tierney almost went into shock — we immediately administered morphine (co-pilot Gil Parker was the first-aid man). We were up pretty high as we had just come off the target so we had to use oxygen bottles while all this was being done.
We laid "Tee" down in the passageway between compartments, put

blankets on him to try to keep him from going into shock. Gil put Tierney's hand together as we thought there might be a chance to save that hand.

Back in the pilot's seat Lt. Nagorka began to take things into his own hands for getting to Africa as soon as possible.

I began to do everything I could to get the ship to Africa ahead of the other formations and there were a number of groups in that effort; groups of twenty or so ships in each and they were strung out in line — a long attack line. We were second in the formation near the front, so I made a point to try to get out in front of the formation to get to Africa first. I wanted to get on the ground first to get "Tee" taken care of.

I signaled our Group Commander visually (we were on radio silence) that I wanted to go ahead. I also signaled my wingman to stay back, so we began to drop our nose a little bit and began to gain a little speed and began to pass slowly under the formation. In the meantime we had a hung-up bomb in the bomb bay racks, and we had to get rid of that bomb! One of the guys went back, but could not get the shackles undone. When he reported that, I said, "Get an axe and chop the damn thing off. Let's open the bomb bay doors and you drop it down — get it out of there." He did that and it dropped as we passed by Lake Garda, Italy. The bomb was not armed and I watched it go down into a very beautiful countryside. I prayed it would not hit anyone. I did not see an explosion.

We kept on going. It had been a rough fight for us and had some attacks after 'Tee' was hurt. We kept gaining ground on the lead group, passing very gradually to the point where we got right out near the front of the formation. By the time we got to Bon (Bon Penninsula in Africa) we just kept watching for the airfield to be sure we got in first. I got on the radio and told them to have an ambulance ready for us as we had wounded aboard. They assured us they would have everything ready. We shot a red flare or two, indicating wounded aboard, and came right straight in, not going around the traffic pattern at all. I pulled around and stopped — no sign of any ambulance — no sign of anyone! I got on the radio to the tower and angrily shouted, "Where's the Ambulance? We called for an ambulance — we have a wounded man."

"We are trying to get one over there," said a voice from the tower. The ambulance soon arrived and two very young G.I.'s got out with a stretcher. They appeared (to us), to be afraid of the sight of blood and were acting very gingerly as if ready to faint. I got very angry. "Get the hell out of here!" I roared. "We'll do it ourselves." The crewmen got Tierney on the stretcher and put him in the ambulance in no time. I jumped in and the ambulance took off. What we did not know was that the hospital was twenty or thirty miles away over a very rough dirt road. "Tee" was passing out and coming to. I sat with him, holding him for comfort. After an interminable ride we got to the hospital. I talked to the surgeon and pleaded with him to save "Tee's" hand! "There is still circulation and the small fingers are warm — please, please try to save it!" The next day when the crew came back to visit "Tee", the hand was gone!

Lt. Francis Tierney, Navigator on *Iza Angel II,* was one of the original crew that flew over with the 388th B.G. in 1943. Lt. Tierney explains:

We went over with the original *Iza Angel* from Salina, Kansas to Goose Bay, Labrador, then Iceland and England. The original bombardier was William Mason from South Carolina. He quit after Hannover. Les Baum of N.Y. was Squadron bombardier, and he was with us from Hannover on. Mason flew with another crew at Hannover, but never flew after that and went back to the states. Les Baum filled in for Mason after that. Les was a real man; on the Paris Raid I had no parachute harness that day and he offered me his. I would not take it of course, but he was real people.

On this Regensburg raid we got off a little late. We were to go first, then the Schweinfurt Groups were to come right in behind us so they would not have to fight their way in. We were late, but the Schweinfurt Group was more than an hour and a half behind us. They had to fight their way in and out again.

We were the low group, low squadron on the first wave of three groups and another two wings behind us. Those had only two groups in them and the last group in the low position was the 100th Bomb Group, and they had a hell of a time!

At the briefing the only map I saw was the one on the big board in the briefing room. They had a ribbon tracing the flight in and out of Regensburg; it went off the map! After the briefing some guy in the back stood up and said, "This raid is so important that Col LeMay is going to lead the whole darn thing!" That didn't impress me a bit. I was more impressed with that line going off the wall map!

Sgt. Jack Harris, tail gunner on *Iza Angel II,* could see the battle the 100th Bomb Group was having, and he said they really got hell. But that was the way it was sometimes. For them it was a hell of a battle; for us it was easy. Some of the Groups didn't think that it was much of a fight at Hannover, but that's when *we* caught hell! At Regensburg the low group only had two squadrons, so that, I'm sure, is why the 100th got it so bad and were picked on.

The guy that attacked us at Regensburg was diving on us from 7 o'clock position and was pulling up when he hit us in the left wing.

Regensburg wasn't a tough raid for us. Some of them are easy and some are tough. You get into a raid like we had at Hannover — we were low group; we fought all the way in and all the way out! At least for two and a half hours of constant fighter attacks. The Germans didn't want us to get to Hannover, but once we were there they did not want us to get out either! It was an overall bad raid! More of Hannover later.

I was the first one to go out of our crew except Mason. Our Group did not have any problems going in, and it was a big fight, too. Got over the target O.K.; coming back we were spread out still; that's when I got hit.

That was one lone FW190. There was no concerted fighter attack. I never saw the airplane that hit me. The hits, there were four of them, stitched the wing and one came in and knocked me down. I jumped up and Les Baum turned around and saw what happened and pulled a piece of wire from an intercom and wrapped it around my arm and hollered for someone to come down. My wrist was pretty well chewed up. Gil Parker was the first aid man for the front of the airplane and he came down and put a regular tourniquet on my arm, put sulfa powder on the wound, and gave me a shot of morphine.

As I recall, we did not get back into formation after that. We were flying below and were under attack a couple times. One time I got up and manned one of the guns, successfully repulsing attacks by German fighters. [Lt. Tierney received a D.F.C. for that effort.]

I can recall some of the trip to Bon, West Africa. Going by Switzerland. Most of the time I was just stretched out in the nose breathing oxygen. I do recall having a bomb hung up in the bomb bay. Les Baum went back, chopped it out and let it drop. I do recall going over the Mediterranean — the trouble we had landing — everybody was out of gas. We left a bunch of airplanes in the Mediterranean Sea because they didn't have enough fuel to make it to Bon, which was the airport right on the coast of Africa. Telergma, the scheduled field, was back off the coast a ways. When we landed Nick did not taxi back to the hardstand. He'd shot flares, so stopped the airplane right away so the ambulance could come right up. I got in the ambulance, went to the hospital, Nick went with me. The next thing I really remember was being on an operating table with a surgeon pinching my fingers to see what there was. I could only feel my little finger, so the nerves must not have been severed in that finger. I could feel him squeeze it. All the nerves, ligaments and blood vessels had been severed. So he told me the next day and said there was no chance to save the hand. The next day I got another shot of blood, then Nick and the other guys came up, also Colonel David. I was in the enlisted man's ward. The Doc said you got better treatment there. The kid in the next cot from me was a wounded tail gunner from the Regensburg raid.

When Colonel David asked me what I wanted to do I told him I wanted to go back to England. He was talking about putting me on a hospital ship. But I had all my clothes and everything else in England. So he told the guy that was running the hospital, as soon as I was able, to take me down to

Telergma and catch a ride. I think I was in the hospital for a few days and was transferred to the 57th Station Hospital, then to the 60th, five or six days later. I was able to travel, of course, and went to Telergma on a B-17 that had been damaged. The flight plan called for going to Telergma, to Marakeesh, and to Prestwick, England. When we got to Marakeesh with this crew, the pilot went in and had the plane checked and decided to have all four engines changed. Well, I went up to MATS, told them what the situation was. I didn't have any orders or anything, I was just hitchhiking.

I went to the flight surgeon's office; there were cots in there and I slept in there. When the guy in MATS told me I could not do anything without priority, I went back to the flight surgeon and told him my problem, and he said, "I can take care of that." He wrote out a letter saying that my physical and emotional condition was such that I should be returned to P of I immediately. So I took that to MATS, and they said they could have me in Miami in two days. I said I did not want to go to Miami, I wanted to go to England. So I got out that night. They put me on a plane to Prestwick. Maj. Gen Brereton was on that flight and he asked what I was doing and where I was going, and I told him and He said, "I'm going down to London and you can ride with me. I'll see that you get back to your base." So from Prestwick I flew down to London with him on a DC-3, and he got somebody to give me a ride back to our base at Knettishall. I was back to the base in ten or fifteen days. I know I was back before the Stuttgart raid.

That's where the 388th lost a lot of airplanes. I got back just before the Group went to Stuttgart. Then I was sent up to the 30th Hospital in Northern England and back to the States on the Queen Mary in November. When I came back I told them I wanted to stay in. I'd had an instructor course in navigation, and rather than get discharged in '43 I turned around and became an instructor and was sent to San Marcos, Texas Navigational School, and in '45 I went back to law school. When I was in a bar one night and ran into a guy named Mulroney, we got to talking and he said he'd been to Regensburg and that he remembered me because I had the cot next to his injured tail gunner.

When I came to start practicing law in Fort Dodge, one of the other attorneys here had graduated six months or so after I did. Arthur Johnson flew B-24s and had flown on the first Ploesti raid. Back when I had gone thru Marakeesh in '43 and had gone to the MATS place, this guy who had told me I had to have a priority to get on those B-24s to go back to England, one of those B-24s that was headed for Prestwick landed in Lisbon. Well, Art Johnson was the navigator on that B-24. Small world?

Meanwhile back at the African base, *Iza Angel II* was found to have a number of holes in the wing and fuselage as a result of the fighter attacks. The ground crew carefully patched the holes with fabric and dope and called it good.Nick Nagorka continues:

Colonel LeMay, General Eaker and some of the other leaders of the raid had a conference right there in the open after we had landed, about an hour later, and they had pictures of the results which were very good.

Just before we took off on this raid I found out that my girl, who was an army nurse, was stationed in Bizerte, North Aftica. Sooo — the next day after they had patched the airplane I said to the guys, "Hey, we're going to take a test flight and check this airplane out. If you want to, you can come along." We took off for Bizerte. I saw a field, a fighter field, so I went down. We had a heavy cross wind so I crabbed it in. All the fire engines and everything in the place came out. They thought I must be having a rough time, but just before I set it down I straightened it out. All these people came up and I said, "Go on home. No problems. We are looking for the hospital!" The driver of a vehicle said, "You are at the wrong field. The hospital is on the other side of town." OK — so we pulled to the other end of the runway and took off again, went over the other side of the hill about three or four hundred feet high.

The hospital was on the side of that hill. I found the hospital and got low and did a zoom, buzzing right along the hospital windows. Some of the patients came out to see the madman. We went down and landed at the nearby fighter strip. A Lieutenant gave me his jeep and we tore on up to the hospital. I found out that Izabella was eating lunch in the mess hall. We strode into the mess hall with our slouch hats, pistols and flight gear. Everybody stopped and looked. We found her, took her down to the airplane, which was named after her. Iza — short for Izabella, her first name, and Angel for Angel of mercy — a nurse. This was the first time she had ever seen one of the B-17s. We showed her the cockpit, how it all worked and then took her back to the hospital and we took off and got back to base, and Colonel LeMay comes up and says, "Well, how is it?" I said, "Fine. She's behaving fine!" He didn't say another word, but gave me the fisheye. Apparently he got wind of what we were doing. He didn't object.

Two or three days after this the *Iza Angel II* took off from Telergma, flew via France, bombing the Bordeauz-Merignac airfield and repair shops. There was mild opposition to this raid, though tail gunner Jack S. Harris shot down a FW 190 on this raid for which he received an Oak Leaf Cluster to his Air Medal, as was the custom at that time.

When the *Iza Angel II* landed back in England the crew chief looked her over very, very carefully. This was his ship. He shook his head from side to side and asked Lt. Nagorka if this plane had been serviced in Africa. Nagorka replied, "sure it was." The crew chief said,

"Well, you have a live 20mm shell in one of your gas tanks!" Pilot Nagorka disgustingly replied, "Well, congratulations!" He thought back to the day at the field at Telergma when the ground crews had found cannon shell holes and had simply applied cloth fabric patches over the hole and that was that. They had found an entrance hole, but no exit hole, so had just put a patch over the hole. Now the crew chief was livid, and the crew was wondering the *what if* sort of thought. They had been flying over Africa and France with a live shell in the fuel tank! They finally had to take the wing off, remove the gas tank to get that 20mm shell out.

We had our share of excitement! The real kicker was that Gydnia raid when we got knocked down. Gydnia was the 14th raid, Regensburg was the 9th, but by the 13th or so raid my knees would start to go for no reason. Well, for a certain length of time you don't go into battle shock — it doesn't sink in, but by the last two raids I was starting to go into battle shock gradually. I got to the plane in the morning and my knees would start to go wobbly for no reason — shock! I was not afraid, but my knees did it by themselves. I didn't feel any fear and I couldn't understand what was happening to me. I flew the raids. I was beginning to go into battle shock gradually. I thought I was coming down with the flu — so I would put my parachute pack down and lie down on the grass next to the plane a while. "I'll just take it easy for a while," I mused. "Must be getting the flu." but I was shot down at Gydnia, so that ended that.

I didn't realize all this until recently when I began working it over with psychologists and we determined what was really happening. But that kind of thing happened to a lot of men and some of them could not function any more at all after that. It happened to one of my crewmen who flew with us from the States. It happened at the end of the second or third raid. He was so frightened, so terribly frightened, he was no longer useful on the crew. He was doing everything wrong, could not get himself together. His eyes were wide — we had to ground him. When you see a great deal of trouble and injury it happens earlier. It goes to work on you earlier. I thought I had done "Ships Captain" functions properly. I didn't think I'd seen that much, and I don't think it had anything to do with my being shot up on the other raids.

There are ways to avoid that "shock", but in training men and preparing them for violence there is not enough done on the psychological level. They are not prepared for death. If they were prepared for death it (battle shock) would never happen. When I say prepare for death, I do not mean expect death. I mean understand it, understand what it's all about.

We had trained as a group, formed as a group, flew the Atlantic and landed at our own base. Terrific morale in that group — terrific! We lost one plane coming over and never heard from it again. We landed in England and started to function as a group. We were told when we took off from the states what the odds were, but it seemed more in the nature of a challenge than frightening. We were simply told, "Look, six percent are coming back." Those were the figures in our time in '42-'43, six percent. With only six percent coming back you can't believe even an American is invincible.

This could have been avoided if the psychology of the air crew had been worked on and they had been exposed to the idea that death is not the end.

Everybody believes that in his own way — in his religion. But it was never touched on in training. As a result you built up tension gradually as you saw things happen. You built up a conviction that you were going to go next — self-induced stress.

When you number is up, you're up, not before. When I was in the water after the Gydnia raid, everything went wrong that could, but it just was not my time to die.

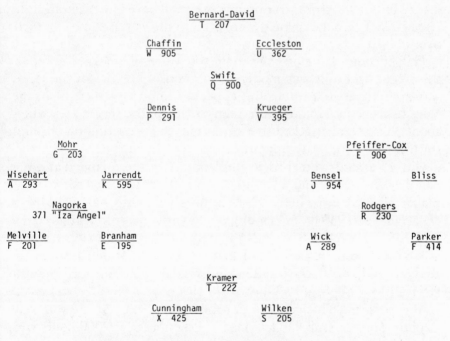

The 388 Bomb Group formation, 17 August 1943.

Date: 24 August 1943
Target: Bordeaux, France
Group: 388th Bomb Group

On the return bombing trip from North Africa 16 of our ships took off from Telergma Field and were joined by six ships of the 390th Bomb Group. One of our ships aborted (Lt. Dennis) due to mechanical failure.

The bombing targets were hangers and dispersal areas at the western edge of the Bordeaux/Merignac airfield. It was difficult to make positive results of our bomb hits as the film which was to be used photographing the target area had been exposed while being loaded in North Africa. Our bombs may well have fallen amongst the large cluster of bursts which were seen in the woods some 200 yards over.

Flak encountered along the route was generally meager, except at the target, where it was moderate to intense. The flak at the target was accurate as to altitude and appeared to be a predicted barrage. Very few enemy aircraft were seen except in the target area where about 15 fighters attacked the formation, concentrating on our high squadron and the group behind.

Our 15 aircraft returned to England, 11 of them landed at home base between 2015 and 2018 hours. Gas shortage forced three of our planes to land elsewhere. Lt. Cummingham, ship #425, landed at Oakington at 1930 hours out of gas and with one prop feathered. He refueled and reached base at 2140 hours. Lt. Bensel, ship #954, landed at Okehampton, refueled and arrived at base at 2110 hours. Lt. Rodgers, ship #230, crash-landed in a field near Foxborough-Stanton after all four engines had died from lack of gas while he was in the traffic pattern. This ship is beyond repair, but the crew is safe. Captain Forrest, ship #362, landed at Lakenheath at 2000 hours with one prop feathered and serious engine trouble.

Key personnel on this mission:

Group Leader	Col. David	Lead Navigator	Lt. Egaas
Deputy Leader	Major Cox	Lead Bombardier	Lt. Bartuska
Lead Pilot	Lt. Bailey	Staff Members	Capt. Forrest
			Lt. Humpries

Date: 6 September 1943
Target: Stuttgart, Germany
Group: 388th Bomb Group

As Logged at the Time of the Mission

Twenty-four aircraft took off by 0547 and effected the Group and Wing formations without difficulty, and the briefed course was followed throughout. One of our ships aborted because of mechanical failure. Two of the spare ships returned when the formation remained filled without them. Twenty-one A/C proceeded to the target, but only twenty bombed Stuttgart, for #289 went down just before bombs away. Bombing was poor. A heavy cloud cover was over the target. Several targets of opportunity appeared but as we were flying the low group to the 96th Group's lead, our lead bombardier dropped on their target.

Fighter opposition on this raid was the strongest encountered in this Group's history. The Group formation was threatened with extinction. Enemy fighters, three at a time barrel-rolled through our formation. Every time this tactic was used it seemed that a Fortress was disabled, destroyed or forced out of formation where it fell easy prey to hordes of fighters standing by for such an advantage.

More than 100 German fighters attacked our Group which desperately repelled attack after attack for several hours. Our low (563rd) Squadron was completely wiped out.

Enemy aircraft included FW 190s, ME 109s, ME 110s, ME 210s, JU 88s, and JU 87s. On the route in, seven enemy aircraft attacked at 0825 hours near Cambrai, but these were dispersed by the fighter escort. The first large concentration of fighters were encountered near the Initial Point. The attacks were very intense from that point to the target, decreased over the target, but regained intensity in the vicinity of the Rally Point. Eventually the tempo of the attacks decreased but the opposition continued 'till Berney was reached on the way out.

The first heavy attack consisted of fighters being two or three miles in front of the formation and then coming in level from 11 o'clock to 1 o'clock. For the first five minutes, while our low squadron was still in existence, the attack momentarily assumed a "traffic pattern," attacking mostly from the left at 11 o'clock. They trailed each other in, slightly stepped up, at about 20 second intervals. At 300 to 400 yards they would start their roll, make their pass at the lead squadron and out. After the low squadron was eliminated, the traffic pattern was shifted over to the right. Some attacks were pressed as close as 50 to 75 yards.

The planes of our lead element flew an especially tight formation. The waist gunner of the lead ship reported that he could have touched the wing tips of the right hand wing ship. Nevertheless, an enemy fighter knifed between the lead and the left hand wing ship, barely evading collision. Immediately upon this attack the Bombardier's and the pilot's compartments burst into a mass of flames and the ship went down out of control. Before the fighter had gone 100 feet further it was destroyed by our guns.

Eleven of our A/C were missing. In addition Lt. Krueger was killed and his co-pilot, Lt. Mayfield, was seriously wounded by a 20mm. burst in the cockpit. His waist gunner, S/Sgt. R. Hill, was also seriously wounded. As many details as are available follows:

378 —Bowen—nothing available.
942 —Roe—Nothing available.
423 —Cunningham—Nothing available.
234 —Miller—Nothing available.
478 —Beecham—Nothing available.
222 —Kramer—Last seen going down out of control in a steep dive. He was on the way back, but the position is not known.
289 —Wick—Just before bombs away at Strausburg it was in flames, but four to seven chutes were seen.
201 —Melville—fire in the nose and the #4 engine. Three to six chutes were seen as the plane went down just beyond Strausburg.
203 —Mohr—Disappeared south of Paris, apparently out of control.
293 —Karnezis—Last seen just after Strausburg, apparently heading for Switzerland.
349 —Wilken—A large fire started in the nose from a 20mm. explosion. Down near Paris.

Our Group claimed 23 e/a destroyed and many others probably destroyed and damaged. The confirmed score was 15-7-1.

Little or no flak was encountered before reaching the city of Stuttgart. At Stuttgart meager flak was encountered but this was low. Between Stuttgart and Strausburg accurate meager to moderate flak of continuous following variety was encountered. Major Satterwhite was Group Leader; Lt. Jarrendt, Lead Pilot.

On September 7th the following message was received from the Commanding General of the 8th Bomber Command: "The 388th Bombardment Group suffered heavy loss yesterday. The spirit of the Group in bearing those losses and coming back with fighting hearts is a matter of great gratification to me. I wish that you would give the Group commander my commendation to the 388th Bombardment Group for their excellent spirit and their confidence in the greatness of the task they are now performing. Signed: Eaker" — the message was endorsed by Colonel LeMay, commander of the 4th Combat Wing, who added his own congratulations to the group.

Yes, at that time our crews were flying another combat mission.

Later information on crews down September 6, 1943: F/O Bowen, 563rd Sq. Plane "Sky Shy" #378 hit by flak after IP. Engineer S/Sgt. Wissner killed in Turret, then with plane on fire, the other nine bailed out. C/P 2nd Lt. Woods broke leg on landing. Radioman, S/Sgt. Redmond was killed by civilians.

2nd Lt. Roe, and C/P 2nd Lt. Thomas were POW's. 563rd.

Lt. Beecham's crew interned in Switzerland. 560th.

Lt. Kramer's crew, 563rd Sq. Pow's.

Lt. Wick's crew, 562nd Sq. Plane *Wolfpack* #42-3289. POW's Ed Wick was captured after three days and released at Moosburg April 1945.

Lt. Melville's crew, 560th Sq. Plane *Tiger Girl* #201, five KIA and five POW's.

Lt. Mohr's crew, 560th Sq. Plane #203. Lt. Mohr KIA., Navigator Lt. Shilliday POW, 560th Sq. Lt. Karnezis and 2nd Lt. Loveless were POW's.

2nd Lt. Krueger, 561st Sq. pilot KIA.

All planes from the 563rd Squadron were lost in action this day.

Mission number 19 for the 388th Bomb Group had been a rough one. Lt. Nagorka recalled this mission:

It was one of the missions in which the Germans got most of our Group. When my element was reduced to two ships we moved up and formed under what was left of the first squadron. There were just four of us flying together out of the 20 aircraft that bombed. We maintained that formation all the way back. Not all of our aircraft were shot down, however. We discovered some had turned back due to battle damage. It ended up with a very heavy loss for our group. The Germans once again tried to wipe out one group and then go after another. That's why we went up under the first group so we would add to their firepower and to ours. Once again we managed to get back without injury, though we had a lot of holes in the ship.

Date: 6 September 1943
Target: Stuttgart, Germany
Narrator: 1st Lt. Raymond Baier
Group: 92nd Bomb Group, 327th Squadron

Written 8 September 1943

Stuttgart, Germany stands in the shadow of the Alps.

We were alerted at 6 p.m. Sunday. The day had passed quietly but I couldn't go to church because Wood (just returned from the rest home) and I had to fly 2 hours of instruments down at Thurleigh — SBA (Standard Beam Approach). I slept a bit Sunday p.m. and at supper we got the news of the alert. It was to be early too. A rumor circulated that Berlin was to be hit by us this month in a daylight raid. This consumed the evening in idle speculation. Finally, I said goodnight to Frankie — he had been speculating too! The place was quiet and there was a tension — you could feel it. We talked some of previous missions but always would drift back to that certain question, "Where do you think we're going tomorrow?"

The orderly came in a 0100. At 0200 we had eaten breakfast and were at the line. Irish eggs and they were half rotten. When we saw the map, the big map in the briefing room, we merely gasped and then, as if in a stupor, asked in after-thought, "Well, where is it?" Our target was Stuttgart, Germany, just 20 minutes by air from the Swiss border. We were further dismayed by our bomb load of 40 incendiaries. Briefing was quite ordinary but everyone was worried about gasoline. Take off set for 0600 and our ETA was 1230. That made 6H hours of formation time — too much, we thought and our thoughts proved only too correct by sundown. Here is the line up for the 327th which again was low squadron of the low group — just exactly like Schweinfurt. Tucker, lead; Woods, #2; Miles, #3; Booker, lead the second element; I was #2 and Bogard #3 with Christenson in the Diamond spot.

```
                    Tucker
         Miles                  Woods
                    Booker
         Bogard                 Baier
                  Christenson
```

Christenson was told to fill in the first abortion and he did over France. With briefing over we went to the ship #165T. We got extra oxygen and ammunition and topped (filled to over-running) off the tanks. We had 1700 gallons. That was just enough to get us back to the English coast, not to our own base. I spoke to Col. Keck but in the last analysis we had to risk it, after all the Swiss border was only 20 minutes away from the target and we could be interned (sorry since I didn't). Take off was set at 0606, station time at 0530. Toombs and I started our engines at 6 sharp thereby saved a little gas.

Off we went, 21 B-17s from the 92nd Bomb Group. The rendezvous at Thurleigh was OK for once. We climbed steadily to 17,000 and crossed the channel. They told us at briefing, "You'll make history today and don't shoot at any ships in the channel." We jumped to conclusions that maybe today was Invasion Day — YES, JUMPED! Not 5 minutes after crossing the French coast Asher left the formation and his cockpit was seen full of smoke. Three men bailed out but the chute of one didn't more than partially open. Since it has been explained he pulled the cord too quickly and the chute caught on the ship and ripped. It is felt that the incendiaries, I mean one incendiary, went off because close to the ground the ship exploded. That would account for the smoke in the cockpit. The big shots have declared it was an engine fire but everyone firmly believes it was the bombs. There was little flak. The fighters came in but they weren't too eager. We flew on toward that weather front half-way down France and to Stuttgart. Those Alps were the most tempting sight I've ever seen. After the weather front we saw no fighters and no flak 'till the target but the flak was heavy there. No fighters were seen over the target. Twice the leaders opened their bomb bay doors and twice they closed them. The second time I ordered my bombs dropped. Five hundred miles with two tons of potential hot fire was enough for me. Booker followed me and then Bogard. Chris filled in Asher's spot over France and that's the last I saw of him. Climbing up off my right wing, up, up, up, where supposedly it was safer. We missed the flak at the target due largely to Booker's evasive action.

Then came the mix up! About 500 B-17s got mixed up while we were still over Germany and the 2nd element followed the wrong group out. But we did better in our position. The lead navigator got lost and we consumed more gas. We went south of Paris and ultimately left the continent at Harve. About 1 hour from Stuttgart, Bogard went down. We were in the midst of heavy fighter attacks by the Abbeyville Kids with Yellow Noses. They attacked in groups as usual. Nose and tail attacks. Plenty rough but thanks to Booker picking a high position, two of us got back. One fighter came in high at about 2 o'clock and dove beneath the formation, then suddenly chandelled up and threw a rocket into Bogard's tail section. The tail gunner was blown from the ship, the rudder was almost all gone and the elevators were badly damaged. I can remember Bogard leaving his #3 position and trying to climb yet higher. It is said he lowered his wheels and a couple of parachutes were seen. Then, suddenly the ship went in to a sickening vertical dive — no more chutes were seen. We were taking violent evasive action all the time, sweating fighters and gas. My ball turret ran out of ammunition, one tail gun went out making the other unstable, so we had no tail guns. Then the upper turret went out and finally the nose guns but not before we had accounted for five German fighters (later 4 were confirmed). Gas was low. Gas was our real worry.

At 1130 I told Johnson to come out of the turret and even up our remaining gas. Number 4 engine had burned more than the others. We were at 21,000 feet and that is 11,000 feet above oxygen level. We were almost out of oxygen, even though we had filled up completely before starting. All the warning lights were on, on the gas tanks. Then the nose guns went out so all we had left between Paris and Barge were two waist guns. Rinko was working madly to keep one of them working. Fighter attacks continued. Of the 7 ships that began the mission only Booker and I remained. One we knew was down, one filled in an abortion and the other 3 were OK the last we saw — somewhere over Germany. At 1145 I asked Toombs for a gasoline check by engines. Here was the answer and the entire crew heard it and began sweating too: #1 engine, 40 gallons; #2, 40 gals.; #3 had 40 gals.; and #4 had 60. The crew chief wanted to transfer gas from #4 to #1 but I rejected the idea because #4 was burning more. I asked Fred, the navigator, "How much longer to the coast (French)?" "Ten minutes." This was at 1145. At 1200 I asked again and answer was incomplete. Still we were over France. I told him we had gas until about 1230 and after that no one could tell how much longer we could last. Then came 1215, 1220 and then 1230! I couldn't save gas by going slower or cockpit tactics because of the ever present danger of fighters. At last at 1242 we were over the blue water and white sands of the French coast. Quickly we pulled the props down to 1500 RPM and cut the engines back to 29" so as to save gas and cut the air speed to 130 mph. Green flares were fired for Spitfire protection if any were around. I asked Dougherty for a course to England — anywhere on the English coast, just to England and how far was it? I got the course but his mileage was a bit off. He said 30 miles and later I found it to be 90. Several miles away we could see the 4th Wing formations leaving us. We were all alone, with practically no guns, nearly out of gas, just limping into port when someone yelled, "Fighters, FIGHTERS, FIGHTERS!" We began firing green flares and the Spits saw us and came over. If any enemy fighters were around they didn't make any passes at us. One Spit came up on the left wing and just sat there guarding not 30 feet away from our wing tip. He stayed with us nearly all the way across the channel. Our 21,000 feet faded to 15,000 and suddenly the fuel pressure on both #2 and #3 engines went to zero. The gas gauges had been at zero so long we had forgotten about them and were sweating the fuel pressures! That left us #1 and #4 engines. Meantime the radio operator was sending out S.O.S. and all hands were preparing to ditch (land on the water). I could see the waves were quite choppy. I told the radio operator to contact our home base and tell them we were out of enemy territory but were also out of gas and probably would ditch. To do this he had to change his tuning unit for the other frequency. Meanwhile, everyone except the pilots were throwing everything out in the channel to lighten the ship and to prevent loose gear from being thrown about in a crash landing. The waist guns went and practically everything else. When the radio operator reached the base, he went to get his SOS tuning unit. Someone had thrown it out, so we had no more SOS! Our altitude gradually faded to 10,000, 8,000. Air speed was a bare 130 just enough to keep from settling to get maximum glide. Toombs and I sweated blood. Everyone prepared to ditch by taking their positions in the radio room and bracing according to previous instructions. Our altitude sank to 5,000 feet, still had 2 engines, #1 and #4, the outboards. Clouds were below us and water — lots of water! We saw no land, it was about 1255. We took off our chutes so we could get out the pilot's windows in case we did have to ditch — and there wasn't much doubt about it at the time. Then, #1 engine quit and the ship washed back and forth momentarily. So we had 3 feathered props! All was serene again except we had to pay with altitude more dearly for our air speed — 130 mph was essential. We had been dropping about 500 feet per minute now that rate had to be increased. At 2,000 feet we saw land! At 1,000 feet we were over it and Toombs spotted an emergency fighter strip. All the way across I had pinned my hopes on an emergency fighter strip such as this. I figured surely the English would have some fields right on the coast for ships in distress. We circled to the right, dropped our wheels, full flaps and then our once precious altitude turned detrimental to landing, so I slipped her! We slipped and half stalled at 105 mph right down to the ground. We had made it. We touched down a few minutes after 1300. I called the base by telephone at 1330 and they flew in to get us at 1700. Tucker, Miles and Wood had also made forced landings at airports for gas but were OK.

At 1300 when our proud 21-ship formation was due to return, just one ship circled for a landing. It is said the Colonel put his head in his hands and walked away.

Now a word about the bomb load. B-17 bomb bays are so built that they can only carry 25 incendiaries but the incendiaries don't weigh very much so the Big Boys order extra ones wired on making a total of 40. Any kind of a jar might prove disasterous and no doubt that's what happened to Asher. Once the pins are removed "Handle with Care".

Before I close tonight this 8th day of September, I want to note that tomorrow we have 2 missions. We carry 30-lb. fragmentation bombs and it looks like the French invasion. Italy fell today. AND SO ENDS THE STORY OF GASLESS MONDAY, SEPTEMBER 6, 1943 — and by the way, Monday is gasless here in Britain!!!!!

Twenty-one a/c of the 388th took off between 0549 and 0601 hours. We lead the 403rd Combat Wing of the 1st Air Task Force. Formation was effected and the wing proceeded on course.

Four of our a/c returned early. Lt. Wisehar returned at 0753 hours because of a runaway prop on No. 1 engine. Lt. Beeby returned because of inoperative guns; he then changed planes and returned with the second one at 0850 when a tire blew out on take-off. Lt. Parker returned at 1000 hours when he was unable to catch the formation. Lt. Felece returned to base at 0746 hours as the co-pilot had no oxygen mask.

The briefed route was followed until the formation was near the IP, at which time the lead bombardier, Lt. Bartuska, was injured by flak and was unable to complete the run on the primary target. There was cloud cover over the secondary target and the bombs were dropped near the target, which was Beaumont/Sur Oise airfield. Bombing results were poor.

Enemy a/c on this mission numbered from 20 to 25. The enemy a/c made only a few passes near the target area at 0855 hours. Our own fighter support P-47s took care of the enemy a/c. Our crews claim seven e/a destroyed and three probably destroyed.

Flak was encountered at four points along the route: at the French coast, at Rouen, at Paris and at Elitot on the way out. Most of the flak was near Paris. It presented a moderate to intense barrage at 24,000 feet, and was accurate as to both altitude and course.

One of our a/c is missing. Lt. Porter's ship was last seen about ten miles from Paris on the way to the target. The ship was first hit by flak and then by a 20mm shell, creating a large hole in the wing by the #1 engine. At this point the bombs were jettisoned and from four to ten chutes were seen. The plane was under control when last seen with the pilot slumped over the wheel.

Lt Nagorka, ship #371, was hit by fighters at 0910 hours at Les Andeleys at 23,500 feet. The bombardier jettisoned the bombs at Vernon at 0915 hours. Due to the hit in the left wing and aileron, the ship broke formation and landed at Ford at 1000 hours.

Key Personnel:

Group Leader	Major Satterwhite
Deputy Leader	Major Chamberlain

Lead Pilot	Lt. Bailey
Lead Navigator	Capt. Egaas
Lead Bombardier	Lt. Bartuska

Missing in action. Plane #362, 561st Squadron, *Wee Bonnie II* .

The 388th did not stand down the day after the Stuttgart disaster, they flew to Watton the 7th. On the 9th day of September, again twenty-one aircraft were dispatched to Paris. Once again the *Iza Angel II* and most of the original crew were aboard. Second Lt. Mickey Mahoney flew as a replacement bombardier on this mission, one of two he would fly with the Nagorka crew.

"Nick" Nagorka relived the mission as he sat at his huge conference table in his office in Washington, D.C. in the fall of 1976. This mission had also made news on the news wire of the United Press.

The official Mission Summary does not make much of the mission as far as the events that took place aboard *Iza Angel II* between the hours of 0910 and 1000 hours. The Mission Summary chronicles facts and statistics.

Lt. Nagorka related:

We had *Iza Angel II* on this mission; it will be a long time before she would go on another. *Iza Angel II* had made nine missions, suffered damage on many but was ready for the next. I had a mixed crew on this flight, as some of my crew were sick and I was filled in with others. One man had never flown with us before and had not done much combat work and was inexperienced up to this time. (He would earn his combat wings on this mission.)

At any rate, we got to the vicinity of Paris flying about 23,000 to 24,000 feet; we thought we were keeping a fairly good watch out. At a given point there was a squadron of pursuit ships up there.They started to peel around and come down, and someone said, "Hey, the British are up there helping us out!" Well, that was wrong — it was Germans — and they peeled down out of the sun so we could not see them to fire at them — very difficult to follow. They came right through our formation, tried to fly between the ships; apparently we were not flying good formation. At any rate, they were aiming at someone and their shots went into my left wing and badly damaged it. The aileron's control wires and the wing began to flop. It was extremely difficult to control the ship and keep it in position. I was afraid the wing might rip off so we slowed our airspeed down and, as I was leading an element, we signaled them to continue with the formation as we dropped back. With a slower airspeed we hoped the wing would stay on.

Second Lt. Gil Parker put his feet up on the dash and his knees behind the wheel of the control column to help steady it a bit from the wild vibration coming from that loose aileron. I did the same thing. We made a gradual slow turn, losing altitude, and headed back toward England.

Second Lt. Mickey Mahoney, bombardier, salvoed our bomb load near Vernon. We did not need that extra weight now that we were not going to be able to continue with the mission. The eight German fighters that had been so nicely formed up above us now made their play for us. You could almost sense the eagerness in them to mark one more "kill" on the tail of one of their Me109s. I had called Sgt. Robert Blankenburg out of the ball turret and Sgt. John Harris out of the tail gun position, thinking they should have their parachutes on in case the wing came off. The whole squadron came at us in pairs from the rear and the sides. I sent Jack Harris back to the tail gun. The ball turret gunner went back into the ball without his chute. I had told him not to, but he did anyhow.

On the first pass, Lt. Mahoney got a Me109 as it came at us from 1 o'clock. We were alone for the first time in combat and it occurred to me, without even thinking about it, that I should be using pursuit tactics — not bomber flight patterns. When flying formation in a tight bomb group you fly steady and straight. I was alone and being shot up by fighters. I decided to fly evasive tactics and to dive and turn as much as the mangled control surfaces would allow. I began to fly like a pursuit ship, turning into the attacks, diving, turning, and it confounded the Germans. They could not get a good clear shot at us. We could see the tracers just missing us, but the gunners on *Iza Angel II* were not missing. On the second attack Sgt. Edward Keisler shot one as it flew over and he actually saw the wing come off. We were down to six enemies.

There were times when all the boys were firing at the same time. The ship continued to jump and shake. Sgt. Claude Whitehead, the right waist gunner, said, "The ship was jumping around so much we didn't have a platform to stand on half the time. We were up in mid-air hanging on to the guns."

Sgt. Blankenburg got one more Me109 as it came in at them at 5 o'clock, just after he returned to the ball turret. "He seemed to stop in mid-air, went down out of control and began to burn," Lt. Nagorka continued.

Sgt. Jack Harris returned to his tail gun position in time to get a good burst into the third fighter and it went down. Sgt. Harris was not built like you would expect a tail gunner to be. He was over six feet tall and well-muscled, dedicated to his crew and to his job. No enemy plane gave him time for more than one good shot. The enemy avoided the twin stingers in the tail of *Iza Angel II*.

Three of the remaining four German fighters peeled off and left the gallant Fortress and its crew to one lone yellow-nosed Me109 with green colored wings. The crew named him Ferdinand. He stayed with them all the way to the coast. "He tried us from every angle looking for a position with a gun out or an empty position. The gunners were excellent in calling out Ferdinand's attacks to us up front," Nagorka stated.

Lt. Nagorka would turn toward the attack and the shells would burst outside of the ships turn. All the while the crew was expecting that fluttering wing to come right off, but not willing to give up the ship until it did.

Lt. Nagorka went on:

Ferdinand finally got disgusted, and made one last approach from the rear. We climbed sharply from him and could see a stream of 20mm shells pouring past us just under the wing. I guess he had used up all his ammo by this time as he pulled off about a thousand yards to the left and flew at our altitude, wobbled his wings at us — a salute — so we saluted back, "See you next time. We won this round."

I believe that he was also checking and calling in our direction, altitude and speed, and we were too caught up watching him to pay close attention to our position.

We were real proud of ourselves — that we'd fought off that squadron. All of a sudden four anti-aircraft shells burst right around us, perfectly bracketing us, one off each wing and one in front and one in the rear. It was a perfect shot! So perfect, that not one shell did us any damage. That battery had struck right around us. I said, "Holy God, what am I doing?" I set the plane on its side and did a falling leaf. They kept trying to get us, firing like mad with those anti-aircraft batteries — 105mm stuff. They didn't get us; we were able to skid out of it. They were not able to follow us exactly while on a skid, so we got down to five or six thousand feet and were finally out over the channel.

All the while that wing was flopping around. I didn't know from one minute to the next whether we'd go another 100 yards or not. I slowed it down as far as possible, kept dropping it very gradually down toward the water using as little power as possible to keep that wing from breaking off.

We approached the English coast and I warned everybody (who were lustily singing, *Coming in on a Wing and a Prayer*), to look for an airfield, anywhere and any size.

Sgt. Jack Harris added his comment to Lt. Nagorka's (whom the crew liked to call "Nick".

After we got rid of the fighter and crossed the channel we all looked for a place to land. We were shot up pretty badly and could not get our wheels to go down, so we dumped some fuel over the channel. We had found a field, it was Ford Field, a Canadian base. the ground crew foamed the runway and we came in on our belly. There were sparks flying 20 feet in the air, but no fire. This base was near a town named Sandwich. When we quit sliding all the fire trucks and meat wagons came roaring out to the ship. We were all ok and no one was hurt and no fire, but this little fighter base was hosting a B-17 Fortress.

Lt. Mickey Mahoney recalls:

The British O.D. came up after we landed and said, "I say you've torn up the bloody runway and the Mosquitoes take off in a half an hour."

I said "The Mosquitoes, why don't you ask how we are?" At this point our relationship with this Britisher was at a very low point.

When things quieted down, the whole crew went up to the base pub for a few jolts of whatever the British have to ease a persons nerves after such an experience. It could have been Irish whiskey or good Scotch whiskey, but it did the trick.

Soon after notifying the home base, a plane arrived and as Jack Harris said:

They flew us around England for five hours so we would not get plane shy. When we got back to the base the other guys in our barracks had divided up my uniforms and shoes. I had twelve pairs of those half-boots I had confiscated from other crews that didn't come back. My shirts and pants had been tailored, so I had to round up all my clothing, plus getting back my four bikes. Three of them I had inherited also. I used to rent out a bike for a dollar a day. I did get all my stuff back eventually.

Sgt. Harris got credit for one Me109 probably shot down and one damaged on this mission, which was not mentioned in the article written by Bob Considine for the press wires at the time.

All the crew members were loud in praise of their fellow crewmen. It showed just how important teamwork really was in the survival of heavy bomber crews under such adverse situations. At this time the average mission life expectancy was six missions and the crew of *Iza Angel II* had more than doubled that. Jack Harris would fly one more week, as would Sgts. Whitehead and Christensen.

Date: 16 September 1943
Target: Bordeaux/La Pallice, France
Narrators: Henry J. Nagorka, Jack Harris
John Baxter Douglas and Jimmy Walker
Group: 388th Bomb Group

Twenty-one planes of this group were scheduled to take off. Sixteen planes were airborne between 1141 and 1152 hours. These planes rendezvoused with the 96th Bomb Group over Snetterton-Heath and proceeded on course despite adverse weather over England. The 388th was lead group of the Second Combat Wing with the 96th tacked on as low group.

Three planes never did take off. Lt. Bensel, #954, developed engine trouble; Lts. Eccleston and Dennis, in #193 and #201 respectively, whose ground crews were unable to fill the Tokio tanks in time for them to join this mission. Lt. Felece in #421 took off late at 1221 hours. He climbed through the overcast and, according to Capt. Goodman, flew off the wing of one of the ships in our group, but mistook the formation for another group, peeled off and proceeded toward Lizard Point. Lt. Felece followed two groups of the First Bomb Division into France to the vicinity of 48 degrees 00'N and 02 degrees 20'W. At this spot a few bursts of flak convinced him he was in the wrong spot and he made a 180 degree turn and headed back for base and landed at 1656 hours.

Lt. Todd in ship #837 took off at 1225 hours, again due to delay in gassing up, and headed for Lizard Point over the overcast at 6,500 feet. He arrived at 1442 hours, saw no formation in the area and headed south. He followed the briefed course for 87 miles out to sea and then, being unable to sight our group, headed back to base and landed at 1820 hours. There were no aborts from the original 16 planes that took off.

The briefed course was followed to the vicinity of the assigned targets in the Bordeaux area. Cloud cover here obscured the primary, secondary and last resort targets and forced the formation to turn north up the coast of France. Our Groups followed the lead Combat Wing into La Pallice as the Target of Opportunity. The lead bombardier synchronized on the sub pens at the eastern end of the Wet Docks. Our bombs formed an excellent pattern, covering the sub pens and the maintenance and supply shops to the north. While it is questionable as to the damage our 500 lb. bombs did to the pens, the damage to the adjacent buildings and personnel made the raid well worth while.

Fighter opposition was moderate when 20-25 fighters were encountered, including FW190s, Me109s and JU88s. The attacks against our Wing were directed on the low group but our gunners claim one enemy aircraft destroyed and one possible.

Flak presented no serious problem, being relatively meager at La Pallice and heavy at Bordeaux only.

After leaving La Pallice, the formation headed out to sea and intersected the briefed course back to base. Just off the southwest coast of England severe rain squalls were encountered, and this, plus the oncoming darkness, dispersed the Group. As a consequence, three planes crash-landed in England as follows:

Lt. Cox, 562nd Sq., 42-5906 *Sondra Kay,* crashed just south of the RAF station at Shobdon. All ten members of the crew were killed.

Lt. Jarrendt, 560th Sq., 42-5904 *Gremlin Gus,* crashed into the side of a hill at North Mounton at 2115 hours. T/Sgt. Ed Baliff, cameraman, was killed. The bombardier, Lt. Dick, and the navigator, Lt. Staples, were seriously injured. T/Sgt. Forsta, S/Sgt. Cunningham and S/Sgt. Hovatter were slightly injured. None of the rest of the crew was hurt.

Lt. Nagorka, 560th Sq., 42-30030 *Old Ironsides,* passed to the north of this base, being unable to identify it, and ditched just north of the Wash. S/Sgt. Christensen and S/Sgt. Whitehead, both waist-gunners, were drowned. Tail-gunner S/Sgt. Jack Harris lost a leg.

Seven other planes landed away from the home base as follows: Lt. Bohne landed at RAF Stratford; Lt. Joho landed at RAF Shobdon; Lt. Rodgers landed at RAF Harrowbeer; Lt. Beeby landed at RAF Colerne; Lt. Pfeiffer (not listed) and Lts. Bliss and Williams landed at RAF Dunkeswell.

Our remaining six planes returned safely to the base by 2224 hours.

Key Personnel: Group Leader-Colonel David; Deputy Lead-Captain Goodman; Lead Pilot-Captain Bernard; Lead Navigator-Capt. Egaas; Lead Bombardier-Lt. McCandless.

Iza Angel II had been damaged on the September 9 mission to Paris, and because of this Lt. Nagorka and his crew were in ship

42-30030 *Old Ironsides*. Once more Lt. Nagorka related a tragic trip over enemy territory.

The briefed targets were in the Bordeaux area. This mission would differ from our usual timing. Our normal pattern for raids was to take off early in the morning, about five or six, hit our target about noon in Germany, and fly back visually. As many thousands of workers in the German plants were forced laborers, we would occasionally announce our raids so that perhaps some would be able to get out. We tried to avoid bombing during working hours if at all possible. Some of our own people thought it was bravado to pre-announce our missions; we were challenging the German Air Force. Nothing of the kind. We weren't interested in challenging that German Air Force; we would much prefer going in there without them opposing us. But at any rate we went into La Pallice by taking off at noon. It was to be a dusk raid — first one ever — and it (La Pallice) was not the primary target; it was a target of opportunity. All the other targets were socked in. So we went into La Pallice, did a good job on the sub pens, came back and turned around. We had a couple of fighter attacks, a single fighter or two, so we got a few rounds off, but nothing serious, no damage to us. We turned back for England and it had begun to get a bit dark. Then we ran into overcast — there was no warning whatsoever.

We were flying formation and the whole formation WHOOP! went right into the clouds. Well when that happens you can't see the man whose wing you are flying on. You know the next thing is crashes — mid-air crashes, and I was leading the upper squadron in this case. So when we hit that thing I just began a slow turn up and away from the formation to lead the squadron away to try to prevent mid-air collisions — couldn't see a thing.

I ordered everybody to watch every window and to scream if they see anything at all. We put our lights on; we did all kinds of things that were not normal to help ourselves — we got completely lost. We ended up being completely alone, no wingman left, no squadron left, no nothing — couldn't see a thing. We began to try and raise our base on the radio, and we got them for a few seconds. They answered and we lost them and never heard a thing after that. So we began to break thru the overcast. We were coming down thru it, not up thru it. We knew that England has some mountains up to three thousand feet and so we had to stay above that altitude. At one point it seemed were were in between two levels of overcast where it was clear. We kept looking down and at one point we saw some land and lights. I thought that must be south England. We kept watching our direction of flight, our headings and everything else. We would fly 20 minutes in one direction, turn 180 degrees and come back. It was impossible to locate anyone. It was as if the whole world had disappeared. Nobody would answer our MAY DAY call — nothing.

Well, in the course of that traveling north and south — the wind was from the west and was pushing us east off England to the North Sea.

Sgt. Jack S. Harris maintained his position in the tail all during this lonely flight for life blinking their alphabet (H) in code — no one would light up a field. But this was an old German trick and no one was buying it.

Lt. Nagorka continued with his story:

I saw what I thought was a river, but it was just a rift in the clouds and I began to go down into that rift as I thought I might be able to see a light or anything, somewhere. Finally we broke out over the water. We could see the water, see the variation of intensity of the darkness on the glint of the water.

I could hear an air barrage signal on my earphone. It was like a siren. As you got closer to it it got louder, and we were getting this signal. But by this time neither I, nor anyone else on the plane, knew where we were.

By this time we had been flying too long. We had been lost for hours. The navigator could not help us — no one could help us. The navigator did not know where we were and so it was up to me. We were flying along in the dark, not knowing we were above the water, apparently approaching a port of some kind where there must be Navy with balloons up. We did not know — German port, Danish port or British port. Scandinavia? — in two or three hours you can go that far. I had warned everyone up front to stare like crazy. Any point of light you see, "give me a shout right away — any light."

Jack Harris in the tail had been blinking back there and up front we were blinking our landing lights. We had been using the Universal SOS and those landing lights can be seen for ten or twenty miles.

During these last very frustrating and nerve-wracking moments, while the crew was tensely straining to see some kind of light, someone had seen that flashing landing light and was very hurriedly organizing a group to give aide to the stricken plane.

John Baxter Douglas related what transpired on the ground that night as the B-17 flew in the rain-darkened skies looking for a landing place.

I am a fisherman and live near the sea front and I am also a member of the Royal National Lifeboat.

On the night in question, my wife and I heard a large plane circling our village (Seahouses) many times before the crash. We wondered if it was an enemy aircraft. I thought the reason was to use up as much fuel as possible before crashing. The time was right about eleven o'clock P.M.

The state of the weather was a moderate to fresh south to southeast wind, together with heavy rain falling making visibility poor, and the swell four to six feet deep.

I do not know from which course the plane was steering when hitting the water, but whatever course it was, it was a very dangerous position when it came down. Everything blacked out. The island from which we rescued the men stands 80 to 100 feet high out of the water and the plane crashed only about one mile from those rocks. Should the plane have hit any one of the group of islands, of which there are 20 or 30, there would not have been one survivor.

While Lt. Nagorka and the crew continued to look for light, Sgt. Jack Harris had moved forward to the waist gun positions and was standing near the right waist window. Lt. Nagorka goes on:

As we were flying one of our fuel lights went on indicating five or ten minutes of fuel left in that tank. At the same time I noticed a pin point of light off to the side of the plane. So I said to my co-pilot, Lt. Gil Parker, "Take the wheel," and I kept my eyes rooted to that pin point of light. Gil gradually moved the ship around toward that light. The barrage noise became louder and in ten minutes we could see the light very clearly. At first I was not sure it was a light or not, maybe a reflection on the glass in the ship; it was so tiny. I held on to it and finally we began to arrive at that light, and it was a light. There in the water I could see dark shapes, ships? Holy cow, we are flying toward an armada of some kind. They are going to open up and knock us right out of the sky. I could hear this growing signal so I had to turn slightly to the right, and as I did, the second fuel warning light went on. I said, "OK fellows, this is it; we've got to land. It doesn't matter where we are. We only have two engines with gas and they are about to go too." I made a turn to avoid this "fleet" and go over the edge of what I thought was land and as I did that the third light went on.

"That's it, everybody get ready for ditching." I hit the alarm button. I told Lt. Parker to give me altitude readings. We showed 700 feet and we were dropping way down now. I flashed the landing lights and could see nothing yet. Gil shouted, "300 feet." I flashed the lights again and there was water right in front of us. We were going right into it. I hauled back on the stick as hard as I could and the tail slapped the water and it broke the ship in half in the bottom.

The two waist gunners were hurled out of the ship or fell out. I'm reconstructing this. Jack Harris, the tail gunner was twisted around and got caught up in something that twisted his knee very badly, tearing ligaments and blood vessels.

Jack Harris detailed what happened to him when the plane hit:

I was standing at the door waiting to get the bail out order. We couldn't see a thing because of the storm. The waist gunners were laying down smoking. I had on my chest chute and Mae West. We hit a large swell with the tail, breaking it off and knocking me forward and unconscious. I came to under water, went up to the ceiling where there was a couple feet of air. I went back under water and found the door. I pulled the pins out that act as hinges and butted the door out with my head. Lucky I have a hard head. There was equal pressure outside as well as inside.

Mr. Douglas filled in the details of the beginning of the rescue.

The Fortress came down into the sea south of a group of islands known as the Farnes. When the crew took to the dingy, they landed on what is known as the Inner Farnes or St. Cuthberts Island. They had flashed a May Day signal SOS by Morse Code.

The lifeboat was then launched at approximately 11:30. The tide was very low at the time of the crash. We had our lifeboat to pull from the lifeboat house quite a distance to the water to get it operational. There were seven of us in the lifeboat and we proceeded to the rescue. The crew of the lifeboat was: George Dawson, Robert Rutter, Michael Robson, William Fargus, John Baxter Douglas, Joe Dawson and Jimmy Walker.

Jimmy Walker played an important role in the initial contact with the crew, as did John Douglas. These two men jumped ashore to get to the crew of the crashed Fortress. Jimmy Walker began his story:

We saw the plane flashing the SOS signal. He was flashing, flashing, flashing, but we dassn't show a light, couldn't say anything in case it was a Jerry. We got the lifeboat underway and got to the south side of the island. The coxswain said to me, "What are we going to do?" I said, "Get in a little further and I'll jump." I got into the fore end of the boat and the boys took it into the rocks and I jumped out and up the rocks, John Douglas right behind me.

Lt. Nagorka again focused on the crash.

When we hit the water we went under like a submarine. The water was going by. We came back up on the water and all the equipment is supposed to work automatically when water hit it, and our ditching procedure is to get out as soon as the ship stops. The doors are supposed to pop out and the dingy come out as soon as there is water. Nothing happened. Not a bloody thing. I started to scream, "Get the hatches open! You on this side, you on that side get those hatches open. Pull the dingy out."

Again Jack Harris recalled.

When I came up from the plane I pulled the handle on the Mae West. It did not work. I still had on my 28 foot chest chute and I had put on some boots in case we had to jump and may hit trees or rocks. These all caused problems being so heavy. Swells must have been eight feet high. It was still

82

First Army photos of the bombing of Hickam Field, Hawaii, December 7, 1941. U.S. planes at bomber airfield. It all started here. (USAF photo)

A formation of Eighth Air Force 306th Bomb Group Flying Fortresses launch their bombs on communications centers during an attack on Germany. (USAF photo)

Hannover, Germany after the Eighth Air Force neutralized it by bombing. (USAF photo)

A 92nd Bomb Group Fortress flies over the Lengenhagen Airfield at Hannover, Germany during a bombing mission on August 5, 1944 (USAF photo)

Lt. Earl Hurd. (Hurd photo)

L. to R.: Capt. R.B. Houston (K.I.A.); Capt. Charles T. Merrill; First Lt. James R. Steeg, Navigator, *Tarfu;* First Lt. Earl Hurd, Pilot, *Tarfu.* (Hurd photo)

L. to R.: First Lt. James R. Steeg, Navigator; First Lt. Earl Hurd, Pilot; First Lt. Joseph B. Clements, Co-pilot. (Hurd photo)

B-24-D *Tarfu* fueling up for Ploesti mission, 1 August 1943. (Stephens archives photo)

Nose view of *Tarfu*. The man is unidentified. (Hurd photo)

Intensity shows in all of the faces at the briefing for the Ploesti mission. In the first row, L. to R.: Col. Ted Timberlake; First Lt. James M. Gill, McBride crew, (K.I.A.); First Lt. Jefferson S. Chadwick, Bombardier, Merrill crew. (USAF photo)

A closer look at some of the faces at the briefing. Closest to the camera at left are 1st Lt. Earl Hurd, Pilot of *Tarfu;* 1st Lt. Carl C. Barthel, Navigator of the Walker crew; Capt. Raymond A. Walker, Pilot. Directly in front of them with his hand on his cigarette is 1st Lt. Joseph B. Clements, Co-pilot of the Hurd crew. (Hurd collection)

These shots give a vivid idea of how low the B-24s flew in bombing the Ploesti field. (USAF photo)

Oil storage tanks on fire as another wave of B-24s come onto the target. (USAF photo)

Oil storage tank explodes. (USAF photo)

88

More B-24's come across the already burning target. (USAF photo)

Close up view of the Columbia Aquila Refinery showing burning storage tanks. (USAF photo)

Schweinfurt, Germany. (USAF photo)

After the bombing showing hits on machine shops (A & B) and power
house (C). Arrows show camouflage to confuse damage assessors.
(USAF photo)

Heading for home and looking back at Schweinfurt in flames.
(USAF photo)

Regensburg, Germany Messerschmitt factory taken four hours after the raid. Virtually all bombs hit within the factory area with hits scored on nearly every building. (USAF photo)

Enlisted crew of *Iza Angel I* in Africa after the Regensburg mission. L. to R.: Sgt. Jack Harris, TG; Sgt. Claude Whitehead, LWG; Ed Keisler, TTG; Sgt. Ed Christenson, RWG; Sgt. H. Antalek, RO; Sgt. Blankenburg, BTG.

Lt. Nagorka shows *Iza Angel I* to Nurse Izabella Helwoski after whom the plane was named. Taken at Benghazi August 18, 1943.

1st Lt. Earl E. Woodward, N, is shown holding a 20mm German shell that tore a hole in his wing. This could have been *Iza Angel I* after returning to England with a similar shell in its fuel tank.

The crew of *E* after a gasless landing at the emergency field in England. Note three feathered props with just a strong #4 engine to bring them in with the piloting skill of Lt. Ray Baier.

92

The happy crew of *E*. Back row L. to R.: Lt. Harold Toombs, CP; Lt. Raymond Baier, P; Lt. Fred Daugherty, N; Lt. William Munro, B; Center row: S/Sgt. James E. Geibeil, RO; S/Sgt. Donald J. Sack, TTG-E; S/Sgt. John Johnson, BTG (POW); S/Sgt. George A. Rinko, RWG. Sitting: S.Sgt. Elwood R. Newton, TG; S/Sgt. Vaughn E. Bowers, LWG.

Bombing of enemy harbor installations at La Pallice, France, 23 May 1943. (USAF photo)

Front, L. to R.: R.A.F. Salvage Officer, Margaret Graham (now Mrs. Moran, owner of Bamburg Castle Hotel at Seahouses), Betty and Ella Graham; Lt. Gil Parker, CP. In rear, Lt. Henry J. Nagorka, P, during the time that they returned to Seahouses to help locate the two missing waist gunners, Sgts. Christenson and Whitehead. (Moran photo)

Life-Boat house at Seahouses still being used in 1983, with the Harbor Master standing in front. The lifeboat is manually dragged 1/4 mile to the water by the crew. (Stephens photo)

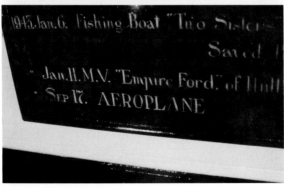

The "Tallyboard" inside the boathouse showing the entry for the rescue of the B-17. (Stephens photo)

94

Mr. Jimmy Walker, age 89, last of the lifeboatmen who took the *Old Ironsides* crew off the Farne Island crash site. He is holding a cup presented to him by the author inscribed with the 8th Air Force insignia and the names of the crew members of *Old Ironsides*. (Stephens photo)

Relics salvaged from *Old Ironsides* crash site by Jimmy Walker. The cigarettes were still fresh when opened in September 1983 when Mr. Walker presented them to the author. They are "Sobranie" straight cut brand. These relics have been returned to England for display in the 390th Bomb Group Memorial Museum in Framlingham. (Jeho photo)

At Bamburg Castle Hotel, L. to R.: Lorraine Stephens; Leslie Moran, R.A.F., Retired "Lancaster" pilot; Margaret Moran; Bob Rutter; Bob Reay, Secretary of the Life-Boat group.

Port bow of the lifeboat. (Stephens photo)

95

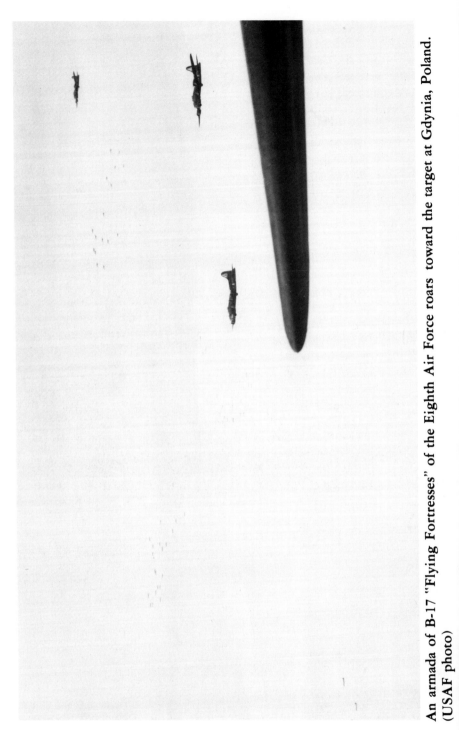

An armada of B-17 "Flying Fortresses" of the Eighth Air Force roars toward the target at Gdynia, Poland. (USAF photo)

Target area at Gdynia, Poland, position of cross marks are approximately in the center of the target area. Note the smoke screen. (USAF photo)

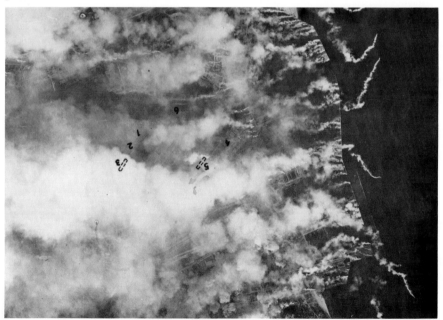

The smoke screen at Gdynia, Poland covers the berths of the cruisers Nurnberg (1) and Leipzig (2), the Gneisenau (3), the Lutzoe (4), Emden (5), and U-boat depot ship (6). (USAF photo)

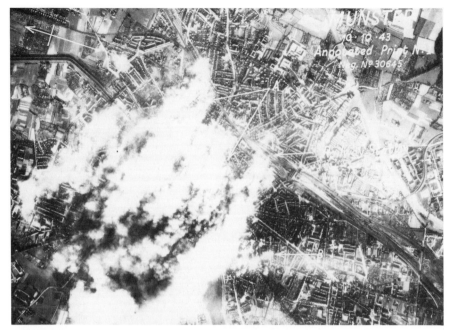

10 October 1943. Munster, Germany in flames. (USAF photo)

Railroad station
and workers
area in Munster
in flames.
(USAF photo)

With only ragged pieces of the tail left, this B-17 was brought back safely to its base at Thorpe Abbots, England. Crews of other planes had seen *Hang The Expense Again III* have its tail almost entirely shot off over France and figured that it had crashed inside enemy territory, but it showed up later flown by Frank Valesh. Frank Gregory was the bombardier on this plane. (USAF photo)

The front end of *Hang The Expense Again III* does not look too bad even though the tail end had been severely damaged. Suprisingly the tail gunner survived the incedent. (USAF photo)

99

Bombing results of the 100th Bomb Group against Marienburg, Germany on 9 October 1943. The first bombs have just hit. Note how perfectly they are being concentrated within the comparatively small area of the target. Picture 1 of a series of 4. (USAF photo)

Picture 2. Bomb bursts and fire have now created an enormous cloud of smoke rising high into the air. (USAF photo)

Picture 3. Marienburg, Germany after the dust and smoke of bombing has stopped enabling this damage assessment photo to be taken. (USAF photo)

The official damage estimate at Marienburg, Germany after the raid of 9 October 1943. (USAF photo)

Back row, L. to R.: Sgt. Otto Trammer, WG; Sgt. Charles H. Hartnett, WG; Lt. David C. Brisbes, N; Lt. Joseph F. Thornton, P; Lt. Arthur A. Carmell, B; Lt. Whitney M. Bray, CP; Sgt. Rolland A. Gallaway, TG; front row: Sgt. Dean W. Sommers, BTG; five ground crewmen, names unknown; Sgt. Lawrence E. Dennis, ROG.

B-17 returning from Trondheim, Norway. A flak hit left his engine smoking. Sgt. Sommers' plane suffered the same damage at Knaben. (USAF photo)

Bombing of bridge near Vegesack, Germany. Forest Norman's copy of this picture has written across it, "Got shot down on this one." (USAF photo)

S/Sgt. Forest "Pete" Norman from Eaton, Colorado, as a member of the 303rd Bomb Group in England.

Forest Norman rides one of the donkeys brought back from Africa on the Regensburg mission. The scene is in his quonset hut barracks.

Forest Norman's membership card in the Goldfish Club.

The radio operator's gun position. This is the position Sgt. Bob Maddox flew when he was forced to bail out after serious damage to his B-17 on a raid to Brunswick, Germany. (USAF photo)

Lt. Cole's crew, 95th Bomb Group. Standing, L. to R.: Lt. McKenna, N (KIA); Lt. Cole, P (KIA); Lt. Graffe, B; Lt. Boswell, CP (KIA). Kneeling: Sgt. Kushnerik, TTG; Sgt. Mendoza, LWG; Sgt. Sam Johnson, BTG; Sgt. Gerniglia, TG; Sgt. Harris, RWG; Sgt. Robert Maddox, ROG.

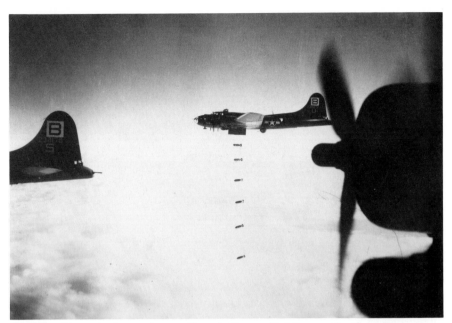

A stick of bombs drops from a Bomb Group B-17 onto Emden, Germany, 2 October, 1943. (USAF photo)

This 95th Bomb Group B-17 shows off the new, more deadly twin-gun chin turret. This mission was over Bremen, Germany. (USAF photo)

P-47 escorts keep their noses pointed away from these 95th Bomb Group Fortresses. It sometimes was fatal to point the nose directly at a bomber in combat as the bombers might mistake the plane for an enemy FW-190. (USAF photo)

95th Bomb Group B-17s leave contrails on the way to bomb Brunswick, Germany. *No Excuse* went down on the way to bomb this target carrying a full load of bombs. (USAF photo)

Dressed with every imaginable display of uniform possible, from knit wool caps with Captain bars to Russian fleece-lined boots, liberated American prisoners of war disembark at a Douglas A-26 Invader airstrip in north eastern France on their way toward a processing station at Rheims in 1945. (USAF photo)

A heavy concentration of bombs fall on the industrial section of the Zeblendorf district of Berlin as Liberators and Fortresses of the Eighth Air Force again strike at the Nazi capital city. (USAF photo)

Blitzing Betsy of the 388th Bomb Group, the plane commanded by Lowell H. Watts which was shot down on the return trip from Berlin 6 March 1944. Sgt. Harry Allert, crew chief, stands in front. (Watts photo)

107

The Lowell Watts crew. Back row, L. to R.: Lowell Watts, P; Bob Kennedy, CP; Murphy; Ed Kelley. Front row: Ramsey, TTG; Ray Hess; unidentified; Bob Sweeney, BTG; Harold Brassfield, TG; Don Taylor, WG.

On an Eighth Air Force raid over Berlin, a B-17 in a lower formation moved directly under another plane which has just released its bombs. (USAF photo)

An instant later and one bomb has crashed through the horizontal stabilizer. The lower plane has also just released its bombs.

108

The stricken B-17 is knocked out of control and loses altitude sharply.

The B-17 continues down, losing altitude. No chutes were seen from this plane.

2nd Lt. O. A. "Jack" Farrar in the co-pilot seat prior to his first Berlin raid. After this mission he took over the pilot's seat.

These 3rd Division B-17s drop their load of bombs on a Nazi fighter
base. Flak bursts mingle with bombs and planes sending shrapnel
through the air. (USAF photo)

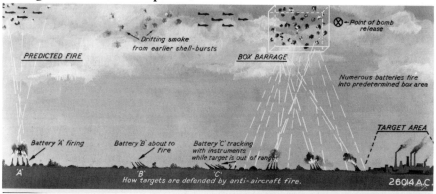

With it's bomb bay doors open, this 381st Bomb Group B-17 is ready to
drop it's load on Averd, France. (USAF photo)

Graduation photo of the Aviation Cadet class of O. A. "Jack" Farrar (first person at far left in the center row).

Photo for phoney identification papers supplied to Lt. O. A. Farrar in his escape kit.

The crew that flew with Lt. Farrar prior to flying the Atlantic to begin their combat missions. Lt. Farrar was the co-pilot at this time and is second from left in the front row. Youngest man on the crew was 19 years old and the oldest was 43. This crew flew a total of 51 missions together. First in the 381st Bomb Group in England and then in the 2nd Bomb Group in Italy.

Lt. Henry Dayton and crew. They flew with the 390th Bomb Group, 570th Bomb Squadron. L. to R. back row: Donald Keohane, TTG/Eng.; Charles Loomis, LWG; Harry Schneider, ROG; Robert Hurley, TG; Clarence de Arman, RWG; Richard Mooers; BTG. Front row: Henry Dayton, P; George Benton, CP; Howard Jones, N; John Reichardt; B.

With engines roaring, Fortresses of the 390th Bomb Group line up on the perimeer getting ready for take-off from Station 153, Framlingham, England. (USAF photo)

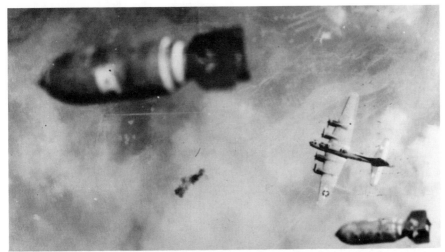

This photograph shows flak bursts and smoke from smoke screens mingling with smoke from fires that mark hits on the target at Ploesti, Rumania oil refineries, 15 July 1944. Lt. A.O. Farrar, flying with the 2nd Bomb Group, 96th Bomb Squadron, flew this mission and his B-17 was hit by flak on the tail surfaces and he was forced to land at a fighter base in Italy. (USAF photo)

One of the P-38 Lightnings that escorted these B-17 Fortresses of the 15th Air Force over Blackhammer, Germany 7 July 1944 was hit by flak. With one prop feathered it returned to its base under the protection of the heavy bombers of the 2nd Bomb Group. (USAF photo)

This photo shows the extent of the Nis, Yugoslavia marshalling yard. This is the south yard with locomotive and repair sheds, rolling stock and stations. The "accordion" roofed structure near the center of the photo is a locomotive shed. (USAF photo)

Nis, Yugoslavia, results of bombing: (1) tracks cut, cars destroyed; (2) siding cut; (3) loading ramp damaged. (USAF photo)

Major Lanford's 483rd B-17 goes down in flames after a direct flak hit over the marshalling yards at Nis, Yugoslavia, 15 April 1944. Lt. Miller was flying off Major Lanford's left wing at the time and his plane also received hits from the same flak guns. (Miller photo)

114

raining with high winds. The radio operator had pulled a handle on the front of the plane since it was not under water. This then shot out a life raft with a 20 foot rope on it. "Nick" had urged all the other guys out onto the wing. They pulled the raft in with the rope and cut the rope, and I came up by the raft and they pulled me in and rowed away from the plane so we would not get sucked under when it went down. After going a short distance, they were all hollering, "Whitehead, Christenson!" — no answer.

Jack Harris was groggy with pain and was given a shot of morphine to ease his pain. The other crew members were still trying to get an answer from the two missing waist gunners. They stayed about forty or fifty feet from the plane shouting all the while for their crewmates until the ship *Old Ironsides* slipped under the water. No sense waiting, the men were gone. They were hurt in the crash and could not get out and had not survived. Lt. Nagorka recounted:

We saw something jutting out of the water. It turned out to be an island. What I had thought were ships from the air were actually small islands. I warned everybody to do no talking when we landed. We didn't know who we'd see, Germans or what, maybe Scandinavians. I intended on telling "them" it was a practive mission, that we had crashed coming home from a practice mission, that we had run out of gas, so they would turn us back to England. We got to the bottom end of that island and rocks were all round, very difficult to walk on, slimy and slippery. We got out of the dingies. We had no choice but to leave Jack Harris in one of the dingies as we could not pick him up. He was in terrific pain. We gradually got the dingy up on the rocks out of the water and the further we got the better the going got as the rocks got smaller. We finally got to the land.

Gil Parker and I decided to go up to the top of the island to explore, to see if we could find markings of some kind to determine what we should do. Meantime a light in the distance that we had seen began to flash. It had seen our SOS signals. They were flashing something. Then we saw another light from the same area. It began to move in our direction. It was a boat. They'd launched a boat. Before walking to the top, I warned all the crew, "Don't talk to these guys until I get back if they get here before I do." I wanted to hear what they were speaking to prepare myself a little bit — to know what kind of story to give them. If they were Germans we would give them one line. If they were Norwegians we would give them another. At the top of the island there was a group of buildings made of stone, rough natural stone. They were of all sizes and shapes. They looked Medieval, centuries old without a mark or sign on them. One was a church made of stone. The door was locked; everything was locked; nobody was there. Completely deserted; no way to identify it. I couldn't believe my eyes. I saw a small tug-like boat come up to a little jetty.

Sgt. Harris told of the aid he was given by his crew mates.

The guys had opened a small kit I had on my chute harness and gave me a couple shots of morphine. Also, they opened my chute and wrapped me in that. The bone in my leg had broken due to the crash.

Lt. Nagorka and Lt. Parker got back just as the two men in the boat were being greeted. They were unable to understand the deep brogue and at first thought the men were Norwegian.

But they greeted us like brothers immediately. Full of compassion and extremely friendly. They first inquired if anyone was hurt. I said, "Yes, one of my men down here." They went on and took a look at Jack and they saw his leg and immediately made a splint of some small boards and tied them together with their scarves. Jack screamed in pain. They paid no attention but said, "We've got to do this." I was then beginning to calm down somewhat and decided that these great friendly men were not enemy.

Jimmy Walker went on:

This fellow, I don't know who he was, (Lt. Henry Nagorka, pilot) came up and says, "Where are we?" Before I could get time to tell him he says, "We have a badly injured man." So we made our way up to the man. He was laying in a dingy near the old lighthouse. Meantime the lifeboat had gone over to the landing on the island. When I saw the injured man, his leg had been tied up crooked. I said, "Who is doing this?" He says, "I'm doing this." I says, "I don't think you should tie his leg up that way." So we straightened the leg out, took some of the parachute his leg was wrapped in and rigged a splint. Mind you, they did not know where they were, they were lost. The language was a bit awkward. This fellow (Lt. Nagorka) kept asking me where they were. I tried to cheer the fellow up and says, "You're in Northumberland." The men thought it was Norway — enemy territory! I says, "Definitely not!" I says, "Newcastle." Still it didn't ring a bell. So I thought I would try something else. I says, "Edinburgh." They had us then. I says, "You're seventy miles south of old Edinburgh," and that did it. They shouted with joy, " England, England!!" They thought they were in enemy territory. Their joy was dimmed by the loss of two crewmates.

I sat by the wounded man when we got his leg fixed up and asked him how he felt and he said, "Not so bad if I had a cigarette." I lit him a cigarette and he enjoyed that.

As Mr. Douglas went on:

We found it necessary to carry the wounded airman over the rocks at which time he suffered a great lot of pain owing to the slippery stones and rocks we had to cover and we were unable to steady our feet. Then, having got the crew and the wounded aboard, we proceeded to North Sunderland Harbor. On our way in one of the lads and the Lieutenant flashed a signal to

116

the pier, "Want a doctor immediately!" I asked the injured man again how he was and he said, "Not so bad now."

Upon arriving, we took the crew and the wounded airman to the Bamburgh Castle Hotel where a doctor was already waiting in case of casualties. After examining the patient he found it necessary to send him to the infirmary at Alnwick, which is a small town fourteen miles from Seahouses. He told us we did the right thing in wrapping the injured man's leg as we did.

Mr. Walker went on to say:

I never saw the men after we brought them in as it was dark and we had to go about trying to find the Fortress and the two missing men.

John Douglas related:

The next morning Jimmy Walker and one other crewman of the lifeboat and myself went out to sea to look for any signs of wreckage or traces of oil which could give us some idea where the aircraft went down. Jimmy Walker chimed in to say, "We knew about where it was and we did find a glove. And the Americans came, The RAF came and one thing and another."

Later a fellow came along with us and he got his operations going and after about an hour and at the finish we got tired of this. We asked him what he was trying to find. He says, "Oh, I'm trying to find the flying fortress." I says, "How do you expect to find it that way? You only got a bit of chain on the end of a rope." Well he says, "Coming over the plane it will make a noise or rattle." Well I says, "It will do the same coming over a rocky bottom." So he says, "Can you find it in any different way?" I says, "I think we can if you give us about an hour. We'll give it a try." We came ashore and got some old ropes. We were all fishermen and we rigged up a drag we thought would work. Shortly we had something and started heaving on the winch. About this time the small forward hatch came open and two heads popped out. My son and another lad had sneaked on while we were getting the ropes. Suddenly they shouted, "Look what's coming!" It was the tail of the Fortress. We could not lift it, but it was intact when we fetched her up. We could see nothing wrong with the tail. We wound the ropes together and put a float on the end to mark the spot. The only float we had, though, was black, so that night the minesweepers sank it as a mine. We had to start over.

Next time we took a diver along and he went down and had a good dive and had radio contact with the boat and he called up and said he was on one of the wings and the plane was setting just like she would in a hangar, the wheels down and everything. It was a beautiful day and the diver was trying to do this and that. He had seen nothing of the waist gunners, but the plane was intact. The next day the same diver could not find it. Just the change in the water current moved it.

Mr. Douglas continued:

In later weeks when location of the plane was determined, salvage operations took place to raise the aircraft in order to try and recover the bodies of the two who were lost. But owing to the big strain of the ropes we used when getting the four engines and the cockpit ashore, the fuselage had been cut off and was never recovered. The missing airmen were never found. The forepart of the Fortress is visible at some extreme low tides to this day.

While in conversation with the Captain, I found out that particular time that his navigational aids had been out of order. He said he was completely lost so far as his position was concerned. When we explained to him that he was in England, he seemed quite relieved that he had been rescued in Great Britain.

Though Jack Harris was in a great deal of pain at the time, he did vaguely recall being sent to the hospital. Lt. Nagorka filled in a few details of the arrival of the crew at Seahouses:

They took us to a small town that was a fishing village. As Mr. Douglas said they had seen our flashes way out in the sea and it was late, so they raised the village and got their team of rescue men and carried that boat, it was low tide, all the way from its shed down to the water. That was a big boat and the carry was a long and hard one. These men were all outstanding men, full of compassion and tenderness toward Jack as well as the rest of us. The villagers were the same. We were taken to what is called the Bamburgh Castle Hotel which was run by the Graham sisters and one daughter of one of the sisters, the men all being off to war.

They took off all our clothing just as if we were their little children and gave us towels and told us to get fixed up. They had already prepared hot rum and tea for us. I called the base long distance. The good people of Sea Houses had warned a nearby RAF base that a plane was coming in apparently hurt, so they sent out an ambulance to the hotel. After the doctor had examined Jack Harris, the ambulance arrived and Jack was whisked off to the civilian hospital. It was necessary to amputate his left leg at the knee. We were told to stay put and the base said they would send someone down for us. We were there for a couple of days as the weather was fierce, raining, overcast, and we would sit in the hotel in the alcove where there was a large fireplace and nearby some small windows that we could look out to the place where we had crashed.

For the life of me I could not stop thinking of Sgt. Whitehead and Sgt. Christensen. The plane was out there under I didn't know how much water. They got the British Air Sea Rescue and the RAF on it. Our people came and picked us up and we left everything. When we got back to Knettishall and they heard our story there, they put us on leave for a week. I was determined to do something to help find the two missing gunners during this week of leave. I managed to get a ride up to Seahouses with a Commodore who was

118

in charge of the air Sea Rescues in that part of England. So I rode from East Anglia all the way up with him. When I got there, there was Lt. Gil Parker. He had beat me up there. He had said nothing about going up there. We both stayed the whole week. We waited for and tried to help find our two missing comrades. The RAF got divers down and found the ship, but could find no bodies. The weather was bad and the sea was rough and it might be a day-to-day situation before they could chance going down to look.

We became good friends of the Graham sisters and the one daughter, Margaret, but it was a bittersweet kind of thing because of the deaths of my two waist gunners and the loss of Jack Harris' leg. We went to see Jack in the hospital, of course, and they told us they could not save the leg as it was gangrenous from the knee down. I could not understand this as I could see no visible wound, but they explained the bone was broken and the veins and ligaments inside were torn and broken and no circulation was in the leg. We had visited him before the operation and this is why I was surprised that he had lost his leg.

Sgt. Jack Harris stayed in the hospital there for a month, then was transferred to an American hospital in Sherwood Forest. After three months there, he was sent to Percy Jones Hospital in Battle Creek, Michigan where he had two more amputations in the eleven months he was there. Jack was discharged December 8, 1944. The rest of the crew were back again a week later flying the missions with the 388th Bomb Group — their time would run out October 9, 1943 over Gydnia, Poland.

Of the lifeboat crew, only one survives, Jimmy Walker, and he spends many hours in the warm sunshine in the boat harbor right behind the Bamburgh Castle Hotel. It was a pleasure of my wife and I to enjoy a long visit with him and his lovely wife, the two of which have over one hundred years of service with the National Lifeboat Service. Mr. Walker is credited with saving fifty-four lives. As are all lifeboat crewmen, it is volunteer work and the men carry on their regular jobs, mostly that of fishermen.

Mrs. Margaret Moran, a very prim young girl at the time of these events, is now the owner of the Hotel. Mr. Moran being a retired RAF Lancaster pilot himself.

All contacts at the village of Seahouses were extremely friendly and helpful in my quest for information, and the Harbor-Master took me on a tour of the lifeboat and showed the "Tally board" where all rescues since 1868 are recorded.

The 388th flew low group in the lead Combat Wing of the 4th Task Force. The 96th Bomb Group led with the 96th-388th composite flying high group.

Eighteen a/c of this Group took off between 0819 and 0832 hours, formed and headed to Splasher #5 and on out into the North Sea, rendezvousing en route without the usual circling. None of our a/c aborted and no spares were sent on this mission.

The briefed route up across Denmark and across the Baltic skirting the southern tip of Bornhorn to the Northeast coast of Germany was followed to the IP. By the time our Group was making its bomb run, the Germans had already laid down a very effective smoke screen over the Port of Gydnia, completely concealing the area in which our assigned target, the Cruiser Nurnberg, was supposed to be lying. As a consequence, the lead ship held its bombs and proceeded to make a wide circle to the right out into the Bay of Danzig, out in front of the 96th, and came back on a second bomb run on a heading of 270 degrees. On this approach, there was really but one hole in the smoke screen. In the center of that hole was located a large ship berthed along the north side of the French wharf. The lead bombardier synchronized on this ship and reported two and possibly three direct hits on the ship. In addition, the bombs did considerable damage to the warehouses on the dock and to the dock itself. On the other side of the same wharf, the Dutch wharf, one medium-sized ship which appears to be a 300 foot freighter and one small ship, possibly a tug, were lying, and our pattern got at least one near miss on the freighter and several near misses that must have done damage. Our strike photos show only one direct hit in the large ship nearest the French Wharf, in addition to the other damage above. British Bomber Command reports by teletype that a photo taken after the attack shows our target to have been the Liner Stuttgart. It was on fire and being towed away from the French Wharf.

Flak encountered on this mission was accurate. As the formation crossed the Danish Coast on the route in, flak was received from guns located just north of Nymendigab, which was accurate at our altitude of 11,000 feet. Some meager flak was encountered at other points in Denmark on the route in and just after making landfall on the German Coast. The Group received very accurate flak again from batteries near Stolpe. Flak at the target was fairly intense but inaccurate. Anti-aircraft fire was also thrown up at several points in Denmark along the route back.

No enemy a/c were encountered until just as the Group was about to leave Denmark on the return route, at which time they were jumped by approximately 35 a/c, about half of which were single engine fighters. The single engine a/c pressed their attacks very vigorously while the twin engine a/c would lob shells into the formation, either from rockets or cannon. Our gunners claim 18 a/c destroyed, one probably and one damaged.

All 18 ships returned safely. Seventeen at Knettishall between 1750 and 1821 hours while the 18th landed at Rackheath. Three crew members were seriously injured and two slightly on this mission.

WOUNDED IN ACTION: S/Sgt. Adolph Hughes, LWG and Sgt. David Houston, RWG in a/c #291, 561st, Sq., Dennis crew; and T/Sgt. Charles Hartman, Jr. RO in a/c #800.

KEY PERSONNEL: Group Leader, Major Reed
Deputy Leader, Lt. Eccleston
Lead Pilot, Lt. Willson
Lead Navigator, Lt. Flor
Lead Bombardier, Lt. Zettek.

An additional six ships from this Group were assigned to form the high squadron of the 96th-388th Composite Group. They took off between 0810 and 0812 hours. Somewhere along the route, the low squadron of the 96th came up and forced themselves into the lead of the high squdron. Lt. Beeby tried to force them back but was unsuccessful. As a consequence, Lt. Nagorka, who was leading the second element of our formation, took his element down to form the low squadron and protect the lead squadron.

Bombing by this Composite Group is reported to have been on a mag heading of 350 degrees and the bombs are reported to have struck on both sides of the harbor entrance.

On the route back, Lt. Nagorka and Lt. Kinney were both lost to fighters off the west coast of Denmark. The remaining four ships landed safely at the base between 1750 and 1754 hours.

KEY PERSONNEL: Lead Pilot - 388th a/c Lt. Beeby

MISSING IN ACTION:

1st Lt. Henry Nagorka	P	Sgt. William Caruso	LWG
2nd Lt. Gilbert Parker	CP	T/Sgt. Robt. Blankenburg	BTG
2nd Lt. Michael Mahoney	B	S/Sgt. Francis Antalek	RO
2nd Lt. John Leverone	N	T/Sgt. John Dugan	RWG
T/Sgt. Howard Keisler	E	T/Sgt. Wilbur Quinn	TG

Shot down over North Sea off Denmark and crew were POW's. Lt. Nagorka was a POW escapee in April 1945. Crew had 14 missions.

2nd Lt. Henry Kinney, Jr.	P	T/Sgt. John Browchuck	Eng.
2nd Lt. Chester Clem	CP	S/Sgt. John Risse	RWG
2nd Lt. William Lawrence	N	S/Sgt. George King	LWG
2nd Lt. William Wakely	B	S/Sgt. Donald Goodin	BTG
T/Sgt. Eugene Tobias	RO	S/Sgt. William Maki	TG

CREW POW'S:

B17F   42-30371   560th Squadron   "Iza Angel II"
B17F   42-30802   560th Squadron

The Mission summary on the October 9, 1943 raid to Gydnia, Poland allows thirteen lines to the effort of the 96th and 388th Composite group. This group was airborne for nine hours and forty-four minutes. The two plane crews that did not complete the nine hour and forty-four minute mission would take some 18 months before they would return — and a few crew men never did return. This is the account of the mission by Lt. Henry J. "Nick" Nagorka, pilot, 560th Squadron, 388th Bomb Group. His words:

When they aroused us early that morning I saw where we were going on the map. I got hold of the Commanding Officer and the Briefing Officer to warn everybody not to drop short, because we were coming from the land side out into the sea and any short drops would kill our Allies. We were after that German pocket battleship hiding in the port, which could do a lot of damage to Allied shipping if not knocked out. So we were to come from the seaward side to make our turn to the I.P. and make our bomb run to the seaward. Gydnia is Polish. I said, "Man, you drop short and you're going to kill all our friends. Nobody had better drop short. If anyone is going to make a mistake, drop long into the water." So the Briefing Officer warned the mission crews to be very careful. These people are our friends, he underlines.

It was the duty of the bombardier in each crew to see that the bombs were loaded and that it was done properly. My bombardier, Lt. Michael Mahoney, came to me as the arming proceeded and said there was a problem with one of the bombs. So we took a look. One of them was not on the bomb rack; not hanging correctly on its shackles. It could slip at any moment. We got the bomb loading crew to come back and rework the loading, and they fixed it up. So we took off and flew all the way across northern Germany, across Denmark and into Poland. As we were making our turn toward the Initial Point to make our bomb run, I felt something go Clunk! Clunk! Clunk! Like it was going down three steps with the whole airplane. Several of the bombs had dropped into the bomb bay — dropped right off the racks! Someone calls me on the intercom and says, "Hey Sir, a bomb fell off." "Holy God!" I thought.

"Quick," I said, "check and see if its arming propeller is turning."

"Just a minute, sir," he said.

A big long pause.

"Sir?"

"Yes!" I barked.

"It's turning."

Now after 700 turns the bomb is armed! The tiniest jar and phoof!

I wanted to salvo the bombs immediately and shouted over the intercom — "Salvo! Salvo! Salvo!" But the bombardier was not anxious to follow orders. He would have to crank the bomb bay doors up by hand if he did. The salvo button unhinges the doors and they fall open.

I was waiting for the explosion.

But Lt. Mahoney pushed the regular bomb bay door opening button. The doors slowly rolled open and all the bombs rolled out. The whole rack had been improperly hung.

I was leading the low squadron, so bombs or no bombs, I had to keep on going. I just hoped the squadron did not drop bombs when they saw mine go. Fortunately they understood and dropped with the leader of the group. I stayed in my position and went around the bomb run with the Group of course. Everyone else had dropped bombs at the right time. I thought we got the battleship and did not get any bombs into the town.

We turned to go back home and got as far as Denmark when the Germans raised a welcoming party for us. Single and twin engine fighters. They were lobbing rockets at us and even dropping bombs on us. They were trying their damndest to wipe us out.

A Focke-Wulf 190 came in and got my left wing man. He was set on fire and began to peel out. Then the fighter came after me and as I saw him coming I knew he was making his pass on me. I did some evasive action. I don't know what he did, whether he misfired or I went down into his fire or what happened, but a whole load of his shots came right into the ship. I could not evade it; the ship caught fire. Co-pilot, Gil Parker, took one look out the right window and his eyes got big and he said, "It's on fire!" "Get out!" Get out!" I said. "Get your chute on and get out."

"Everybody bail out," I ordered, "the ship is on fire! Everybody out!"

The ship lost power on the right wing with the engines shot out. Smoke and fire were coming into the plane. The bombardier and the navigator had jumped immediately. As I was responsible for the crew, I had to make sure everyone was out, and I took my responsibility seriously. We were wearing parachute harnesses, but the chest packs for the pilot and co-pilot were supposed to be under the seats. Here it is — the ship is on fire as I'm flying it — and let go of it for a second. It starts to keel over on that bad wing trying to go into an upside down flat spin. So I have to keep righting it all the time. Whatever I'm doing and with the ship full of smoke, I could not see a thing, if everybody was out. I waited what seemed like a hell of a long time — maybe three or four minutes — but plenty of time for the men to get out. Gil Parker was gone; there was nobody up front left, and I couldn't see anybody in back, so I said let's get the hell out of here. I reached down for the parachute. No parachute! Don't tell me someone has taken my parachute pack — I thought aloud. But no, when I reached way under the seat, it ws way under there close to the wall. I got the pack out and then had to right the plane again so it would not go over on its back. I had to do this every 10 or 20 seconds. I'd get one snaplock on, straighten the ship, with the fire licking in here, I got it level, got the chute pack on and then got in between the seats and reached up to the steering gear to get the ship flat again and got caught between the seats because the pack was too thick for me to get through that way. I had to turn around and get through another way down in between the seats. I reached out and straightened the ship up the last time. I dropped down to the escape hatch, which was open. I sat in the hatch for an instant. I would not fly *Iza Angel II* again. This was our last mission. The propellers were purring, not roaring like they always did. They were windmilling — no power left. I took a quick look around, leaned out and left.

As I went out I began to look around for to see where everybody was. I saw four chutes. When I looked back down to the plane, it had exploded. Just smoke and pieces left. I was dropping without my chute open yet — in free fall. The last time I had looked, the water was like tiny little ripples. This time the ripples looked real big so I pulled my ring, the chute popped open and just about that quick — smack! I hit the water. At the same time I inflated the Mae West. It was under the harness and thus pressed in against my ribs. The combination of that Mae West pushing in and me hitting the water broke a couple ribs — but I didn't even feel it yet.

I had my flying boots on and all my flying equipment, everything. I'd gotten rid of the .45 caliber pistol, but could not get out of my flying suit. I kept pumping my legs, but even the Mae West did not keep me from sinking to my chin. I knew I had better get out of the harness somehow. I tried to unbuckle the harness one buckle at a time. I had to go under water each time I undid a buckle. It must have taken me fifteen minutes to get out of the harness. In the meantime I was moving my legs and pumping. Unnoticed, the cords of the chute wound around my legs above my boots. I could not pull them off. Oh man! I'd let the harness go and it was sinking.

124

The chute was sinking with it and the whole thing began to pull me down. A comedy of tragedies! The next job was to reach down to get those boots off, to get those cords off my legs. They were wound too tight above the top of the boots. I tried to get the zipper open on these heavy lined boots, but under water they didn't want to zip. Finally, after many, many tries and much dunking, I got the boots off and got those cords off somehow. All the while I had swallowed a lot of salt water.

The estimated time of survival in the north Sea in October is one hour before going into exposure. I'd been in the sea maybe 3/4 of an hour. I could still sense the direction of the land and knew it was eight to ten miles away. (We had just passed Denmark where we were doing the fighting, headed for England, when we went down.)

"Well, God helps those who help themselves," I thought. I'm going to start doing what I can and start to swim toward Denmark. I'm not much of a swimmer. I swim and watch in that direction — you could only see 10 or 20 yards. You were down in the water among 10-15 foot swells. After a while I start seeing something that looks like a little stick. I started to watch that like crazy and it turned out to be a mast. It looks like it is coming my way about a half mile away or more. Soon I could see the hull. They got with a half a mile and made a turn and started going away.

What am I to do if they leave me out here? I decide to make believe that I'm swimming an exaggerated Australian crawl with my hands way up over my head. The crew men of the German Air-Sea-Rescue boat were scouting the water with binoculars. They saw my hands and turned toward me, got to within about ten or twelve yards of me, and threw me a line. I couldn't even hold on to the line I was so far gone. They then threw me a life preserver. I managed to get up into it and they pulled me aboard.

They got me up on the boat and when they put me on deck everybody scattered like a gunshot. They expected me to pull out a gun and start shooting everybody — you know 'American Gangster' — Air Gangster. We were called American Air Gangsters by German propaganda. I was so far gone I could hardly stand up. I was in shock, I was shaking and could not stop. I was aware of it, but I could not control it. I tried to get the zipper open on the flying suit. I could not even get that open, reeling unsteadily on my feet. When they saw that I was no threat, they started to come out from behind the masts and other cover. The German sailors started to help me get the flying suit off. One brought a towel and another handed me a pair of pajamas. After I got myself organized, they took me below and put me in the Captain's bunk. It wasn't a big ship. It had a crew of maybe ten. I'm laying in the bunk shaking violently from exposure and shock. "What the hell is this?" I thought. "Why can't I control this?" I'm aware of what is going on, but unable to change it.

They gave me a shot of rum and ersatz coffee. It was terrible — undrinkable. Then the Captain came in. A typical 30-35 year-old Aryan blond,

125

straight-laced type, good looking, he came over and greeted me like a gentleman and said, "How are you?" in German. I could not speak German, but could understand what he was saying. "Are you alright? Can I do something for you?"

Proper treatment, but it didn't cut any ice with me because he was the enemy as far as I was concerned. I was well indoctrinated. He was the enemy. He was the enemy, a damn German!

They gave me blankets and a tray of food — sort of like hors d'oeuvres, trying to help me.

The Captain excused himself. "Look I've got to go on duty," he said. "Please excuse me."

He was no sooner out of sight when a sailor came in, looked carefully around, opened the Captain's little cupboard next to the bunk, took out the rum and gave me another shot. He wanted information.

"I'm from Bonn," he said, "my mother and father are in Bonn. How is it there?"

"Kaput!" I replied in a hard voice. You don't always need language. You can explain with gestures.

"My God," he said, "my father and mother.!" I began to think twice about what I was saying.

"Hamburg?" he asked. I signified — half gone.

"Berlin?"

I gave him a thumbs down sign — and because the head of the German Air Force, Herman Goering, had boasted that if any plane ever gets as far as Berlin, his name would be Schmidt. I added, "How is your Mister Schmidt?" I had to explain as best I could what Goering had said. Later, when I repeated this to a German guard, the guard took deadly offense — turning purple and red. He brought up his sub-machine gun, cocked it and was about to execute me right on the spot. He didn't carry it out — but that's how angry he got about my ridiculing Goering.

The rescue ship got back to Denmark in about two or three hours. I was the only one picked up by that boat. Four of my crew were killed and six were taken prisoners.

During the time I was going down in my chute I could hear machine gun fire from the German fighters. They were trying to kill the men as they came down in their chutes or were already in the water.

I was taken to an airfield in Denmark, near the Port of Esbjerg. The Luftwaffe was based there. The Germans used the facilities for interrogating the flyers they shot down in that area.

My dog tags carried my first name Henry, my second name Joseph spelled Jozef, the Polish spelling, and Nagorka, a Polish name. They had us — shot down Americans and British — standing out in the hall. At one point somebody opened the door where they were conferring and I saw that they had my dog tags as they were talking to one another — Jozef, the Polish

Jozef. Why the Polish Jozef if he is an American? A Major and a Captain were going over details. Later when they called me in for interrogation they didn't say a word about that, not a word.

I was a much better soldier than they were. I stood at rigid attention in spite of the crash down and the ribs.

"At ease," one of them said. "Thank you," I replied coldly and remained at rigid attention. I wanted to be as unfriendly as possible and to show disdain for the enemy.

They asked questions and I replied with my name, rank and serial number, almost machine-like.

"Come on, don't you want us to notify your family or anyone?" the Major said in irritation. "What's your address? You can give that you know. We know who your crew is, you don't have to worry about that. We have all their names and everything."

"If you were in my position," I said flatly, "What would *you* say?" Again — I gave my name, rank and serial number.

They finally gave up and put us in a room about 14 by 14 with triple bunks in it and straw pallets. Those pallets did not do my bad ribs any good. Every time I took a breath it felt like a knife in my ribs. I tried to find a position in which that would not happen.

We were there for three days, then they started us via train on our way to Frankfurt, Germany, an interrogation point called Dulag Luft — the central interrogation point in Germany for captured airmen. While we were in this interrogation center the Germans used all the devices they had to extract information. One trick was the mounting of executions. The cells had windows that overlooked a courtyard. They were too high so you couldn't hardly get to them in the cell. A fake execution would go like this: they would march out somebody in an American uniform, give all the appropriate orders for a firing squad — and POW! The guy would fall over and they would carry him out. Right after this they would come in and say, "OK, ready to talk now or not? or do you want to be next?"

The Germans put real pressure on us. We kept up our morale by singing and raising hell as much as we could — that is, those of us who were healthy.

They did not even want to let us go to the toilet. There were no facilities inside our cells, so we would just about have to beat the door down to get a guard to come open it so we could use the outside facilities. We cursed them to their face and screamed bloody murder. We told them that this is no way to treat a Geneva Convention POW. When a German Officer came in later and we would object loudly, "You people are not treating us according to the Geneva Convention." They ignored us. The Germans played it cool trying to extract information. They played one prisoner against another for any tiny scrap of information.

Generally they would keep the prisoners there from one or two days to one or two weeks, depending on the rush they had and what kinds of raids

127

were occurring. Then they moved them out to permanent camps. I was sent to Stalag Luft III, (Permanent Air Camp 3) on the Polish border. (It was from this camp that "The Great Escape" was made with the loss of 50 lives.) This location was made to order for me. I speak Polish. Most of the people in that area, even the Germans, spoke some Polish or broken Polish.

But these advantages ended abruptly in February of 1945. The Russians were coming close so we were ordered into a forced march with whatever we could carry. February in Bavaria is very cold. Snow storms cost us many good men.

The Germans finally put us on trains — 50 to 60 men in those small cattle cars, leaving no room to lay down. One had just enough room to stand, with everyone scrunched in. Usually there were one or two guards in the cattle car with us. The guard in our car was not very alert. He was 55 or 60 years old, and very tired. Well, we got his rifle from him without him realizing it, stripped it down completely and scattered the parts all over the car. When he discovered his rifle was missing, he got very angry, began to curse and stamp his feet and swore he'd get the Captain if we did not give his rifle back. So we called all the pieces in and put it all together for him while he was watching. The guy was dumbfounded. We had a great laugh.

Many of the men suffered and became ill because there were no toilet facilities and no provisions for stopping the train. We were not permitted to urinate or defacate on the train, but many men could not contain themselves. It was a mess.

We finally arrived at Stalag 17 in Bavaria, all the way across Germany. The play and movie was about this P.O.W. Camp.

The very first night ten of our officers escaped. The guards were not used to dealing with officers, but with enlisted men and were more lax and with poor security. So ten of the officers went over the fence and disappeared. The next night six more did the same. The guard was doubled and dogs were put inside a third row of fences around the place.

That didn't stop us. I made special arrangements with one of the guards. He turned out to be a Pole from Northern Poland who had been forced into German service. He allowed me to go out of the camp through the main gate and meet with the Poles in the Polish Compound, exchange information and make plans for an escape.

"OK," he said "but they are coming to check me off duty in two hours exactly. Get back in plenty of time or there will be hell to pay."

"Don't worry about it," I reassured him. He agreed to do this for a bar of soap. Four or five cigarettes would have bought off most guards.

I went out and had tea with the Polish officers. They wanted to know everything....including our government war policy, which I could in no way answer. They had posted their own guards all around the place to keep my presence secret and to observe the change of guard. I would be told when changing of the guard took place in time to get back safely. We discussed

128

ways and means of escaping for some time. When the change of guard got within an audible distance, the Polish guard interrupted our meeting and took me out. I made the pass over to the main gate myself. The guard I'd bribed was pretty shaken up due to the fact that he could hear the new guard coming. I went in, and that was that.

Another time two of us broke out of the camp by cutting our way through a side fence at night and penetrated a Canadian camp. There were five to seven camps all in one area, all separated from each other by wire fences. We were trying to get information to help ourselves escape.

When we got into the Canadian camp we walked boldly into the barracks and they thought an invasion had taken place. We were dressed in clean uniforms, boots on, the works and walked right down through the middle of the barracks.

Holy God, the paratroopers! The Canadians shouted. "Relax men, no paratroopers," we explained. "We want information."

The head of that Canadian bunch turned us in to the Germans the following morning. The German Commander called on our Senior Officer.

"Look, you better keep your boys at home," he blustered, "because we are going to start playing rough." Our Senior Officer told us all to cut out the fun and games.

But to me it was not fun. I was carrying out instructions. Prisoners of War were directed to escape if possible or cause trouble behind the enemy lines. I finally traded places and identities with a G.I. in a work party who came in as a resulting of our cutting through the fence. They came in to put up a third row of fencing and make a fence and to put rolled barbed wire and dogs between the other two. This was meant to insure that we would stay put.

We created a diversion about 2:00 p.m. I got a friend to go into a barracks and create a fight with a lot of cussing and screaming, yelling and throwing of things outside. It drew off the German guards. I was standing at a window next to where a G.I. was digging post holes for the new fence. We had made our arrangements the day before.

"OK, this is the time," I whispered loudly, "let's go!"

We exchanged places. I picked up his shovel and just kept shoveling. The guard came back, started to stare at me as though he noticed a difference. I paid no attention, just kept shoveling and even shoveled some earth on his shoes.

They marched us out and the guard never did notice that I wasn't the same man. That got me into the major open camp and from there I escaped. It was a successful escape. There were three of us. Another American, a Canadian and myself. We stayed in the outer compound for a week where we managed to get three others to cover for us. We three went out and the other three came back in. The Germans were interested in numbers, so despite the fact that three American types went out the gate and three Sikhs' came in — the count was right.

We went Northwest across Germany toward the approach of Patton's 3rd Army. We had that information from our nocturnal visits. It took us three weeks to escape through woods, German road blocks and everything. We walked right through a half dozen German patrols by daytime. I wore civilian clothes and carried a pitchfork, walking right down the middle of the road. One of the fellows had a pail. If anybody came close or a patrol tried to stop us I'd say, "We're from this farm up here, what you talking about escaped prisoners?" I would say this in Polish as we were playing Polish forced laborers. I taught my two colleagues three Polish words — yes, no and maybe. Anything I said they would answer with one of those three words and would react to anything they said. Many Germans understood some Polish, so they would hear the Polish and assume that these were Polish forced laborers.

Hell, we didn't fool the French one bit though. We went through one town where French forced laborers were working in a lumber yard. They picked up their heads, took one look at us, and gave us the victory sign.

We got a lot of good help from the Yugoslavs. The Serbs, too, were prisoners, but in full military dress they were forced to work the land. They had to plow and do that sort of thing, but they gave us all the help they could — food, water, directions, and brotherly encouragement. We carried with us an order from their Commander, who we were able to communicate with. He ordered everyone of his soldiers to give us every possible help in our escape. "These are American officers escaping," went the order.

Of course we had that piece of paper ready to chew up and swallow at any moment if there was danger of being searched. At one time we were completely out of food, out of shelter, with no way to help ourselves. This bunch of Serbs organized a meeting with us about 7:00 in the evening. About 20 Serbs came and met in the woods with us. Everyone of them brought either a loaf of bread, two eggs or some cheese or milk, or something else to eat. By the time they finished assembling their food we had a fine supply which lasted us the rest of the escape.

Then we found some Polish forced laborers just below Ingolstadt, working on the railroad. We got together with them, became Polish forced laborers ourselves and walked with them right through the German Army as it was retreating. They stopped in a town, to rest, and we'd walk right through — bumping them! We went to the dairy to get skimmed milk as Poles were not allowed whole milk. The three of us went to the guard to get our supply of skimmed milk for the day. As it happened, the German Army was retreating and they stopped right in the middle of town. They were all over the place, must have been 5,000 of them. So we had to go right through the middle of them to get to the diary. We paid no attention and they paid no attention to us. We went and got the stuff and took it back to the barracks.

One lady on that street, the houses on the street that lead to the barracks where the forced laborers were quartered, had a visit two nights before of a flying squad of S.S. and Gestapo, and they had with them their own supplies. Among these was a dried soup mix — beautiful stuff — and they asked her to make soup for them. She made a big pot of soup, five times more than they could eat. They had their supper of that soup. Well, the next day when they were gone and we went by, she invited us in for soup. She said, "Come in, I've got more soup than I can use." She was a good woman. Her husband had died on the Eastern front. She'd had enough of war. She thought she was talking to Poles when she invited us in.

"But you are a young man," she said to me, "why are you in forced labor?" I do not recall exactly what I answered her, but something that satisfied the logic. And we all sat and had some of that fine Gestapo soup.

We were able to hear the heavy guns pounding in the area, and two or three days later the American troops started down this same road, and I was finally able to convince them I was not a German civilian. General Patton had ordered them not to talk with any Germans. The G.I's were giving them the same treatment the Germans had given the conquered people. So the Americans were not talking to any Germans. If a German said something, the G.I's just did not hear it. I ran alongside the leading jeep of a long column of American G.I's. The Sergeant driving the jeep would not turn his head because he thought I was a German. Well, I finally began to cuss at him and said, "Look, I'm an escaped American Pilot. I'm a Captain in the Air Force and you so and so, if you don't stop this jeep, I'm going to court martial you!" He looked at me, stopped the jeep, got up on the seat and yelled, "Hey Lieutenant!" There was a whole string of 105's, halftracks behind him, ten or twenty of them.

"What's the matter?" says the Lieutenant running up.

"This guy says he's an American." The Lieutenant comes over to me.

"Lieutenant, I'm Captain Henry J. Nagorka, serial number so and so. I was a POW and escaped with my two companions."

"Hell, Captain, you take my place in the jeep," he said without hesitation.

Then I had a few misgivings. Here I am in the lead jeep wearing civilian clothes, and every German sniper is going to think I am a German traitor. They are going to go after me first. This didn't occur to the Lieutenant, but it was the first thing that went through my mind.

"You been around here for a day or two?" The Lieutenant asked.

"Yes," I said.

"Where is the nearest bridge?" He asked. (The night before the Germans had destroyed all the bridges.) "There is an old wooden bridge," I said, "but it won't hold up any of these halftracks."

We have to give it a try. We've got to get across this water.

"OK," I said, "Come on."

Suddenly there was shouting from up front. "Hold up, hold up! Snipers!"

"Yeah—sure!" I thought.

The Lieutenant turned to his men and said, "Fellows, we need a couple volunteers."

131

"OK," a couple guys sing out, "I'll go," "Me too."

Hurry it up, will you fellows, Two guys take off in a trot. There are a few rifle shots. Two minutes later they come back.

OK Lieutenant, all clear.

The whole column of men and guns held up by sniper fire and two young kids go up and in two minutes clear them out.

I was dumbfounded. The guys marching with the column looked so young, 20 or so, looked more like Boy Scouts. Some were carrying two guns and whistling, walking through Germany. They were tanned and looked very fit in contrast to us after a year and a half in POW camp. My comrades were all wane and skinny, underfed.

We got to the bridge and stopped. A couple of farmers were there and they looked at those halftracks, the old wooden bridge, then back to the halftracks again, then at each other, and began shaking their heads.

The Lieutenant looked at the piling and it was in bad shape. A horse and wagon was about all that bridge would hold. Well, the lead jeep went over with the Lieutenant in it. So they yelled for the first halftrack to come over. The tank-like halftrack got just a portion of its weight on the bridge and the wood broke up and collapsed, the halftrack falling into the stream. They were stalled. A messenger came from the front. A rifle company spearhead had come through during the night chasing the Germans, but was now stopped by some German artillery.

The Lieutenant drove me to that forward command post and introduced me to the Commander, who was a Major. Without even thinking the Major whips out a telegram and hands it to me and says, "Here, what should we do with these guys?"

I'd been in prison camp for a year and a half and didn't know what was going on. The telegram read, "SS man so and so, SS man so and so, confirmed."

"We've got these two out back here. We caught them," explained the Major, "What shall we do with them?" "Is this a test?" I asked him. Don't ask me to make a court decision on these guys or give a death warrant on them."

One of my escape buddies spoke up abruptly.

"AH, shoot them!"

They were shot immediately.

According to orders, there were to be no SS prisoners. I felt as if my guts were going to drop out. After a year and a half as a prisoner of war you're no longer in the war. You've been getting it from the Germans so long you don't want to hand out the same thing. On our way back from that command post we encountered columns of German prisoners being marched back to the rear. As we were driving by them I looked at them and darned if I didn't feel sorry for them. It didn't matter that they were Germans, but the fact was that they were prisoners and I had just been a prisoner. I knew how they felt.

Well, from that forward point the Army took us back to Nuremburg where there was an airfield. General Patton had just landed. We saw him get out of his plane, pistols on his hips. From here on it was movement to the rear. We kept moving to the rear until we got aboard a ship in France and sailed for New York.

We were sent to Miami for a medical checkup and thirty days rest leave for all POW's. I was reassigned to the Japanese theatre after my leave was up. Apparently I was in pretty good shape for a returning POW. Things were going so well in the Pacific on my return from the leave that I was reassigned to a training school near Atlanta.

This school apparently was run by Military Personnel who had never been overseas. They sat us all down in a mess hall, and sitting there were General officers, Colonels, etc. I was just a Captain. Everybody was back from overseas duty or ex-POW's, men with decorations all over their chests, who had been in this thing for four or five years and gone through hell.

The training Lt. Col. gets up — and speaks to the officers.

"You guys are going to do what we tell you. If we need KP, you'll do KP." this to battle-scarred Generals and Colonels. I couldn't believe it. Listening to this insulting and degrading treatment, I decided that I want no more of this Air Force.

I went to the base Adjutant's office and asked for immediate release.

"The way you treat us is a clear indication that you don't want us and I don't want any part of such an outfit as this. I'm a freed POW and I know you've got to let me out on my request."

I was released the next day.

It is a bitter-sweet story. I returned to the Juilliard School of Music, earned a B.S. in composition and violin, went on to Columbia and received a Master's degree in composition and music education.

I have always enjoyed flying and still do. Although I have not piloted recently, I still enjoy flying. I always regretted not being able to take time to enjoy flying while in combat. In the Air War one needed to be super alert and could not enjoy just flying while in combat. It was a constant fight to keep alive to fly again. Training was the only time you could enjoy flying for flying's sake. Preflight, primary, basic and advanced training lasted about eight months, and it was difficult and enjoyable. But in combat you had to keep your mind not only on the technique of flying, but also on what was going on right then — battle! If you didn't, you took your life in your hands.

When I was in the water, trying to save myself there off Denmark, I made some commitments. That is one of the reasons why I am doing what I am today. At the National Spiritual Science Center we have no dogma, no regulations, very few affirmations, and we are a non-denominational group. Our program of progressive training is designed to expand the consciousness, heighten awareness, and guide the individual into higher levels of spiritual activity.

We could have used these concepts as bomber crewmen when we were challenged with those discouraging odds against making a full tour of combat missions. However, we learn as we live. While remaining an unshakably loyal American, I am learning to respect and live with a higher order of allegiances — and to achieve inner growth through loving service.

Lt. Mickey "Mike" Mahoney was asked to recall the 9 October 1943 raid to Gydnia, Poland and he did so with eager clarity.

I had a ten day leave waiting for me in England and a beautiful American nurse, a jeep filled with gas and a fabulous holiday in Scotland planned, to no avail.

We made the raid on Gydnia and headed for home, but were jumped by German fighters on the West coast of Denmark. We were shot up pretty badly and lost several men. I later learned that someone lost a leg. A 50mm shell tore through my chute and exploded between me and Lt. Leverone, the navigator. I had gotten the fighter at 12 o'clock level and I think we nicked his aileron or it was the shell explosion, but Leverone and I were hurled back from the nose right over the escape hatch. The oxygen lines were burning and we didn't wait but jumped. On the way down I could see daylight as eight sections of my chute were missing where the 50mm shell had gone through my chute and exploded.

I landed (lucky me) on the beach of one of three small islands a mile or so off the west coast of Denmark near the town of Esbjerg. It is the largest of the three small island and is connected to the mainland by a causeway. Leverone landed 30 yards off shore in about three or four feet of water. He was white as a sheet and praying and had been hit very badly in his leg. I helped him from the surf and laid him down and cut his pant leg back and he had a hole the size of a half dollar that had gone clear through the upper thigh.

I took my brand new white silk scarf my girl friend had given me and tied a tourniquet, jabbed him full of morphine and took off to find a doctor. I walked through a cemetary, I thought, with all the crosses. I found out seconds later it was a mine field. It was about 100 yards off the beach to the island where a German soldier jumped me with a machine gun and screamed, "Dumkopf! Das ist minen, minen!!!" I passed out cold.

I woke up on a gurney in the hospital where they rushed me into surgery and removed pieces of shell fragments. Then I got a nice room, good food and a German guard.

In my descent my chute was buzzed by a fighter, who leveled off at me and I had heard rumors of guys getting machine gunned, it scared hell out of me. All he did was buzz me and waved at me.

After three or four days in the hospital we had a mild interrogation, followed by a long passenger train ride to Germany, headed for Frankfurt.

We passed through Hamburg where we saw a number of British airmen hanging from telephone poles from the raid the night before. The town was leveled and the Germans were throwing kids into cattle cars, evacuating them. The crowd was surly and threatening and our guards kept pushing them back telling them we were American flyers not British. If we had been British I don't think we would have made it through.

When we got to Frankfurt we went through interrogations, were classified, and sent to Stalag Luft III.

On the train from Denmark to Germany a POW was removed from the train at, I believe, Flensburg for a leg amputation. I thought for years it was Leverone. Only six men got out of the plane. At any rate, I contacted Leverone in 1980 and found that his leg had not been taken off but had been fixed up.

As a P.S. on this story. I had tried for 30 years, half heartedly, to find the name where I landed and could never find the name of the island. In 1977 I was in Berlin, a guest of Herman Glemnitz's daughter, Gerda (Glemnitz was our Feldweble in Stalag Luft III). I met a lady on the Ku'dan Strasse who asked if she could share my table with her girl friend. We rapped in German for a minute and switched to English. She then explained she was teaching English to the German hotel employees. She told me she was from Denmark and floored me by knowing the name of the island I had landed on. In Danish it is MANO, in English it is MANOE. She worked in a bakery in Ebsjerg and delivered bread to the hospital I was in. The bread was delivered by bicycle.

On the morning of October 10, 1943, the briefed target was the built-up section of Munster, a rail center north of the Ruhr Valley.

There was nothing unusual about the importance of the target. The Royal Air Force had been unable to disrupt this populated area as they had other parts of the Ruhr. The idea of the operation was to wipe out the built-up area and disrupt the people as much as possible.

Within a radius of a hundred thirty miles, the logical striking distance of German fighter planes in preventing a bomb run, the crews were told that a maximum of 245 single-engine and 290 twin-engine aircraft could oppose the operation.

As they approached Munster, the three groups that composed the 13th Combat Wing were hit in the most violent and concentrated attack yet made on an Eighth Air Force formation.

Nearly 250 enemy planes engaged the Wing and fought viciously until the Fortresses had bombed. The attacks, which lasted for forty-five minutes, appeared to have a definite method. The enemy approached in groups in formations of from 3 to 6 planes, and flew straight and level at their targets. The attacks were pressed up to fifty or seventy-five yards, before the enemy aircraft turned and took violent evasive action, and kept coming back in for the additional attack.

They showed definite tendencies of concentrating attacks on one group at a time, even to the point of flying through the lead group to attack the low one (the 100th Bomb Group). After disposing of the 100th Group, the attack switched to the 390th, and then to the low squadron of the 95th.

When first encountered, the German fighters flew parallel to the formation, out of range, in groups of from 20 to 40 planes stacked in echelon formation. They would fly on ahead of the formation, and then peel off one or two at a time, to attack the lowest bombers. Many beam attacks from 4 to 8 o'clock were also made by groups of 20 to 40 aircraft at a time.

At the time the fighters first hit the 100th Group, the formation was average. In two minutes the formation was broken up, and within seven minutes 12 of the 14 planes from the 100th Group were shot down. Ultimately, Lt. Robert Rosenthal was to be the only survivor of this mission from the 100th Bomb Group. His plane and crew made it back to their base at Thorpe Abbot In England.

The Luftwaffe then turned on the 390th and added some tactics never seen before by B-17 crews.

While the FW-190s and ME-109s were slipping through the formation, twin-engine fighters stayed out of range and fired explosive cannon shells from twelve hundred yards to fifteen hundred yards. JU-88s attacked with rockets from eight hundred to a thousand yards, and a new feature was the use of Dornier bombers, which flew parallel to the formation and fired rockets from a fifteen-hundred-yard range.

Back from the fiery skies over ancient Munster, in the Ruhr, came 10 out of eighteen 390th Group Fortresses assigned to the target. Eight were gone, shot down by the enemy.

If the fighting men of the Luftwaffe had been less thirsty for the kill, they might have seen the price tags on those big Yank bombers. It was a fabulous sum — 8 Nazi fighters for each Fort. The German Air Force paid and with interest.

The heaviest price of the aerial war over the continental Europe was exacted from the hundred men who rode those 10 returning Forts. In a white hot battle with the longest single concentration of enemy fighters ever encountered on an 8th Air Force operation, they conclusively proved the Fortress to be the greatest fighting machine of the War in Europe. In destroying 62 enemy planes, the 390th Bomb Group established a record for heavy bombardment groups that was never equaled.

The raw statistics shows the concentration of the attack: unfeeling words and numbers on paper. In actuality they were sons, uncles, brothers, dads, buddies, husbands and sweethearts; both sides were the same, both sides became M.I.A. or P.O.W.

At this time no reconstruction of the claims will be made, the numbers will remain as they were written on the "Mission Summary" those many years ago.

A/C Dispatched	A/C Lost	Claims
3rd Bomb Division 133	29	180-21-49
13th Combat Wing 53	25	105-13-28
100th Bomb Group 14	12	2- 1- 1
95th Bomb Group 20	5	41- 5- 9
390th Bomb Group 19	8	62- 7- 8

In 45 minutes 10 Fortresses and 100 courageous crewmen annihilated the equal of six German fighter squadrons, scoring the greatest bag by a single Bomb Group on mission in the war. Officially destroyed were 63 first-rate interceptors, while credit for the probable destruction of 6, and damaging 8, was announced with confirmation from Bomber Division.

At that, the final count failed to include the Hun fighters blasted into perdition by the guns of the ships which fell.

The chronicles of the great events of WW-II will tell the history of the American Air Force. They would be missing a bet if they fail to dedicate a paragraph or two to these hundred heroes who came through the hell that was Munster; 10 October 1943, and the 80 who did not come back. To those heroes this chapter is dedicated.

The battle wagons of the 390th that weathered all the Luftwaffe could dish out and proved themselves worthy to carry the heroic men who brought them back from Munster were: *Betty Boop—the Pistol Packin' Mama* piloted by Captain James R. Geary, Jr.; *Rose Marie* piloted by 1st Lt. Kenneth E. Daugherty; *Eightball* flown by 1st Lt. William M. Cabral; *Cabin in the Sky* skippered by Captain Robert D. Brown; *Norma J* piloted by 1st Lt. Bruce R. Riley; *Miss Carry* flown by 1st Lt. Paul W. Vance; *Spot Remover* piloted by 1st Lt. Keith E. Harris; *Geronimo* piloted by 2nd Lt. Robert G. Schneider; *Rusty Lode* flown by 1st Lt. Robert W. Sabel; and *Shatzi* flown by 2nd Lt. Harold W. Schuyler.

Missing at Munster were: *Tech Supply* commanded by 1st Lt. John G. Winant, Jr., son of the American Ambassador to Great Britain; *Miss Fortune* flown by 1st Lt. Wade H. Sneed; *Short Stuff* flown by Captain Robert B. Short; *Spider* piloted by 1st Lt. William W. Smith; *Pinky* commanded by 2nd Lt. Frank E. Ward; a nameless ship flown by 1st Lt. Edward W. Weldon, Jr.; *Cash and Carrie* skippered by 1st Lt. Robert A. McGuire, Jr.; and last, *Miss Behavin'* piloted by 2nd Lt. George E. Starnes.

Munster, the story of a hundred heroes, began like any other mission story — the roar of powerful engines at dawn, men shivering with the anticipation of combat.

138

But inside the Fortress *Miss Carry,* as it circled to gain altitude over its station, two waist gunners and the radio operator were squinting into the sun, attempting to verify what they thought they saw there — an ME-110!

Staff Sgt. Ross W. Farris called the observation to the attention of pilot Vance over the interphone commenting, "Two to one the fighters will be out on this run." Farris was never certain about the enemy scout, but he was right about the fighters — they were out!

The first appearance of German fighters was spotted as the formation turned into its bomb run. Escorting fighters having reached the extemt of their range had left the bombers with the skies looking quiet over the target.

Then the interphones exploded as the tail gunner shouted, "Enemy fighters at 5, 6, 7 o'clock low hitting the group behind us." The Germans had launched a coordinated attack, striking the very moment our fighters escort was out of sight.

Captain Gordon-Forbes related:

We caught the brunt of that first attack on the 390th Group. 2nd Lt. George Starnes' plane was hit at the middle by a rocket. The plane started to break in half. It nosed up and crashed into another, just above it in the formation. Both planes fell away and went down in a column of smoke. A ship on our right blew up with a great red flash. I saw the right waist gunner come out of his window in a grotesque swan dive. His chest was shot away.

All around them the great battle raged. The sky filled with debris of men and planes. It ceased to be a battle in any organized sense, and became a nightmare of attacking fighters and burning fighters and bombers. At one time close to 50 planes were burning and going down. The sky was so full of parachutes that it looked like a paratroop invasion.

As they neared the target, Colonel Dolan sighted a large formation of planes off to the right. At first he mistook them for Forts, because they were stacked up in a formation similar to ours, but then as they turned in and fanned out like a Prussian infantry company, he identified them as twin-engine German planes. They were JU88 planes that layed off out of range of the bombers guns and lobbed rockets into the formations of bombers.

"We had fought every inch of the way to the target after the bomb run had started," Gordon-Forbes said. "The railroad yards were wide open. Bombs splattered all over them."

After calling out, "Bombs Away!" Gordon-Forbes manned his gun. I didn't have to look for targets," he recounted. "They were everywhere."

Until the formation was halfway home, under cover of strong escort, its fate was in the balance.

"Munster was a nightmare of burning Forts and exploding fighters. I am confident that those we lost were fully avenged. They must have taken a terrific toll before abandoning the fight," 390th Group Combat Leader Major Ralph V. Hansel reported to his Commanding Officer, Colonel Edgar M. Wittan, shortly after the mission.

The men of the *Rose Marie* evened an old score with the Luftwaffe at Munster. On August 24 they had watched their first ship *Hot Rocks* sink out of sight in the English Channel, taking a dead comrade with it. They named their second ship after the wife of that comrade, killed by German flak over France. Lt. Daugherty, whose skillful exhibition of flying is credited by the crew as the most important factor in bringing them through the great victory, was a flying mate and close friend of Lt. Winant who went down with *Tech Supply*.

Captain Bill Cabral, pilot of the *Eight Ball,* had a huge hole in his right wing, big enough for a couple of men to crawl through. The ship had been hit by a rocket and was in plenty of trouble.

The crew of *Cabin in the Sky* defined the Munster battle as the "Battle of Britain wrapped up in thirty-four minutes." Skipper Brown told the story in a brief few sentences: "No one can say how many fighters we knocked down. If we had taken a scorekeeper along, perhaps we could claim twenty. They fell fast, I know that. The boys held their fire until the Huns were right on top of us, and then they blew 'em to bits. We're certain we got eleven — they exploded!"

Brown asked his tail gunner how the squadron was holding up, and the latter answered, "What squadron, Captain? We're all alone up here!" They had lost 5 ships in about ten minutes. The other squadrons fared little better.

Seconds later, Brown spotted 36 fighters just ahead. Enemy fighters! And for the first time Gordon-Forbes felt like throwing in the towel. The cause seemed hopeless. They had been battling for what seemed like hours, though actually the fighting over Munster lasted just thirty-four minutes. The Group behind had been literally blown out of the sky. This would be the Bloody 100th Bomb Group.

The ammunition was almost exhausted, shell casings were piled up a foot deep on the floor, and still the Jerries came. Although they did not know it at the time, a pair of empty guns which the plane's ball-turret gunner was waving was the only protection left for the ship's belly. He kept off the attack by tracking the fighters.

Directly ahead, streams of white vapor trails appeared — P-47's charging in. "It's difficult to express the feeling that swept over me at that moment," Gordon-Forbes commented. "All the weariness of battle seemed to drain every ounce of strength I had. I felt like yelling and praying at the same time."

The battered German forces whirled away in a hurry and hightailed it in disorder. The Thunderbolts caught a few and shot them down. Then they returned to herd the remnants of the bomber formation home.

A landing through zero-zero fog, without radio aid, with both starboard engines dead, topped off the harrowing mission for the crew of the *Norma J*. Only a few hours before, over Munster, the crew and *Norma J* narrowly escaped destruction when a live German aerial rocket whizzed through an open waist window and lay sputtering on the floor. Lightning-like action by Staff Sergeant George T. Rankin saved the day. Rankin, decorated with the DFC for extraordinary achievement on the Regensburg shuttle attack, grabbed the rocket and heaved it overboard, watching it burst below. To the gunner the rocket, a closely guarded German secret weapon, looked like an ordinary dry-cell battery, with a foot of stove pipe stuck on one end.

The *Norma J* carried an enlisted man as its bombardier on the historic flight, an almost unheard of procedure in the European Theatre of Operations. Staff Sergeant James H. Shields was commended highly by Pilot Riley for laying his bombs "right on the button". Skipper Riley's landing was just short of a Hollywood take. With two engines useless, unable to bail out because of a wounded tail gunner, he came through a blanket of fog in a "field or nothing" try, and landed safely.

Meanwhile, the curtain was falling on a private little drama in the cabin of *Miss Carry* as the returning bombers rolled in. Star performer was pilot Vance, who though seriously wounded over Munster, coached his co-pilot through the rough ride.

Hitler had scornfully said Americans were soft. He would have had acute indigestion had he been with Lt. Vance over Munster. When a heavy flak fragment ripped through the left side of the plane and tore a jagged hole in his thigh, he motioned his co-pilot, 2nd Lt. Burgess W. Murdock, to take over.

Using the rubber extension cord from his interphone connection as a tourniquet, and wrapping his white scarf around the wound, he retained consciousness to direct Lieutenant Murdock through the bombing run, and aided him to hold the protective formation during the withdrawal from the target. During the run four Forts on *Miss Carry's* wing fell out and went down.

None of the other crew members knew that Lt. Vance had been hit. "It might disturb them," he told Lt. Murdock. He left his position only after the arrival of fighter support assured him of the ship's safety.

Rusty Lode recorded the grimmest experience of all, landing in England with a two minute fuel supply left, upwards of seven hundred and fifty holes in its fuselage, yawning holes in both wings, with the rudder, left aileron and both flaps shot away, and all regular controls severed. Engineering officers shook their heads in agreement. To them, the return of the *Rusty Lode* was a miracle.

The courage and determination of Pilot Sabel and his crew were responsible for the miracle. Under violent fighter assaults shortly before reaching the objective, the plane sustained terrific damage, but Lt. Sabel dropped it out of formation, put it on automatic flight control, made a lone sweep over the target, and headed home through the fighter hordes that barred his way.

Staff Sergeant William L. Ellet, who described his experience on *Rusty Lode* en route home from Munster as "Thirty minutes in hell," spoke slowly and in a low voice:

We had been battling fighter swarms for what seemed a lifetime. Suddenly, below, I saw three 'chutes open: I knew they must have come from our plane, so I climbed out of the ball turret to be certain. The waist guns were hanging limp, both gunners were gone.

I listened for the sound of guns, but all I could hear was the grinding of our engines. It was a queer feeling, standing there — like being in another world. I walked over to the waist guns and then looked back into the tail. The tail gunner was gone also.

I almost ran to the radio room, but when I reached the door I stopped short. Mac was hanging over his gun. It looked like a twenty mm shell had burst in his face. I laid him on the floor and then kinda stumbled toward the waist door. All I could think of was getting out. I looked down at the flak suit on the floor. There was a big splotch of blood on it. Then I heard the guns going in the upper turret. I knew then that the fellows up front were still there, and that my place was with the ship. I went back to the waist guns and started firing again.

Eightball contributed its share of color to the Munster saga. With 1st Lt. Cabral at the controls, the Fortress, whose adventures on fifteen bombing missions over Europe read like fiction, came in virtually on a wing and a prayer.

The action started when a German all but sheared off the ship's right wing twelve feet from the tip. Cabral, using all his strength and aided by the co-pilot, Richard Perry, and the bombardier, Dean Ferris, held the ship on course and flew it home while his gunners held off the attacking swarms of fighters for nearly an hour.

Climax to the *Eightball* episode came over Britain. With his gas supply almost gone, Lieutenant Cabral arrived at his home station to find it completely fogged in. Climbing to two thousand feet, so his crew could have a chance to bail out if the gas were exhausted, he headed for another station. Finding it, he brought the battered *Eightball* rolling in for a crash landing which the crew termed "sensational" to add the happy ending.

The spotlight which flooded *Eightball* also fell on 2nd Lt. Dean C. Ferris and Staff Sergeant Joseph G. Pouling. Lt. Ferris, bombardier on the ship named after the black pool ball, saved the plane and crew from doom when he jumped from his guns in the heat of fight, and with bare hands beat out a fire which threatened to set the nose ablaze. Flames had been sparked by red-hot shell casings falling on a pile of flying clothes.

Meanwhile, Sgt. Pouling stayed with an inoperative ball turret through most of the battle, waving his guns in a silent threat to protect the approach to the ship's belly. The crew of this ship was given credit for 5 enemy aircraft destroyed, 2 probables and 1 damaged.

The crews who returned were unaware that many Groups bombed that day without seeing an enemy plane. All that they realized was that they had scored some sort of "Pyrrhic Victory." They had shot round after round of ammunition at enemy planes. As one gunner put it, "We didn't have to aim. We just pulled the triggers — something was bound to get hit."

We have read what it was like from those who came back. What about those who became guests of the Third Reich?

What is it like at that last second when all hope of returning that B-17 to base has been removed by more flak, more 20mm cannon shells? It just has to be a feeling that cannot be adequately described by anyone who has not himself gone through that experience.

Major John C. "Bucky" Eagan, 100th Bomb Group Command Pilot, remembers the Munster mission; two days prior to that mission he had lost his good friend, Major Gale "Bucky" Cleven, on the mission to Bremen. Major Egan was ready and willing to get his "B-one-seven" into the air over Germany to drop out some destruction onto the Germans who had brought his friend down. To Major Eagan:

The briefing was the same as usual until the photo picture of the target was flashed on the screen; it was Munster. The Aiming Point and Mean Point of Impact are the center of the old walled city. We were to sock the residential district. At this point I find myself on my feet cheering. Others who have lost close friends in the past few raids join in the cheering, 'cause here is a chance to kill Germans, the spawners of race hatred and minority oppression. It is a dream mission to avenge the death of a buddy.

The mission had not been set up for me to kill the hated Hun, but as a last resort to stop rail transportation in the Ruhr Valley. Practically all of the rail workers in the valley were being billeted in Munster. It was decided that pursuit and fighter-bomber attack could not effectively stop up the Ruhr Valley. A good big bomber raid could really mess up the very efficient German rail system by messing up its personnel.

People who never witnessed the exploits of bomber pilots on missions in the ETO during the summer and fall of '43 really missed seeing boys who were for a short time big men. Mind now, all of these boy-men weren't fighters, i.e. professional soldiers or adventurers. They were people who were in the Air Corps for various reasons: better food, better pay, better ratings, better glamour, better kind of discipline, better chance to slug Adolph, better chance of being killed . . .

These boy-men commanded no less than nine other individuals and booted four thousand horses in the tail with their right hand to get their big-gas birds into the air and keep them there in the face of the toughest, roughest opposition mankind ever faced.

We became airborne and start our climb, our formation scraped together by the best Service Groups in all Bomberdom . . . Nothing unusual in climbing, except for supercharger trouble. This isn't too bad if you don't pick up too many holes in the wrong places. It's Tail End Charlie that needs the manifold pressure, not the stoop that leads the formation. (I say 'stoop' because 2nd Lieutenants believe that every time a senior officer is promoted he is required to turn in part of his brains.)

There are abortions. The J.D. Brady crew is leading the group with me as incommodious kibitzer. It's Brady's first time in the number one position, so he's enjoying the easy flying the 'one' boy enjoys. Later, of course, the unholy Hun tries most desperately to knock number 'one' to galley west.

The coast comes up and Brady makes a sign of the cross just as the first burst of flak goes off . . . one of those close ones with the pretty red centers. We're being covered by P-47s, and the dive and zoom boys couldn't take us all the way to the target because they didn't have the range.

From here to target things weren't dull, and occasionally a "large bird" would leave to land in a place he had not signed a clearance for. Just as we approached the I.P., I called out to the group that our high cover was leaving, watched them go, looked straight ahead and said: 'Jesus Christ! Pursuits at twelve o'clock. Looks like they're on us!'

Those were the last and only words I was to broadcast for many months, with or without CAA or Army Airway approval. A flak battery of six or eight guns, whose officer in charge must have bore-sighted them on a captured B-one-seven, went off directly below with integrated second timing by a bee-hive of about 150 . . . that's right, 150 . . . German fighters who went through us. The results of this flak and fighter episode can best be expressed by mathematical formula:

$$\frac{(13\ B17 + 131M) \times (100\ FW + 50ME)}{3R} = 120PW + 3R - 20E/A \quad Or \ldots$$

Thirteen B-17s plus 131 men times 100 Focke-Wulfes plus 50 Messerschmitts divided by the Third Reich equals 120 prisoners of war in the Third Reich minus twenty enemy aircraft that were destroyed.

This whole thing was disastrous more than somewhat, as of the thirteen ships that reached target area, only Lt. Robert Rosenthal piloting *Royal Flush* got back to England, and he only on an engine and a half!

As for our ship, it was obvious that we'd had it. Brady pulled off his oxygen mask the same instant I did to say, "Number Two has quit . . . there goes One . . . and there goes Three." Number Four proceeded to run away. Dave Soloman came up from the nose looking quite messy to tell us that we have to leave the formation because Hambone Hamilton has numerous holes in him and wanted to go home. I assured him that we had left the formation. After he left, Lt. Hoerr, co-pilot, made certain that the boys in the nose got out while Engineer Blum checked the after end. Brady was having difficulty keeping the ship on an even keel while I ran the administrative end of the abandon ship.

The goons were still shooting at us from above, below and both sides. I asked the co-pilot how we were doing, and he says, quote, "Everything is alright, and besides we just caught fire," unquote.

We scramble to the bomb bay where we discuss who should go last, me as senior man or Brady as Captain. Brady says, "No, go ahead." I didn't see Brady from that day 'till two years later, when he confirmed that he wanted to be out last because it was his ship and crew. Anyhow, we stood there, me with, "Go ahead Brady," and Brady with, "After you." We prattled some more, when the nicest spaced holes you ever saw, a row about six inches apart and about six inches below our feet appeared along the entire length of the bomb bay door. They were thirty calibre punctuation marks, and I said, "I'll see you, Brady," stepped out, counted one and pulled the rip-cord about the time I went by the ball turret.

The 'chute opened without a jar and the family jewels were safe. Looking around I saw three of our little chums, the 190s. They came in, and do you know what, they started shooting at Mrs. Egan's little boy, Johnnie. My 'chute is now full of holes, and so was Mrs. Egan's boy . . . They came back for another pass at me, and I took a very dim view of the whole thing. They finally left, thinking that I'm very dead, not knowing that I'm Irish.

Coming down three miles takes a bit of time, so I light a cigarette. This was not an uncommon occurrence among descending American airmen, who through government purchase owned the right kind of lighters. The longest feeling any living person has ever experienced is the feeling one has suspended in a parachute over enemy territory upon which is raining B-17s. It looked like I was going to land in a town, so I was forced to slip the 'chute, then slip it again to avoid a woods.

My landing, like that of most first jumpers, was unexpected at the time it happened. I landed lightly on my feet, my 'chute buckled back toward me, so I detached it from my harness and took off on the double, mainly because about 350 of Adolph's bosom buddies were interested in my ill-being. En-route for the woods, I shed equipment on the double, flying boots one at a time, goggles, harness and Mae West. I made the woods and gave the Krauts the slip.

Major Egan was eventually captured and joined his pal, "Bucky" Cleven, as guest of the Third Reich.

Flying to Munster in the 92nd Bomb Group, 427th Bomb Squadron, Lt. Raymond W. Baier, pilot, began his 12th mission. His words:

I flew my old crew on this raid as Julian Brown had flown the 11 hour mission the day before to Danzig, Poland. The take off and climb was normal, so was the crossing of the Channel and trip over Germany. This was the 25th mission for Captain Basler and his entire crew, and one other pilot. Slim Turner was in command and rode in Basler's ship, which lead the

146

Group and the 40th Combat Wing. Sgt. Donald J. Sack, top turret gunner-engineer, lost his oxygen at 24,000 feet and passed out trying to tell us something was wrong. All he could say was, "I can't breathe; it's on the right side," repeating this over and over, with his voice becoming weaker and weaker, sounding very strange! Finally co-pilot Toombs got to him and released him from the sling seat Sack was trying to use in the upper turret. Tombs gave him some oxygen and fixed his oxygen hose and Sgt. Sack was fine, but the crew was listening to that weird sound of a man in distress and that made everyone's blood tingle.

Nothing of importance happened until we reached the Initial Point of the Bombing run. We had not planned on going over Hulse, which is on the edge of "Happy Valley," but we did. And the edge is quite close enough—thank you! What Flak! not in quantity, but quality. It was really accurate — would have made the coldest Prussian smile with satisfaction. The first burst or groups of them appeared about 100 yards off our nose a little to the right and slightly above. We made a left turn, and those flak gunners helped us complete it! We got three hits and I think all of them right there during about 3 minutes, and it seemed like the second hand got stuck on the 3rd minute and started all over again! Strangely there was no flak over the target. We hit the wrong part of town. but it made little difference as there were German rail workers living all over town.

Somewhere en route (we heard the next day) Ambassador Winant's son, John C. Winant, was lost!

On the way out I looked back and saw one lone B-17 between us and the Wing behind us. He was straggling along obviously hit by flak and trying to get home. I then saw a FW-190 fly ahead of that Wing and for a moment it looked like he would come on up and attack us from the tail, then he turned and went back after that lone straggler in a direct nose level attack. He was getting closer and closer and just as it seemed he would open up with those "thousand little lights" on his wings, a flash came down from above; it was a P-47. Then came another flash as a second P-47 hit this Jerry and all that was left was a pall of black smoke — he had blown up! The prop wash of his intended victim soon scattered his smoke.

Another B-17 was seen in a spin. I saw him make at least four turns and he probably made 4 to 6 more. Then the pilots brought her out and my ball turret gunner, Sgt. John I. Johnson, saw many of them bail out. Nice work! We made the rest of our return with no further attacks and landed at our base in fine shape. Of course others did not fare as well.

We had determined from talking to others that the German Air Force has developed a new defense against the Blistering firepower of our heavy B-17. First is an abundance of single seat fighter aircraft which do not go into action until our escort had to turn back because they are low on fuel. They, the Germans, have the air to themselves.

Secondly, a rocket firing Group of twin engine ships, firing rockets that are estimated to be as much as 18 inches in diameter. The tactic is thus: single engine fighters attack from the nose, continually, with their usual fire power — deadly 20mm and 40mm shells, while the slower twin engine JU-88's attack with the rockets, continually, from the tail and both beams. While the single engine ships must close to assure success of their shells, thereby exposing themselves to the fire of the .50 calibre defensive guns of the B-17, the rocket ship can place their rockets from a point far beyond the range of our guns. If you fly a tight formation the rockets have a wonderful target. If you fly loose, then the single engine fighters have a picnic. Evasive action is now useless. The idea behind the rocket is to lob it into the center of the formation where it explodes, no doubt from a time fuse. If it hits a B-17, fire and explosion follows immediately; if not, the flak or shrapnel effect can easily be disastrous.

That tactic was without doubt the same one used on the October 14th mission to Schweinfurt — often called "Black Thursday." That was a mission on which 60 B-17s were lost. Of the 48 ships from the 40th Combat Wing participating, 29 were lost. One Group entered the French Coast with 19, were seen over the target with four, and got home with three! The 92nd Bomb Group lost 6. Two from each of the squadrons. So very much has been written about this well-chronicled mission that I shall not delve into it any further logistically. However, I would like to tell of some of the very sad and heart-wrenching duties that befell those who did not have to go on that mission or those who were lucky enough to come back. On this mission to Schweinfurt Lt. Baier stood down and was not called to go. His crew flew the mission under the command of Lt. Julian Brown.

For the ground crews, the pilots and other crewmen when they have buddies out on raids and on escorts, it is a long and tedious day of uncertainty. It is especially hard when you have a very good friend piloting your ship with your crew. Lt. Julian Brown's crew had gone down with Lt. Sergeant as pilot, on the August 17 mission to Schweinfurt, and we had heard that the plane had exploded. You just can't believe that they will not come back. The night before the October 14 mission to Schweinfurt, Lt. Baier, Lt. Brown and Duke had supper together with expectations of going to Northampton to see a show. Coming from the dining room they met Harvey and as usual asked him if there was a mission on for the next day. His reply was an immediate affirmative. The weather was bad, murky, low grey scudding clouds. They decided not to go to town after all, and did not feel

148

too cheerful about that. Lt. Julian Brown's crew had gone down with Lt. Sergeant on the August 17 mission to Schweinfurt, and we had heard that the plane had exploded. Instead they went back to the barracks and had a quiet evening reading. Julian and Duke went to the Squadron orderly room and got a couple of books out of the meager library (5 shelves). Lt. Baier stated:

After Julian and Duke returned, I took my log to the orderly room to do some typing on it. As I typed I talked to M/Sgt. Kowalczik — he and I had been in the 39th Bomb Squadron back in 1937 at Langley Field. He left, but returned shortly and I heard him say over the phone, "The wing tip tanks should be filled with 250 gallons each." I thought, "A long trip."

I returned to barracks and sat listlessly before the fire. It was still drizzling outside. At midnight we all began to drift to bed. I stepped outside for a last look at the weather. I jokingly told Julian, "The moon is shining — a big harvest moon." He shot back, "No can't be." I kidded on and never changed the story.

At seven in the morning I was awakened by Booker when he got up the alerted officers of the crews. Not being included I just turned over. About 0900 Julian came into the barracks and said, "Schweinfurt" in a non-committal way. I just did arouse myself enough to say, "Well, it won't be too bad," and then "Good Luck" when he left.

At 1030 they began taking off. Julian's position was lead of the second element. The 92nd Group was lead Group and the 327th (our) Squadron was low. On take off, Willie Steward blew his right tire. Somehow he managed to get her into the air with all that extra gas and 6 one thousand pound bombs! Visibility was zero and ceiling was zero. The others in the Squadron were Tucker lead, Julian, Steward, Talbot, McKennon, Oliverio and Miles.

The day WORE on. Duke, Frankie, Willie Monro and I ate lunch and talked around the fire in the barracks. One topic of conversation we covered was the law of averages and I said I thought we were due for a loss in the 92nd. Frankie expressed his thought that the law of averages worked differently in combat and that a successful Squadron or Group did not necessarily have to lose a ship every so many missions. He pointed out the marvelous record of an outfit running 35 missions without a loss. At 1430 someone went out for the mail and we all hit the jackpot with at least four letters apiece. I received one from "E". After reading mail we again fell into conversation. I wrote a whole page to "E". The feeling persisted that I would not feel like writing that night. At 1720 we went to operations, all four of us, and checked the Groups ETA. It was 1741. We continued on to the end of the runway to watch them come in. We were all anxiously awaiting their appearance over the field. We who don't go, wait around with the ground

149

personnel; smoking, talking. Several always have field glasses and they scan the horizon. When they get closer they try to read the big letter on the rudder and the number. The weather was still bad; visibility here at Poddington was fairly good — about a mile, but the ceiling was a scant 300 feet and lower in spots. Nash was standing by with a Verry pistol waiting to shoot some flares to help guide the ships to our field and right end of the runway, which was already marked with smudge pots burning brightly.

A stiff cross wind was blowing from the South. 1741 came and went. We then learned they were 16 minutes late crossing the British coast. That automatically advanced the ETA to 1757. But we could see some ships circling in the haze over Thurleigh. About 1800 a ship came in very low headed straight for us. It proved to be the lead ship of our Group with Col. Peasley aboard. Slim Turner was at the control tower with the Colonels from our base. That ship landed OK. A second appeared and it turned out to be Brown from the 407th Squadron. A third appeared and circled once to the left. As it passed we saw a large Z on the rudder. Willie Steward was flying a Z 496, but there was a second Z ship and as he made his first pass we couldn't positively identify this Z as Willie. This ship made a beautiful approach with power and as it passed over the end of the runway, we saw that it was Willie. He made the nicest landing imaginable, first the left wheel and tail wheel touched, then the right wheel touched and gradually the flat tire swerved him off the runway to the right. No other ships appeared in the traffic pattern or were heard around the field. At first no acute apprehension was felt because we knew many would seek other fields due to the weather, and furthermore, they undoubtedly used the let down procedure and were quite separated. We thoroughly expected more any minute. NO FOURTH SHIP EVER APPEARED. Then the name SCHWEINFURT began to loom ever larger in my mind. All of us walked in to Squadron Operations expecting to ask Steward about the raid and how many came over the British coast.

Floyd saw me as I stared toward the office and said, "J.T. Brown had it." I asked how? Where? What happened? Any 'chutes? One answer satisfied all my questions. An ME-210 had crashed Julian's plane #654 from the left side and set the bombs off. The German pilot had apparently been killed. Dougherty; Toombs; Sack; Geibell; Johnson; Rinko; Bowers; and Simeroth, a new crew's tail gunner; Harrison, an enlisted bombardier; and Newton, as my original tail gunner was in the hospital with an eye infection; had all been blown to pieces. Ships in the formation were shaken tremendously and much damage was done to them by the explosion. The story of the raid gradually came out. Today the 14th of October, 1943 the B-17 became an old fashioned bomber. It no longer will ever be the destroyer of enemy fighters and feared by them. This new tactic the Germans used at Munster proved effective there and was used again at Schweinfurt as many of the ships that went down had exploded. We lost Talbot also, but he was seen to crash land

150

in Germany. It is said German fighters escorted some of our bombers down and they were also seen to circle some of our men in parachutes. They were not seen to nor did anyone accuse them of firing on anyone in a 'chute.

Lt. Baier continues:

That night our barracks had 3 empty bunks: Julian's, Tooms', and Dougherty's. That night was the saddest night in many years. The blow fell on us so suddenly. The fact that no one had a chance to use their 'chutes. Not one of ten men. We talked to Willie Steward and got the story direct; still it seemed fantastic, unreal. As I walked into Willie Steward's barracks someone handed me a letter from my wife, "E". it had somehow strayed over there. There was a poem enclosed and for what it is worth, here it is:

THE THING THAT COUNTS

When pilots fare forth on a mission
Of service for me and for you
This one thing apart each man
    knows in his heart,
"All of us can't come thru":
But there isn't a one of that gallant band
Lest that thought interfere with his zest,
Whatever betides, it's destiny rides,
And we know that he'll give us his best.
It's precisely the same in the battle of life —
All of us can't come thru,
The halo of stars and the place in the sun
Are marked out for only a few;
But taking our tip from the Pilots,
    that dauntless, inspiring crew,
When life hands us a test, let's give it our best
E'en tho all of us can't come thru!!

I had several drinks of scotch in the club between dinner and 2100 when we found Willie Steward. At midnight I went to bed while the other guys were still over there. Chuck Bennett came in and I called him over to my bunk and said, "Glad to see you back." Earlier I had told Tucker, Steward and Bob Carlson the same thing. It seemed a miracle any of them got back. Sleep, despite the scotch, simply wasn't to be. The others came in and we gathered around the fire and just talked. Finally one by one we drifted off to bed. I was last — turned out J.T.'s table lamp and went to bed. We each had a corner bunk; his was the southeast and mine southwest.

On the morning of the 15th we had to get their small personal effects together. Duke removed Julian's silver bars and wings from the blouse and we pinned them to the little blue hand book we had received as cadets at

151

Maxwell Field. It is called Take Off. His candy, cookies and chewing gum were added to that of Toombs and Dougherty, which will go the the Chaplain for the crippled children's Christmas party. Ironic that a party should be held with our buddies' things, yet what better disposition could have been done with it? From all three — soap, razor blades, cigarettes, shoe polish and so many little things were brought forth. Someone here will use these things as there is no use sending it home. In Julian's Pilots Log — I entered his last flight — will go home.

Sgt. Bowers, my right waist gunner, had had a second child born just before were shipped overseas, but did manage to "promote" a leave of ten days and for that I am thankful to God. Toombs had gone home in May. I don't know when Dougherty had been home last nor any of the others.

It is a strange coincident that Julian and I were graduated on January 14, 1943 after 9 months training in the cadets, and on October 14, 1943, just 9 months hence, Julian failed to return from Schweinfurt where *his* crew on August 17, 1943 had gone down on their second mission, with Captain Sergeant in command of ship #835. This was Julian's 8th raid. I had known him only since May '42, but we were fast friends throughout our cadet training, Sebring, 2nd Air Force, Bovington and here in the 92nd Bomb Group, 327th Squadron, we had been together. Eighteen months is a short period in normal times. In war, a month is a year and events and relationships are magnified proportionately. My crew, my best friend in the ETO and in bomber work and the Best Man at my wedding all in the same breath. One explosion took them all. That's almost too much!!

It was learned months later that Sgt. John Johnson, the ball turret gunner, did indeed survive that explosion and was a P.O.W. in Germany.

Tour Summary
Narrator: Captain Frank C. Gregory
Group: 100th Bomb Group

As Lead Bombardier I did not fly mission after mission but only when called on to fly as Lead Bombardier. I did go on as many missions as the other guys but it just took me a lot longer to do that.

My first missions were milk runs. During the winter, and in most cases on the Continent you had from 7/10 to 10/10 cloud cover. This was in the days before the radar and radar crews. We would go over to hit primary, secondary and third, or targets of opportunity. With 10/10 cloud cover you didn't see anything. Just go over and try to see an opening and if you did try to see a target to drop your bombs on. You hated to bring those bombs back if you could help it. We always tried to find something, railroad tracks or anything enemy that could be destroyed, but you always had three targets charted out, all of importance.

Going in on the bomb run from the Initial Point to the target might be 10 miles on a straight run. All the flak in the world was over that target and at first we tried evasive action for the first part of the run, by swerving back and forth, it put the flak off. We also found out, since our primary object was to put the bombs on the target, by swerving around we could not get lined up and zero in and do a good job. We got to the place that when we got to the Initial Point we flew straight and level. You could not change speed or altitude because we had put all this into the bomb sight and could not change this. As soon as the bombs were dropped we turn right or left (our briefing notes told us to rally right or rally left), close the doors and go home.

We had intervalometers which are electrical-mechanical devices that would drop out one bomb every second or whatever it took to make a chain of them. I never used that, in fact, that is why I think I got back.

The procedure was that I would zero in on the target, we did not use the intervalometer or anything else, so when the cross hair was on the target I salvoed the whole thing. When I as Lead Bombardier dropped, the whole 21 plane Group dropped. Also to our advantage was that as lead group, we had a group above us and one below us and Enemy Aircraft had to get through both of them before they could get to us. This is one reason I got back. Another is we always had the best crew, we had lead and deputy lead. The responsibility of the whole mission was mine and this bothered me the most, because if I goofed up on the target or we did not get good results it meant we had sent 21 planes and 210 men and the whole works there for nothing. When we did get a good bomb pattern and came back, it made us feel it was worth it regardless of what happened. That meant one more factory or one more something else that would be out of operation for a while. They seemed to get them back in order pretty soon though. The main thing about it was the responsibility of it. If something happened to us the deputy was to come in and become Lead and everybody dropped on the Lead. So all dropped when he did, that way either the whole group hit the target or none did. Most of the other bombardiers were busy protecting the nose of their airplane and no way could they all zero in on the target.

One of the big problems was keeping ourselves oriented all the time. Except with good navigators, once in a while someone would get off line — like the "bend in the river," well, there were a lot of bends of the river. We always had certain points that we were looking for that were near the target or lined up with it. We were given enlargements of our targets and the area around it so we could familiarize ourselves with the target, in the meantime we didn't have much time. We would go to the briefing where they would give each crew member his special information: bombardiers, navigators, etc. The navigators and bombardiers would study this information as long as they could, take it along and work back and forth to make sure we both knew what we were doing. When your formation is stacked in good and flying a tight formation you are going to get good bomb runs and hits.

As a matter of fact, it is just as easy to fly tight formation, say 2 feet from another plane, as it is 20 feet, because everything is relative. Just a little movement on the controls or the throttle. It would be the same as driving a car down the road close to another one. You can't believe it until you see it. You could almost reach out and touch wings we were tucked in so close. The tighter the formation and the closer you were to each other the more firepower you had to bring to bear on enemy aircraft. Enemy aircraft had trouble getting through tight formations and so they would always hunt for a loose formation to go after. If they did come in at you they would have to come up or down or some other way to keep from running into a bomber because they did not want to do that.

Normally, it was a quick unforeseen action that would cause planes to touch each other. In all this time there was never any possibility in most cases, probability I should say, of planes touching each other. This whole idea, formation flying, was new and impressive.

We were operating with the British all this time, we can't make fun of them. Though, they had a tougher deal than we did, in fact, there was a time when they bombed by daylight. Later, we bombed Berlin in the day-time and the RAF hit them the next night, then we again in a daylight raid. The RAF did not fly formation as we did. They flew in a straight line using the navigation lights of the plane just ahead of them. The tail light was a blue light. So they would be a long string of planes stretching for miles across the sky. When they bombed they bombed one at a time. There was no way for E/A to get to them except from the sides when they flew this way and they,

154

too, had side gunners. The RAF had special equipment: radar to see each other and the ground. This had to be the toughest flying in the world, a plane right in front and one right behind, all the way across, and they never did get credit for what they did. The RAF put bomb after bomb in there. We got so much more credit because we did it in the daylight. Our idea was to present a solid wall of planes and guns, and until they broke it up, which some times they did, and scattered the planes, then they could pick the planes off like picking cherries. Until that time they could not penetrate this defense because we had at least six guns trained on them at all times. As Bombardier, I operated the nose guns, later the chin turret, up to the bomb run. The navigator was busy at all times with his job, getting us to the I.P., after that he says, "There's your target." We worked together all the time. He could not work the chin turret or nose gun either when I was on the bomb sight, he was directly above me. The rest of the time he could work it or I could work it. Meantime, he is the next most important member because he has to get the planes there and get them back. In fact, his was a primary responsibility. Unless he got the plane crew and bombardier to the target area the mission was a failure.

Capt. Gregory was one of a small number of men who had a double rating. He was also rated as a navigator.

Once in a while someone would say, "Where's the navigator going?" "He's on course." "No, he's not on course, he's 100 miles off, we should be up there." Everything looks the same up there. We had no radio aids, we went strictly by visual as much as possible. When we were holding a certain heading and knew where we should be, then by our ground speed we knew where we should be as far as penetration was concerned. Whenever we got a clearance all we had to do was look around and look for something to identify our position, then check from this point to this point and determine how long it took us to get from here to there, we could tell our ground speed again.

When Headquarters set up our missions they would tell us the time we would take off and they could tell within five minutes of when we'd be coming back and that is when they would start looking. They had the winds aloft, our cruising speed and knew our ground speed at out altitude. Everybody was there waiting for them and when that mission didn't show up they began to worry, or a few would show up and they would worry. Sometimes the planes would be scattered.

When they did get back all the crew went to de-briefing and gave all the information they could give while it was still fresh in their mind.

When we left England to go to Europe on a mission we were told exactly where to cross the enemy coast — specifically where. We crossed at the exact place they told us to. At that time the flak was weak there or was not as strong as it was in some other places. Wherever we would make a crossing or two, the Germans would put some more guns there and we'd have to cross some place else. That's the way we flew, if there was a bad area up ahead we'd scoot around it. We would never fly over a city on our way to a primary target because a lot of time you would pick up flak you were not supposed to have. Normally you would not pick up flak until you got to your target area. Along the way we would try not to get close enough to anything to get flak.

The 88 mm flak gun was the one that did the most of the damage. For a time there were no guns that could reach up to 27-28,000 feet. We were given instructions to fly clear up north over the islands or come back around another way. Our problem was still the range of the bombers 2,700 gallon fuel capacity. In fact, when we flew that shuttle mission to Russia we dropped a few in some corn fields because of a miscalculation of the fuel. They could not fly after they ran out of fuel so they set them down the best they could. Later, they went back and repaired them and brought them back to the field, flew them out as best they could. It had been anticipated that we could get all the way to Kiev, and my plane made it, others didn't. Planes are like cars in a way, some get better gas mileage than others. A certain percentage made it and a certain percentage didn't. It was perfectly flat country so when they had to crash land they would do a wheels-down-landing, unlike when they had battle damage and had to land on the belly. It takes a lot more room to get one off than it does to get one down. If you had 4600 or 4700 feet you could get one off. I heard a B-17 pilot that put one down at a small airport in Ft. Collins, Colorado and was unable to get it off again so they had to haul it back to the base (Lowry Field, Denver).

The Norden bomb sight was a gem. We had experts trained in maintenance of the sight who would check it out. We did leave the sights in the planes all the time. By this time there had been so many of our 17's knocked down that surely the Germans had the sight. On the other hand we carried a .45 pistol and were told to put a couple rounds into that sight if we were going down. By the time the Germans would have figured it out, it would not have done them any good so we were not concerned about it. The sight was mounted, levelled and kept in this same position all the time. The sight was a real good one and if you were aiming at a factory there should be no reason you would miss it. If they wanted you to bomb an office in the northeast corner, that would be different.

In training we had very small targets, and of course, were scored according to how close we came to the target with the bombs. We spent many hours practicing night bombing, but we never did any night bombing. We were supposed to be home at night because the field had no landing lights. Due to a miscalculation from time to time we had planes come in after dark and so had to send up flares to show them the field. One time a group was late and it was a dark dreary night so the lights and flares went on. At the same time some German fighters moved in on those heavy bombers and

156

shot them up very badly. This was never let out though, and thereafter no missions were sent out that would present the chance of coming in after dark. The German night fighters knocked those bombers down right on our base, just like sitting ducks. Our bombers had no protection at all. They were on final approach, flaps down, wheels down. We had no night fighters, the British had a few. This was a bad ending of that day.

When we first started flying missions we had fighter cover for only one third of the penetration, from then on we were on our own. After the Eighth got the P-47s in, then we got a little more cover. The British Spits would take us across the channel a ways and leave us after we got across the flak line, because they had to go back for petrol. The P-47s would then pick us up and take us in a little further. When we got to our target and came on back the 47s would have gone home, refueled and came back to pick us up and escort us the rest of the way home. Then they got the P-51s and they carried wing tanks, and could fly further. Sometimes they could fly all the way to the target with us. Sometimes when going in we would see them drop their wing tanks and we'd say, "Oh, oh, trouble!" This meant they would not have enough fuel to go all the way with us and would have to go back to refuel and come back again.

Fighters bothered me more than the flak — you could see it, you could see where it was coming from — it didn't bother me. The fighters would invariably come in out of the sun. In fact the mission to Berlin on March 6, 1944, when our Group was all shot up, we lost 15 planes, the remnants joined up with the 390th Bomb Group. We tried to crowd in and not be up from the sun and somebody else crowded us out, so we had to go down in the lower echelon and be tail end Charlie. We thought, "That sun of a gun, you worked us out of that." It was not thirty minutes later that a German fighter came in on him and he was shot out of the position we tried to take.

On these missions to Berlin: We went into briefing and all sat down. This was the third of March, 1944. They start off with a few preparations then they pull the curtain. We could tell by looking which direction the red tape went just where we were going we didn't need any name. We could tell if it was in the Munich area or what. And they opened the curtain up that morning and nobody said a word. It was quiet. Boy, this is it! Big B! Funny part of it was that on that mission we had fighter cover all the way in and out. It wasn't bad, we had some come in at us but we never got knocked out or anything. So the 100th Bomb Group flew all the way to Berlin, dropped their bombs over 10/10ths cover, and we didn't know where they went. At that time we still did not have radar. We thought, "That's no big deal." We went back again the next day, then we had to lay off due to weather and then went in again. That is when we got the hell knocked out of us. We got over that and we had to go again. Seemed like all we ever did was go home, go to bed, get up, and fly again.

I had a pair of shoes inside a pair of flight boots and rather than take them

157

out each time, I just left the shoes inside the boots. Each morning I jumped right into the boots. Later on when I did take the shoes out of the flight boots, they were all slimy and green with mildew.

We thought that every mission we got in was one more we figured we wouldn't get. So if we got any time off between missions we lived it up.

The first time we went to Berlin the mission was recalled because of that 10/10ths cloud cover but we were the only Bomb Group to make it and I don't know yet if they heard the recall or not. Somebody said, "Well, the radio was out and we didn't get the recall." We don't know to this day if the radio went out or the lead plane decided to go in regardless. But they claimed they never got the recall because you were supposed to follow orders. Did they get the recall and just bowed their neck and went in anyhow? Don't know. That was an easy one.

Our shuttle mission to Russia was nothing, as we had no fighter opposition. But Berlin was different. Hitler had made the statement that no one would bomb Berlin and I guess that is why everybody wanted to get there first. I don't remember our particular target, but we always had one, rail yards, ball bearings, Schweinfurt!

I went to Schweinfurt. Anytime we made those deep penetrations into Germany they were quite obnoxious about it. The Germans could read the handwriting on the wall paper. That is, if we got their factories etc. they were not going to be able to put out much in the way of war products. As a result the Germans would put up everything in the world to prevent it. They were beginning to let the marshalling yards go, and the oil, etc. But we found out later when the ground forces moved in, that the Germans had brand new planes sitting on the ground but no gas for them, they were just sitting in the revetments.

The Germans made a great effort to keep us out of Regensburg too, it was so far down there. The shuttle to Africa was a surprise to them, but when the B-17s started to run out of fuel after crossing the Mediterranean Sea it got to be a mess. I was not on that mission but I know that they had problems. If you get a change of wind or something is wrong with your engines, your fuel consumption is going to change for the worse. If you do some maneuvering around along the way, or can't hold the same course you were holding before, everybody is in trouble. By the time they got there they are out of ammunition, gasoline and everything else. Those are the tough missions.

One time we even bombed Poland (Gydnia). We flew clear around the North Sea and over that way; in fact, the fighters had time to get us in the North Sea, go back down, rearm and refuel and catch us on the way back. Trips like this made us sure we could make it to Russia. Something went wrong because by the time we got to Kiev we were out of gas. In fact, some of those jokers were four or five weeks getting home. They went all the way to Egypt on the way back. I don't know how they got back to England, but some of them didn't show up for a long time. On this Russian shuttle we had fighter support all the way.

On the mission that we lost our tail, we were flying *Hang the Expense III*. Lt Frank Valesh was the pilot, he was the third pilot I had had as I was changing crews all the time and had at least four crews. Frank was a real good pilot, kind of a daredevil, but a good pilot and that made all the difference in the world. The name for the plane came about this way: All during the time we were over there, money meant nothing. We were given electric flying suits instead of sheepskin, we got special fancy thin flying gloves from the RAF so we could work the controls better. They were such good gloves there was no comparison with our G.I. gloves. Cost meant nothing, so we got to the place where we said, "Hang the expense." The airplane was named the same. Oh well! Get new engines, get a new tail, hang the expense.

We had been to our target, dropped our bombs and were on the way home. I saw the Germans shoot when they hit us. I was sitting up there in the nose and those black puffs below, those 88's were winking and blinking at us. I said, "Oh, oh, we're in trouble." I no sooner said that when they hit the back end. For a while we didn't know what was going to happen to us. It was touch and go, we talked it over as to whether we should bail out or ditch it or try to make it in. We kept getting different reactions from the plane. It would fly alright for a while and all of a sudden it would start mushing again. We finally used the Automatic Flight control and got the thing levelled out pretty well. I don't know how Frank Valesh got that plane down but he did. He brought it down at an RAF base. The tail gunner had been blown out of there and the guys flying our wing and behind us said he went all to pieces, in all directions. However, some weeks later we got word that he was in Stalag I or II. I can't recall which. He was a prisoner. Then we got to thinking on it and the tail gunner had had so many close calls and been shot at so many times that he had begun to stack ammo boxes all around himself. We got to thinking — the flak knocked everything off, but he wasn't touched by the flak itself. The flak blew the whole tail section off and him with it, but no one saw a chute. He could have been half unconscious anyway and not opened his chute for quite a while. We saw the card that came back from him via the Red Cross. He said he was well except for his two ————— The word after the "two" was blacked out by the Germans. But he was OK except for something he had two of was either missing, injured or damaged.

I didn't say a word about this to my parents or anyone at home. I always told them I was getting along fine — no problems, no nothing, no use for them to worry. But someone sent a picture from a Canadian newspaper to the folks, and they found out all about it. Then it was published in the U.S. over the Associated Press wire.

When *Hang the Expense III* got home it was junked out — hang the expense! Get number IV.

The incident illustrated by the photographs of *Hang the Expense*

159

was given wide publicity by the newspapers of the time and promptly forgotten, by Captain Gregory. As he had mentioned previously, "All the missions were the same to me." The mission was flown into Germany on a day in late January 1944, *Hang the Expense* was listed as missing at the base and was presumed to have gone down, however, several hours later it did return to England and landed at an English RAF base.

Lt. Frank Valesh of St. Paul, Minnesota granted an interview to a reporter and is quoted: "I'm getting damned tired of this business." This had been his third crash landing in three weeks. Lt. Valesh went on, "It looked like everything in France hit us at once. The plane reared up, out of control and started climbing steeply. I found my hand controls were gone, and snapped on the automatic pilot. Luckily there was enough tail surface left to straighten us out."

"When that flak hit us, it felt as if somebody had hit me in the stomach with a plank. I picked myself up from the floor of the plane about seven feet from where I had been standing," commented S/Sgt. Herschel H. Broyles the right waist gunner, from Chatanooga, Tennessee. The photograph shows the almost complete destruction of the tail of the plane, and clearly shows the absence of the tail gun position.

Struggling over the Channel *Hang the Expense* was picked up by a P-47 escort and escorted to an RAF field that was expecting a large flight of their own planes. Lt. Valesh could not contact them by radio and since he was loosing altitude rapidly the Thunderbolts just kept buzzing the runway to keep anyone else from landing. The ship was brought down in a picture-perfect landing.

The rest of the crew included 2nd Lt. John E. Booth, Haverhill, Massachuttes, co-pilot; 2nd Lt. Frank C. Gregory, Greeley, Colorado, bombardier; T/Sgt. John Mytko, New York, top turret gunner; T/Sgt. Ernest A. Jordan, Keller, Texas, radio operator-gunner; S/Sgt. Louis Black, Jr., San Diego, California, ball turret gunner; and S/Sgt. Paul J. Carbone, Newburg, New York, left waist gunner. The missing tail gunner and navigator were not identified.

I wasn't flying with Lt. Valesh on the other junkets, instead I was flying with Lt. Helmick. I had lost my original crew some time before that. They were all alive, but POW's as they went down soon after we first got over there. The fact is, that was the main problem I had. We were in barracks with four to eight men to a room. They kept changing crews on me. This guy was here today and gone tomorrow. I didn't know most of them over there.

We had to put up three squadrons on each mission with one left at the base. Whenever we led the wing would be the only time that I would fly, so I missed a number of missions. It was hit or miss. It took me a lot longer to get in my 25 missions. Some made their's much sooner than I or never did make it at all. I was fortunate in being held back in this way. This lengthened the time I was over there, but at the same time it was the only reason I got back. I don't remember anybody who went over with me that returned to the States. Out of the original bunch we started out with at Kearney and Moses Lake, I don't think any of them got back. Oh, some of them got back after spending the duration as POWs and we had a bunch of them in Switzerland. If you were over in the area and in trouble you had the option of heading south into Switzerland. We had some down there. I'm not sure if they had battle damage, or if they just headed south. I don't blame them. We threatened to do it half the time. Everytime we had a little flak damage we'd ask, "What's the heading for Switzerland?" It got to be down right funny at times, but not often. We got to the place where we just did not see how we were ever going to make it, that is the 100th Bomb Group. We were losing crews and planes faster than could be replaced. Later on it got to the point where we would make the whole mission and maybe see an enemy aircraft and maybe not.

On D Day I don't think we saw an enemy plane. We had the white "Invasion Stripe" on all our planes, and we had strict instructions that we were to fly South and that anything flying North would be shot down. If you had one engine left or no engines left, keep it headed South. You were to do this at least until the landing was over with. We never saw an enemy plane.

One thing that isn't much talked about are the No-Ball runs. We considered milk runs except that we lost some crews on them too. These No-Ball runs were just across the Channel to a wooded area. This we liked. We were briefed as to exactly what to hit. A No-Ball is a ski run for launching the V-1 and V-2 rockets. They were beginning to cause a tremendous problem in London in particular. It got to the point that when we were on leave in London we were more afraid of those flying bombs than we were of flying combat missions over Germany. Those bombs could land anywhere. The Germans did not care what they hit when they got to England. When I was in London on several occasions, I tried to stay in the area of a bomb shelter. One night I was invited out to an evening dinner with a family and, of course, could stay the night if I liked. I asked where the family lived and was told, out in the country near Wimbolton. So, fine, I'll go out there. I found out later that it was on a direct path from the French coast to London, and most of those bombs flew right over. As long as you could hear that engine, no problem, but as soon as it stopped making noise you better duck because it was coming down. The Germans put in enough fuel to get them to London and when the fuel was gone, down it came. Some of these were blockbusters and did a great deal of damage. At these folk's place at Wimbolton I heard one coming and then I didn't. My host family all ran for a staircase and got under that. I was told this is where they went for safety

161

during air raids so that is where I went too. This flying bomb hit about a block away and really shocked and rattled things. I went to the impact area the next day and could hardly believe the destruction it caused. This was very upsetting to the British population psychologically as it was to everyone else as you could never tell where or when they would come.

The primary purpose of the No-Ball missions was to knock out these launching sites, which meant we only had to fly to the Coast and back. The way our missions count was kept was that when you crossed the enemy lines you got credit for a mission. We had recalls where we would get up, load the planes, form up and get over the channel and then be recalled, so no credit for a mission. But we did get a good breakfast out of it. The flight crews got real eggs for breakfast, the rest got dried eggs. Missions were most often scrubbed for bad weather. As it was difficult to form up, with everyone around it was too easy for mid-air collisions. There were times coming back from missions we would get within 100 feet of the runway before we could see it. We had three runways. At one time or another we had as many as four or five B-24s at the end of our runways that had crashed trying to get in with battle damage or trying to take off or for other reasons. When your plane is damaged and you might have injured aboard, you try to get in as soon as you can.

Most people don't realize just how cold it was up there at combat altitude. The temperature could be as much as minus 62 degrees on the outside. When we took off on a mission and were over the channel, the pilot would say, "Everybody test fire your weapons." and everybody would give a short burst to see that their guns were working properly. When you'd get over the continent in a combat area we'd have a number of weapons that would not operate, just froze. Eventually the gunners got over this and would use little or no grease, of course, the guns got hot but were still operating. Once in a while at altitude some joker would let off a short burst to test his guns. Right away over the intercom would come, "Where are the bandits?" So he says, "Just test firing." When anyone fired that way over the continent you assumed there were bandits in the area and everybody wanted to know what was going on. Most of the time bandits were called off before they got to you, in fact, you could see them or their contrails and the lead planes ahead would tell you bandits at such and such a clock position. We would keep a wary eye on them. Sometimes they wouldn't even bother us, they would look us over and go on. If they did not like the looks of the formation they would go on and pick another one. They especially picked on stragglers. If you lagged behind and couldn't keep up you were in trouble, the formation could not hang back. If a plane had trouble or malfunction or whatever early enough, he could just abort and return to base and have fighter protection. On the other hand, when you got in there a ways with no fighter protection you would have to stay with the group for protection. If you could not keep up you were a sitting duck for a bandit. That is one thing you worried about — those engines working. Being in the lead crew we always had the best plane

162

available, best crews and best ground crews. They wanted to be sure that lead plane was working. That made a difference in surviving, I'm sure.

Speaking on "special" load sequences in the gunner's ammo boxes some of the gunners may have had special loads in their ammo boxes, I don't know. The fighter pilots did. All the ammo belts had tracer ammo in them every fifth or tenth round. Since in air battles the closing speeds were so terrific you had just seconds to shoot. With the tracers you could see where your bullets were going and could compensate accordingly if you had time. Our crews always had plenty of ammunition. We had it stacked from hell to breakfast, all we could get in. I can only remember one time that we ran low on ammunition. When we would see enemy fighters close enough to us we would give a few bursts just to let them know ahead of time that we were alert and waiting for them and watching them. Some times they would go look over another group which is what we were after, we wanted to keep our group intact. The Germans still had some of the best fighter pilots, few in number but good flyers.

We had some good men in the 100th Bomb Group in high positions — fearless. And then there were some (Colonels and Majors), a couple of them anyhow, that didn't want to fly missions. They had had their fill of it so in most cases they were grounded. In nearly all cases when a high ranking officer was in a formation he was in a particular position where he was more or less operating the group or wing or whatever it was and he was responsible for it. There were cases when a Colonel or a high commanding officer would be flying in the tail gun position. He would be watching the formation and giving information on closing the gap and trying to keep the whole unit operating as well as possible. The C.O.'s and the rest of them would fly a mission every so often. They didn't fly all the time because it would be senseless to put your best men up there on every mission and all of a sudden you're going to lose all your chiefs and all you have left are the Indians.

On very important missions where they were after a definite target, they wanted to be sure and penetrate and get it (Regensburg, Schweinfurt, etc.), so they could send a good man. As a rule he would be flying co-pilot of the Group or Wing lead plane. He would be making the decisions on what they were going to do according to weather and according to what the navigator said. On everything in general he was making the decisions. Command actually tried to use the good officers as best as they could without taking a chance. On those short missions they would just leave them at home — no use taking a chance on it. You have no way of knowing which plane is going to get shot down, if any. You could lose a good man that way and they did not have enough good men to go around.

We had some men who would go to great lengths to keep from flying. They didn't care about flight pay or anything — just staying alive. Some would put on so much equipment that I don't think there was any way they could get hit if they had to. They would have a flak suit on the front, a flak

163

suit on the back, and a parachute over that. They had stuff all around them.

Oh, everybody was afraid all the time. Each time we went out we were not sure we were going to make it. The thing of it was it looked so hopeless. All we wanted to do was get one more weekend, maybe one more mission. There was no way of knowing. All the fellows I had bunked with across the States during training and every place else, all of a sudden were gone. New people came in and they would ask, "How is it?" Well we would not want to flak them all up as they would get enough of that later on, so we would say, "Sometimes good, sometimes not so good." Some guys were disturbed when they were sent to the 100th to begin with.

We had to have so many replacements, people were coming in all the time. It was strictly, I think, tough breaks because the 100th was a good Group, good personnel — fine personnel. But we had bad breaks. We could never find out if it was true about that "wheels-down" incident that had the German fighters so irate at the 100th Bomb Group in particular. This is still talked about at Group reunions to this day.

After I got in about 15 or 16 missions I was put into Intelligence briefings etc. I was being saved for specific missions where I did my job as Lead Bombardier. I talked to other intelligence officers about the "incident" and never did find anything to verify this. The story goes like this: A 100th Bomb Group B-17 had some battle injury or damage and dropped down away from the Group and in so doing, the enemy fighters picked on him as they would do in such cases. Since he had so much battle damage and it did not look like they were going to make it anyway, he dropped his wheels. This is supposed to be a signal that, "We give up and are going down." Thats all there is to it. Though, actually, when two German fighters came along side to escort them to the field they wanted them to land at, the guys inside the B-17 shot the two fighters down. So after this, the Germans began to pick on the 100th Bomb Group. We never got any more than this story: true or not?

In debriefing after a mission the debriefing officers would want to know everything that happened. There would be a number of tables with one D.O. and five combat crew members. The D.O. want to know it all, anything and everything. Intelligence could put it all together, maybe it was important that this happened or that happened and they could make something out of it. One thing the D.O. wanted was a direct count on battle damage.

They wanted to verify exactly how many planes went down, how many chutes were seen, how many enemy aircraft seen, how many claims for shot down enemy aircraft. Intelligence theory was that had this "Incident" really happened around any of the Groups, somebody would have seen it and say "We saw it happen." Evidently this plane had dropped down behind the Group and there is nothing in the record to indicate that anybody had seen this.

A lot of times when you get back from a mission you say this happened, this is what we saw and somebody else will say something completely different. The debriefing officers and Intelligence piece it all together and figure out what they can. The one thing they stress is that when a plane goes down, how many chutes were seen? They want to come up with a total of ten. There may be one or two and then an explosion and that will be it. Later they will find out that six more got out.

Never-the-less, the 100th Bomb Group had tough luck. I say tough luck because a Group gets picked on and its a good Group and the 100th was a good Group. They were flying well and they got shot out of the sky, then that's tough luck. Of course the 100th had that big square D and I'm sure if anybody over there wanted to know who the 100th was they would know. Axis Salley never did tell anybody about it.

It was true on some missions we would lose more planes and maybe just one or two, other Groups would get shot up (the 390th at Munster, the 388th at Hannover), it varied from mission to mission. If we lost just three planes that too was a bad mission, I don't care what you say. We would stand on the deck at the flight line counting them as they came in, red flares meant injured aboard and they got priority in most cases and came right in. We would count them and keep looking and count more. Then every now and then we would count one or two more. Often times somebody was in trouble from another Group and landed because they could not make it back to their own base. Until we got them all down and counted up we did not know what kind of mission we had. Usually the Group would call ahead and give some information on the mission, when they had bombs away, their ETA, etc. But our guys might be over with another Group too. Anytime you get in trouble you'd stack in with somebody else, you didn't care who it was, even if they were B-24s, anybody at all, you needed cover and you had to work together. If you had three planes together they were a lot better than one, you tripled your firepower. In some cases on the way back from a mission the Groups would try to slow down for stragglers. On the way in it was a different story entirely, you simply could not do it. You had to keep together, keep things moving. When you are flying mostly full throttle and you get behind, somehow it is awfully hard to catch up, especially when you've lost some altitude. In most cases when this happened, you've lost an engine or maybe two, if you have you're in dire trouble! You can fly and you can get home, but you can't gain altitude and can't keep up with the Group as a result. If your controls were OK and your remaining engines were strong many crews would come back to England right on the deck, tree top level. They were so low no one could see them unless they were flying at a much greater altitude and if they pass over they probably were doing something else and not paying any attention to what was going on at ground level. So some of our people got back that way except they had some trouble with the gun towers near the coast. They would be zooming along and all of a sudden they would be getting ground fire. Nevertheless, on returning the Group would try to slow down and let somebody catch up if they could, otherwise they were strictly on their own unless fighter cover would come in and pick them up.

We encountered the jets toward the last, but didn't know what they were. They didn't give us much trouble because this was too much toward the end and the Germans didn't get them really operational. They were so fast when they went by we'd never seen anything like it. We would see them mostly in the distance and were never attacked by them, only the prop planes. I don't know if there weren't enough of them or if they were still experimental or what they were doing. We brought back the tale the first time we saw them and the brass said, "No way," just did not know what they were. None of our planes could come close to them as to speed.

Our fighters developed a system of shooting down the jets. Chasing them down proved futile, so our fighters would vector around the Me262 landing fields and attack them as they were taking off or landing — at which time they were vulnerable.

One other problem we had in flying missions besides the flak and the fighters was the Ju-88's. They would fly off your wing and out of your gun range lobbing rocket shells or cannon shells into the Group. They would use whatever heavy artillary they could get into the plane. Sometimes they were even worse than the flak because they were closer, but threw a smaller shell. The Ju-88's would also call down our speed and course and altitude to the flak batteries and they in turn would shoot right into the formations. But I don't think we lost anyways near the planes due to flak as we did to fighters. A lot of the planes damaged by flak could get home, but the fighters did so much damage once they got a cripple. To me the flak was more psychological than anything else, but if you got a direct hit it was bad all the way around. So many times the flak would get a wing or engine or tail. A close hit could break a wing surface or fuselage or something like that where it looked like a lot of battle damage. It wasn't nearly as bad as the fighters themselves when they came thru they could tear a plane up, they threw so much firepower at one time. Of course we were putting out firepower, too.

When we came back from a mission and had encountered fighters, the shell casing would be ankle deep on the floor. There was a deafening roar when there was battle action. You could hardly hear yourself think. I could hear the jar of the tail guns going off clear up in the nose of the plane. No matter who was firing, ball, side, top or tail you could feel that vibration. We always had a lot of ammunition. To let the German aircraft know we were alert we always shot a burst at them even at extreme range just to let them know we were alert.

Speaking of such things as fighters and flak etc. I picked a couple of inch square pieces of flak from my parachute harnass strap once. As in all these missions I do not remember which one it was but at any rate we were on the bomb run and I was at the bomb sight. The flak was fairly heavy at the time, but no worse than any other mission. I felt a couple of taps on my shoulder and thought it was the navigator wanting something back there, but I waved a "I can't be bothered now motion." When we completed the run I turned and asked him what he wanted and why he had tapped me on the shoulder when I was on the bomb run. He said he did not want anything and further more did not tap me on the shoulder! I then looked at my harness and here were these two pieces of flak that had gone thru the plane and spent the last energy imbedding in my harness. Like I said I do not recall the mission, to me they were all the same — no difference. Unless we had real battle damage we did not remember one from the other. The only thing I recall about this mission was that it was to knock out a bridge so the Germans could not use it.

Wilhelmshaven, and those up there that we had heard about before we went on the mission, their defenses were very strong. When we went on the mission we found this to be true, strong going in and strong coming back out. Some of these, except Big-B, I don't recall ever going back to again. Many times if you hit them good one time you would not have to go back again.

Marienburg is a very classic example of really precision daylight bombing. We went in there and did a fine job on that one and finished off right away. If a target was not completely destroyed somebody else would go in and finish it off.

Many times we would have to wait to get a report from the Underground as to the damage to the target and if it needed a second strike. So we would hear, "Boy you really hit that one." or "You missed that one. You'll have to do it again." We always had recon photographs of the results of the missions, but we also got word from the Underground, and I can't say how we did this as I don't know. The Underground would have complete information on how good or how bad we did. The Germans did a lot of camouflage work, which didn't help that much. They did do one thing that was very effective at times and that was the wide use of smoke screens, particularly on the smaller targets that did not cover a great area. They had their problems too, the wind would shift and the smoke would go the wrong way. The Germans would do everything in the world to throw us off the line — try to confuse us — even as to building fake factories. But so much of the time we were confused anyhow, mostly because of bad weather. Cloud cover would drift in and you would lose your target. We'd bomb where we thought it was and wait for a report to come back from the Underground to find out how we had done. I do not recall a mission where we brought bombs back unless it was a scrubbed mission before we got to the coast. We did not like to land with bombs aboard. There is no danger in bombs whatsoever, they have a little propeller in the front and that has to turn so many revolutions before the bomb is armed and will detonate on impact. Until then it is

167

considered safe. We just did not like the idea of going all that way and bringing them home.

When we went to Russia on that first shuttle mission we had a certain type of bombs aboard, but the target was changed so we had to change bomb loads. The Russians said they would do this and when they did they just salvoed the bombs onto the ground! The bombs banged into each other while we stood off at a distance and watched this and said, "Those crazy jokers!"

Our bombing missions were meant to destroy anything that would help the Germans win the war. I don't think our people realize just how much it did add to the winning of the war. The Germans got to the point they didn't have anything to work with. There was no way they could keep in operation with so much of their resources having been taken out of commission. Many of their manufacturing industries went underground and were able to produce manufactured goods right up until the end of the war. The production of aircraft went up, as a matter of fact, but they were not able to get any of the new planes up. We'd go over there and maybe we'd see a few E/A and they would look us over and go back down again. They could not bring enough force to make any difference in the bomb run.

It was found after the war that the lack of fuel kept most of the planes on the ground. The German oil supply had just been bombed off the map. They had no fuel to even train new pilots but with a minimum of flying time. These ill-trained pilots were shot down immediately if they tangled with our fighters.

Our thousand plane maximum effort raids were put up in order to do as much heavy damage as possible at one time. It was also found out that it was bothering the German people to see formation after formation headed for Berlin and those areas that Hitler said would never get bombed. At the same time the people were being told they were winning the war. They knew better. That was part of the reasoning behind the big thousand plane raids. The other was that we were not suffering losses to where we could put the planes up and not have to depend entirely on fighter escort. The Germans could not muscle enough planes to really bother the big raids like this as opposed to the smaller ones before. If you go with 400 planes, actually the Germans could pick them off one at a time as they go by and they could get at each Group. When you got a thousand planes or even twelve hundred it was more confusing to the enemy fighters, "Where do we begin?" If we are holding a tight formation they could not find a place to start in on us. All this added up to make a difference. I'm sure it was confusing to those Germans over there trying to get into those big formations, because when you are tight they can't get in.

When we went to Russia the very best crews were picked to go and were told, "We don't care what you do, but fly the tightest formation you can —

make it look good." And we did, we flew wing tip to wing tip all the way in. We lost 43 planes on the ground. I don't think we lost a man. The Germans had our number from the beginning and they came in at night. The Russians did not fight at night so had no night fighters. We sat up on a hill and watched the whole show. The Germans dropped flares and systematically blew up the B-17s and some of our P-51s, all we could do was sit and watch. The loss of these planes made no difference at this stage of the war, although it was just after the invasion of Europe. Despite our reputation the 100th Bomb Group lost no planes.

Eventually we all got back to England, more missions and finally we did some of the food missions over Holland where we dropped food parcels to the Dutch people, who were in dire need of food. The Germans had taken most of the food from them to feed the German army. The Dutch helped save a good number of American airmen during the war. We appreciated that and they appreciated these food drops.

The 100th Bomb Group was a good group, good flyers, brave men, and loyal men. There were times we had bad luck maybe more so than other Groups. But there were missions that we did not lose a plane and others we did. We just had that reputation for losses.

Thanks for the memory
        Of flights to Germany
        Across the cold North Sea
        With blazing guns
        We fought the Huns
        For air supremacy
                How lucky we were!

Thanks for the memory
        Of Me 109's
        Flak guns on the Rhine —
        They did their bit
        And we were hit
        They ended our good times
                We hate them so much!

    Chorus:
        We drifted far out of formation
        We jumped and what a sensation —
        And now to sweat out the duration
        Our job was done
        We've had our fun

Thanks for the memory
        Of days we had to stay
        In Stalag VII A —
        The cabbage stew
        Which had to do
        Till Red Cross Parcel day
                How lucky we were!

    Credited to
        Staff Sergeants   Davies
                            Dougherty
                            Knudsen
                            Edwards

Date: 16 November 1943
Target: Knaben, Norway
Narrator: Dean Sommers
Group: 92nd Bomb Group

On November 16 the second mission of the month was flown by the 92nd Bomb Group. Due to bad weather only one other mission had been flown. A very brief summary states:

NOVEMBER 16, 1943, THE MONTHS SECOND MISSION (DUE TO BAD WEATHER), WAS TO THE MOLYBDENUM MINES AT KNABEN NORWAY, AND 21 A/C LED BY MAJOR MCGEHEE WARD JR, FLYING WITH CAPTAIN BLAIR BELONGIA, PARTICIPATED. THE ENTIRE 8TH AIR FORCE ATTACK WAS CONCENTRATED ON NORWAY, WITH THE 2ND DIVISION BATTERING THE AIRDROMES NEAR OLSO AND THE 3RD DIVISION ATTACKING THE HEAVY WATER PLANT AT RJUKEN. PART OF THE 1ST DIVISION ATTACK WAS SUCCESSFUL, BUT THE 92ND'S BOMBS FELL ABOUT 1500 YARDS SOUTHWEST OF THE MPI. ONLY 12 A/C BOMBED, THE REMAINDER JETTESING OR RETURNING EARLY. THE AIRCRAFT PILOTED BY JOSEPH F. THORNTON OF THE 407th SQUADRON FAILED TO RETURN.

Sgt. Dean Sommers, ball turret gunner on this mission:

I had a cold at this time but this mission was supposed to be one of those "milk runs" so I decided to go along rather than turn in to sick bay. We were hit going into the target. We were 15 or 20 miles off the coast when they got us.

Two enemy fighters put some 20mm stuff into #3 engine and hit my ball turret. I got some scratches and fragments from some of that 20mm stuff, but nothing bad. I got a good hit on my nose and there still is a knot there, a chipped piece of bone, I guess. No one else got a scratch and we all bailed out safely and were captured except the navigator. He was exchanged later on.

We began to straggle, the #3 engine was bad and then the prop started to run away, but we thought we could make it to the target. We had a peculiar situation. When the prop started running away, the pilot said something about everybody being alert. But down in the ball and the rest of the stations, we didn't know what was going on. Every little bit we'd hear the pilot call the navigator and get no answer. This was after we dropped our bombs. Finally they sent the engineer down to see what was wrong with the navigator. When the engineer got there the bombardier was sitting there with his headset off and just staring. He had his hands to his face. The

171

engineer looked down and saw that the escape hatch was gone. We didn't have a navigator — he was gone! Come to find out, he had left when the pilot gave the first alert. When the pilot had called him, he had in mind getting a course for Sweden. He didn't think we could make it all the way back. We lost a lot of time. The navigator did get to Sweden. The Norwegians hid him out and got him to Sweden. This was in November and days were short. We'd have had a good chance but we'd gone a long ways while the pilot was trying to get hold of the navigator to get us a fix.

We all landed safe. I had no sensation of falling after the chute opened up, but that ground hit you just like that! It was a little after noon. We were to hit the target just after 12 so all the workers would be at lunch or be out of the target area.

The tail gunner, Rolland Gallaway, and I landed close by. He was tangled up on a bridge. We walked up a little hill and looked down in the valley and saw a little farm house. It was a sunny afternoon. We watched the house for any activity for a while and we saw this Norwegian man get his horse and wagon and go someplace leaving his wife and kids running around doing chores. It appeared there were no Germans, so we thought we would go down and make contact with these people just before dark. We went down and went through all kinds of antics explaining that we were flyers, pilots, etc. The lady was very scared. She kept shaking her head and saying "NO." Of course we could not understand. There were three little kids, all girls from six to twelve, all blonde. The seemed to be enjoying it. They were smiling, but the mother was scared, so we left then. We didn't know which way to go. We came to a lake after a while and followed it around. It was beginning to get dark and there was a house and a light. We knocked on the door and these people invited us in. An older couple and a younger woman in her late 30's. They fed us, but we still could not communicate. When we had finished, a younger lady and her husband came in. She could speak broken English and told us that they had one of our men who had hurt his arm. That is where they had been. Eventually we found that the first Norwegian had planned to leave with his horse and wagon to help pick up our crewmate, but he said that he would take us to him. It was about six o'clock I guess. They took us back in the woods where we came to a little hay shed. They had Lt. Carmell, our bombardier, in there. He had caught his arm in his chute harness and hurt it so they were going for a doctor. Eventually the doctor came and he could speak English. Carmell's arm was dislocated and we had a heck of a time getting that arm back in place. We took a board, tied it to him and put a rope around him. The doctor said to hold him and he took a belt and tied around his arm and that big Norwegian doctor began to pull in a circular motion. He broke that belt, but did get the arm back in place. From our escape kit we gave Lt. Carmell a shot of morphine for the pain and we laid him down in the hay. Sometime during the night I heard someone say, "Dean, Dean." That turned out to be Mike Dennis, the radio operator. He had landed in one of the several lakes in the area. The

Norwegians had fished him out of the lake and dried his clothes.

The grapevine must have been working pretty good because they got four of us grouped together that night. Then way before daylight here come one of the Norwegians back, the one whose wife was so scared. I know why she was so frightened now — because he was helping us. They loaded us up in his wagon, took us way back in the hills, and gave us some hot milk and potato cakes. He indicated by his watch he would be back sometime that night. We spent the whole day sitting up on that hill. We were in a pretty tight situation and we knew and the Norwegians knew it. Our bombardier was having a hard time of it. He was cold, his arm hurt, and he wanted to build a fire.

We saw some people way across the canyon moving around. Well, it wasn't long until we could hear Germans. They had a search party out. They were coming down the valley looking for us. We all ran like hell and hid in the trees. Some of the search party came within 100 yards of us. I had been on sick call the day before the mission as I had a bad cold, but when I heard about this milk run up to Norway I thought I could go on that one. After a night and a day in the cold I had a fever, but I was not ready to build a damn fire. The other guys tried to talk me into going down and give myself up for fear I would catch pneumonia. But I didn't want that. So we sat up among the rocks that night and the next day it began to snow., and here comes the Norwegian with a sled. He put us in his sled and took us down to the barn and we slept in his barn that night.

Before daylight the next morning we loaded up in his sled again and he took us to another hay barn. Now I've lost track of the days, but one day a fellow came there who could speak very little English, but he had a letter from a school teacher who could. They were going to try and get us into the interior of Norway which they called back up in the mountains. There would be an old bus that we could hide in at a certain time, and wherever they would let us out we would find a cabin. We'd have to break into it but there would be supplies there so we'd be able to stay during the winter months. They said they could not get us across the mountains and into Sweden because of the winter, and because of the enemy they would have to sneak us across rather than use any public roads. They said we could stay there that winter.

I assume this was about the fifth day. We kept waiting for the bus and the next day the Norwegians came back and said they had found our pilot, Thornton, and they were going to bring him over and take him with us. That would make five.

During the day we would leave the shed and go up on the hillside and hide among the trees and bushes so we would be hidden in case the Germans came through hunting for us. The day after the Norwegians left nobody came by so we headed for our hiding places before daylight. Shortly after daylight the Germans came and caught us, Mike Dennis, Art Carmell, and myself. Rolland Galloway had gone further into the brush and timber to

173

relieve himself. The Germans took us to the hut and they kept putting up four fingers, indicating there should be four of us. We knew what they but said and did nothing. They didn't spend any more time there. They took the three of us, with our hands over our heads, and marched us about a mile to a farm house. This farm was the headquarters for the search. We had managed to evade capture for seven days. We were taken to a little town, the name of which I do not recall, and were put in jail. Sgts. Otto Trammer and Charles Hartnett were already there in jail. They had been picked up almost immediately. Lt. Bray, the co-pilot, and our pilot, Joe Thornton, had been picked up right away also.

We found out later on that right after Lt. Thornton had been caught, they had taken his clothes away from him. The Germans told us that Thornton had come through this small village looking and asking if anyone had seen us. No one had. When we were interrogated, it was by a tall guy who could speak good English. It was he who had put on Thornton's clothes and made that pass through the village to see if he could smoke us out.

Meantime, Galloway, the tail gunner, said the Germans criss-crossed that hill all day long and stepped on every bush except the one he was hiding in. After dark that night he went back to this hay shed to sleep until about midnight, then headed for other parts. Well, he was laying in that hay pile, all covered over. Soon he heard somebody come up — it was a German. This German carried a metal case. He got up on that hay mound, took his bayonet and jabbed around here and there into the hay. He was satisfied no one was there, sat down and opened his case and took out some bread and bologna. After this he decided to bed down for the night in the hay, so he started to dig down in the hay and bury himself, just like Galloway had done. The German made a few scoops with his hands and there was Galloway. It scared the hell out of the German when Galloway said, "I guess you got me." When the German had punched into the hay with his bayonet he had put a small nick in Galloway's ear. When the German recovered, he marched our tail gunner down to join us.

We were taken to Oslo and put in solitary confinement for a few days. In fact we spent Thanksgiving Day in solitary. Our next ride was on an old dirty boat that took us to Denmark. We next went to Frankfurt, Germany, the centralized interrogation point for all prisoners. Again we were in solitary for three more days. Our interrogation did not amount to much, really. By this time they knew more than we did. The guy in the interrogation room opened up a big book about the 92nd Bomb Group. About the only thing I think I knew that he didn't was that the 92nd was experimenting with the pathfinder group — a radar group. Other than that, he told me more than I knew.

It was early December when we got to Krems, Austria. I do not know how many miles it is, but it is a long way in those little cattle cars. They had a double deck. One deck was up about high enough that you could crawl under there and sleep. There was another group above. Out by the door they had

174

kind of a sand box with a fire so you could heat up your soup, etc.

We were in Krems until April 8th, 1945. At that time the Russians were already in Vienna. We could hear guns and at night you could see fires. This was Stalag 17. On the 8th of April we hit the road. The Germans said they didn't want the Russians to get us and they were going to turn us over to the American Army. We were going along the Danube when we heard that President Roosevelt had died. We marched all the way to Braunell, Hitler's home area. We crossed a river and were at a junction of two rivers. The Germans cut a circle around a patch of woods to observe us, I guess, in case we tried to escape. They told us we would be better off if we stayed together in the group. We had guys escape, though, the first couple of days and after they were out a few days they were caught and brought back, and darn glad to get back. The Austrian people and even the German guards weren't much better off than we were. The S.S. had already gone through the area cleaning everything out — they didn't want to leave anything for the Russians. There wasn't hardly anything to scrounge. After we'd been on the road for a week, one of these Red Cross truck caravans came out of Geneva with parcels. The Swiss heard we were being marched in that area so we got Red Cross parcels — two men to a parcel.

These were mean days, especially when you were marching. The first few days it was hot and some of the guys threw their O.D. coats away. Then it began to rain. It rained night and day — just enough to keep you soaked. After that we were in a wooded area and we made lean-tos. It snowed a little.

On our march we took the back roads and bypaths. The main roads were congested with German Army and civilians. We came through Lenz, Austria. We saw a sight at Lenz. One afternoon just before dark we came to a factory and industrial area. We had to bed down there for the night, sleeping in bomb craters, etc — there were a lot of them around there. The next morning the Germans took us through the town. The guards asked us to be very military like and not be smarting off because the people were quite hostile to American flyers as they had been bombed quite often. We were the American air gangsters. After we got all the way through the town and out on the west side, we started to meet guys from the concentration camp going into town to work in the factories. That was a pitiful sight. Some of them were so weak that their buddies were trying to carry them. We were the second group through that morning. The group ahead of us said that the guards had a wagon out there to pick up the ones who fell and could not get up. The S.S. would club them to death then pick up their bodies by the head and feet and throw them on the wagon like a sack of feed. Eventually we went on by the camp and out from there a ways we saw a lot of women and children. The children ranged from very small on up. A pitiful sight and we realized that those children had never known anything but cruelty and starvation all of their short lives.

On May the 2nd, the 13th Armored Division came up to us. And what a great sight that was to see. We were turned over to the Army, who then arranged to have us flown out of that area to Nancy, France. They had what they called a tramp camp. All of our clothes were taken away from us, and we, and the clothes, were deloused. We went by train to a camp called "LUCKY STRIKE", which was near LeHarve. This was another staging area, a tent city. They said that there were 40,000 of us there. Eventually we caught a boat out of LeHarve. It was nearly June. I didn't get home until the 16th of June.

I had been a P.O.W. for eighteen months. It had taken me eighteen months to finish my eighteenth mission. Some of the guys on my crew had 19 or 20 missions. The navigator who had bailed out had one or two more than I. Our original bombardier only made five missions and was grounded. We never had a regular navigator or bombardier. We dropped as a group, so we had the gunner as a toggler drop the bombs on signal from the Lead Group or Lead Bombardier.

Sgt. Dean Sommers related some event that took place at Stalag 17-B during his eighteen months stay:

The Red Cross gave out large bound books that had blank pages in them. We could write down in them anything we thought important — names, poems, drawings and the like. There was one guy in our compound that was a real artist, a guy named Phelper. In prison camp we had all kinds of guys and all kinds of talent. I think this Phelper had been with Disney. A couple of the guys in the compound made up the stage play script that later became the movie, *Stalag 17,* with William Holden.

We had about 130 men in our end of the barracks which was "A" end. In "B" end there were less because that end had a common wash room with troughs and spigots to wash in, also the latrine. I seem to recall we had about 150 in a barracks. I could be wrong.

It was a drag. We slept a lot. When we got books we did a lot or reading, had classes organized and did a few plays. I remember doing *Charlie's Aunt* and *The Man Who Came to Dinner.* We also had a nice band when we got musical instruments. A fellow named Baker, who was a professional from around St. Louis, was a real trumpet player. When we got musical arrangements he had a fine band. He was Paul Baker who passed away in Texas a few years ago.

Hartnett and I pooled our Red Cross parcels. What allotment the Germans gave us was handled in the kitchen. Rutabaga soup, and not much more, was our standby. Once in a while we'd get a stew with some kind of meat in it. We'd have been in bad shape if it weren't for the Red Cross parcels. We got hungry a lot of times, but it was not critical or severe. When we were short of Red Cross parcels the Germans would tell us, "If your planes would not bomb the trains your parcels would be here." As it was we were to get one parcel a week, and sometimes we would go two or three weeks without a parcel. The Red Cross parcels kept us in as good a shape as we were in, though we did lose weight. Surprisingly there was not too much

176

sickness, and as I recall, not many deaths from natural causes — one or two. Two or three were shot.

Through the winter of 1944 and into the spring of 1945 the Germans carried dead Russians from the compound every day. Out in a wooded area there was a cemetery. The procession had to come right by our compound, and there was hardly a morning they didn't come by carrying a dead Russian or two. The Russians were dying from disease and starvation, and the Germans shot a few of them. The Germans had a warning wire betweeen the American compound and the Russian compound and there was a 50 yard no-man's land in between. Our boys would crowd that line real close and try to throw packages of cigarettes over to them. The Russians would sometimes pick up an onion or some beans or something and there would be some trading back and forth. The Russians would even come up with pipes and knives, etc. I guess they would steal them when they were out on work details. If a pack of cigarettes would land between the warning wire, the Russians would make a dash for it and the Germans would, of course, shoot at them. Sometimes they would miss and sometimes a Russian would be killed, but the body would be left laying there most of the day while the Germans investigated the incident.

On of our guys got it one day. He'd had some problems and was losing hold of himself. The Germans had had him up in the hospital and back to camp. One day he and a guard were on the way to the hospital again and he tried climbing a fence right by a guard tower. The tower guard shot and killed him. The escort guard had yelled not to shoot because he was crazy, but the tower guard shot him anyhow.

Another guy got killed right in the barracks. Some guys had some wire cutters out one night and were trying to cut some wires to escape when the lights went on and they got scared and made a run for the barracks. The guards started shooting at them and a guy in the barracks was killed by a stray bullet.

Date: 17 November 1943
Target: St. Nazaire
Narrator: Forrest Norman
Group: 303rd, 385th Bomb Group

President Franklin Roosevelt, Prime Minister Winston Churchill, and their top advisers met at Casablanca, French Morocco in January 1943 to outline the strategy to be used to defeat the Axis powers. General Ira Eaker proposed the British by night, the American by day "round the clock" bombing of Axis targets. A system of target priorities was agreed on by the Combined Chiefs of Staff, advised by industrial analysts. In order of priority, they were the German submarine construction yards, aircraft industry, transportation, oil industry and other war-related industry.

The Eaker plan, officially called "The Combined Bomber Offensive from the United Kingdom," with some modifications, was approved by the Combined Chiefs of Staff in May, 1943, with the codeword "Pointblank".

One of the intermediate objectives was the need for the destruction of the German fighter strength. It being necessary to get the bombers to the targets with their bomb loads before the main objective could be realized. The Luftwaffe had to be neutralized. By means of direct confrontation as well as destruction of aircraft factories and those factories manufacturing aircraft components, and the fuel they required.

The operations by Allied Bomber Offensive was aimed at one thing, the future invasion of the continent. The Combined Bomber Offensive was geared for the destruction of the German war machine and thus remove its ability to wage war.

The selection of targets was not a hit or miss proposition, but well-planned, with secondary and alternate targets for each bombing mission. Every mission had to be a paying proposition, some target aiding the Axis war effort had to be destroyed or damaged. The Germans were, however, able to disperse a great deal of the aircraft manufacturing industry.

Under the Speer Ministry the Jaegerstab (Fighter-Staff) countered the raids by reorganizing inefficient management, reducing the

178

number of types of planes and, most important of all, in subdividing production into small units that were comparatively immune from attack. This seemed to work well, for the German Air Force accepted a total of 39,807 aircraft of all types in 1944, compared with 15,596 in 1942. Even so the Luftwaffe was not a serious threat to Allied superiority during the winter of 1944. The attacks were escorted by P-51's and P-47's. They were now instructed to not only protect the bombers, but to invite opposition from German fighter forces and to engage them at every opportunity.

Sgt. Forrest "Pete" Norman, Tail Gunner, 303rd Bomb Group, became a "Lucky Bastard," a Goldfish as well as a Caterpillar on his tour with the 8th Air Force. He flew missions with the 303rd Bomb Group, the 385th as well as the 2nd Replacement and Training Squadron. When he finished his regular tour as a combat gunner with the 8th he then went to the 9th Air Force in the supply and evacuation squadron as an engineer.

"Pete" was a short, wiry man, very quick and alert and very hard to get down. On a mission to the sub pens at St. Nazaire, November 17, 1942, the Germans put up an accurate flak barrage, but all planes returned to base. Sgt. Norman returned to base very briefly before going to the hospital for treatment for flak wounds on the foot and right arm. He returned from the hospital to join the 2nd Replacement Squadron for several missions before going back to the 303rd, where his station was changed to top turret from tail gunner.

January 1943 found him flying with the 385th Group on the long mission to Wilhemshaven. This was a terrific fighter battle and plenty of flak added in to make it more interesting. Fifty to 75 enemy fighters were encountered, with 22 claimed by the bombers.

March 18, 1943 was a "milk run" to Vegasack. Once more the Germans put up an accurate flak barrage. Within a few minutes "Pete" Norman's B-17 had numbers one and four engines shot out by flak. The pilot tried to get out along the enemy coast, but enemy fighters found them, as they usually did, and finished the crippled B-17 off. Sgt. Norman had his top turret shot up. It collapsed on him, breaking both of his legs. He also said the Germans strafed them as they drifted down in their chutes. Bombardier Lt. Strobel was lost on this mission, and Sgt. Norman was to spend six more months in the hospital.

When his hospital "tour" was over, Sgt. "Pete" Norman returned to combat with the 385th Bomb Group and flew on the October 10th Mission to Munster which was a disaster for some groups.

The B-17 Sgt. Norman rode in suffered damage to the hydraulic system as well as the electrical system, and 20mm hits damaged the vertical stabilizer. The rugged B-17 was flown on and landed safely at the base at Great Ashfield. As it happened to Sgt. Norman at Vegasack, a crew that was forced to bail out of plane number 155, was fired on in their chutes by an Me 109.

The second mission to Schweinfurt, well known to those who flew that day as "Black Thursday," was also flown by "Pete" Norman. Flying as tail gunner on this mission it seemed like the Germans had it in for "Pete". Fighters came in at this ship and so many others in this second air battle over the ball bearing plants. His plane suffered damage to one engine and a FW 190 came in on the tail position and "Pete" Norman was determined that he was going to "bust this German's ass". The 190 came in from about five-thirty and the twin guns of Sgt. Norman fed a steady stream of .50 caliber death at that enemy fighter. The German was determined as well to send this B-17 to the ground. Sgt. Norman won the battle and the 190 went down in flames, but not before doing severe damage to one of the twin 50 guns, the same shell cutting a long gash in Sgt. Norman's right arm. The left waist gunner, Sgt. Tomosko, was badly hit, and before anyone could offer him aide he bled to death at his gun.

On D-Day, June 6, 1944, Sgt. Forrest "Pete" Norman again took to his chute and was fished from the English Channel, and later with due ceremony was awarded membership in The Goldfish Club.

In talking with the veterans that went on the bomber missions many subjects were covered.

"Pete" Norman was not a great admirer of the electric flying suit. He states:

We had electric flying suits. In the tail they were not so good. When I sat, it burned my butt, and when I bent my arms at the elbow it burned there too, so I put paper in there." Asked if it was cold. "Cold? I hope to tell you. I had a malfunction on my gun and took my glove off, and when I touched the gun my finger stuck to the gun. I pulled my finger away and a piece of skin stuck onto the gun.

I always took good care of my guns too, because the guns could save my life. And if they did not work you were helpless. I would take the feeding pawls on my guns and shine them with crocus cloth. And when I came back from a mission I would clean my guns and keep them under my bed.

You could use a set of barrels up in a couple of missions or even one if you used them continually, but if you did not use them a lot they would last pretty good. My ammo belts were loaded — one tracer, three armor piercing, incendiary and then tracer again. Most side gunners fired by tracer rather than sights as you did not have much time to use sights, that is until we got that optical sight and it was a fine sight.

I got a lot of shots from my tail gun position at first. They really worked on the tail, but then they started coming head on. They wanted to get the engines. We only had about 60% field and not much time to aim and shoot. The top turret gunner would call the E/A off to us as he could see pretty good. He'd call one coming in at 7 o'clock so I'd swing that way and wait for him to come and fire at him going away. We just had a little window to see out of and it was steamed up and smoked up from the guns. It was like shooting quail with a rifle.

Once when we had fighter escort, one officer at debriefing held up four fifty caliber slugs and said, 'Anybody know what these are? Well,' he said, 'those came through into my cockpit. You damn shoot-happy gunners lay off them S. O. B.'s when they come up to you. You're going to knock off our own people.' So we were pretty careful, though I've seen Germans come right up into the group and fly with us. They were sending our speed, altitude, direction and that sort of information to the ground. If it would have been over our territory he might not have been so brave. If we shot him down he would be picked up by his own people, but over our country he would not have stuck his neck out.

Sgt. Robert Maddox enlisted from Bakersfield, California in September of 1942. After basic training he was scheduled for link training, but there were no openings and he ended up at Radio school at Scott Field, Bellville, Illinois. He volunteered for gunnery school and was sent to Harlingen, Texas. A barracks mate of his was killed in a training accident and Bob was terminated to accompany his barrack mate's body to Salina, Kansas. Shipped up to Ephrata, Washington, he became a member of a bomber crew with a pilot who was a graduate of West Point, but who was pulled after third Phase training to become a Group leader.

Sgt. Maddox got a new pilot who had already been through training.

We had no idea where his crew was or what became of them. His name was Charles Cole and he was from Colby, Kansas. He could fly rings around the West Pointer. He was a 1st Lieutenant. We went on up to Walla Walla, Washington for more training then down to Kearney, Nebraska, where we were to leave with another group for overseas, but out pilot got sick so they sent us up to Grand Island, Nebraska by ourselves. When the pilot got well we flew solo to Philadelphia and then on to Bangor, Maine. Ours was a new plane, but it was one of the O.D. colored ones.

When we arrived at Bangor they'd had three feet of snow and when they plowed the field they had not plowed enough space at the end of the runway to turn the plane around, so our pilot had to gun the engines to get it turned around by sliding the tail. It was slick and the tail slid into the snow bank, so we had to push it back around by hand. When we did this we found two big holes in the tail. The pilot and co-pilot talked it over with us all, and they decided to go on with a damaged aircraft since probably the pilot would have been fined for damaging government property. We left for Labrador and laid over at Gandor for three days while the tail was repaired.

We picked up an extra crew. I do not know what became of their airplane. Anyhow, we had just half enough oxygen outlets for our trip over the big pond to Prestwick, Scotland. When you are on oxygen things are fine, but when you do not have any, there is no sensation, you just keep on breathing but have an urge to sleep. If you do not get any oxygen, that is what you do, just go to sleep — permanently. We had to swap oxygen outlets among us

182

for six hours while we flew over 16,000 feet.

Sgt. Maddox relates that oxygen outlets were exchanged every three or four minutes among the two crews until a weather front had been cleared and Pilot Cole was able to drop down to five thousand feet where no oxygen was needed.

Arriving at Stone, England the pilot went to a school to get updated on procedures and the crew went to other schools. Sgt. Bob Maddox went to Radio School for a brush up to learn new radio procedures for the combat zone: frequencies, codes, tuning, etc. The planes at this time were equipped with tuning boxes that had the required frequencies installed already. When the plane went out on a mission they would use one frequency and a different one on the return trip. There was no effort made to tune in, just put in a different tuning box. Sgt. Maddox quotes:

They sent a message from our base every thirty minutes, and I had to keep a log of these. If I did not have every broadcast recorded I caught all Billy Hell. The broadcasts were not of any great importance as a rule, usually weather or inconsequential stuff. However, they wanted us to handle these broadcasts just in case they did have important information. One trip we did get an order for a diversion to the sub pens at Wilhelmshaven.

But back to Stone: we spent a week there, then were sent to the 335th Bomb Squadron, 95th Bomb Group at Horham. Lt. Cole flew several days to familiarize himself with the area and the other fields, tower procedures, emergency procedures and things like that. When he was done with that, we were considered ready to go. And our first mission was on January 1, 1944 to Paris.

Bob Maddox tells what went on at the briefing:

You are posted for a mission the night before. There is a red flag flying over Squadron Headquarters if the squadron is flying the next day and if you are posted for that mission you go to bed early. A guy wakes you up and you go to the mess hall about 0300. Oh, you would so like to get a couple more winks of sleep, but you are a bit tense, too, so up you get and on with the flying clothes and on to chow. One good thing was the meal, you had your eggs prepared the way you want them and with bacon or ham or both or sausage, whatever tickles your taste buds. It might be your last good meal period, or maybe the last one for a long time. So you eat for those reasons if no other.

The whole crew went to a general briefing to see what the target was. Here's a big wall with a map all covered up. When they pulled the cover back there was a red string from our base to our target, the longer the string the bigger the groan. There was always a groan. When they uncovered the map for the Brunswick mission there was a LOUD groan. We had been there before and no one felt good about it.

We also learned what to expect in the way of flak, enemy fighter opposition and where we would pick up our own fighter escort, if any. We would also be warned to familiarize ourselves with our escort types as our own escorts had often times been shot at and even downed by bomber crews. The fighter pilots were also cautioned not to come straight into a bomber formation, but to come in sideways as a P-51 could very well be mistaken for an ME-109.

After a general briefing, the pilot, co-pilot and navigator went to separate briefings, radio operators to another, where I got the radio code sheets and frequencies. Then I would check out my .50 caliber gun and I would install it in an open hatch above the radio room. We also got an escape kit which we also had to check out. The kit had money, maps, and compass, they were sealed, and if you brought one back unsealed, you were in trouble. I never got a chance to open one.

On the Brunswick raid I got up front with the truck driver when he picked us up to take us to our hardstand. This particular morning was a bad morning. It was cold and spitting snow. I did not know this would be my last ride for a long time. Anyhow, when we got to the plane and assembled our guns, we waited for our turn to take-off. Every thirty seconds a plane took off. On this day we had one crash on take-off. Assembly was as usual, fly circling until altitude. We flew over the Zuider Zee, Holland to Germany.

I had no different feeling on this mission than any others. Maybe the first one was worst, though. We came in all shot up by flak and fighters, in bad shape. But this one had no feeling of pending disaster. On our previous mission to Brunswick we found on returning and in the landing pattern, we had only one wheel down and we only had three engines. We just barely made it up again. That B-17 did shake and shudder. I could see trees going by, looking through the top gun hatch of that plane. When we got up again we were low on gas. We cranked the wheel as far as we could, about one quarter of the way down. Lt. Cole told us we had fuel for one more turn so, "Lock that wheel in place and get to crash landing positions." Lt. Cole did a fantastic job of landing that B-17 on one wheel and with only three engines and kept it up on that one wheel until we had slowed down as much as it could, then the wing dropped down and the props went into the ground. We slid off the runway. That scared hell out of us. That was our first crash landing.

Sgt. Maddox related more close calls:

One other time we picked up some 20mm shell hits. We did not get any struts or spars, though. Usually we were going into the sun so the enemy aircraft would fly high and parallel to us then come around and hit us head on. But they would and did, at times, come from all directions. A couple of times we got hit by the "Abbeyville Kids." They would hit you just before you got to the Channel and sometimes after. They got our wing plane one time. Once it was so quick, we were in the landing pattern and they shot down a plane in back of us. I don't know if this was the "Abbeyville Kids" or not, but they sure had nerve. A couple of deals like that put everybody on their toes. Usually when you reached the Channel you kind of relaxed.

Continuing on the February 10 mission to Brunswick, Sgt. Maddox said:

They jumped us going into Germany. If we had an escort that day, they had not picked us up yet. The first I was aware from my position, which did not give you much vision, my gun was on a manual swivel-not turret. The crew started to call, "Fighters, fighters high, 2 o'clock!" I could see them out my hatch, but they made their turn and came through the squadron, and it is incredible how fast they came through. We got hit once on the first pass and caught fire on the right wing. It seemed like no time at all and they were through again and we got hit on the other wing. At that time I could not get anybody on the intercom. I could not find out how bad we were hit. I turned around and opened the bomb bay door. I was going to see what was going on up front and possibly go up there. When I opened the bomb bay door the fire was coming from the wing into the bomb bay. I just figured it was time! I was excited. I did not wear my chute. It was on the radio. I picked up my chute, a chest type, snapped it on. I forgot to break by oxygen connection, which would normally have broken. I started dead away and came to the end of that oxygen tube and came right back to the radio room. So I had to undo that. By that time It was beginning to be a real rough ride. I made it to the ball turret and the gunner was not up yet. I pounded my foot on it but he still did not come out. I had to go on. I then got to the waist, one waist gunner was just standing there watching the fire. One was kneeling at the door having kicked it out. He had hold of both sides of the door jam, but would not go out. We were flying as 32,000 feet, But I didn't figure I could stand around very long This fellow at the door kneeling was an original crewman and I hollered at him, "LET'S GO!" By now the fire was going clear to the tail. He still did nothing. He had his chute on, the plane banked way up to the left. When it came back down level I kicked him out and I right behind him!

The other waist gunner was still standing at the other door when I left. The plane went up and over and down and into a flat spin. The other fellows who got out were lucky. I did not see the plane break in two. The other fellows told me about it later. That flat spin held the other guys in until the plane was about halfway to the ground before they could get out. The other waist gunner; Sgt. Maddox; the ball turret gunner, Sgt. Sam Johnson; and the tail gunner, Sgt. Cerniglia; got out after the plane broke in two. Sgt. Kushnerick made it out somehow. Lt. Graffe, the bombardier, went out a large hole in the plexiglass nose of the plane. Lt. McKenna, Navigator; Lt. Cole, Pilot; and Lt. Boswell, the Co-pilot, were killed. We had lost three men.

At training sessions they had harped to us about delaying opening of our chutes because in a group of bombers you could drift into another plane and that would be it. They said watch the ground and when you think you are getting pretty close, then pull the rip cord. But you're not experienced so you do not know what to expect or what happens. Well, the first thing, it becomes awfully quiet. You're used to a lot of noise, engines, guns, fighters coming through your squadron, etc. It suddenly got real quiet. I had no sense of falling, just the air going by and no sense of turning. It seemed to me I was still and the ground was going around me. I watched the ground go by once, then twice, and I began to see a little difference. The third time it went by, buildings began to stand out and I could see the Zieder Zee and the trees alongside it. I thought now is the time. I pulled the rip cord. I was up pretty high. It jerked me hard and I lost one shoe and a flying boot. I had never jumped before so I did not know how it worked. I looked at the rip cord, nothing happened! I threw it away and said outloud, "The son of a bitch isn't going to open." I just started to reach for the chute pack and a little white thing came out and the chute came out and darned near cut me in two. It was good I did not free fall anymore as I was drifting over the Zuider Zee. I went over a farm house and just about cleared a tree, but hit a big limb in a tree and broke four ribs right at the back bone. I had turned away to protect my face, but when I hit that tree I was also knocked out. When I came to there· was a Home Guard watching me with a gun pointed at me. It took me a long time to get out of that tree because of the chute harness and I was hurt and it was a big tree.

There was quite a group of Dutch civilians watching the goings on. The Home Guard took all my possessions, escape kit, candy bars, everything. A little Dutch boy saw I had only one shoe and he ran to the house and brought out a wooden shoe for me — it cost him dearly. The German Home Guard hit him with the butt of that gun and knocked him sprawling. And the Guard made him take the shoe back to the house. I had to walk a couple miles to the nearest village in the snow with one foot in just a sock.

I did see our plane hit the ground and explode. Several went down on that mission, but not as soon as ours did. Our plane had a figure of a stork carrying a bomb in a diaper and 'NO EXCUSE' painted on the side. We had a full bomb load when we went down.

This was the beginning of a very long and painful ordeal for Sgt. Bob Maddox. In his words:

We were taken to a small town and stripped of all our clothes. They kept some of them apart and gave part of them back, but not after they gave us a going over, even to examining our rectums. At a small jail near the railroad station is where I first saw some of the crew, the tail gunner and the ball turret gunner. I did not see the rest of the crew for some time later. Here we stayed overnight and the next day we were put on a train and taken to a German air base where we were locked in a machine shop in a hangar. I slept on a metal work bench the first night here. The next morning the hangar was full of airmen. They had been coming in all night. I still just had only a sock on one foot and my ribs were really hurting, but nothing to what I would hurt before I got them fixed.

We all were shipped to a Dulag Luft for interrogation. And of course it was solitary confinement in narrow cells, a cot, no window, but with a light. We each got a form to fill out to send to the Red Cross to notify the U.S. Government that you were a POW. I sat for three days in that room before I was called in for interrogation on the fourth day.

The guy sat at a desk with a number of chairs like a waiting room. He said, "Take a seat over there. I'll be with you in a minute." He worked for a while, a lot of conversation, some of this for my benefit I think. "Come on over here. We have to talk to you," he said. He started with, "Where you from? What base you from?" I said, "I can't tell you that information." I just gave him my name, rank and serial number. He jumped right straight out of that chair and yelled at me, "Don't you speak to me like that! You address me as Sir!" He changed from friendly to very angry in a split second. And those Germans know how to holler. He said, "You better give me some information." He wanted the names of my crew, target, base and that sort of thing. He then added, "If you don't give me that information I will turn you over to the Gestapo." I said, "I can't do that." And he said, "We'll see." They took me back to the cubby hole in solitary where I sat for two more days. I went through this same procedure again, then the third time he brought me in he said, "Who the hell you think you are? Hap Arnold?" He went on, "All we have to do is identify you and put you in a prison camp. I don't know, you might be a damn spy."

I had thought before on the other trips to his office that I could not tell him anything anyhow. I didn't know anything. He knew as much as I did. He said, "You won't tell me so I'll tell you. Your pilot, co-pilot and navigator are dead. One of the others is hurt bad but is going to live. You were flying with the 95th Bomb Group and your target was Brunswick. Isn't that right?" I said yes. He said, "You could have told me that to begin with and we wouldn't have had to go through all this."

But when I was sitting in that cubby hole I had a lot of time to think. I just could not see where I could tell him anything that would do him any good or that he did not already know. I was a Sergeant, I had no classified information. I was scared, so I did what I was told, and I was still hurting real bad from those busted ribs. I told them about my ribs and they said I would get medical attention when I got to where I was going. Up to now I had not received any medical attention. The time I spent in the cubby hole did me good because I rested. I laid down and I guess the ribs started to knit and they moved me out of the interrogation section to a shipping area. Here were all my buddies. We had to stay there two days or maybe three. I learned here about the plane breaking in two.

We were sleeping on old bunk beds with four or five slats covered by a big sack of straw. One night I raised up and coughed at the same time, and it felt like someone stuck a knife in me. I had busted those ribs all loose again. Just about that time they shipped us out of there on box cars. We spent two weeks in those box cars. They divided the cars in the middle, with prisoners on one side and guards on the other. We were packed in so tight we had to take turns sitting down and standing up. This was in February, it was cold and we had no heat. We rode through Poland into East Prussia. The nearest town I could hear the Germans talk about was Memol.

We got an issue of old black bread and a bowl or can of soup each day. That's all you got out of the Germans was one meal a day. The Red Cross supplemented that. At the interrogation center we had received a cardboard box, like a suitcase, from the Red Cross and it had a toothbrush, razor, soap, a pair of pajamas and other toilet articles that we needed badly. It was a good sized box. After we got into the camps we got playing cards, musical instruments, etc. And of course in the very important Red Cross parcels there were G.I. shoes, overcoats and that kind of stuff. In transit we got nothing. Memol was a good sized camp and was a new camp. There were large sized barracks and in those there were two large brick stoves that were really something. If they want to conserve fuel nowadays they should talk to those people that built those places. Up there they built the stove like a miniature L. The bottom leg was not as long as the letter L, but it had a little fire box at that end. You could put coke or coal or whatever they gave you to burn, and the flue went all the way through this L shaped stove. Forty or so feet long and four feet square. There was one on each end of the barracks building. And it took about three days for that sucker to get warm, but once it got warm it did a good job on a minimum of fuel. We learned after we had been there awhile, that the way to get our feet warm was to get on top of that stove in our bare feet.

I'll never forget the 31st day of March, 1944. We were locked up in the barracks at 4 o'clock, as it got dark early and they wanted us locked up after dark. It was snowing then. There was maybe three or four inches of snow on the ground. In the morning when the Germans opened the door of the barracks, everybody was absolutely amazed — there was three feet of snow on the ground.

188

We used to have to go out and stand roll call in the snow and if they couldn't get their count straight, you would stand and you would stand and you would stand and your feet would get like two icicles. So as soon as they would get the count straight, everybody would turn and run as hard as they could go to get on top of that stove. There were fifty men all trying to get on top of those stoves at once. Not everybody could stand on top, but a lot of men could.

Memol was a new camp, a lot of new people were coming in and we did have touch with the outside world. It was winter time and we just hadn't gotten organized. It was a permanent camp and we stayed there for some time. It wasn't until the Russian front became a threat that they moved us out of there. That was the next fall.

We walked out of there to a port where the Germans loaded us on a ship, which was a lousy deal. It was a freighter with a big black hole (hold). They had issued us duffle bags, smaller than our Army duffle bag. We got these at camp and we were to put all our belongings in them — everything. When we got to the boat, they ran us up the gangplank and said, "Put your bag there." Everyone wanted to know how they were going to find their own bag. They told us not to worry. We would each get a bag and we could trade around until we found our own bag. We did have our name on our bag. The Germans were not about to worry about something as small as mixing up a whole prison camp of men and their bags.

They put us in the hold and just kept putting more and more until there wasn't any room to turn or sit down. We were in that hold for two days with nothing to eat. They lowered water in buckets on a rope, and I think they used the same bucket to take the urine out. When we did get out of there we did not know where we were, as we had not seen daylight. There was one little hole; the one we came down through. The port we reached was Schwienemunde on the Baltic. We were all unloaded and everyone got a duffle bag, but not your own. The Germans next loaded us in boxcars and handcuffed us together in pairs. Each man had a free hand to carry his duffle bag. While we were in those box cars there was a bombing raid in the rail yards. That was miserable. The bombs hit all around us and the Germans just let us sit there. We were locked and chained together and couldn't get out. I guess we were real lucky we didn't get hit. The whole trip was bad. We went from there to a little town, which I don't know the name of, but when the train got there you could hear a man who sounded like a maniac hollering. They very roughly got everybody out and lined up. They said, "You are now going to run four miles to the camp and we mean run, not walk!" They had police dogs with the guards who each had rifles with fixed bayonets. They started us running down the road and ran us and ran us, and if you got off the road at all you had a police dog snipping at you or a German bayonet pointed at you. I was chained to a little Frenchman, Sam Johnson.

He got excited and dropped his pack real quick. He wanted to go real fast. I told him, "Sam, slow down. We've got four miles and just stay in the center of the road and you're not going to get stuck or you're not going to get bit." He calmed down a little bit and I held on to my pack and carried it almost to the top of a hill, and boy, I'll tell you I was beat and figured I wasn't going to make it. There were guys falling down and the Germans were bayonetting them, and the dogs were biting them. I just didn't figure I could make it with that pack. I dumped it and it wasn't another fifty yards before I could see over the hill and there was the camp. I was really sick that I had dumped my pack even though it wasn't my own. Whatever the bag held would have been mine, that is, what was left of Red Cross parcels, clothes, etc., but like most of the rest of the guys I didn't make it to the camp with a bag. I think the whole purpose behind it was that the civilians were looting the packs. There were people lined up all along the road watching this march or run. I could not see what happened after we got over the hill to the camp, but I am sure they allowed the civilians to go through all those bags and take what they wanted. The Germans were showing the population just how they treated these American Air Gangsters.

Several men died on this forced run-march, but I don't have an exact number. There was a Tennessee boy right in front of us. Through the Red Cross he had gotten a banjo and he dropped his pack but still held on to his banjo. He was just one nip ahead of a big German police dog and he kept looking over his shoulder and trying to drag the guy he was chained to. Finally, just as the dog got to where he could nip him, he hit the dog just as hard as he could with that banjo and all he had left was a little bit of the handle and the strings. I watched that whole thing develop and it was really humorous. I laughed at the time even though it was a serious situation. I couldn't help but laugh.

This was the first move we had made and it was fairly warm weather at the time. This was a new camp or one that the Germans were expanding, as we lived in tents for three or four months while they were completing another section of camp. We had quite a time in that tent area. The Germans did not have guards in the perimeter or compound at night. They turned these mean German police dogs loose to roam around at night. A tent is not much protection from a hell of a big dog. It made a difficult situation because when you had to relieve yourself at night you either had something in the tent or you were out of luck. If you stepped outside your tent the dogs would be on you immediately. But we finally got out of there and got into barracks like the ones that were shown on the TV series "Hogan's Heroes." We had a big can right in the middle we called the slop bucket for use at night. Each room had five double bunks, five slats and a round sack of straw. You had to get yourself with the slats rigged so you wouldn't fall through. We started out with ten men, then before we finished

190

we had a man on the table, a man under the table, and a man sleeping under each bed or on the floor by the bed. The Germans were unable to build barracks fast enough, and don't think they really gave a darn anyhow. We stayed in this place until the fronts started closing in again. This was Stalag Luft VI. The latter part of January 1945 they moved us out of there and from that time on until we were liberated we didn't stay any place very long. The Germans marched daily.

We went through Schwienemunde again and they ferried us across to the other side. We moved pretty steadily. I guess we must have moved 30 kilometers a day, though not every day. But right in the heart of winter they ran us into a big open field that had snow on it. It was an evening about dark. There were a bunch of other men there already. We all tried to break branches off the trees to make beds, and we had a miserable time trying to sleep.

The way we made packs on this trip was by taking a G.I. shirt, sew it across the tail and up the front, except for two buttons, and we tacked the two sleeves to the tail. If you had a towel you rolled it up for each sleeve, and poked it through there and then you took one sleeve over each arm then you tied it together using a shoe lace and this made a good pack. Your food and clothing and all your belongings were in that pack.

We'd been on the road a month, and the first month we walked I never had my shoes off. That was the longest I ever went without having my shoes off. I did take them off the first day or two but we found that when you took your shoes off, the skin of the blisters came off with the socks and your feet got worse. So the biggest part of us just left our shoes on. When they ran us into that field at night it was bitter cold. We tried to make a bed. I had a buddy named Hathaway that I was bunking with. We laid our overcoats over the tree limbs and we had two blankets left. We tried to get in the best we could and were using our packs as pillows. We climbed into that makeshift bed and cover up completely including our heads to keep warm. I was just dozing off to sleep and someone jerked my pack as well as my partner's pack right out from under us and got off with them slick and clean. By the time we got untangled we couldn't see a damn thing. That was all our worldly goods — gone. I'll tell you about being on relief and destitute! We were it. We walked for three days and we had nothing, nothing whatsoever. On the fourth day when they stopped us we found what we thought was a potato mound. Over there the farmers hollow out a pretty good sized hole in the ground. They line that with straw and put potatoes in it, and cover it with dirt. The thickness determines the temperature at which the inside air of the mound stays. They had found they could keep it cool enough to keep, yet not cold enough to freeze. They could keep them all winter that way. We found a mound and managed to dig through that thing and we could just barely reach through the dirt and straw and get hold of some potatoes. We

191

filled our pockets and our shirt and every crevice that would hold potatoes. In fact we were able to trade some of the potatoes for some of the things we didn't have, like extra clothing, cigarettes, etc. We got back into a little better shape, but the thing is, it is surprising how cold blooded everyone can be. You can be generous when you have plenty, but when you don't have anything there aren't many generous people. I really don't know what we would have done if we had not found something to eat. I guess we would have just gotten sick and starved. The Germans were giving us only one bowl of some kind of soup every now and then. And only when they had time to set up a field kitchen. On the road we did not get much of anything from the Germans as far as food goes.

We wound up in a transient camp near Magdeberg. We could hear the artillery fire that was east of us. We stayed there a couple weeks. It was the longest we stayed any place since we had started the march. We watched the artillery fire until it was noticeably closer, then they finally broke us out from there. When we got on the road and back on our walk, we met German soldiers going by us. Some were riding German tanks and coming from the west. At that time the two fronts in Germany must have been awfully close together. We were marched for five or six days and we came to the little town of Omanberg. There was a pottery factory there. As we went in to the town we got strafed. There was a railroad that came through Omanberg, and we were marching down the center of the road through the village when four big old P-47s came down and strafed a railroad engine and train and on into us. A lot of the fellows got so excited that those planes were ours, they yelled to them telling them that they were getting the train. All the while those fifty caliber bullets were hitting all around and ricocheting around us and in amongst us. No one was hurt. We ended up on the outskirts of the town in this pottery factory, which had several floors. We were held in there for a week or ten days and while we were there we were bombed.

Just down the road was a couple of benzine dumps. There was a raid by some twin-engine B-26s. They made their run on the benzine plant right over the pottery factory. The first group that hit the benzine dump laid some bombs in too close to the pottery factory. I was on the second floor of the pottery factory and when the bombs hit they broke every window in that factory. How we ever avoided mass panic I'll never know, because there was only one stairway down and there were three or four hundred men in that building. Everyone held their cool and went down this big flight of stairs, and when we stepped out the door there was a great big smoke stack. I looked at that, then I looked back and here came the second wave of the bomb group. This group could not really tell where the benzine plant was because of all the dust from the bombs of the first wave. Around this pottery factory was a big chain link fence, and everybody headed for that fence. By the time I got to it, it was flat on the ground. I was running as hard as I could and I was right behind a German guard and he, too, was running all out rifle slung over his shoulder. Right next to the factory was an ancient grave yard, and we ran until the bombs started to hit. The guard just plopped right on the path. I went over him just a little bit and dropped between two graves. They were the old mounded graves. I laid there between those two graves throughout the bombing. The dirt flew all over us, and when it was over I needed a cigarette. The guard says to me, "Haben Zigarette?" I handed him one and I took one. He lit a match and he was shaking so bad he could not get his cigarette lit. I lit a match and I was shaking as bad as he was. We had a time getting those cigarettes lit. That was quite an experience. The benzine plant was just a ball of fire. A couple of stray bombs hit the pottery factory, but it was not demolished.

I had stayed with the guard. During and after the bombing there were prisoners running, as far as you could see there were running prisoners. I could make out a little German and guard spoke a little English. I asked him what he was going to do and he said in effect, "Nothing. They will be back. It is safer here than out there." I would think that 99% did come back. The war was nearly over and the prisoners did not know where to go. They had no extra food nor anything they would need to make an escape.

We walked for just two days more — all night one night, the next day and the day after that. We were out in the middle of no place and met a jeep that was flying an AMERICAN FLAG, and everyone went crazy. In fact they went so crazy, it scared me. They knocked the guards off their bicycles, took their rifles, took their pistols — took everything they had when they realized they were liberated. I was still with some of my crew mates in the group of POWs that I had been with all the time. We walked another four or five miles and came to the Elbe river. The bridge was out so we slid down the bank and there was a pontoon bridge that the 101st had set up. They were in a town where there was a big Luftwaffe supply center with clothing, etc. for the German Air Force. We stayed there which was the established line for the Americans, as there was an agreement with the Russians not to cross the Elbe River. The jeep that found us was a scouting party looking for the Russians. Evidently the Russians were not too far behind us, and the Germans did not want to turn us, nor themselves, over to the Russians.

We stayed there for about a week, then were flown to Rheims, France where they deloused us, issued us new clothes, and interrogated us very briefly — name, serial number, etc. They were compiling a list to notify people back home. To my nearest recollection this was May 19, 1945. From here they took us to Camp Lucky Stike near LeHarve, France. It was right on a harbor on the French coast and it was a mess. We were offered leave to go any place we want to: Paris, England, Switzerland or anyplace, because they had so many POW's to transport. A lot of them went. I was ready to go home so I never left camp — didn't even go into LeHarve. I'd seen all that country I wanted to. All the survivors of my ship stayed together through the POW camps and all the marches. I was 21 years old when I was in those camps.

I never ran into anyone else in the camps from the 95th Bomb Group. Most every other one though. This march we were on was in the neighborhood of 1200 miles. I weighed 115 to 130 pounds after the march — not much for a man six feet tall. Some years ago a book was written about this march called "The Black March." I will say there were a lot of fellows that did not fare as well as I did. A lot of them got sick, got dysentary, and a lot of the guys died. Except for that deal with the dogs, we were not treated too badly. The Germans did not have anything to eat themselves. As a whole we were not badly abused.

I never did get any medical attention for my broken ribs until I got to East Prussia. I had reached the point I could hardly walk. The Germans finally took me into the compound medical room and taped me up and I slowly healed, but those ribs still plague me to this very day. That is why I quit smoking, because when I would cough it would hurt and if I coughed too much they would bust loose and I'd have to go through the whole thing over again. There is no way I will ever be able to forget that fifteen month period of my life.

Target: Berlin, Germany

This is the story of a day already forgotten in the annals of aerial warfare. For a few brief hours, the date March 6, 1944 flared across the headlines of embattled nations and then faded into the musty files of history. Forgotten or not, that date will live forever in the hearts of those American men whose sixty-nine battered, flaming bombers left a hideous trail of twisted metal and broken bodies from Berlin to the English Channel and earned for that day the nickname "Bloody Monday." The following is an account of one of those crews as seen from the eyes of one man who was more fortunate than many, but who will never forget what it cost to carry the white star of the U.S. Army Air Forces above the capitol of Nazidom for the first time.

Sixty-nine bombers were shot down. In the 388th Bomb Group only one ship returned from the low squadron. This is the story of that mission as seen by the pilot of the ship that led that ill-fated low squadron through a manmade hell in skies defiled by blood and bullets.

Date: 6 March 1944
Target: Berlin, Germany
Group: 388th Bomb Group

The 388th furnished A Group and the lead and low squadrons of B group which was completed by the 452nd Bomb Group. These formed the two-group 45th A Combat Wing, the last wing in the 3rd Division formation, the second division over Berlin. Our assigned target was the subsidiary plant of the Robert Bosch Electrical Equipment Factory at Stuttgart, located in the southwestern portion of Berlin. The 1st and 2nd Divisions were assigned targets in the southern and eastern sections of the city. In all, 504 B-17s were dispatched plus 226 B-24s. Of these, 474 Fortresses and 198 Liberators attacked German targets, dropping 1,199 tons of general purpose and 450 tons in incendiaries with generally poor results. The bomb forces were escorted by 19 groups of USAAF fighter planes. Three of the P-47 groups flew a second sortie. Further support came from 2 squadrons of RAF Mustangs.

	Losses	Claims
1st Bomb. Division	18	41-24-45
2d Bomb. Division	16	5-0-0
3rd Bomb. Division	35	47-20-21
13th Combat Wing	24	93-48-66 (total)
45th Combat Wing		
388th Bomb Group	9	4-5-0
	69 (68 confirmed)	
ASAAF fighters	11	82-9-32
	80	175-57-98

Thirty-three of our ships were airborne between 0751 and 0824 hours. Seven of these aborted for mechanical reasons. Formations were effected without difficulty and the aircraft proceeded to the target. The lead a/c of our A group aborted over Cambridge and the deputy lead took its place. The groups changed position with B group taking the lead of 45th Combat Wing "A." The briefed route was followed until the formation reached the vicinity of Berlin. Instead of attacking the assigned target, the formation continued to the south, making a left turn and circling completely around the outskirts of the city from West to East and thence to the North. The B group bombed Oranienburg on the Northern outskirts of Berlin. Strike photos show hits in the residential section of the town between the marshalling yards and the Oranienburg Canal just east of the Heinkel Plant at Annahof. The A group, following, did not drop its bombs on that target but attacked Wittenberg, northwest of Berlin. Bombs were away at 1407 hours from 19,400 feet while on a magnetic heading of 279 degrees. Strike photos show a tight pattern in the center of the factory area of a priority textile works located on the banks of the Elbe River, just east of Wittenberg. Reconnaissance photo shows that the target was the Kurmarkische Zellewolfe factory, three of whose four building groups received direct hits from our bombers.

The wing formation then proceeded to make good the briefed course on the return route. Eighteen of our Forts landed at base at 1646 hours, and F/O Dopko landed at 1745 hours after hitting the deck in the target area and returning alone to England. Seven of our a/c failed to return.

Approximately 15 to 20 FW 190's were first met on the route into the target in the vicinity of Dummer Lake. The attacks, which started at 1200 hours, lasted until 1220 hours, were mainly directed at the groups ahead. No serious enemy fighter attacks were again encountered until the formation was again in the same area on the return route. Here the same number of FW's plus several ME 109s pressed home vicious, daring attacks for 30 minutes. It was from these encounters that six of our a/c were lost. The seventh was lost when one of our crippled ships collided with it. Attacks were from all clock positions but mainly from 10 to 2 o'clock high, with e/a coming in line abreast and diving through the formation. Two to six e/a in line astern would also attack from the nose high. Crew members report that the 20mm cannon which were used exclusively, fired both incendiary and time-delay shells. Many bombers shot down were observed to burst into flames immediately after attacks by the enemy fighters.

Inaccurate scattered flak was encountered from Amsterdam, Quakenbruck and Vechta. In the Berlin area an intense barrage was seen over the center of the city. Over the outskirts of the capital, flak was continuous, following, accurate and intense. Approximately ten rockets were observed from the ground defenses at Berlin.

Seven crew members were wounded during the mission, one of whom, Tech. Sgt. Sartin, died in the hospital.

Lt. Col. Hayes led the A group (45th CW officer); Captain Job of the 388th led the B group.

At interrogation of Lt. B.K. Land's crew, several instances of conduct beyond the call of duty were revealed. A/c 907 was flying in No. 3 position, lead element, low squadron, and was violently attacked by enemy fighters at 1200 hours on the route to the target.

In one attack by an FW 190 the ship was racked by 20mm shells which knocked out an engine, damaged rudder and controls, hit oxygen lines, thereby forcing the plane to return alone. In this attack Sgt. Sartin was fatally wounded. The LWG, Sgt. H.E. Kellner, was wounded but continued on his guns and is credited with destroying the attacker. The TG, Sgt. C.S. Momeyer, was badly wounded in legs and face but continued at his guns while the attacks persisted and is credited with damaging an e/a on a later attack. He later crawled back to the waist to assist the wounded waist gunners. Lt. Land brought the plane back safely, constantly losing altitude and taking evasive action against flak, receiving excellent fighter support until near the coast.

From DAILY BULLETIN NO. 69, dated 9 March 1944:

3. The following TWX is quoted for the information of all concerned from Gen. LE MAY, Commanding General, 3rd Bombardment Division: — QUOTE. THE CREWS OF THE 45TH COMBAT WING DELIVERED A PUNISHING BLOW TODAY TO THE MORALE OF ALL GERMANY. IN SUCCESFULLY PUTTING BOMBS ON THE ENEMY'S CAPITOL AND HIS VITAL PLANTS THEY FURTHERED THE WAR EFFORT MORE THAN ANY OF US CAN ADEQUATELY EVALUATE AT THE PRESENT WRITING, THE MAJOR PART OF THE HURT TO THE 3RD DIVISION FORCES FELL ON THE GALLANT CREWS OF THE 96TH, THE 388TH AND THE 452ND BOMB GROUPS. THE SPIRIT AND FIGHT THESE UNITS DISPLAYED TODAY MADE IT EASIER ON THE OTHER TWO WINGS WHO WANTED TO SHARE THE BRUNT OF THE BATTLE WITH THEM. CONVEY TO ALL THE OFFICERS AND MEN WHO PARTICIPATED MY DEEP ADMIRA-TION FOR THE COURAGE AND DETERMINATION WITH WHICH THEY PUSHED THE AIR ATTACK INTO THE HEART OF THE ENEMY'S TERRITORY AND BLASTED BERLIN. SIGNED LE MAY UNQUOTE.

Key Personnel:

A Group		B Group
Lt. Col. Hayes (45 CA)	Group Leader	Capt. Job
Lt. Sullivan	Deputy Leader	452nd
(Lt. Zengerle (aborted)	Lead Pilot	Capt. Brown
(Lt. Travis (aborted)	Lead Navigator	Lt. Duprey
(Lt. Batectae		
(Lt. Barnett (aborted)	Lead Bombardier	Lt. Gill
(Lt. Turner		

MISSING IN ACTION

P	1st Lt. M.D. Givens	(16)	BT	S/Sgt. T.H. Foulds	(16)
CP	2nd Lt. H.J. Teat	(17)	TT	T/Sgt. R.E. Kesanen (18)	
N	2nd Lt. K.H. Betts	(17)	TG	Sgt. D. Walstra	(0)562nd Sq.
B	2nd Lt. L.G. McMilliam	(16)	RW	S.Sgt. W.R. McGee	(16)
RO	T.Sgt. J. Geraghty	(17)	LW	T/Sgt. J.W. Karr	(13)

In the area between Dummer Lake and the Dutch-German border, a/c 135 was reported to have gone down in flames as having been hit by enemy fighters. No chutes were reported.

P	1st Lt. L.H. Watts	(24)	BT	S/Sgt. R.H. Sweeney	(23)
CP	2nd Lt. R.N. Kennedy	(23)	TT	T/Sgt. J.B. Ramsey	(21)
N	2nd Lt. E.J. Kelly	(21)	TG	S/Sgt. H.A. Brassfield	(24)562nd Sq.
B	2nd Lt. E.J. Murphy	(24)	RW	S/Sgt. R.E. Hess	(23)
RO	T/Sgt. I.N. Finkle	(21)	LW	S/Sgt. D.W. Taylor	(24)

On the return route, in the vicinity of Quakenbruck, at 1500 hours, a/c 886 was hit by enemy fighters. Flames were seen coming from the cockpit and the #3 engine, and the vertical tail fin was partially shot off. The a/c seemingly pulled out of formation slightly and 3 to 5 chutes came out. Then the a/c started to climb and went up into the lead a/c of the lead squadron.

P	2nd Lt. C.P. Wallace	(3)	BT	Sgt. D.T. Balut	(3)
CP	2nd Lt. E.B. Gilroy	(3)	TT	Sgt. W.C. Cortes	(3)
N	2nd Lt. R.P. Kuhn	(3)	TG	Sgt. H.E. Davis	(3)
B	2nd Lt. M.A. Korn	(3)	RW	Sgt. W.R. Amos	(3)
R	S/Sgt. D.J. Fumagall	(3)	LW	Sgt. E.E. Whitman	(3)

There is no definite information on this a/c, but it is thought to have gone down as a result of the enemy fighter attacks when the formation was in the vicinity of Weskenbruck on the return route.

P	2nd Lt. J.W. McLaughlin	(7)	BT	S/Sgt. L.S. Birt	(6)
CP	2nd Lt. G.R. Keller	(6)	TT	T/Sgt. J.F. McClure	(6)
N	2nd Lt. A.W. Wallis	(6)	TG	S/Sgt. W.L. Lacky	(6)
B	2nd Lt. J.P. Stomany	(6)	RW	S/Sgt. W.V. Taylor	(6)
R	T/Sgt. F.D. Moneau	(6)	LW	S/Sgt. J.E. Black	(6)

There is no definite information on this a/c, but it is thought to have gone down as a result of the enemy fighter attack when the formation was in the vicinity of Quakenbruck on the return route.

P	Capt. G.C. Job KIA	(6)	BT	S/Sgt. E.W. Pfannar	(11)
CP	2nd Lt. J.P. Leichowski	(11)	TT	T/Sgt.R.E. Joyce	(19)
N	1st Lt. J.W. DuPrey	(21)	TG	S/Sgt.W.A. Marcario MIA	(13)562nd Sq.
B	2nd Lt. R.T. Gill	(12)	RW	S/Sgt.E.P. Moyer MIA	(17)
R	T/Sgt. J.B. Blatz	(13)	LW	S/Sgt.W.S. Reed	(10)
X	Capt. P.E. Brown MIA	(14)			

On the return route, in the vicinity of Quakenbruck at 1500 hours, a/c #054 was struck from underneath by the a/c which was leading the low squadron. The lead a/c of the low squadron apparently out of control, came up under hitting it underneath on the left side. The ball turret was seen to fall off and both ships immediately dove earthward. Some crews report seeing a/c 054 explode shortly going into the dive. Several chutes were seen in the area, although none can be definitely identified as having come from #054.

P	2nd Lt. A.B. Christiani	(5)	BT	Sgt. R.G. Smith	(6)
CP	2nd Lt. C.D. Farrington	(5)	TT	T/Sgt.S. Ciaccio	(6)
N	2nd Lt. Leo Levy	(6)	TG	S/Sgt.J. Griscom	(24)561st Sq.
B	Ray R. Newmark MIA	(7)	RW	S/Sgt.W.A. Pope	(6)
R	W.B. Mayne	(6)	LW	S/Sgt.W.N. Kline	(6)

Very little information is known about this a/c but it is thought to have been last seen in the vicinity of Zwolle on fire, still under control and with its wheels down. No chutes were reported.

P	1st Lt. C.A. Gridley	(19)	BT	S/Sgt. B.E. Liebman	(19)
CP	2nd Lt. E.V. Alander	(20)	TT	T/Sgt.J.H. Parker	(19)
N	T.Sgt. R.W. Fanning	(22)	TG	S/Sgt.S. Thompson	(18)562nd Sq.
B	2nd Lt. D. E. Mecum	(20)	RW	S/Sgt.B.R. Tucker	(19)
R	T/Sgt. G.H. Hockenbarry	(19)	LW	S/Sgt.J. W. Johnson	(19)

On the return route, at approximately 1455 hours at 52.44 N-07.20 E, a/c #194 was hit by enemy fighters. The a/c was last seen on fire, gradually descending. Five to six chutes were reported.

Perhaps I should have had a premonition of disaster as I pulled my clothes on in the inky blackness of early morning on March 6, 1944. If not then, maybe the briefing should have left me anxious and worried. We were all set for our final combat mission, the mission which would relieve the strain of combat and give us at least a month at home with our friends and families. Now we had looked forward to going home again. That trip was almost within our grasp. Just a few more combat hours — that was all. But those hours were to be spent deep in Germany over a city the 8th Air Force had twice before tried to bomb without success. The city was Berlin — "Big B" — defended by the full force of the Luftwaffe and by hundreds of flak guns manned by some of the best gunners on the European continent.

On the previous recalled missions to Big B a dog-leg route had been planned. There would be no bluff on this mission. We were to fly straight in and straight out. In addition to this grim prospect, we were to lead the low squadron of the low group of the second section of our combat wing. In short, our squadron would be the lowest and farthest back and therefore the most vulnerable spot in the wing to aerial attack.

As I walked out of the briefing room Major Goodman, our squadron C.O. gave me a pat on the back and his good wishes. He was assured that our plane, *Blitzin' Betsy,* would be back on the line that evening and if not, it would have cost somebody plenty to bring her down.

I then walked under a faded white half moon through the pre-dawn darkness to our equipment room. The stars seemed cold and unfriendly. I had gradually grown calloused to many of the dangers of combat. Sure, the fighters and the flak brought out the sweat and a tingle of nervous energy, but the thought of actually being shot down seemed like something that just wouldn't happen. Still, there was one thing certain . . . no chances would be taken on this last mission.

I was deadly serious in checking over every detail of our plane and equipment. Still, I could show plenty of confidence when I told Harry Allert, our crew chief, to expect a first class buzz job over his tent when we got back.

The sun crawled up and peeked over the eastern horizon casting a pink tinge on the fluffy, scattered clouds that seemed to forecast a clear day. Had we known . . . could we have seen a few hours into the future — we would have taken that pinkish tinge as a portent of the blood that was to be shed above those clouds. But then, it just looked like another day with better than

201

average weather.

At 0730 the big planes, full of bombs and gas, began lumbering toward the runway. Ten minutes later, they were following each other off into the sunrise.

Our takeoff was perfect. We slid into our formation position without trouble, the rest of the squadron pulling up on us a few minutes later. Everything was working perfectly, engines, guns, interphone. Every man on the crew was feeling well and in good physical condition. We were well set for this final and greatest combat test. I wondered then if all this was a harbinger of a smooth mission or the calm before the storm. That question was to be answered very definitely within a very short period of time.

While we were assembling the wing and division formations, the lead ship of our section of the wing aborted. Our group took over the wing lead. I felt better then. At least we weren't in the low group now.

We crossed the English coastline, the gunners tested their 50 calibers. The channel passed beneath us. Then the Dutch coast dropped under the wings and fell away behind us. Then we sailed over the Zuider Zee and were almost over the German border when the storm broke.

About two or three miles ahead of us was the 13th Combat Wing. Their formation had tightened up since I had last looked at it. Little dots that were German fighters were diving into those formations, circling, and attacking again. Out of one high squadron a B-17 slowly climbed away from its formation, the entire right wing a mass of flame. I looked again a second later. There was a flash — then nothing but little specks drifting, tumbling down. Seconds later another bomber tipped up on a wing, rolled over, and dove straight for the ground. Little white puffs of parachutes began to float beneath us, then fall behind as we flew on toward our target.

Our interphone came suddenly to life, "Enemy fighters, 3 o'clock level." "Enemy fighters, 1 o'clock high." Then they were on us. One could feel the tenseness, the electrifying impulse that swept through each individual crew member when the Focke Wulf 190's sailed through our formation. We now were fighting for our lives, for the plane and the crew, and for the formation, the group upon which much of our safety hung, for should that formation be badly chewed up now, we'd catch a great deal of Hell during the next six hours.

Roy Island, flying on my left wing, peeled off and headed West. His place was taken by another ship flown by a swell kid with three missions behind him. This fourth one was all he'd get. Another of our planes feathered an engine and began dropping behind, the target for several of the fighters.

Two silvery streaks flashed past us — P-47s came in, the Jerries dropped away, making only sporadic passes. Once again we could breathe a little easier.

The rest of the way in we had good fighter cover. Violent dogfights flared up ahead of us forcing several of our fighters to drop their tanks and head for home. When their cover spread more thinly the FW's picked up the pace of the attack. They hit us hard twice before we reached the I.P., taking several of our bombers out.

Near the I.P. I looked off to the left where Berlin lay, just north of a heavy, low cloud bank. One bomb wing, the 13th was making its run, just entering the flak. A dark, puffy veil that hung like a pall of death covered the capitol city. It was the heaviest flak I had ever seen. It almost seemed to swallow up the bomber formations as they entered it, but somehow the planes kept coming out the other side. True enough, there were losses. One ship blew up from a direct hit and three others dropped away from their formations . . . but still the formations went on to drop their bombs. It didn't seem like anything could fly through that, but there they were, Flying Forts sailing proudly away from the scene of their devastation. It wasn't too comforting to realize that we were the next group over that hellish scene.

Our group leader opened his bomb bay doors and we followed suit. However, the turn into the target was not made. Instead we were making a wide sweeping circle to the left around the city. Our leading groups were already out of sight heading home, but still we swung on around Berlin. Precious seconds mounted into minutes and still we flew without a bomb run. Tempers mounted and the radio crackled with curses and challenges to the men aboard our lead plane. "Get that damn thing headed toward the target. What in hell do you think this is. The scenery may be pretty, but we're not one damned bit interested in it. If you ain't got the guts to fly through that, let somebody else lead this formation," and so went the radio challenges to a crew who through incompetence or some error had lost us precious time and muffed a lead responsibility that posed no peculiar problems other than courage and a clear head.

Finally, northeast of our target, our lead ship turned toward the center of Berlin again. Our bomb doors came open and we settled down for the bomb run. This was it with a capital "I."

For maybe a minute or two we flew on, flattening out and tightening up the formation. Then the flak hit us. They didn't start out with wild shots and work in closer. The first salvo they sent up was right on us. We could hear the metal of our plane rend and tear as each volley exploded. The hits weren't direct. They were just far enough away so that they didn't take off a wing, the tail, or blow the plane up; they would just tear a ship half apart without completely knocking it out. Big, ragged holes appeared in the wings and fuselage. Kennedy, the co-pilot, was watching nothing but instruments, waiting for that tell-tale story on some instrument that would indicate a damaged or ruined engine, but they kept up their steady roar, even as the ship rocked from the nearness of the hundreds of flak bursts.

"Pilot from tail gunner. Oxygen's going out." Pilot from left waist.

203

Oxygen gone here too." Pilot from radio. Mine's out too." "Pilot to crew. Check oxygen. Get on a walk around bottle if you don't have oxygen. Give me an oxygen check."

In quick succession the crew reported from nose to tail. Everybody was okay with four of the crew on walk-around bottles.

Flak was coming up as bad as ever, but increasing in intensity. Above and to the right of us, a string of bombs trailed out of our lead ship. Simultaneously our ship jumped upwards, relieved of its explosive load as the call, "Bombs away," came over the interphone.

Our left wing ship, one engine feathered, dropped behind the formation, leaving only four of us in our low squadron. A few minutes later, it seemed like a long time, the flak stopped. We had come through it and all four engines were still purring away. After getting through that, nothing should be able to knock us down.

A call came on the VHW radio from our low group. They still had their bombs. As if things hadn't already been enough of a nightmare, we still had another bomb run to make. Wittenburg lay off to the northwest, a big, easily spotted factory visible on its outskirts. We headed over it with our other group and took another blast of flak while they dropped their bombs. A big column of smoke began pouring out of the factory as the bombs hit.

By this time we were thirty-one minutes late. Thirty-one minutes can be an eternity. It proved to be for a good many men. Our fighter escort had long since headed for home and our other bombers were nowhere to be seen. There we sat, two lone and shot up groups in the heart of Germany with no friendly fighters in the sky.

I checked the ships in the formation. We had fifteen. We should have had twenty-one. Only three ships still flew in our low squadron where there should have been seven. A check of our low group showed only fifteen planes there, a total of thirty in all. Off to the south of us lay Brunswick, a well-defended target on previous missions. It lay under a screen of smoke from smudge pots.

As we settled down into the routine of the trip home, I began to feel a glow of happiness. We had come through hell without an injury on the crew. Shot up as we were, the plane was still flying smoothly. We had been over Berlin and contributed to the carnage that was to be almost complete by May, 1945. Now we were headed home. There was an immeasurable relief in knowing that a target had been crossed for the last time, at least in our present combat tour. No longer would we worry about the alerts that meant fitful sleep before another mission.

On into the west we flew while the minutes turned to hours and the miles clocked beneath us in endless and fatiguing procession. The sun swung low into our faces, streaming through the windshield in a bright but eerie light. Off to our right we could now see the much bombed cities of Bremen and

Hamburg. In a few minutes Holland would be beneath us.

The interphone came to life. "Fighters at 10 o'clock high — hey, they're '47s." Oh what a beautiful and welcome sight they made as they swooped over us, dipped their wings, and wheeled away. With our first sight of them, a terrific sense of relief swept away the horrible feeling of aloneness and danger that had ridden the skies with us all the way from Berlin. We were now protected and in twenty minutes would be over the English Channel. I began to think about the buzz job I was going to give Harry and also to wonder how I'd word the cable back home to Betty when we landed. For a second a wave of extreme and indescribable happiness swept over me. Completion of our combat tour in the "big league" of aerial warfare seemed at hand.

For us, that mission was a lot nearer finished than we realized. The P-47s, after their first pass over us, turned tail for England. We didn't know then that they had been sent out looking for us. Not until they were just about to return for lack of gas did they spot us. But the sight of them had been reassuring with only 15 to 20 minutes flying time to the channel we felt we could fight our way through anything. . .and we hadn't seen a Focke Wulfe for almost an hour.

I had just settled wearily back into my seat, relaxing from the first tenseness of seeing the fighters and subsequent relief of knowing they were friendly. I noticed the high squadron leader was relaxing too much. He was flying back out of position with his squadron by what looked to be four or five hundred feet. Things settled down for that last weary haul across Holland and the channel.

The interphone snapped to life. "Focke Wulfs at 3 o'clock level." Yes, there they were. . .what seemed with a hurried count to be about forty fighters flying along just out of range beside us. They pulled ahead of us, turned across our flight path and attacked from ahead and slightly below us. Turrets swung forward throughout the formation and began spitting out their 50 caliber challenge to the attackers. Some of the FW's pulled up above us and hit us from behind while most of them dove in from the front, coming in from 11 to 1 o'clock low to level in waves so close that only every second or third plane could be sighted on by the gunners. Still they came, rolling, firing, and diving away, then attacking again. As the first of these vicious attacks began to ease off, flame shot from Gridley's plane, flying our left wing. Chutes began dropping one after the other from it.

"Those poor guys," somebody said. "They've got in 21 missions too." Attacks were made from above and behind by Me109s.

The stimulation of mortal combat took hold as we wettled down to see this last battle through to its bitter bloody end. I had old *Blitzin' Besty* pulled into the tightest possible formation and was cursing the high squadron leader who still was trying to get into a decent position.

The fighters began their second attack. I saw only what was visible from the corner of my eyes. I was flying formation, as steady and as tight as humanly possible. The FW's swept through our formation, especially between our lead and high squadrons. Somebody would pay for the gap left up there by lax flying. They couldn't get between us and the lead squadron, so began concentrated attacks on our ship; now the lowest on in the formation. Enemy fire swept the nose and front of the cockpit. Dust began flying and smell of powder from the exploding 20 millimeters was strong and pungent in my nostrils. The second wave passed and the fighters qued up for still another attack. Two more of our planes had been badly damaged and were dropping in flames from the formation.

Brassfield called from the tail position, "I got one! I got One!" Then with almost the same breath, "I've been hit." No sooner was the interphone cleared from that message when one even more ominous crackled into the headsets, "We're on fire." Looking forward I had seen an FW come at us from dead level at 12 o'clock. Our top and chin turret fire shook our B-17. At the same instant his wings lit up with the fire of his guns. Twenty millimeters crashed through the nose, exploded beneath my feet in the oxygen tanks. At the same time they broke some of the gasoline cross feed lines. Flames which started here, fed by the pure oxygen and the gasoline almost exploded through the front of the ship. The companionway to the nose, the cockpit, and the bomb bays were a solid mass of flame. While this happened, the fire from Ramsey's and Kelley's forward turrets began tearing the attacking plane apart. flames could be seen, and as the fighter fell apart, throwing pieces of metal in his path, he swept a few feet over our cockpit, obviously finished and out of control.

I took a last look at Clark's plane, on my right wing and our only remaining ship in the squadron. Then the flames blotted out all vision. I called the crew to bail out and started to set up the automatic pilot to fly the ship after we cleared the formation. I looked over to Kennedy's seat for help He was gone. Ramsey had left the top turret, now nothing but a furnace. I had been too busy to even see them leave the cockpit.

Still, I was not ready to give up. I shoved the nose down to clear the formation and reached for the auto pilot with my left hand. Just as I touched the switches and noticed the two inboard engines flaming out of control and no hope of stopping it; the ship jarred, shuddered, and went out of control. Just what had happened I didn't know. I could tell we rolled over upside down. My safety belt had been unbuckled after the P-47s found us. I fell away from the seat, but held myself in with the grasp I had on the control wheel. After a few weird sensations, I was pinned to the seat, unable to move or even raise my left hand to pull off the throttles or try to cut the gas to the inboard engines. My left foot had fallen off the rudder bars while we were on our back. I couldn't even slide it across the floor to get it back on the pedal.

Flames now swept past my face, between my legs, and past my arms as though sucked by a giant vacuum.

Unable to see, I could only tell that we were spinning and diving at a terrific rate of speed. With all the strength I had, I pulled back on the wheel. Horrible seconds passed and the controls failed to respond. I knew that Sweeney could never have gotten out of that damned ball turret. I fought the controls with no response. The fire was too heavy to even bother trying to jump from the nose hatch or bomb bay. My chute would have been burned off in nothing flat. I pulled my side window open gasping for air. Then the G's began easing off. I thought of trying to jump out the side window, but at best that was a tight fit and a rough way to bail out. I was still worried about Sweeney. He couldn't possibly have gotten out yet. Then I noticed that there was no windshield, no top turret, and no roof to the cockpit. At least I could bail out by jumping through the roof. The ship felt like it was levelling off, but still the fire kept me from telling just what our real position was. I thought I'd fight it out a few seconds longer to give the men in back a better chance, then jump. I fully expected to see the earth crashing through the front of the plane. Which would it be...that or death from the flames that were searing past? I couldn't help but feel sorry for Betty and her baby boy. I remembered with a flash of pain that Don Taylor had called from the waist less than ten minutes before we were hit to tell us his boy was a year old that same day. Death in itself didn't seem so frightening as I had imagined it might be. That wild eerie ride down the corridors of the sky in a flaming bomber was to haunt my memories for the rest of my life, but it wasn't just the terror of death that would sear those memories across my brain...it was the unending confusion and pain of a hopeless fight and worry of nine other men who were my responsibility. Contrary to the usual stories, my past life failed to flash in review through my mind. I was too busy fighting to keep that life.

As these thoughts combined with the struggle to maintain control of the plane, I felt myself catupulted through space, spinning so fast I couldn't pull my arms and legs into my body for several seconds. Something jerked heavily past my face. That was my flak suit. Then my oxygen mask flew off, followed by my goggles and helmet.

I reached automatically for my chest. Yes, there was the rip cord, right where it should have been. Until then, I hadn't once thought about my chute. I jerked the rip cord and waited. Nothing happened. I jerked it harder. There was a soft swish, then a hard, sharp jerk, and I was suspended in space, hanging in the most complete silence I had ever known. I anxiously looked up at the billowy white nylon of my chute, fully expecting it to be on fire. I knew a great relief when I saw it intact. Above me the formation roared on into the west, the battle still raging. I looked for our plane. An engine went by, still burning. A few pieces of metal wrinkled on down, and

207

farther away I caught sight of the bright yellow of the dinghy radio falling through space. What a screwy time to notice that radio, but ever since, the sight of it has stayed in my mind more clearly than anything else.

I could see nothing else of our plane. Up above me were three chutes. There should have been nine. Just three. Damn! And Sweeney never had a fighting chance.

Off to the west our formation faded from sight. As the sound faded, a surge of anger and helplessness swept through me. I had flown a solid eight hours of formation. I took no chances. Our gunners had taken their toll. We had taken at least two, probably three, and possibly four German fighters down with us. We had done everything possible; yet here I hung on the shroud lines of a parachute. There were three more chutes . . . and what of the others?

A Focke Wulf swept towards me in a slow deliberate circle. Then he came straight at me. "Damn. Do these Bastards shoot guys in their chutes?" I thought. The fighter flew on until he was almost on top of me. I tried to swing the chute, feeling very helpless. Then I noticed he was still turning, going on by me. A few seconds later he crashed. Not until then did I realize that a dead pilot had just flown past me. I saw three other planes burning on the ground from my chute.

With a start, I suddenly realized that I wasn't just hanging in space. I was drifting, and backwards at that. My burns, which I had begun to notice, were forgotten as I swung up, hanging to the shroud lines. The ground came up faster, faster, faster. I jerked on the shrouds. In a very definite but unceremonious manner I had set foot upon the European continent.

As I tumbled onto the wet, snow covered earth the wreckage of *Blitzin' Betsy* fell in scattered litter around me, and with it also fell the hopes, the faith, and the efforts of everything I had trained, and worked, and built for during the past year and a half. The miles back to Colorado seemed farther than human comprehension as I looked hopelessly into the western sunset.

Lowell H. Watts continued this story in his office at Colorado State University some thirty-four years later. It was easy to determine that his memory of that day had not diminished.

Those FW190s had shot up our tail and put us out of trim, and when I was out of trim and trying to get the auto pilot on I came up under our lead ship. I talked to the crew. Some of them got out. They were in the POW camp with us. One said he heard his bombardier screaming at him and the next thing he saw two props come up through his left wing. It set them on fire, sheared the top off our plane. I don't know how many of them got out, but they lost some. I didn't realize what happened until I talked to someone who had seen what happened. When we hit that plane that flipped us and put us out of control, both inboard engines were burning like mad and we were

208

burning inside. So it was impossible to see anything and things happened pretty fast. All that G pressure and you're not used to flying a B-17 upside down, so it was kind of a bummer. Six of us got out of *Blitzen' Betsy*. We came down about four kilometers from the border. That FW190 came down a little way from where I came down.

I got on the ground, got rid of my parachute and dove into a ditch. There were people milling around. There were airplanes all over the place. They knocked down a bunch, both Germans as well as ours. I saw four airplanes burning, and my chute was not over 1,000 feet over the ground when it opened. So it was pretty congested — people were out. I saw one farm family come by. I stayed in the ditch until they got over there. I could not talk with them and vice versa, but I did understand that it was just four kilometers to the German border. I was trying to get them to give me some clothes and get rid of my flight suit and stuff. The guy said, "Deuchlander!," pointed east and drew his finger across his throat. They did not turn me in.

The screwy part of it was that we had our escape kits. We had them secured to the pant leg of our flight suit. One had money and a map and compass. The other kit had emergency first aid, rations and stuff. The pant leg with the map and money blew off, so I didn't have it and I didn't know where I was. But when the farm family told me I was in Holland I sort of relaxed a little. I thought if I headed southwest — I knew we were east of Amsterdam — I didn't want to go there because it was heavy with Germans. I thought I could walk to Spain or somewhere to get picked up by the Dutch underground. Well, that night I started walking southwest and spent an hour trying to get across a river and a barbwire fence, and I guess I walked myself right back into Germany through that process, because when you look at a map of Germany and Holland, you come down from the North Sea side, south there is just a little jog into Holland. Germany just sticks out west about 20 miles. By going southwest I'd walked into this part of Germany. I was just about to get to the other side when I was picked up a day later. They took me to a farm house and the guy was pointing to a photograph of three sons that were in the Wehrmacht. I thought, "What a sneaker to have three sons in the Wehrmacht." This guy was a German of course, but it was a year later when I got a map of Germany and found out what I had done. If I had gone straight west I would have been better off. Funny things happen to you, distances look different when you are walking as compared to flying. By the time I got picked up I was tired. I was hurting and hungry and you don't give a damn. I'd been trying to duck these guys and I'd made a mistake. When it was daylight I tried to get across this bridge. I think someone must have seen me when I went across. I'd been hiding out all afternoon in a bunch of brush and just took off a little too quick. I was cold, a bit careless. They had some dogs for a while — I got away from that routine, but the next day they picked me up way out in the tules. They were a civilian defense corps deal of some kind. One of them had a pistol and I think he was a lot more scared of me than I was of him. I really didn't give a hoot. They wanted me to put my hands up, but I was just too tired, so they were willing to settle. If they'd been SS I don't think they would have.

They took me to a little country jail — dumped me in. I spent that night trying to figure how to get out of it. It wasn't all that big a deal. They came to pick me up with a Luftwaffe pilot in the car — a staff car. There was a German 1st Lt. and a couple other German officers in the car. The Lieutenant could speak good English and he wanted to talk. By then I didn't trust anybody so I didn't talk, but now I wished I had so that I could have gotten his side of it before I got to Frankfurt to interrogation. They took all POW's to the center, Dulag Luft, for interrogation. I didn't even get interrogated they had so many people there. My radio operator, bombardier and navigator did get interrogated, though. They piled us up on a floor. Hardly enough room to lay down all at the same time. Finally, they shipped us all out, sent us to Stalag Luft I on the Baltic. I never got an official interrogation, though I got a good going over by a Major when I was first picked up.

They showed me a billfold of Captain Job, who was the Operations officer for us. He was flying the lead ship as command pilot. They thought at first I was flying P-47s. I didn't even talk to them so I didn't admit to that or to anything else. Then they showed me the Captain's picture. I wasn't aware he'd gone down, so that was a kind of shaker. I didn't let them know who it was.

Another crew that was in our hut flew this same mission. They saw us go down and they got it right after we did. So they wound up there too. This was 1st Lt. M.D. Givens and his crew. We were in Stalag Luft I in the south compound for about 10 months, then they moved us to another new compound that had just been opened up. We'd been digging a tunnel for months in the first compound and it was never discovered. Then they moved us, so we just had all that exercise for nothing. I guess it kept us busy. I can't recall how long it was, but we had 200 feet to go to get outside the compound. When you haul that dirt out in your pockets it goes pretty slow, but in that building in our room we had a brick foundation like a hearth under a fireplace, and we took the bricks out of the back and got under the building that way. We were inside a brick enclosure so they could not see us from underneath and it worked pretty well, but it was just exercise. We had a few funny things that happened in POW camp, but not too many. I think it was the 4th of July we spent all night in the compound half-dressed. They had some identity cards, and a dead file index card, a 4£ x 6£ card with your picture, Kriegie number and vital statistics. If they came up short on the prisoner count, they'd get out these I.D. cards. They'd put everybody back in the barracks, come there and identify everybody. They could identify who was missing. Well, they'd come in for one of these checks at one of the roll

Concordia Vega oil refinery at Ploesti, Rumania, after bombing by the 15th Air Force on 24 September 1944. (USAF photo)

As huge clouds of smoke billow up from this target, more bombs fall to add to the destruction at Astra Romano oil refinery at Ploesti, Rumania during a mission on 28 July 1944 by planes of the 483rd Bomb Group, 815th Bomb Squadron, 15th Air Force. (USAF photo)

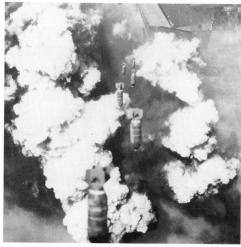

Fire breaks out on a B-17 while on a mission to Ploesti on 9 July 1944. A few minutes after this picture was taken, members of the crew bailed out. Lt. Farrar also made this mission to Ploesti. "It was always rough there." (USAF photo)

211

Enlisted crew of Lt. Nivens and Lt. Miller. (Miller photo)

Cadet Ray Miller, at top of photo, with other squadron cadets are being shown what makes the prop go round on the Stearman trainer. (Miller photo)

Back row, L. to R.; Lt. Brice Nivens, P; Lt. Ray Miller, CP; Lt Jack Reed, N; Lt. Bert Doan, B. Front row: Sgt. Eugene Casebier, TG; Sgt. Vecchiola, BTG; Sgt. Lipshitz, WG; Sgt. Lewis, WG; Sgt. John Larkin, ROG; Sgt. George Kryloff, TT/E.

Airmen who made their way back from France to Switzerland with the aid of the Marquis board a transport that will return them to England and their Eighth Air Force bases. The 15th Air Force also picked up evaders such as these. (USAF photo)

Sgt. Everett S. Allen, second from right, with ground crewmen after he had flown missions as a gunner with the 483rd Bomb Group. (Dave Jehu photo)

The lower level of the top turret gunners position. This is the position of Sgt. Kaz Rachak, 486th Bomb Group, when he was forced to bail out after a mid-air collision over Bremen, Germany. Photo is of the TTG on *Hell's Angels* of the 303rd Bomb Group. (USAF photo)

Back row, L. to R.: Lt. Ingerson, N; Lt. Walthall, P; Lt. Myers, CP; Lt. Graham, B. Front row: Sgt. Rachak, TT/E; (man not on crew); Sgt. Faber, RO/G; Sgt. Danno. BTG; Sgt. Lambertus, TG; Sgt. Dold, WG. Only Sgt. Rachak and Lts. Ingerson and Graham survived the mid-air collision on 4 August 1944. (Dave Jehu photo)

214

This formation of the 486th Bomb Group is on its way to bomb road and rail points on air/ground cooperation with the Allied armies only a few miles away on 23 December 1944. (USAF photo)

Damage to the storage tanks at the Bremen/Oslebshauser oil plant on 4 August 1944. The priority beginning in May 1944 and especially after the invasion of the continent was the destruction of German oil sources to starve the German war machine of fuel. (USAF photo)

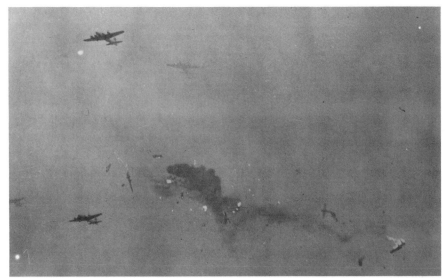

Photo of a mid-air collision of two B-17s. This collision occured over England as planes were returning from a mission and encountered dense fog as indicated by the fact that only a few of the planes can be seen in what was a formation of more than a score. (USAF photo)

Embroidery done by Kazmer Rachak while in Stalag Luft IV-C. from parachute cloth and thread from argyle socks. The original measures 16x17 inches.

216

Back row, L. to R.: Sgts. Perrin, Jim Abrams, Bob Manderchide, unknown, Tom Kokley. Front row: Lts. Rolf Dinwoodie, Broods, Art Williams, Raynard.

"Luckye Bastardes Club" certificate of 1st Lt. B.M. Bittle, Jr. from the 100th Bomb Group. (Dave Jehu photo)

Crew of *Everythin's Jake.* Standing L. to R.: Lt. J.C. Ramsdell, CP; Lt. Mike Burns, N; Sgt. Reid, TT; Lt. Phil Reed, P; Sgt. Berry, LWG. Kneeling: Sgt. Moskowitz, AAE; Sgt. Pulcinella, BTG; Lt. Larry Zeigler, B; Sgt. Hess, TG.

Hundreds of bombs dropped by Consolidated B-24s of the 467th Bomb Group descend on the enemy at Dole, France, 14 August 1944.

218

Lt. Miller's plane takes a direct hit from flak over Magdeburg, Germany, 16 August 1944. (Ramsdell photo)

Moments after Lt. Miller's plane blew up, bombs away over Magdeburg, 16 August 1944. That plane was directly in front of J.C. Ramsdell who recalls the mission vividly. (Ramsdell photo)

Woippy, France, the second mission flown by Lt. Phillip Reed in *Everythin's Jake.* 18 August 1944 (USAF photo)

Lt. J.C. Ramsdell's photo for his escape kit. Lt. Ramsdell was co-pilot of *Everythin's Jake.* (Ramsdell photo)

P-47 escort with 467th Bomb Group on way to Magdeburg, 7 October 1944. (Hess photo)

A compact concentration of bombs from U.S. Eighth Air Force heavy bombers neatly covers the Buckeu tank and motor transport works at Magdeburg, Germany about 60 miles southwest of Berlin during the 7 October 1944 large scale daylight assault. (USAF photo)

One of the "Rest Homes" for combat weary flyers. (Hess photo)

Bomb damage to synthetic oil plant, Magdeburg, Germany. (USAF photo)

Marshalling yards at Bingen, Germany were the target of Eighth Air Force bombers on 10 December 1944. Damaged round house and cratered yards show the effect of precision bombing. Destruction of the bridge was believed to be due to enemy demolition. (USAF photo)

Bombed bridge at Coblenz, Germany. Planes of the 467th Bomb Group made a 52-minute bomb run on this bridge with good results on 31 December 1944. (USAF photo)

Bombs away over Hamburg, Germany's Rhenania-Ossag and Ebane oil refineries. Bombing was through partial cloud cover and despite the intense flak barrage, the Liberators dropped heavy concentrations within the target area. (USAF photo)

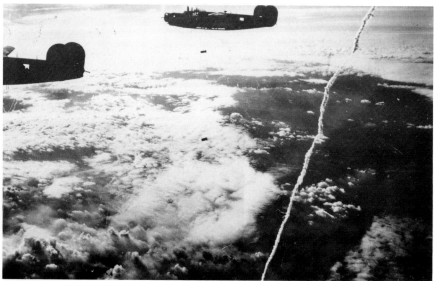

B-24s of the 467th Bomb Group drop bombs on smoke markers over Monheim, Germany, 15 October 1944. (USAF photo)

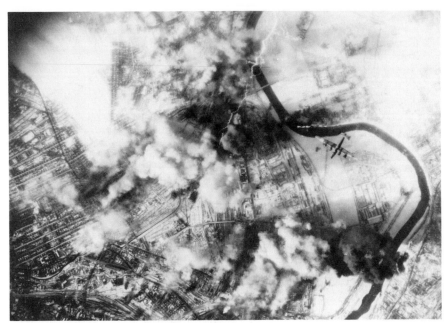

Dresden, Germany, 16 January 1945.

46th Bomb Group drops its bombs on the Hespe airdrome near Onsa-
bruck, Germany 21 March 1945. 1300 heavy bombers plus 700 P-51 and
P-47 fighters took part in raids on nine different airfields that day.

The 467th Bomb Group over Schwabiach-Hall airfield in Germany on 25 February 1945. (USAF photo)

The 467th Bomb Group heads for Schwabiach-Hall airfield, 25 February 1945. (Hess photo)

467th Bomb Group headed for Halle, Germany, marshalling yards. Circled are a pair of Me109s ready to make a pass on the Group.

The B-24s "tuck in" for more fire power while on a mission to Halle, Germany. (Hess photo)

Bombing of the Bielefeld-Herford railroad bridge in Germany. Four runs on the rail bridges were made with clouds drifting over the target on the first three passes. The bombers were over the target area for one and one-half hours. Shadow of the P-38 9th AF photo plane can be seen. (USAF photo)

The approach to the bridge is also destroyed. (USAF photo)

Sgt. Larry Barbier, former combat aerial photographer examines the destruction of the Reinmetall-Borsig production plant which procuded machine guns, anti-tank guns, guns for submarines and destroyers, AA guns, 88 and 128mm field guns, shells, torpedoes, as well as oil refinery equipment. Here he examines unfinished torpedoes. (USAF photo)

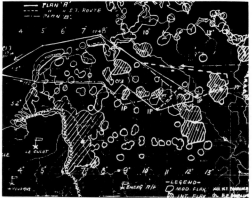

Mission route and flak map of one mission to Berlin flown by the 467th Bomb Group. Alternate target is Koblenz. (Stephens photo)

Bursts of flak dot the sky during a raid on Lutzkendorf, Germany, by B-24s of the 467th Bomb Group, 7 July 1944. (USAF photo)

Widding district of Berlin just north of the famous Tiergarten seen as clouds open during a raid.

Magdeburg, Germany, 7 October 1944.

Bombs away at Magdeburg, Germany, 7 October 1944.

Monheim, Germany, 15 October 1944.

The Hermann Goering engineering works at Hallandorf, south of Brunswick, Germany, after being bombed by B-24s on 14 January 1945. (USAF photo)

On the 25 February 1945 raid to bomb the Me262 factory at Schwabiach-Hall, Germany. (USAF photo)

On the way to Halle, Germany, 27 February 1945. (Hess photo)

The ball turret of a B-17 showing S/Sgt. Kenneth A. Long who completed 50 missions. (USAF photo)

The top turret gun position of the B-17 shown by T/Sgt. Harry Goldstein of Bronx, NY. (USAF photo)

S/Sgt. Otto A. Sobanjo of Hibbing, Minn. shows the tail turret position on a B-24 bomber. (USAF photo)

Waist gunners position on the B-17 of *Hell's Angels* of the 303rd Bomb Group. (USAF photo)

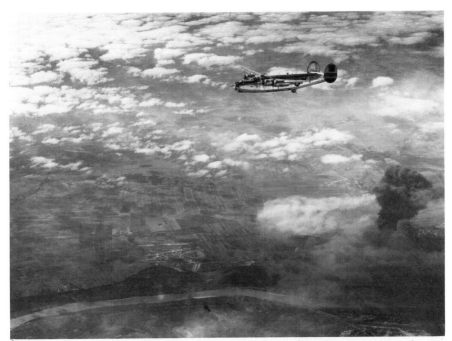

A fine picture of a 15th Air Force B-24 leaving Vienna, Austria, 10 September 1944. (USAF photo)

15th Air Force B-24s "pulling the string" over Vienna, Austria during their winter oil campaign. (USAF photo)

B-24s of the 15th Air Force strike at enemy oil reserves in Vienna, Austria in the campaign to destroy the oil supply of the German war machine. (USAF photo)

One smoking B-24 Liberator of the 15th Air Force peels off prior to crashing, while another stays in level flight with a smoking engine as both are hit by flak over oil targets in the Vienna area, 10 September 1944. (USAF photo)

A B-17 of the 15th Air Force over the Lobau Oil Refinery southeast of Vienna, Austria. (USAF photo)

Bombs from a 15th Air Force B-17 head for the target, an oil refinery near Vienna, Austria. This was one of the few remaining sources of oil for the Germans. (USAF photo)

Over the smoke of fires started by the RAF the night before, B-17s of the 381st continue the blitz of Hamburg. At lower right Nazi fighters rise to challenge.

Battle damage to the nose of a Boeing "Flying Fortress" of the 381st Bomb Group, 9 April 1944. (USAF photo)

Columns of smoke rising from bombs bursting on Germany's most important source of molybdenum in the mountains of Knaben, Norway.

236

This picture emphasizes the obscurity of the Knaben, Norway target.

The sun glistens on a 92nd Bomb Group Fortress as huge explosions reach skyward from the I.G. Farbendustrie chemical plant in Ludwigshaven, Germany, 27 May 1944. (USAF photo)

The combat formation of the 92nd Bomb Group makes the final turn on the approach to the target at Wilhelmshaven, Germany. At right is the lead squadron followed by the larger-appearing first planes of the second squadron, and at left are the rest of the second squadron, 11 June 1943. (USAF photo)

Boeing B-17s attack Bremen, Germany without target visibility, 16 December 1943 and leave contrails behind. (USAF photo)

238

Damage to the Ploesti, Rumania oil refinery from the ground view.

A wrecked submarine in Germany's largest submarine-building plant in Hamburg, Germany. (USAF photo)

239

Bombing of Deurag-Nerag plant at Misburg, Germany (USAF photo)

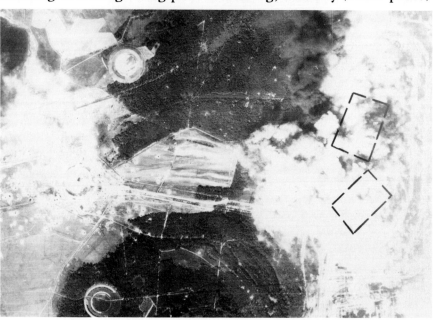

Peenemunde, Germany electrostatic plant is shown demolished in 25
August 1944. Location of the main buildings is shown by the lines.

240

S/Sgt. Charles A. Haygood, tail gunner of *Laces Aces* of the 96th Bomb Group, shows the 3x6 foot hole torn in the tail of his ship by a 20mm shell that barely missed his head. (USAF photo)

Squarely on the target of the Atlas Werke, Bremen's main ship repair yard, part of the 1200 tons of bombs dropped by the Forts and Liberators of the Eighth Air Force on 23 December 1943. (USAF photo)

Blechhammer, Germany, 27 December 1944 shows holes in roof of water gas plant (1); blower houses (2) damaged; main compressor plants (3) severely damaged; low temperature carbonization plants (4) damaged; H2S removal building (5) damaged; gasholder (6) destroyed; boiler house (7) damaged; refinery (8) damaged; tanks (9) heavily damaged.

The Magdeburg Ordnance Depot during attack on 12 September 1944. It supplied the German Army units with tanks and guns. (USAF photo)

calls one afternoon. Some guys got to flubbing around. The guards had, I think, all the cards for our barracks, about 200 guys, and probably for four more barracks. They put these on the ground and turned around to talk to another of the guards. A bunch of us were there and a couple of guys grabbed those cards, got them back into the barracks, got a fire going and burned them up. There was hell to pay for that. They just about tore the place up, so we spent all night out there while they just about tore through the buildings trying to find those cards, trying to find out if there really was somebody missing.

What we'd do when we had started our tunnel — we weren't digging just to have something to do — you'd leave two guys down in the tunnel during roll call and you would come up short. Then you'd get them out, and then you'd have the identity roll call. Everyone was there, and they would spend all day at this. It didn't bother us as much as it did the Germans.

The funniest thing, I think, concerned one of the German guards. He was a funny little guy. He wasn't very alert, and this was in the fall. Somebody got hold of a big bushy weed. There was a wire about ten yards inside the main barbwire enclosure, and you were not to get inside that wire. Somebody reached over and just pulled out that old weed that was growing there and sharpened the end of it. The guard came out. He had been standing guard in front of our barracks. A couple of us got out there and were scruffling around as a diversion. He was watching us so that one of the guys was able to get behind him and stick the sharpened weed in the guard's rifle barrel. He was standing there during roll call — with this big old weed sticking out of the barrel of his rifle. They turned around and called his detail to attention to march out after roll call. The German Major took a look at him, and OH! We thought the day was made. I guess if you didn't have any sense of humor you could really drive yourself crazy in a setup like that POW camp.

As for food, we had turnips and some barley cooked like cereal part of the time. One time we got a horse leg when an R.A.F. Mosquito came over, strafed the area and killed a horse. We got one leg to eat and found a .303 British bullet in it, but by and large we got no meat. The Kriegie bread was like eating sawdust. That was our staple, plus some potatoes. From March of '44 until the Battle of the Bulge it wasn't so bad. From then on it was really tough. We didn't have a Red Cross parcel after that that I recall. They were getting erratic before, when the transportation system began going to pot. They were doing pretty poorly themselves. We had Red Cross parcels once a week for quite a while. While you would get a little hungry, it was adequate. The parcel gave us a "D" bar, some Klim, Spam, raisins or prunes. It really made a difference, but then we lost that and they cut down on their own rations too. From then on we would get pretty darn hungry. It wasn't like the guys in the Pacific that had the same conditions for maybe three or four years. All in all, I thought our treatment was better than you might expect. We harassed them in ways I'm not sure I would have taken had I been a guard.

After our planes got to flying over there a little bit, we'd stand out and cheer every time the 8th Air Force came over. Finally, they put out an order that there would be no more of that. When there was an air raid we'd have to go inside and shut the shutters on the windows.

One Sunday we were having Chapel outside. I was walking back and we were scheduled to eat at noon. We'd eat once a day. I wasn't about to stop until I got to my barracks, but they'd put that order out. An air raid had started while I was walking back. I was two barracks away from ours when the guard let two slugs go right over my head. I decided maybe I'd better be careful and after that they were pretty touchy.

We had some guys that got out of camp and the compound, but did not escape. They were caught and brought back right away. One got out in a laundry cart. Two or three got out, but the Germans put dogs on their trail and they caught them. It was pretty tough to try and figure out how to escape. After you got out you still had no money, knowledge of the country, etc.

The Russians liberated us. The first Russian officer that came in to the camp wanted to march us to Odessa and put us on a boat. One of the guys in our room that could speak enough Polish-German to get by did some trading with the Russian. He said he was not about to walk to Odessa one way or another. He traded his supply of cigarettes for a horse and a motor bike, but nothing happened for four days. Then another Russian officer came in and took over. He didn't know what they were going to do. Finally, we were flown out in B-17s. We did not have to walk out. My radio operator had been in a camp in Poland but ended up in our camp. As the Russians came from the east, the Germans kept evacuating to the west. Our radio operator was on one of those marches, however, and it was not all fun and games. We kind of escaped that.

The Russians were crazy. They were a screwy bunch. They had half tracks, tanks, bicycles, horses. Those guys would have wrist watches from wrist to elbow that they had taken off the Germans. They would take everything they could get their hands on. The Germans were really scared of them. The Germans just pulled out the night before the Russians came in. We woke up in the morning and there was nobody there, though a day later the Russians came in. They were friendly. There was a herd of holstein cattle across the bay and the Russians asked us if we'd had any meat, and of course we said NO! So they said they'd get us some. Next morning a bunch of horsemen came down the road with some fine milk cows. "Here's your beef!" I was raised on a holstein dairy farm and I hated that. I even got up at 3 o'clock in the morning and went out and milked some of them. It was a sad

244

waste of dairy cattle.

We went to a place called Lucky Strike. It wasn't on the coast. Then they took us to LeHarve, where we were put on troop ships and came home that way. V.E. day was May 8th, so it was probably late May when we got out. Kelly, my bombardier, took off with the Russians and he had quite an experience too. He finally reached the British troops and got back that way. They were trying to keep everyone in camp together so they could get everyone out. They were quite good on discipline as far as the camp went. Our senior officers were trying to exercise all the military control they could under the circumstances. I felt it was better to wait than to take off because things were pretty chaotic. This was an all-officer camp, but at the end of the war the Germans had brought in some of the G.I.'s from the east. Ours was an American and R.A.F. camp. There were R.A.F. that had been shot down at Dunkirk. Some of those guys had been in quite a while. I had only direct contact with two British officers, a chaplain and a medical officer. They had gotten some typhoid shots for us.

I didn't have a purple heart on my crew until the day we got shot down. We'd had some close ones before, but no injuries. The day we got shot down one waist gunner went over to get another belt of ammo and when he turned back, where he had been standing there was an 88mm hole right there. It got to where the rougher the mission, the better you liked it because you think you are immune. You either go flak happy or settle down. I'd gotten to the latter point. I was in line to go on leave, and if they would have sent me to London in place of Berlin, I would have been incensed. The Berlin mission was my 25th, I could finish and get out, but as it was, I could have done without that mission.

I guess fighters bothered me more than flak. My tendency was to try to fly as tight a formation as I knew how, and so concentrated on flying and all I got was peripheral vision. I guess that is why a co-pilot goes crazy. He is seeing all that and you are busy flying the plane. You'd get spooky when that flak was close enough to hear, because if it was that close to us, it was putting holes in our plane. Fighters worried me more because their accuracy was better. We went to Poland a couple of times, and at least once we flew across the Danish penninsula, where a bunch of Me110s with rockets would sit back and lob those rockets at us. They had machine guns, but just didn't have enough to combat us directly. The 109s were the ones that bothered me. Our P-51 was our best cover. I thought the P-38 in the ETO wasn't much good. They couldn't turn tight enough, were fast but that was all. The P-51 with drop tanks could go all the way to Berlin with us and did, but if they got in a dog fight before, that would not give them much time with us at the target.

The FW109s that shot us down were good. We called them the Abbey-ville Kids. They were great pilots. They scared H--- out of me. Flak is kind of spooky and you see all that black stuff and you think you got to fly through

245

all that stuff and you think you can't. But after you've done it a few times, it's not so bad. But that day going across Berlin, the sky was just black. I swear a formation couldn't go through there. Sometimes they'd get on target and they would bust up some airplane. Usually you'd get a malfunction such as loosing oxygen or a hole in a gas tank, and you'd have to sweat out the fuel. I've listened to some of the people that are so darned concerned about some of the problems they think we've got in this country, and I've thought about it ever since I came home. If everybody in this country had to spend 90 days in a POW camp and not know at the time whether they would get out of it or not, we would have a lot fewer problems in this country. We really would. You would appreciate what freedom really means to you. Some of the things we fuss and snort about wouldn't be so important. In some of these countries where we have programs, poverty is so abject that people have no clothes, and sleep in the streets. You wonder just how much despair there can be in this world. You begin to understand why people get discontented. I guess discontent is the thing that we use to gain progress. In that context I think it is good, but just to be griping because you want it easier or because some little thing bothers you — I have a little trouble relating to those things.

A German Report of the 6 March 1944 Berlin Raid

Narrator: **Ab. A. Jaonsan**
Written March 9, 1974.

Thirty years ago the world was still entangled in the Second World War. Day and night big formations of allied airplanes on their way to and from their targets in Germany passed over our country.

There are quite a lot of inhabitants of the southeast corner of Dreuthe who still can vividly remember that 6th day of March, 1944. This was the day when the 8th American Air Force stationed in England attacked Berlin or as the American pilots called it: "The Big City."

This day was like so many air raids in the past, extremely hectic. Strong units of the German Luftwaffe were vigorously attacking the American bomber formation without cessation. Subsequently, both sides suffered heavy losses, especially in the southeast corner of Dreuthe and just across the border in Germany many airplanes had crashed during the air raids.

The report of this specific historical raid was written by Air Force amateur history writer Ab A. Yousex from Gromingen who now lives in Oudorp (H-H) and who has previously contributed articles regarding the air war of the years 1940-1945.

It was an historic date for the 8th American Air Force. Already for months the airmen had been looking forward to this first big air attack on Berlin, which had been postponed for several reasons. Finally, it was decided that March 6, 1944 would be the target date.

The planned air formation was spearheaded by the 1st Bombardment Division immediately followed by the 3rd Bombardment Division. Both divisions were equipped with heavy 4-engine type Boeing B-17s better known as "Flying Fortresses."

The flanks were made up of the B-24 Liberators of the Second Bombardment Division. An enormous strikeforce of more than 700 bombers with a total crew of 7000 men and equipped with 8000 heavy machine guns was breathtaking to see flying over in the sky protected by a very large amount of additional fighter planes.

The direct route to Berlin, without the possibility of misleading detours had of course the disadvantage that the Germans already in the early stages could guess which city was chosen to be the target. Nineteen fighter squadrons among which four were US Air Force, were to protect and escort the bombers starting at 35 km east of the Dutch coast.

On the return flight extra support was to be supplied by four groups of American fighters of the P-47 Thunderbolt type, and, on their second flight, three squadrons of English Mustangs and two squadrons of English Spitfires. In case of overcast skies over Germany, all formations were to be accompanied by radar equipped "Pathfinder" aircraft.

In order to distract the Germans from this planned big Berlin air attack, 300 medium heavy bombers were to attack simultaneously targets in northern France.

Targets

Each part of this gigantic air "armada" had its own carefully predetermined task. The main targets singled out in and around Berlin were roller bearing factories in Erkner and the electrical equipment factories of Robert Bosch in Klein-Machow, also the Daimler-Benz aircraft engine factory.

During this short period of time it is of course not possible to report in detail of the activities of each bomber unit. We, therefore, will limit reporting on one group of aircraft of the 45th Combat Wing which was the closing unit flying in the center of the huge air flotilla's Third Division. This 45th Combat Wing consisted of about 60 bombers and was led by the 388th Bombing Group. The bombing target of this wing was the Bosch factory in Klein-Machow.

First Air Battles

At approximately 10:45 A.M. the first formations passed the Netherland Coast over Bergen. Sometime later part of the aircraft passed over the northern part of the Province of Overijssel and southeast Drenthe, where at that time 23-year-old Mr. H.F. Van der Griendt living in Nieuw-Amsterdam wrote in his diary: "The biggest air activity ever observed here in history."

In the beginning it stayed fairly quiet; there was hardly any activity noticeable from the German fighter planes. But as soon as the American air formations had passed the German border with Lake Dummer visible west of Hannoever, hell broke loose. Suddenly the biggest air fighter attack force of the Germans ever seen before came into action. They were meeting head on over and around Lake Dummer: 120 to 150 one-engine fighters coming from air strips in Holland and northwest Germany. In no time it was clear that the target of their attack would be the Combat Wings of the 3rd Division, which was flying in the center of the big group and which included the 45th Wing. This was a very unusual tactic by the Germans because usually they would attack at the head end of the enemy formation. Immediately the American escorting fighter planes among which were the red nosed Thunderbolts of the 56th Fighter Group came into action launching fierce attacks against the German planes.

Friend and Enemy

Lt. Robert Johnson who at that time was in this 56th Fighter Group describes the bitter fight that took place in his book *Thunderbolt* (by Robert

248

S. Johnson and Martin Caidin) from which we took the following excerpt: "When the Germans approached us at extremely high speeds and when our Thunderbolts met them in an attempt to intercept their attacks, also our own aircrafts (Thunderbolts) were frequently hit by the gunners of the US bombers; they thought we were Germans because with their enormous speeds and under these circumstances it was hard to identify our own fighters from the German's attacking planes. Then hell broke loose and the dark sky came to life with a fury of countless sparkles and fire; fire which danced and whirled sparkling through the air. Sixty bombers using a volume of one cubic mile opened fire. In sixty bombers one hundred gunners were turning their guns in the direction of the Germans, but sometimes it happened also to be in our direction.

In the few seconds necessary for my Thunderbolt aircraft to go across this cubic mile with all our bombers in it I saw several German fighter planes, pilotless, going down. They were either hit by our canon fire or the pilots were killed still sitting in their plane which swirled down to earth and crashed.

With so many airplanes concentrated in one cubic mile, crashes were inevitable. Sometimes the Germans flew their planes with the black crosses on their wings and fully loaded with explosives head into the "Big Friend" (US heavy bomber) because their plane could not be navigated anymore. It was like metal hitting metal. The planes were ripped apart causing big fire balls. Parts of human bodies were torn apart and were flying through the sky, with pieces of aluminum and steel." This is quoted from Robert Johnson's book.

Drawback

This attack was only the beginning of the best. Close to Berlin the first and second "Task Force" was again heavily attacked by two-engine type German fighters and again heavy losses were suffered. Thereafter the formations were approaching their IP, from where they would start launching their bombardment into the chosen targets.

Returning to the story of the 45th Combat Wing which at that moment were having difficulties. Their commanding aircraft could not find the target, which made it necessary for the complete Wing to make a 360 degree turn over Berlin. It was decided to bomb the second target Oranienburg which was at the northern outskirts of Berlin; a decision that created a chain reaction with fatal after effects. Because of this delayed action our return trip back "home" was without the protection of our fighter planes, which made us extremely vulnerable against enemy attacks. It had soon been noticed by the Germans and two "Staffeln" (approximately 24 airplanes) were trailing us.

Nothing happened until again we had reached the vicinity of Dummer

Lake, a location where the German fighter planes seem to be concentrating and where the American formations always were attacked; then suddenly hell broke loose again. In the area of Quakenbruck the 388th Bomb Group — which as we know was in command of the 45th Combat Wing — was heavily attacked by the German air force.

About the same amount of Fokker Wulfs FW190s as we had encountered on the way up, including several Messerschmitts, staged bold attacks at the "Dicke Autos" (big cars) as they called the 4-engine US bombers. They came up in front of our formations, attacked in the front, rolled after firing salvo's with a "Split S" through the formation and then dived to return again for a renewed attack.

Battle Field Dremthe

When the American formations reached the Dutch border, the enemy attacker approached us from all directions, mainly from the front position. Some of the fighter planes were diving from across through the formation while other ones, two or six of them also in sequence, attacked from the high nose position.

One of the Boeings that was hit during these attacks was the 42-3708-6 *Blitzin Betsy* under the command of 1st Lt. Lowell H. Watts who flew on the left side of the commander of the lowest flying squadron. The crew members of some other aircrafts reported later that flames came out of the cockpit and the starboard motors (interior), also the vertical part of the tail end, was partly blasted way. It appeared that the aircraft was leaving the formation and three to five parachutes were sighted. Then after the airplane, which appeared to fly with navigators, started to climb and hit the underside of the aircraft of the commander of the squadron (a B-17 No 42-40054). Captain G.C. Job was the squadron operations officer.

The belly dome was torn off and both aircrafts took a dive.

Returned flyers reported that the 054 shortly after it had gone into a nose dive had exploded. Despite the fact that several parachutes in the area were sighted, it could not be established that anyone had safely come out of the wreck. The 42-40054 came falling out of the sky in pieces near the Schoonebekerveld southeast of Emmem. There were at least two dead, Capt. Job and the formation navigator, 1st Lt. J.W. Duprey who had already made 21 missions. The *Blitzin Betsy* came completely down at Zquartemeer (Emmem). From this aircraft three men were killed: Staff Sergeant Ray E. Hess, the right hand gunner; Staff Sergeant Robert Sweeney, the belly dome gunner; and Staff Sergeant Harold A. Brassfield, the tail gunner. The fierce attacks of the Germans claimed more casualties. The B-17 No 42-31135, *Suzy Sag Titz*, with 1st Lt. Monty D. Givens was also hit during the fourth attack near the Dutch border.

When the German commander of the attacking "Rotte" (four aircrafts) started to open fire, Givens was slipping towards his attacker. This maneuver thwarted the carefully chosen attacking position of the Germans to such a way that he missed completely. But the second attacker was more successful and he put the two starboard engine of the *Suzy Sag Titz* out of operation. Also a 20mm grenade penetrated the radio room and exploded near the left hand gunner, Sergeant Daniel Walska. The radio operator, technical Sergeant J. Geragbity, was hit by flying pieces of metal, but was not seriously wounded.

Abandon Aircraft

The *Suzy Sag Titz* was in bad shape; two engines were on fire and there was also a fire in the hull and heavy smoke was getting into the cockpit. It was clear that the crew had to leave the aircraft, but not before one of the attackers was downed by one of Givens gunners, Sergeant Roy E. Kesenen (other crew members had confirmed this.). After Lt. Givens, who was afraid that the fuel tanks would explode, had given the order to "abandon aircraft" the crew members reported to him one by one that they were going to jump. The gunner at the tail end, Sergeant Jack E. Karr, went through the small escape hatch in the tail because he could not reach the center section of the plane due to the damage. During the confusion Givens did not notice that Sergeant McGee had not reported to him. The bomb guide, the navigator and the second pilot all left through the front escape hatch. Givens then put the automatic pilot in action; this way he could keep the aircraft level for a certain time. Then, however, it started to climb and had the tendency to "slide down". Givens then quickly followed the other crew members through the escape hatch. Givens pulled quickly the lever of this parachute, which opened with a shock. When he looked around he counted eight parachutes. Thus, eight men except for one had been able to leave the aircraft. At that time he did not know that Sergeant McGee was killed. Where Givens exactly came down was not known.

Following is the story as was told in his own words: "After I was able to rid myself of my parachute I looked around and I saw two other members of the crew close by; my navigator (2nd Lt. K.H. Betts) and my tail gunner. We joined together for a short discussion and decided to go in opposite directions to find a hiding place for the night. Then two boys of about 15 years of age came to meet us and they took us to the nearby farm house. There we saw two older men and a few women and children. They gave us bread and coffee. We were trying to find out from them if they were planning to hide us when a young man of about 20 years came in who spoke a little English and told us that we had to disappear immediately. The older men, however, told him to leave and were keeping us (under custody) with axes in their hands. In the meantime several people had assembled near the farm house. Then a Dutch policeman came to us and searched us for weapons. A few minutes later a German soldier arrived on a motorcycle and ordered us to follow him. On the way a lady teacher, who followed us with other people, told us that the farmers had reported us (to the Germans) for money. She told us that these were the "bad" type of Hollanders. Now I can only sympathize with them, but at that time I had other thoughts. We then were loaded in a truck and driven to Leevwarden, where we were interrogated. It was then that I learned that Mr. McGee was dead. Most of my crew members and roommates were also there. From Leevwarden we were all transported to Amsterdam and from there to Frankfurt where we were assigned to Stalag I in Barth (Germany)," according to Givens.

More Casualties and Losses

These B-17s of the 562nd Squadron of the 388th Bombing Group were not the only American bombers that came down on that day in the southeast corner of Dreuthe and across the border in Germany. The B-17 No. 42-31194 with 1st Lt. Clarence A. Gridely was also downed by the German fighter Daus at approximately 14:55 P.M. in the same vicinity. When the aircraft was sighted last it was on fire and it was descending slowly. Five or six parachutes were observed. This would check out while at least seven men were able to jump safely to the earth, among them was Lt. Gridley. After that the aircraft exploded and came in pieces down to earth near the town of Schoningsdorf, just across the border from Holland, in Germany and opposite the "Zwartemeer" (Black Lake) in Drenthe. Three of the crew were killed, among whom was the tail gunner,, Sergeant Selmer Thompson, while there was also one who was seriously injured and who later died. There is the possibility that he could have been the second pilot, 2nd Lt. E.V. Alexander.

Another two aircrafts of the 388th Bombing Group went down in approximately the same area; namely, a B-17 (no number known) under command of 2nd Lt. J.W. McLaughlin. It is not known where his engine came down, possibly across from the Dutch border in Germany. Also, the aircraft (number unknown) with 2nd Lt. C.P. Wallace did not return that afternoon to its base in Knettishell. Of this airplane it is also not known when it crashed, however, it is assumed that it was attacked by the German fighter planes when it was approaching the Dutch border. Just in a matter of minutes the 562nd Squadron had lost seven aircrafts and 70 men who did not return to Knettishell, which meant a very dark day for this unit.

The Germans, however, suffered substantial losses on that same day. They lost over Dutch territory, three and possibly more planes among which a one-engine fighter plane near Sleem, a one-engine fighter plane near Coevordem, and a one-engine fighter plane near Oldebroek (Gelderland). The aircraft that had crashed near Sleem was a Fokker Wulf 190, of the 7th Staffel of the fighter plane Squadron 11 and it killed the well known German Captain, Hugo Frey, who had downed many "Flying Fortresses." After he had downed four 4-engine bombers he himself was hit and he crashed at Erm in the Province of Drenthe (townsite Sleem). Frey had at that moment 32 victories recorded in his name among which were the four B-17s which were shot down on March 6, 1944. So we can assume that some of the downed flying fortresses of the 388th Bombing Group were the last casualties caused by this "ace". Afterwards on May 4, 1944 he was awarded a post human cross for bravery (Riddercross).

No Primary Targets

The "Reichsbauptator" (Capital) was for the first time hit by the full impact of the US air force. Despite the fact that the population had prevented primary targets from being hit, widespread damage was done all over the city. This was achieved, however, at the expense of heavy losses; 80 airplanes did not return to England, of which 69 were 4-engine bombers and 11 were fighter planes. The 1st Division had lost 18 B-17s, the 3rd Division lost 35 B-17s and the 2nd Division lost 16 B-24s, of which 11 were shot down by fierce and accurate ground fire.

It cannot be denied that the German defense through careful planning had built up a tremendously strong attacking war machine to meet the enemy bombers in the sky. Most of their success was credited to the one-engine fighter planes, who were intercepting and attacking the enemy over Dummer Lake. For the Germans, however, this raid (on Berlin) was a taste of what they could expect in the future.

The Germans viewed the attacks as catastrophic. In a series of letters to Hitler, among documents seized by the U.S. Strategic Bombing Survey (USSBS), the developing crisis is outlined month by month in detail. On June 30 Speer wrote: "The enemy has succeeded in increasing our losses of aviation gasoline up to 90 percent by June 22. Only through speedy recovery of damaged plants has it been possible to regain partly some of the terrible losses." The tone of the letters that followed were similar . . . . .

Consumption of oil exceeded production from May, 1944 on. Accumulated stocks were rapidly used up, and in six months were practically exhausted. The loss of oil production was sharply felt by the armed forces. In August the final run-in-time for aircraft engines was cut from two hours to one half hour. For lack of fuel, pilot training, previously cut down, was further curtailed. Through the summer, the movement of German Panzer divisions in the field was hampered more and more seriously as a result of losses in combat and mounting transportation difficulties, together with the fall in fuel production. By December, according to Speer, the fuel shortage had reached catastrophic proportions. When the Germans launched their counter-offensive on December 16, 1944, their reserves of fuel were insufficient to support the operation. They counted on capturing Allied stocks. Failing in this, many Panzer units were lost when they ran out of gasoline. In February and March of 1945 the Germans massed 1,200 tanks on the Baranov bridgehead at the Vistula to check the Russians. They were immobilized for lack of gasoline and overrun.

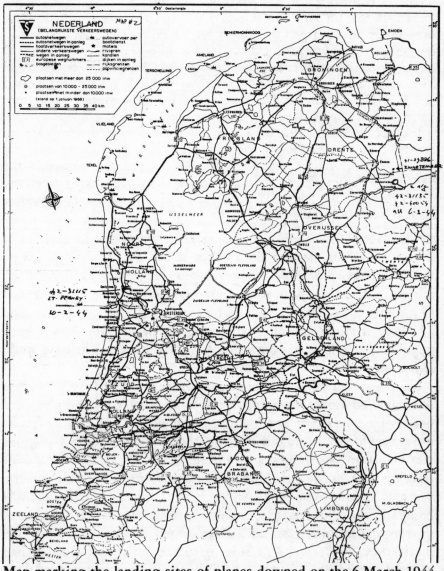

Map marking the landing sites of planes downed on the 6 March 1944 Berlin Raid.

254

Four Missions to Berlin in One Tour

Narrator: O.A. "Jack" Farrar
Group: 381st Bomb Group

Lt. O.A. (Jack) Farrar, pilot of the 381st Bomb Group flew to Berlin four times:

The first Berlin mission was in heavy overcast. The weather people said it was cloudy from the ground up. We were staggering along at 30,000 feet and were in and out of cloud. We were throwing out chaff or window, whatever you want to call it. This was throwing off the German radar and the gunners were following the chaff. We could see the flak going right along with the chaff. They were tracking the window, had no trouble with fighters as they could not get up through the stuff.

The next day being a Sunday, we came back down again. The whole 8th Air Force. It was clear from the ground up. And that was the longest mission I ever flew — bar none — it was clear and we'd been there the day before. The Germans knew we'd be back and were ready for us. They had pulled in their fighters, pulled in the mobile flak guns. We made virtually the same trip. We did bomb from north to south to take advantage of the wind. We turned on the I.P. somewhere north of Berlin. But we started picking up flak even before the I.P. and we were in constant flak on to the bomb run. We were in solid flak all the way across Berlin and out the back side. By my recollection we were in solid flak for very close to an hour, constant flak. We bombed the same way as we did the day before. We simply set the intervelometer that triggered off the bombs. Open the bomb bay doors and every few seconds trigger off a bomb. We were simply tracking them off. No question what we were trying to do — kill people. And the bomber stream was spread out so it was fairly wide. Most of us started with the railroad marshalling yards, started stringing bombs out. We had fighters and flak for more than an hour.

What made it long for me was my co-pilot. The day before he had been the pilot but now he had been put in the right seat and I had been given the left seat. He was on the verge of a nervous breakdown or combat fatique. The system we had when one guy flew, as we approached the I.P. the other would go down below and get on his flak suit, come back up and let the other guy get his on. On this second Berlin mission he just came unglued when we started picking up flak. I happened to be flying and he got up out of his seat to get his flak suit and I never saw him again until an hour and a half later when we had made the whole circuit.

I was so nervous on this mission that my feet would slip off the rudder pedals, they were set pretty high. My feet would fall off and I'd get them up again somehow. With my hands on the throttle, at this altitude it was almost a constant minus 60 degrees, you did not notice the cold. We wore those long flying gauntlets. I was sitting there with the gauntlets upside down on the throttle quadrant. I can still see the sweat running out of that gauntlet, falling down on the base and at sixty below zero it would freeze. When we came out on the other side there was a great big glob of ice, and I mean a glob. That's how scared I was. Just sweat — that is fear. But I worked, watching instruments, the bomber stream, getting hits, watching fighters, watching flak, back to watching instruments. You were watching a lot of things and flying formation. With all that going on it's not that easy. Things get hectic with the bouncing around, flak, fighters could cause you to bounce around. You are trying desperately to stay in close, to keep the fighters off you, and get a good bomb pattern on the target. So it was work, but more fear than work. If the flak and fighters had not been there, we'd have been working a third as hard, if that much. I had the engineer check on the co-pilot and he found him underneath the catwalk below where the pilots sit. He was wrapped up in his flak suit and mine and whoever else's he could get. He'd made a little igloo of all the flak suits.

I made four Berlin missions and they never got better. That minus 60 degrees didn't mean a thing. I didn't use a heated flying suit. They were great for climb out and flying formation. Once I wore one up, we were getting flak and getting shot up and all of a sudden I felt something go "Whump!" I smelled fire and I knew I was dead. All the smell was coming up through the oxygen. What had happened was a piece of flak hit the flak suit, ricocheted to the front of my oxygen mask and shorted out my flying suit.

That was the tough part of it, flying into flak and fighters. You just tuck in and hang in there, no place to hide. I think that is what drove the pilot I went overseas with off the end. He could not stand it, it just got to him. He couldn't resist the urge to fly evasive action, and you can't do that and fly formation. He couldn't hang in there. He became more dangerous than the enemy airplanes. You just can't have a guy in formation flying circles all over the place, and out and in. So they moved him out of first pilot position and 2nd Lieutenant Farrar was made first pilot. His evasive flying could have caused a mid air collision. I saw him pull out of formation trying to dodge flak, which you couldn't do, not by yourself. He lasted eight missions, then finally the crew refused to fly with him. Other pilots in other crews complained they could not look out for enemy aircraft and his B-17 too. But I can understand it, that's a lot of pressure on you.

Flak was a very terrifying thing. You would get those great big puffs of black smoke and if it was close you could see that orange flame in the center. And if closer yet you began to get hits from the flak and you could actually

256

hear it hit the airplane. They fired 88mm and 105mm, and would seem to be in a series of four — like one, two, three, four. If they were tracking on CAVU it was not that good. Much of the time they used radar, though I don't know how good it was, but their tracking wasn't that great. They had what they called a box formation. All the guns would fire into a box — just bracket the Bomber stream and somebody was going to run into it — no question about it.

I guess one of the most tense moments of flying into flak was when you could start counting those flak bursts — one, two — maybe the first one was right in front of your nose, number two was somewhere underneath you, so you knew darn well three and four were directly under you. It's the ones you couldn't see that you really "sweat out." if you could see them you didn't worry as much. If you could see one and two you wondered where three and four were going to be, particularly if you were in one of the box formations where you were flying into it and they were putting up a barrage. You knew darn well it was going to be under you. And you'd get close enough to it where you could pick up the noise, the smell, and the sight of the orange explosion. The booming and popping all around you, and you say there is no place to go — you just hang right there. You become a little apprehensive about this, there's nothing you can do. You are sitting there counting on good luck because flying isn't going to do anything. You can be the best pilot in the world. That isn't going to save your life because you're flying straight into it. You just hope they have lousy gunners and this isn't your day — far more terrifying than fighters.

Fighters was a different kind of fear, and if you had a combination of the two, it was fascinating. Fear, yes, but fascinating too! the difference was with fighters you could fight back. Later when I flew fighters, my stomach didn't tighten up that much because I was doing something. It was sort of one on one like two prize fighters. Sure I respect that you can shoot me down and kill me, but I also know that I'm pretty good too and you make one mistake and I'll get you. So you are working. It becomes a different kind of fear. At least you think you have a fighting chance and you feel cocky about this. I think most of us were. We just waited until you (German) made a mistake, and we knew you would do it, and we would shoot you down. There's no way that you could get me, but in that bomber? NO! I've seen the fighters queue up. We could see them queue up. That old B-17 would be dragging along in a big 100 mile bomber stream. The fighters along in March and April of 1944 were using the technique of not trying to sneak up on you, two, three, or four fighters at a time. Because of the number of guns we had in a bomber stream, we could give them a good fight from almost any angle. So they tried a technique and it worked for them. They would queue up, and I've seen as many as fifty 109s. They would parallel you and the leader would decide which group to hit. Then they would turn into you and here they would come, all fifty in trail, spread out with the whole gaggle coming for the one. The leader went in first, so now it's maybe fifty fighters going into a group of 18 B-17s. They had numerical superiority. They hit us, I would say, 90% of the time head on. *Rarely* did they come at you any other way and it was after they had really gotten in on the first pass. Things were so confused (early in '44) and they would come back and make a second pass at you, and they would come in at any angle. Later in April and May they had the technique of queuing up, making one pass only, not coming back.

It was a head on pass, all of them in trail, coming right at you, and just as they'd get right in front of you, they'd roll it up and give you their belly as they went under you in a sort of modified split S. Occasionally, if they were in too close where they couldn't do that, they'd roll over and turn down, again they would give you their armor plated belly, go over the top of you and pull away, firing all the time until they turned the nose away. Generally, if we had a pretty loose formation they kept on firing as they left because they'd be firing into somebody, but that was quite a show.

I can still see the airplanes as far as you could see, the wing guns flashing the 20mm. It looked like Christmas tree lights, those things winking at you. We had nothing else to do but fly. We'd reach up and hit the landing light switch, blink back at them. I don't think we fooled anybody. From a distance they looked similar, a wing light blinking at you and a gun firing at you. I've heard accounts where this has broken up some of the earlier head on attacks. They thought we had a wing gun there. That is a pretty fearful sight, those wing guns, a big bunch of them, and one after another, the odds are sooner or later you're going to get hit. All you can do is fly the airplane. The pilot — just close your eyes to that and concentrate on flying good formation, tuck it in as tight as you can. We'd actually overlap the wings. Actually, that is the easiest way to fly formation. The closer you are, the easier it is to fly. Trust your luck.

The fighters would usually pick the loosest formation, a wider target. You could spread your fighters out and give yourself more shots too. And too, the looser the formation the fewer guns will be on you from the B-17. Our combat to that was when we saw fighters or had fighters called out to us, start tucking in, and you really have incentive to really tuck it in if you believe they are going to hit the loose group. You don't want it to be your group.

Picture yourself in a fighter looking the bombers over. You'd take the loose formation. The more loose the formation, the fewer guns would be bearing on you. So they would pick the loose group.

But at 25 to 30,000 feet in the old B-17 a group could really spread out pretty quick, but you could tuck it in pretty quick too. No matter how good you're flying, there was always someone flying better than somebody else. Fighters would always fly to the right of the stream, make a turn to the left back into the stream, so you could look up to your right and they'd be milling around, gaggling around and here they'd come! Kick the tires, light the fires, and here they'd go. A mixture of that and flak coming at you — this was sporty.

D-Day, June 6, 1944, Lt. Farrar flew his last of 25 missions with the 8th Air Force. He and his whole crew volunteered to go down to the 15th Air Force and fly another tour.

We went into the 2nd Bomb Group, 96th Squadron, 5th Bomb Wing, 15th Air Force. The Group C.O. was John D. Ryan, later Chief of Staff.

On August 16, 1944 we flew 9.5 hours and of our squadron just two airplanes made it back. They simly ran out of gas. Nine point five hours isn't so much flying time, but for the fact that we were flying formation and we were just jazzing around waiting our turn to go in and bomb. We were simply burning fuel we hadn't planned on doing. We were flying lower than we had planned. We were operating out of Manfredonia, Italy just a ways out from Foggia.

This was for the invasion of Southern France, St. Valliere, France. General Hodges made the landing on the soft underbelly of France that was supposed to coincide with the British 8th Army, under Montgomery, coming down through the low countries. This was also my last mission. I came back to the States having flown 51 missions.

This was not a hard mission, we were hitting a target with the 8th Air Force, bombing from their side. We simply had to wait our turn to bomb and we would queue up and circle until they did their thing and flew out, then we went in and did ours. We had so many formations of planes, big bombers, fighters, little bombers. We had been briefed on bridges and this is always bad for heavy four engine aircraft to be bombing bridges. We dropped down and were flying around 14 or 15 thousand feet trying to find bridges. Zig-zagging around and burning up gas like crazy. That is what happened to us. We saw a little flak, no one really frightened us, we frightened ourselves.

Tour Summary - 1944
Narrators: Henry H. Dayton, and Richard Mooers
Group: 390th Bomb Group, 570th Squadron

Henry H. Dayton arrived at the recruiting office at Binghamton, New York the day after Pearl Harbor. At the time he was working on his father's dairy farm at Stamford, New York, but like so many young Americans, could not wait to get into the service of his country. "Hank" Dayton immediately applied for duty with the Air Corps but was denied entry into that service. When taking his physical it was found that his "bite" was off and was not compatable with the oxygen mask in use at the time. The Infantry had no problems with that and he was soon on his way to Fort Niagara, then to Camp Groft for basic infantry training. After transferring to Fort Devens, Mass. he continued to keep in touch with the Air Corps and in the fall of 1942 his application was accepted. The oxygen equipment had been redesigned. he began his flight training at Westover Field.

As did many who went before and after him, his tour took him to Santa Ana for pre-flight, to Ryan for primary, Marana for basic, to Douglas for advanced, to Roswell for B-17 transition school and thence to Salt Lake City for crew assignment, finally to Ardmore, Oklahoma for combat crew training school. Here he would get his crew: George Benton, co-pilot, Afton, Minnesota; Howard Jones navigator; John Reichardt, bombardier, Fort Smith, Arkansas; Donald Keohane, engineer-top turret gunner, Angola, New York; Charles Loomis, assistant engineer-left waist gunner, Seattle, Washington; Harry Schneider, radio operator-gunner, Gambrills, Maryland; Robert Hurley, tail gunner Santee, California; Clarence de Arman, right waist gunner; Richard Mooers, ball turret gunner, Haverkill, Massachusetts.

Lt. Henry Dayton and his crew would be flying in the 390th Bomb Group 570th Squadron, station 153, Framlingham, England. this crew was to complete 32 missions with no injuries even though their planes on many missions came in with a great amount of flak damage, and the fought off attacks by enemy fighters. The first mission was on April 11, 1944 to the marshalling yards, and Heinkel assembly works at Rostock, Germany followed the next day by a mission to Leipzig,

260

however, bad weather prevented the assembly of the group and covered the target,and the mission was recalled.

In preparation for the proposed invasion of Europe, Bomber Command had been concentrating on aircraft factories and airfields since early February 1944. The attacks made on the Augsburg Messerschmitt factory in mid-March had been ineffectual, and by April 13, 1944 the factory was in full production.

The 390th was alerted for a mission on this date with Lt. Dayton again piloting ship 927, flying #3 in low squadron (570th). The weather was clear and allowed for a visual bomb run. The official summary of the mission is very brief, as they all are:

On this occasion enemy fighters were absent. Incendiary bombs from "A" Group covered a wide area, including their assigned MPI while "B" Group's high explosives fell in fields west of the factory. The operation was marred by the loss of 3 aircraft to anti-aircraft fire. Flak over Augsburg was intense. On the route back the "A" Group swung wide around Brussels, and came into the heavily defended area around Brussels airfield, northeast of the town. Of 38 planes dispatched 13 suffered extensive damage, 9 had moderate damage, and 13 had slight damage.

Ship 927 was one of those to receive extensive damage. Lt. Dayton, with the help of Sgt. Richard Mooers' diary put together what this 'heavy' flak damage really was:

On reaching the target the flak started to come up to us and the flak gunners were "hot as hell." No other mission was as traumatic as this #3 to Augsburg. Perhaps because it was so early in the tour and others were "tame" by comparison, we were just ten green, scared, patriotic boys. We got our 10-500 pound bombs dropped just in time because if we would have had them aboard they could have been hit and we would be all over the German landscape. There were 170 heavy flak guns protecting Augsburg. We first got hit in the gas tank of number two engine, Sgt. Mooers reported it spewing out of the tank. He was ordered out of the ball. Number 3 supercharger was hit and that engine began to lose power, #4 engine began to vibrate and the prop ran away. Meantime flak holes were appearing throughout the ship, but no one was hit. With the help of the whole crew doing their jobs as only a team can do, 927 limped toward Brussels behind the rest of the formation. At Brussels more flak came up and the oxygen system was knocked out. Lt. Dayton dropped 927 down to 12,000 feet, Navigator Lt. Howard Jones gave a heading for England and Dayton put 927 into a long glide for the "closest field in England." This turned out to be a P-47 base.

Lt Dayton recalled:

Lost a runaway prop on landing, number 1 engine and brute strength brought us through, when we landed the engine quit — we had 25 gallons of gas left. Our plane was out of commission until May 29th. 927 had over 200 holes.

D-Day was fast approaching as the Allies made every effort to neutralize the German Luftwaffe. With two exceptions all the missions flown by the 390th in the month of April were to airfields and V-1 installations. The two exceptions were a railway station at Berlin and the huge marshalling yard at Hamm, Germany. The diary of "Hank" Dayton and his ball turret gunner were quite brief when things were really going rough for them and even more so when all they could record was:

April 22, 1944, ship 7041. Ten five-hundred-pounders on marshalling yards capable of handling 20,000 cars per day. Number 1 prop ran away, lost left aeleron. Landed at Marston, a P-47 base. Plenty of flak and the flak gunners were hot.

The next eleven missions mentioned only "lot of flak holes." "Electrical shot out and also left aeleron." "Lost Corky today" (a very unassuming pilot beloved by all).

The Story of the 390th Bomb Group (H) describes Mission 112, Strasbourg, 27 May 1944:

Coming in at 23,000 feet with unrestricted visability, 33 planes from the Group set up a pattern which covered the southern end of the plant. Fifty percent of the bombs were within a thousand feet of the MPI and 99 percent within two thousand feet.
Fighters did not oppose the operation, and flak at the target area, moderate but accurate. One 390th plane was lost for unknown reason. When last seen it was flying at ten thousand feet near Brussels, with several friendly fighter planes hovering about.

Coming as it did just before D-Day, the elimination of this repair unit helped ground the Luftwaffe in the coming days. The heart of the German aircraft industry was situated in "Junkers Valley," in south central Germany. It had been placed there by Goering in pre-war days, under the assumption that serious Allied bombing could never become a threat. Cities like Bernburg, Aschersleben, Dessau, Gotha, and Leipzig were largely devoted to aircraft production. It was a system of component factories whereby one would furnish wings, another engines, while another would do the assembling. Leipzig with its Erla, Mockau, and Heiderblick factories, was the most important of the Junkers towns.

"The Dayton Crew" would be on this mission, once again the diary was very brief:

We dropped 10 five-hundreds. Both turrets were hit and flak was bad.

Closer examination of the situation shows what could have happened hadn't this crew been working as one in the behalf of all. The ball turret was hit badly by flak and shattered. The gunner, Sgt. Richard Mooers, was not injured but was unable to use the turret. Had there been enemy fighter opposition, ship 199 and the Dayton crew would have been in a very bad situation as the Germans liked to pick on cripples. The top turret also took such hits that it came loose from its mount and Top Turret Gunner-Engineer Sgt. Donald Keohane had to hold the plexiglas turret in place with the twin fifty-caliber guns to keep it from flying off, possibly crashing into the tail surface and thus making the pilot unable to control the plane. Sgt. Keohane held the turret in place for four hours until safely landing at Station 153.

May 29, 1944 was a red letter day for the Dayton Crew — they got old 927 back again, devotedly called old *Skillet* by their line chief, Sgt. Arthanasis "Pop" Cummings. Again refering to the 390th Bomb Group History:

Mission 114, Leipzig, 29 may 1944. The weather was right for a visual attack on Leipzig, and the Mockau plant was assigned as the primary target. Like many of these aircraft factories, the Germans provided effective smoke-screen defense. The Mockau plant was well covered, obscuring the assigned MPI. (Mean Point of Impact).

The 390th bombardiers selected their own aiming points. Bombs were in line with the Heiterblick factory, which was about two and a half miles southeast of the Mockau. They landed in the smoke pall. Five aircraft flew with the 95th Composite Group, and left a pattern which crept across the factory airdrome, and walked over buildings of the Junkers Factory.

Forty single-engine enemy planes engaged the formation in a ten minute lapse of fighter escort. The attacks were made by experienced aggressive pilots, and in the shooting the 390th lost two planes. The crew of one returned to England several months later. The Group was credited with 16 enemy planes destroyed, 7 probables, and 10 damaged, about one fourth of the total number of enemy aircraft claimed by the force of a thousand bombers.

Lt Dayton recorded for this day:

Ship 927 — back to the old plane and the first time since Augsburg.

Thirty-eight one-hundred pounders on the aircraft plant. We were hit by fighters and dropped our bombs just before the target as we lost a couple of superchargers. We had both tail and nose attacks, and we got at least three enemy fighters from our plane.

Number 927 was flown for two more missions, May 30 and 31, then June 2 the diary recorded:

Third maiden plane we flew, hit a train switch with 12 five-hundred-pounders. We really broke this one in, tokyo tanks on left were shot out.

For several days weather kept the bombers grounded, then on June 5, 1944 Lt. Dayton was again given a "virgin" plane and as he reports: "This one really caught it." He was in a force of 17 aircraft that sought a secondary target after finding Abbeville airfield socked in. That secondary was the coastal installations at Boulogne, France — again. To every uninformed soldier in England there seemed but little doubt where the landings would be made. The coast around Boulogne — shortest line into occupied territory — had been pummeled as no localized area had been before. It had been thoroughly softened. Two planes were lost to flak but bombs were placed in the target with good results.

The virgin plane #849 was badly hit by flak and with piloting skill and a strong aircraft, the crew came back once again with major flak damage done to their plane. This time the #3 gas tank was shot out, the main spars in the bomb bay shot out, the main bulkheads shot out completely. This will justify the pride the B-17 flyers took in their planes' ability to sustain heavy damage and still have the air worthiness to get the crew back home.

On the afternoon of June 5 the secrets of the pending invasion were released. Group commanders and intelligence officers were summoned to higher headquarters, and supplied with details of the coming operations. Upon returning to the Base, action replaced speculation. Lead navigators and bombardiers were summoned for special target study on a strip of the coast near Caen, in Normandy.

It now became clear that all the bombs dropped on Boulogne had been but a feint. The real operations were to take place in Normandy — a place where hardly any missions had been run.

D-Day was the acme of aerial planning. Twelve thousand aircraft of all types were dispatched that day, and every one was sent out with a specific course and timing. The R.A.F. bombed in the early morning hours and returned to England as the Eighth Air Force went out at a different altitude. Airborne paratroopers and glider troops had been dropped before heavies were sent out. To ground observers, the night preceeding D-Day was a galaxy of fireworks. Planes roved back and forth the length of England dropping colored flares that denoted traffic lanes.

With dawn, the clear skies changed to overcast. Briefing brought significance to the poor weather. A telegram from General Curtis LeMay, old "Iron Ass," of the Third Division was read.

"Every individual keeness, every refinement of technique, and every aid to accuracy must be exploited so that the pattern of our attack is exactly as ordered, and so that there are not gross or avoidable errors to bring disaster to our troops on the ground. The necessary hazards have been accepted. They can be minimized only through exalted performance on the part of our air leaders and bombardiers. I have every confidence in you."

The crews were told that all bombing must be accomplished by 0725 hours, flying in Group column formation, 36 aircraft of the 390th had all bombs away at 0708 hours. This first mission of the day was uneventfull. No planes were lost, and in bombing through cloud on instrument there was no indication of the success or failure of the operation.

The 8th and 9th Air Forces had every available plane that could get off the ground in the air on June 6. Again Sgt. Forest Norman, of Eaton, Colorado was in his tail gun position this day flying with the "Hells Angels," the 303rd Bomb Group from Molesworth, England, station 107. Though Sgt. Norman was to fly with the 95th Bomb Group and later the 2nd Replacement and Training Squadron during his flying career in heavy bombers, June 6, 1944 found him with the 303rd. His ship was badly damaged by flak and forced to ditch in the English Channel. Sgt. Norman's notes state that the ship was *Sway Back* and went into forty feet of water, was later raised and put on display in Fort Worth, Texas. The writer has been unable to substantiate this information officially, photographs from his album have his "Goldfish" membership card for June 6, 1944. Also there is a photo of *Sway Back,* with the notation written on the front, "My ship."

Credit the small loss of ships this day to the successful effort to destroy as many operational units and airfields of the Luftwaffe

265

within operational distance of the landing zone. Few Luftwaffe planes were seen this day, however, the flak batteries were able to put up enough defensive fire to damage a number of aircraft. Consider that the Allies had 12,000 aircraft of all types in the air, June 6, 1944.

Back in 927 again Lt. Dayton and crew made the first of their two missions for the day by delivering 12 five-hundreds and 2 one-thousands to the coast at Caen. The second mission was to Falaise. Bombing from 15,000 feet using pathfinder because of undercast. Ship 927 delivered the same bomb load to this target. The Caen coastal bombing had paid off immediate dividends. It was learned that ground troops made landings in this area without too much opposition. Of course, much of the success of the landings was due to the fact that the Germans had been caught off balance. Even as the rest of the world had erred, the Germans were fooled by the previous saturation of the Boulogne area.

As for the bombing at Falaise, it was learned that a German Panzer division had been caught in that hell by accident. The tank division was in this locality on maneuvers, and lost much of its equipment because of being in the wrong place at the wrong time.

By softening up the German defenses, heavy bombardment had given good support. Now the task switched to maintaining the bridgehead — to ward off the Luftwaffee, and to chip up the German communications which would bring reinforcements into the area to face our ground troops.

The first assignment was June 7. Photo reconnaissance spotted two German divisions in the Bordeaux area in southern France, headed northward. The immediate role of heavy bombardment was to delay them, to keep them from joining Rommel's army in Normandy. The Loire River became the line of interdiction. Every rail and road bridge across the Loire was slated for destruction.

The 390th's target was a bridge at Nantes. Sgt. Mooer's diary records: "Ship 927 railroad bridge — six one thousands. Plenty of flak, and we caught our share." The official report states:

Bombing was to be done by three 12-plane Squadrons, with each Squadron sighting for the bridge individually. "A" and "C" Squadrons made one run each, with 100 percent of "C" Squadron's bombs landing within a thousand feet of the bridge. "B" Squadron, with three runs over the area, missed completely. The bridges at Nantes were finally made impassable by other heavy and medium bomber units. Several days later, when the German divisions finally arrived at the scene of battle, American troops were firmly entrenched.

Airfields again became a priority target for 927 and crew. Dinard-Pleurvit advance airport was bombed on June 11. Ship 927 carried 22 two-hundred-pound fragmentation bombs with good results. The next day a target-of-opportunity, St. Omer airfield, was bombed with the same sized bomb load as the day before. Twenty-four 390th planes attacked without loss, however old *Skillet* took a flak hit in the left wing resulting in the main spar being shot out, as well as the left tokyo tanks. Back to the repair shop for 927 until June 29.

Target, Bohlen, one of the major refineries in the Leipzig area. Twenty aircraft of the 390th encountered accurate flak, but bombing results were good as indicated by great clouds of black smoke seen rolling up thousands of feet as they came off the bomb run to the Rally Point. An estimated 95 percent of the bombs landed within two thousand feet of the MPI, with strikes and near misses on the refinery.

The 390th was the Lead Group that day and got into the flak the Germans sent up soon after approaching the target. Old 927 took a hit in the #1 engine and Lt. Dayton feathered that prop and later dropped the lower ball to lighten the load in order to keep up with the group.

A navigator, who was flying in *G.I. Wonder* on his first combat mission, observed this incident. His plane was flying off left wing of 927. His name is William J. Robinson, publisher of this book.

The German flying bomb sites, called "Q" sites, had been one of the important strategic targets along with the airfields. These sites in the Fressin and Crepy area were the last available to the Germans.

London at this time was subjected to constant day and night attacks by these flying bombs. The Germans were driven to use the sites in the Pas de Calais that were still in their hands. Knock them out was the order. Lt. Dayton again sat in the left seat of 927 for this mission with a new bright left wing, and 20 250-pound bombs in the bomb bay. The official report states: "Weather was good, and flak was absent." Not quite True! Again the diary of Sgt. Mooers was not in agreement with that report. His report: "Heavy flak today, hydraulics shot out," Sgt. Keohane went around with a bucket for everyone to make a donation of urine. The results of which were poured into the system in order to maintain the hydraulics. It did apparently work well enough to get them home and everything worked. No mention is made of how the system was purged of this "custom" hydro-fluid.

The last mission of Lt. Dayton and his crew was flown in 927 also, this was a mission that everyone felt good about. The diary of Sgt. Mooers simply states: "Area 9,"

With the invasion of Continental Europe the Partisan movement came out in the open. These French Maquis had delayed the 2nd S.S. Panzar Division in moving from Toulouse to the Normandy bridgehead. Their next objective was to tie down two other tank divisions in southern France. On June 20 this message was received, "We are being attacked by two divisions coming in on all roads. We ask urgently for assistance." On June 25, 1944, eleven B-17's of the 390th dropped containers of arms and ammunition in central France. At Area "5", the drop zone marked by large bonfires. Before the planes got back to base a message came, "Supplies from American planes received in good order. Many thanks. When may we expect you again?"

This would be a drop to "Area 9", on July 14, 1944. Additional planes had been added to this force, the 390th dispatching 34 planes. The target, Area 9, was again in the Limoges area, where the Maquis had gained control of an area a hundred miles square, the equivalent of a whole French department. The Maquis had kept the Limoges-Orleans rail line cut since D-Day, and were exceptionally successful in cutting communications. The drop was made from 2,300 feet with the containers landing in the desired spot.

This was final mission of Lt. Henry Dayton and his crew, they had gone through flak and fighters 32 times. The original co-pilot was not with them at the finish, however. He had been temporarily assigned to another crew and was forced to bail out, a different co-pilot flew the remaining six missions. As for plane #927, Hank Dayton wrote:

After the war 927 flew home to the USA with returning service men, among them my crew chief who proudly related, "She was the only painted wagon among all those silver jobs, so all and all she saw the war and came home with 90 missions, 1100 hours (better than 800 of those hours were combat hours), so we figure the tax payers got their monies worth out of her."

The War Against the German Oil Industry

With the reduction of German air power, oil became the priority target in the German economy. The bomber force for several months had been adequate for the task. A preliminary attack was launched on May 12, 1944, followed by another on May 28; the main blow was not struck, however, until after D-day. In the months before D-day and for a shorter period immediately following, all available air power based in England was devoted to insuring the success of the invasion.

The German oil supply was tight throughout the war, and was a controlling factor in military operations. The chief source of supply, and the only source for aviation gasoline, was thirteen synthetic plants together with a small production from three additional ones that started operations in 1944. The major sources of products refined from crude oil were the Ploesti oil fields in Rumania and the Hungarian fields which together accounted for about a quarter of the total supply of liquid fuels in 1943. In addition, there was a small but significant Austrian and domestic production. The refineries at Ploesti were attacked, beginning with the daring and costly low-level attack in August, 1943. These had only limited effects; oil deliveries increased until April, 1944, when the attacks were resumed. The 1944 attacks, together with mining of the Danube, materially reduced Rumanian deliveries. In August, 1944, Russian occupation eliminated this source of supply and dependence on the synthetic plants became even greater than before.

Production from the synthetic plants declined steadily and by July, 1944, every major plant had been hit. These plants were producing an average of 316,000 tons per month when the attacks began. Their production fell to 107,000 tons in June and 17,000 tons in September. Production recovered somewhat in November and December, but for the rest of the war was but a fraction of pre-attack output.

The 15th Air Force vs.
The German Oil Industry

Again in March 1944 Ploesti became a prime target of American bombers.

Italy, seven months after surrendering to the Allies, Italian airfields were crowded with growing American air might. From rebuilt Axis bases the Allies were able to attack Nazi targets beyond the working range of bombers based in England.

Out of many sky battles the Allied Air Forces gradually achieved air superiority. Now theatre Air Commanders, General Carl A. Spaatz and Ira Eaker, arrived at Foggia, Italy to plan a new strategy with General Nathan Twining, the Commanding General of the 15th Air Force. Spaatz and Eaker were handing General Twining the biggest job his bombers had ever undertaken.

The 15th Air Force soon got the news — they had been ordered to fly through Hitler's back door and destroy his oil industry. General Twining and his staff took the job. "Gentlemen, we've just received a directive of top priority. The decision has been announced — we will destroy oil refineries and synthetic oil plants."

With in the bombing range of the 15th Air Force bombers existed more than 50% of the oil refineries and plants that produced gasoline, and 25 to 30 percent of total Axis gas production is represented by the ten large refineries around Ploesti.

While these refineries were seriously damaged the previous August by the B-24 task force from Egypt, photo-recon reveals that, with one exception, all refineries were currently operating at full capacity. "We knock out Ploesti and Germany will be deprived of its oil resources." Thus Ploesti was handed to General Twining's 15th Air Force.

On the morning of April 5, 1944, 94 B-17s swung into formation, close by were 136 B-24s. The force was strong, but expected the enemy coastal radar network in Albania and Yugoslavia to spot them as they made their approach over the Adriatic Sea.

Although it was early in the 600 mile run to target, some men began to get into flak suits, a kind of insurance. Climbing to altitude they skimmed the Yugoslav mountains, mighty peaceful until they bristle with flak guns. The force was to find out that Ploesti was the third best defended spot in the continent.

This mission was to be a high altitude mission — 21,000 to 24,000 feet. As they neared the target the groups edged into tighter formation. They had top cover, but they still remembered the 1943 mission with 177 B-24s, of which 54 were lost. Would this be like last year's mission? This one might be worse, with 250 enemy fighters outnumbering ours two to one. Two hundred fifty-six heavy flak guns filled the sky with black deadly mushrooms. To this intense flak the enemy had added smoke — 2000 smoke pots effectively covered Ploesti. Accurate visual bombing was impossible.

At headquarters they knew something had to be done. On June 10 a new tactic was tried. They were going to dive bomb with P-38s. After four hours of flying right on the ground, the smoke screen had to be lit. They climbed to bombing altitude and some dropped their wing tanks as they got close to the enemy. After hitting the refineries they attacked the German fighter units on the ground. Our P-38s got through the smoke, and the mission was successful. We had destroyed 29 enemy planes and had damaged three refineries, but the job wasn't done. Refinery operations increased and repair and servicing went around the clock. The new bombing plan called for the bombers to be on target during the morning hours and stop Ploesti's working day. Now the 15th Air Force began to prepare for a 600 plane mission. They tried new electronic devices for blind bombing. Everyone hoped the sheer concentrated weight of explosives would crack German and Rumanian defenses. Ploesti got under everyone's skin. After hitting it from the air the fliers rehashed it on the ground. The men ate it, slept it, cursed it — especially the flak and smoke. The four months campaign since April had cost 1900 men and 189 bombers and fighters.

Early in August General Twining called a meeting of Group Commanders. "I have you here today to discuss future air operations against Ploesti oil refineries. The Strategic Air Force, during the next three days, will attack intensely, night and day for maximum effort against all refineries in the area." The 15th got over Ploesti alright, but the enemy gave them a warm welcome. They rammed up more than 45,000 rounds of flak. That didn't stop them. During the next three days of smoky air seige, thirty more planes were lost, 23 to flak, but now we had over 100 P-51 Mustangs for escort. Some of these were the 325th Fighter Group — the Checkertail Clan. The enemy jabbed and our Mustangs swooped into battle. Hit hard, enemy fighter strength fell apart. Displaying courage beyond the line of duty, our pilots drove the enemy into the ground strafing their field. Flak kept our bomber crews on their toes. They waded through it all the way to the target. The full weight of our attack fell on Ploesti. That did it, the steady pounding whittled away fully 90% of Rumanian oil production. The global greed designated by the Axis was consumed by the blazing oily Ploesti. This was the crowning climax of the air seige — in only five months this had become a graveyard for one third of Hitler's oil. Oil — a prewar weakness in the Nazi military supply system — became a bottleneck under repeated Allied blows. The bombs had crushed gasoline production, storage and shipping centers. Vainly Germany's 350,000 slave laborers tried to repair the damage, but now all the refineries in the rich Ploesti cluster were damaged or knocked out.

We hurt them, but they hurt us too. The Ploesti campaign had cost us 270 heavy bombers, 49 fighters and crews. Each plane and each man helped to shorten the war. As we hit the donut line we were still flying the missions and we were wondering about our missing crews. How many would come back? The answer came sooner than we expected. Twelve days after the last bombing of Ploesti we got a real thrill — an airlift of 56 transport-converted B-17s were bringing back our buddies who had been forced down. Rumania had surrendered to the Russians. In just three days more than 1100 returned as part of "Operation Reunion." this was the first mass POW liberation. Of the first 600 only ten were stretcher cases. All in all, considering what they had been through, they were a light-hearted bunch. General Twining saw to it that his men got medical attention and food, then he sent them on another mission with the checkpoint the Statue of Liberty and the target HOME!

The 15th Air Force by burning Ploesti off the target list did more than just destroy enemy oil production. They brought eventual disaster at compound interest — the German war machine was stalled for lack of oil.

Tour Summary — 1944
Narrator: Lt. Ray Miller
Group: 483rd Bomb Group

Ray Miller enlisted in Brighton, Colorado. He was a clerk with the Federal Government in Washington, D.C. He could sense something with all the hustle and bustle and people coming into town in the fall of 1941. Things looked like we could be in war, so he worked a transfer to Flight Service Office at Lowry Field as:

I wanted to go into the service from my home town.

I'd always had a low blood pressure, didn't worry too much, never got excited. So the Flight School told me I'd better start eating a lot of salt and pepper, catsup, and rare steaks and then go enlist. I did and in two weeks my pressure was just right. In May of 1942 there was quite a wait — so many enlisted in the Air Corps they could not handle them all. I had to wait 6 months before I could go. There just were not enough facilities to train or house the people that wanted in. I went to Santa Ana for my initial training, pre-flight; to CAL-AERO Airfield, Ontario, California, primary; Taft Air Force Base at Gardner Field, basic; Douglas, Arizona, advanced. All this took about a year until I was commissioned. I think our training was good. I don't know how they put so many people through and did such a good job with them. It was unbelievable of course, we had nine months of training from primary through advanced.

We were assigned to Hill Air Base to get a crew, then to Ellsworth Air Base, Rapid City for B-17 training. I was the co-pilot, as the pilot had been through the training before and somehow lost his crew. I didn't know why and never asked. But he was more experienced so he was pilot and I co-pilot. Then the first part of January we were sent to McDill Air Force Base, Tampa, Florida. The 483rd Bomb Group was formed here at McDill. We flew our planes to McDill from South Dakota. From then on we were to keep our planes and be their guardians etc.. We had a B-17 that cost a quarter of a million dollars, and thought we would never have a plane that would cost more. So we guarded it with our lives. Now a B-1 is a billion.

We went over to Savannah, Georgia for debarcation procedure, then to West Palm Beach. We left from there for overseas. The day before I left Georgia to report to West Palm Beach for overseas, I got a telegram that my wife had been taken to the hospital to deliver our baby. Seven months later I got to see my new baby daughter. I tried to get back to see her, but I was quarantined, I couldn't go anyplace — well, you couldn't do anything about it. I even thought of taking a B-17 to Lowry Field in Denver, but I never made it. So we went overseas via South America, Puerto Rico, Belin, Natal, French West Africa, and Dakar.

On our way over, when we hit each and every one of these stops, every time, every leg, we turned on the radio to listen to something. The Germans would welcome the 483rd Bomb Group to Natal, to Tunis, to Morocco. They'd say, "We're waiting for you, come on up." They were trying to psych us out. They knew who we were and where we were and where we were going.

We lost an oil line on our way over and had to shut down an engine and come back to some small island, Fernando, the Navy had taken over as a base. They repaired our ship after delaying it as long as it would take for us to stay overnight. We were new faces and they wanted someone to talk to. Next day we went on to Tunis, then into the big air base at Foggia Main, Italy.

The 483rd Bomb Group (H) arrived in April, 1944 and was welcomed by "Axis Sally" at the time. Impotent to do anything other than announce their arrival. The first air echelon began flying missions from another base until April 22, 1944 when the remainder of the ground and air echelon arrived. The next day the whole group began flying missions from its own field, crude as it was. By August the base was in such good shape that Undersecretary of War Robert Patterson gave the men a compliment on the progress. This even after they fed him a meal of vienna sausage. Also on the inspection tour was former Brooklyn Dodger great Lt. Col. Larry McPhail, who took time off to look for any of his Flatbush fans to visit with them.

Our base was near a town called Lucero, located on a plateau. The runway was constructed of the steel matting. We had a nice place to take off from. You'd get that B-17 going 90-95 miles per hour and came to the edge of the plateau — you flew — one way or another.

Proceeding with the Mission Summary of Lt. Ray Miller. His first mission for credit was April 15, 1944 to the marshalling yards at Nis, Yugoslavia. This being his first mission he flew as co-pilot to Lt. Brice Nivens, who had flown several missions. The green pilots always went on a couple of missions as co-pilots before taking over as first pilot. At a later time this would be Lt. Millers main job. The formation for this mission was as shown on next page.

Lt. Miller was one who very carefully recorded his missions and a summary of each. Giving details of the formations, the call signals, the bomb load and pertinent information as to routes etc. His summary was very condensed. To quote from his diary for this day:

Summary of the mission; Lone B-24 returning Italy at 10,000 feet at

274

-473-
Major Lanford

-604-		-842-
Haley		Laughtner
	-817-	
	Mott	
-066-		-178-
Nivens-Miller		Macklin
	-408-	
	Rowe	

Places—08:45; Start—08:55; Taxi—09:05; T.O.—09:15; Assembly—10:10; Target—12:00; E.T.A. Home—14:00; Avoid Manfredonia. Load: 12-500 lb.-G.P., Channel "B"—Bombers; Burglar-56-Call, Yis-Emerg. 16 deg. 10 min, No Escort.

The 483rd Formation on 15 April 1944.

10:15 near landfall.

Over Nis 12:15, Flak accurate — lost one plane. Our plane had 34 flak holes. Number 2 engine knocked out, oxygen system destroyed. I was hit in left buttock. Target was missed — return home 2:30 P.M. (Col. Barton hit.)

Not too much detail in that summary. What is left unwritten is a very desperate situation in 066 that could have proven fatal for the whole crew, but for Lt. Miller. On returning to base the crew of 066 made out a number of affidavits and reports recommending Lt. Miller for some kind of award for his actions on the mission. Pressed for detail Lt. Miller related:

We had every time check done at the right time, our take off and everything was good. This was the first mission for me and the crew and we hoped it would be a good one. That first take off we had made to go on a mission was good too, but we lost an engine at land-fall over Yugoslavia so we had to come back. We all hoped we'd get a better mission this time. We were over the target a few minutes late. The flak was thick and very accurate and we were getting hits all thru our formation. We were getting quite a few hits throughout the plane, We could hear it rattling against the plane. Then we got a real close hit and lost our #2 engine, and the oxygen system on the left side.

Just a split second before this burst of flak hit, Lt. Miller asked Lt. Nivens what the target was, so Lt. Nivens said, "Look right down over there to the right," so Lt. Miller loosened his seat belt so he could raise up and look out over the wing and cockpit —

275

WHAM! that flak burst hit and I felt this sharp pain in the butt. A piece of flak about a half an inch square had penetrated and lodged in my hip bone - the same flak burst that had severed the oxygen lines and hit #2 engine.

The plane was out of control for just a little bit. Brice was over in the pilot seat gasping for air and trying to get to an auxillary oxygen tank but could not reach it because of the violent movement of the plane. He yelled to me that he needed oxygen and that I should take over. I was sitting in a pool of blood, but the pain was not so bad so I took over and tried to help him find his oxygen, give him some of my oxygen, and feather the prop on #2 engine. Things happen awful fast. We then came under fighter attack and I disregarded what could happen because of Brice's condition as well as the bombardier and radio operator, they were on the same oxygen line and were having the same problem that Brice was. I thought, "This can't be," so I broke formation and took that B-17 down to 13,000 feet real fast! Low enough for the crew to survive if they could not find their oxygen. With the fighters on us it was kind of a foolish move because fighters always like to find a lone crippled bomber — that was just fresh meat for them. But we made it work and got on back.

That ended his flying for about forty days. By the time he got out of the hospital the crew had told of his quick action and he was awarded the Distinguished Flying Cross and of course the Purple Heart. Lt. Miller feels he does not deserve that award because he was "just doing my job." But he was proud of the Purple Heart and had some appreciation for it until so many were handed out for little pin scratches such as you could get working in your yard. Pin scratches, a few drops of blood, a Purple Heart.

My original crew, by now had flown 15 or 18 missions and I was eager to catch up with them, and after I had flown a few missions I had enough experience to fly as first pilot. I would fly as first pilot for crews that had just come over, to break them in as I had been. I also flew as first pilot for old crews whose pilot was not flying for one reason or another. I never got back with my original crew. It worked out to be fortunate for me because they were flying off my wing over Budapest on July 30, 1944, got a direct flak hit and went down. More about that later.

After I got back into flying after being hit, I didn't seem to be shaky or anything, but as we got closer to the target I started sliding down in my seat. I had my flak suit and helmet on. When we got near the target I couldn't even see out from under my helmet — trying to get away from "it." I was flying with Brice Nivens again and he tapped me on the shoulder and I looked over and he smiled and again patted me on the shoulder. I came out of it and it never bothered me again.

276

Lt. Ray Miller returned to active mission flying on May 27, 1944. The 15th Air Force had been pounding the German war machine In France; Hungary; Rumania; Poland and, of course, Germany itself. On his return to flying the main objectives were the marshalling yards in an attempt to keep supplies from reaching the proposed invasion site in southern France. Following this pre-invasion softening up there followed a systematic destruction of the whole German war machine.

May 27th found Lt. Miller bombing the Avignon, France marshalling yards, which he described as light to moderate flak, no fighters.

Of the next thirty missions Lt. Miller flew with the 483rd Bomb Group, 10 were oil refineries or synthetic oil plants, of that ten, four missions were to that "Hardest target of all" — Ploesti. It was bombed until the Russians captured that part of Rumania. Five missions were to marshalling yards, seven to aircraft factories and airdromes. Bomber Command had decided to eliminate the German Air Force, either on the ground at airdromes, at the factories or in the air. To meet this end the Allied fighter escorts were given free choice to seek and destroy Luftwaffe aircraft wherever it could be found. After completing their escort duties the fighters dropped down to work over airdromes, trains, convoys or anything else of a military nature. However the fighter pilots were most eager to go after the Luftwaffe, which they did with great success.

The briefing officer on Lt. Miller's first mission to Ploesti stated the reason for the mission was first to knock out German oil supplies and secondly to bring out the Luftwaffe so our P-38 and P-51 fighters could work them over. By this stage of the war the skilled, deadly German fighter pilots had nearly all been shot down, killed or captured. There were a few old die-hards, but not enough in numbers to make it count against the hot young pilots of the mighty 15th, 8th and 9th Air Forces.

Still flying as co-pilot to Lt. Brice Nivens, Lt. Miller lifted their B-17 off the ground at 06:15 with twelve 500-pound general purpose bombs, on a heading of 47 degrees 50 minutes for Weiner-Neustat, Austria and the target to be the Wollersdorf Airdrome. Over the target at 10:00 the flak was heavy and a B-17 was lost. This May 29, 1944 mission proved uneventful otherwise.

The campaign on German airpower continued as Nivens-Miller

returned to the flight line June 13. Briefing began at 04:30, start engines 05:35, take off 05:50, rendezvous 06:45 at 6000 feet, P-51 escort, bomb load: 12 500-lb. demo. Flak over the target, Oberpffaffenhoffen Airdrome and factory at Munich, Germany, was moderate to heavy. Though briefing notes said to expect 170 AA guns and 120-140 enemy fighters, no mention is made of fighters. Their plane did receive flak holes in wing and stabilizer. As it happened in hundreds of missions the flak damage might not be known until the crew chief looked over his plane after the mission.

The following day June 14, oil was again the target. Oil being the life blood of the war machine. Bomber Command wanted to dry up that oil supply. The Fanto Oil Refinery was located at Budapest, Hungary and was the selected target for the 483rd. This was a successful mission as far as the bombing results. Lt. Miller reported "six huge fires with smoke rising to 10,000 feet in Hungary and Yugoslavia, mission successful." Flak over the target was intense and accurate and the group lost four men killed.

Veinna, Austria, always a tough target, was listed for June 16. The target was the Floisdorffe refinery, protected by 315 flak guns. Another very brief summary by Lt. Miller: "Very heavy intense flak over target and during entire bomb run (wall of flak at least 30 miles long). Lost several planes. Three enemy fighters shot down. P-38, P-47 and P-51 escort. Huge fires started at target."

June 24 was a run every crew lived to fly — full credit for two sorties, no opposition — a "Milk Run." This is the summary for this day: "Piatra Otul R.R. bridge, Rumania — Milk Run." The following day they flew to Setf, France and the marshalling yards. Summary: "No flak, no fighters but a long hard flight of 9 hours." After a day off Lts. Miller and Nivens were after another marshalling yard. This one at Budapest, Hungary. However that target was weathered in and the alternate target at Brod, Yugoslavia was taken. This too was a marshalling yard and a bridge.

July started out with a July 2 trip to Aimos Fuzite Oil refinery in Hungary, with excellent bombing results. No opposition and light flak, though the target was in the Budapest area. Smoke went as high as 10,000 feet. A large railroad bridge, the Piatra bridge in Rumania, was one more milk run. Lt. Miller flew as first pilot on this mission of July 3, 1944. The Fourth of July fireworks were dropped on the

Brason, Rumania oil refinery. Summary: "Moderate flak over target. Five enemy fighters made one pass at us. (No score either way.) Flight of 7 hours 40 minutes, made a swell bomb run."

Oil targets were to remain priority targets followed by airdromes. With these priorities the big bombers hit the oil center at Ploesti time and again as well as other Rumanian oil targets. Nothing was left alone as the 483rd mixed in raids to plants and factories throughout Italy, France, Austria, Rumania, Hungary and Germany. The remaining missions in Lt. Miller's log book list torpedo factories, steel plants, tank factories, ball bearing works, chemical plants and even a couple of missions to knock out some of the big shore batteries in preparation for the invasion of Southern France.

The railroad bridges and viaducts were described as "Milk Runs" by Lt. Miller, but he said maybe one train a year would go over those bridges across those canyons. However, the Germans were using small out-of-the-way rail lines and "off the beaten track" routes in an effort to get as many supplies as they could to their lines.

Lt. Miller went on to say:

This type of airwar I could understand and do. On the other hand one of the sorriest things I saw was in Southeast Germany. Our group was weathered out of our primary target as well as our alternate target. I do think they were oil refineries. It was a Sunday morning and nothing to do but find some place to drop some bombs. They chose to bomb some little town nestled in some beautiful mountain valley — a town like we have here in Colorado, green and pretty. Here's a little town sitting down there and you could almost hear the church bells ringing. We were told to drop on that little town. That was sickening to me. You lose friends in battle between men, but little mountain villages? Sickening.

When Lt. Miller began to fly as first pilot one of his first missions was supposed to be a "milk run," but as in so many cases of those milk runs they turn out to be anything but. This was a mission to take out a viaduct.

Lt. Millet, co-pilot; Lt. Bloom, bombardier; Lt. Ninfo, navigator. The enlisted crew was the regular crew of Lt. Laughtner. The distance of this mission was 891 miles. Comments on Lt. Miller's summary: "First time I flew with other than my own crew. Heavy and accurate flak at target, almost every plane hit several times but without severe damage. We were hit three times. Lt. Doan (in another plane) hit on arm and about face with flying glass."

Thursday July 6, 1944 Mission #13, Sortie #19

Stations:0700
Start   :0715
Taxi   :0720
T.O.   :0730
Bomb Alt:24,000
Rally   :Left   Aviso, Italy (viaduct) 46⁻ 07′N
                                                         11⁻ 05′E

                                   Ascani
                                    422

                Gleason   Johnson
                 856   671

                                   Jackson
                                    403

                Gussarson   Dooney
                  179   172

                                  Smithers
                                    111

        Hemsley   Boggs
         044   706

Griffen   Van   Hattenhauer   Miller
 017   927   491   852

        Teasley   Mott
         081   170

Waldron   Scwaderer   Nivens   MacSparran
 166   029   922   156

        Ray   Maclin
         043   107

                                  Bentley
                                    849

                Hyde   Orton
                 999   143

                                   Whited
                                    841

                Swanson   Whitaker
                 109   792

                                   Owens
                                    429

280

July 8, 1944 found Lt. Miller and the 483rd briefed for a mission to Vienna, Austria and the Zwolfixing airdrome. As the 27 B-17s approached the target the black and orange flak bursts started to appear all around and thru the formation. It was described as the heaviest, most severe and accurate flak ever experienced by the group to date. The bomb run was a nightmare. Lt. Miller noted that he..."could hear the flak exploding around the ship and could even smell the smoke and gases they gave off. At the target we had several fighters come in on us and my gunners got a few rounds off at them with no known results, they only made one pass. My co-pilot was Harry Millet (I was glad to have him). Lt. Moye was my bombardier and I had my regular enlisted crew."

The following day, July 9, Ray Miller got his first taste of Ploesti, one of the largest suppliers of oil for the German war effort and one that had to be eliminated at any cost. This was the first of five missions he would fly to Ploesti.

As in every mission so far, the warm up and pre-flight check-outs went without error or fault, the usual precision in Lt. Miller's crews. The 483rd formed up and went out over the Adriatic. Coming into the target area the flak came up also with the usual precision. German General Gerstenberg and trained his flak batteries into a well-tuned organization, able to get the flak guns manned and firing very quickly. The "Tidal Wave" of B-24s that went into Ploesti August 1, 1943 found this to be an irrefutable fact. The flak batteries had put in many more hours of practice since that day. The formation chart and code signals are duplicated from Lt. Millers original briefing sheet.

The Summary:

Heavy intense flak. Fighters at target and 20 to 30 minutes after bombs away. Our escort plentiful and they knocked down a number of enemy aircraft, do not know the number. Our #3 box was hit badly. Target was covered by smoke from smoke pots but we blasted it just the same. A B-24 crashed over Yugoslavia and nine men bailed out of a burning B-17 just before target. Flight of 7 hrs. 55 min. 1246 miles, bomb load twelve 500-pound G.P. Had my regular enlisted crew; Harry Millet, co-pilot; Lt. Hicks, navigator; Lt. Floyd Moye, bombardier.

The 15th Air Force, of which the 483rd was one of many B-24 and B-17 Groups, operated out of bases in the Foggia main complex. One combat wing might be bombing a marshalling yard in Yugoslavia while another wing would be after an oil refinery in Hungary. After a

Stations	0530			
Start	0550			
Taxi	0555	B. Alt.	22000	
T.O.	0605	Rally	Right	
Tar.	1000			

Bomber call—Exceed 3   Ploesti, Romania (Xenia oil Ref.)

Fighter call—Surething   44deg 58min N

Recall—Robbin   25deg 59min E

```
                              Barton
                               727
                 Miller              Jeffs
                  922                 161

                              Laughtner
                                706
                 Rowe                Krisman
                  156                 923

         Ascani                               Kilpatrick
          584                                    841

   Gunn          Smithers              Owens        Vlahovich
   008             172                  792            429

       Hammel                              Whited
        403                                 257

  Goesling     Johnston              Long          Swanson
   856           671                 999             109

      Dooney                              Orton


       836                                 010

                              Stein
                               044

               Schwaderer        McNary
                  933             029

                              Berger
                               166

                 Waldron             Ray
                  077                043

                               Van
                               927
```

The formation 9 July 1944.

few days off Lt. Ray Millers' 817th Squadron bombed the ball bearing works at Orbassano, Italy, July 24. The next day the target was the Hermann Goering Tank and Steel Works at Linz, Austria. The B-24 groups took a beating on this mission as Millers' diary reports that

282

"some bailed out after reaching Italy."

On July 27th there was a mission to the Manfried Weiss Steel Works in the industrial area of Budapest, Hungary. Heavy, intense flak was encountered but no damage. The groups skirted the flak over Brod, Yugoslavia.

The oil target at Ploesti was the briefed target for July 28. This mission for Ray Miller was almost a milk run as he had "only one" flak hole in his plane even though the flak was described as being "heavy and intense" over the target. One B-17 exploded over the target after a direct flak hit. Lt. Rackley, co-pilot; Lt. Ninfo, navigator; Lt. Bloom, bombardier; and the enlisted men were the crew from ship 705.

It had been described that Lt. Miller was training new first pilots and often did not have his own designated crew. Lt. Miller flew as co-pilot to Lt. Brice Nivens and the "original crew" until July when he began to get into his pilot training duties and that of substitute pilot, pilot-on-demand so to speak. But he always considered that crew as his own "original" crew including Sgts. George Kryloff, John J. Larkin, Eugene Casebier, Clarence Sinclair, Vecchoila, and Lipschitz. Officers were pilot, Brice Nivens; co-pilot, Ray Miller; bombardier, Lt. Bert Doan; navigator, Lt. Maher.

July 30, 1944 would be the "end of the war" for this tight knit and very loyal crew, still under the command of Lt. Brice Nivens, Lt. Miller flew with Lt. MacSparran's crew with Lt. Scholl as his co-pilot. Lt. Nivens described as "a very good pilot that wanted to be at his very best in order to get the war over as soon as possible." The target on this bright sunny, Sunday morning was the Kotol aircraft factory and airdrome at Budapest, Hungary.

Lt. Miller recorded in his mission summary:

Target really plastered, moderate but very accurate flak. Lost my old crew — Nivens, Doan, Reed, Casebier, Larkin, Veechiola, Lipschitz and Kryloff, with substitutes, Lt. Flanagen, co-pilot; bombardier, Lt. Burt Doan; navigator, Lt. Jack.

Ship in squadron 840 went down too, with Andy. Received a number of hits in my ship. Lts. Gorman and Markland hit badly but limped home on 3 engines, two others also lost an angine but made it home alright. No fighters. Niv and my old crew were flying off my right wing. They got a direct hit right up through the fuselage radio room. They must have had a hole in that plane as big as a wash tub. It flipped them over on their back.

They all went down.

Loyal to the end, Brice Nivens was master of his ship, he was serious about that. The crew went out first, and as the pilot he stayed till last. He went down with the ship. He stayed to help push the others up the escape hatch, and there wasn't time for Niv to get out. First the navigator, then the co-pilot, then the bombardier were helped out. The top turret gunner had ammunition belts wrapped all around him and he was fighting to get free of these and struggling to get to an escape hatch or bomb bay door. He finally made it and got the bomb bay doors open.

Sgt. John J. Larkin, radio operator wrote to Lt. Miller after the war to relate to him what happened that day inside that mortally wounded B-17.

When the flak hit us I was thrown off my chair and landed on my belly on the floor. For a minute I was unable to move. As I understand it we were headed straight down. When I did get up I tried to get out thru the bomb bay, but the ship had turned over on its back and the handle of the door just wasn't where it should have been. Since I was in a little bit of a hurry along about this time, I started to find another exit. I glanced back toward the tail and saw some daylight, and said "that's for me." In the meantime Vecchoila (ball turret gunner) had already bailed out. Can't figure how he got out of the ball in such a hurry, but he did. On my way to the exit I fell over Lippy (Sgt. Lipschitz) or Kryloff (Sgt. Kryloff), who were lying side by side in the waist. The next thing I knew the ship gave a flip and I was on my own in the wild blue yonder (incidentally the chute opened).

I never did see Maher but he must have been killed instantly. Here's the way I got what happened up front from Lt. Flanagan (co-pilot): When we were hit we started straight down and Flanagan managed to get his foot on the four feathering buttons and feathered all four props, we than came out on our back. Lt. Nivens (pilot) and Flanagan made their way up front to the escape hatch, which, since the ship was on its back, was now "up." It was extremely difficult to get out, and each man had to be boosted up. Flanagan, Burt and Jack went out in that order, but Niv had to ride her down. In the meantime Casey (top turret gunner) found himself standing on his head in his turret with about 500 rounds of caliber .50 ammo draped around his neck. He finally got out, opened the bomb bay doors and started to climb up, as he did he noticed Flanagan stuck on the open doors. Flanagen opened his chute, however, and was pulled off. The next thing Casey knew a body hurtled into the bomb bay and — well I guess it was like throwing an egg up against a wall — that was Jack (navigator). Burt Doan (bombardier) got stuck in the escape hatch and had to open his chute to get out. Casey climbed out of the bomb bay, rolled out on the wing and fell off.

We all landed within a quarter mile of each other, and were captured immediately. I learned later that Casey's captors took him out to the wreckage of our ship and pointed out Kryloff to him. George, by some miracle, had survived the crash and recognized Casey as he said, "Casey I can't move my legs," but Casey was taken away then and the Germans reported that George died a few minutes later. Another body was lying near the wreckage, and we figure that must have been Lippy or Niv.

I was taken to a small town near Budapest and about five minutes later Burt was brought in. We both thought we were the only survivors until about three days later when we met Flanagan, Casey and Vic in a Budapest jail. A few days later Burt and Flanagan left for their officer's camp and Casey, Vic and I for ours. I haven't seen or heard from the officers since. Burt was in pain from a swollen knee suffered when a woman hit him with a boulder on the day we were captured.

In closing the letter Sgt. Larkin made a couple of personal remarks and observations:

We had a darn good crew, Ray, and may God bless every one of them. I won't forget the day over Nis that you got hit. You took us down to 10,000 feet in a hurry. You looked over at Niv and said, "Looks like I've got the Purple Heart."

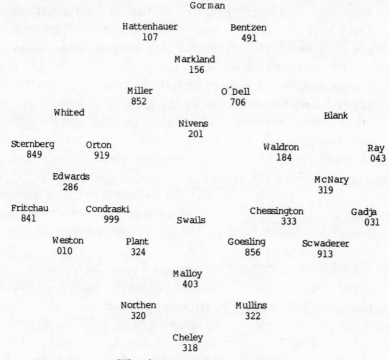

The formation 30 July 1944.

285

This personally disasterous mission was followed by a "Milk Run" to the torpedo factory at Valences, France on August 2, 1944. No flak, no fighters. The next day involved a trip to the Ober-Palerach Chemical plant at Bregenz, Germany. This was not a good mission in that only credit for one sortie was given and the target was missed. Oil targets at Odertal, Germany were to be hit on the 8th, but the weather caused this mission to be scrubbed. Brod, Yugoslavia was the alternate target for August 9, 1944 when the primary at Gyor, Hungary was socked in by weather.

The previous nine days of comparatively uneventful missions was just a lull before the storm. On August 10 the 483rd formed up for a mission to the Romano American oil refinery at Ploesti. The Russians later marveled at the fact that we bombed American refineries even though they were in the hands of the enemy. As in all missions to Ploesti the flak was intense but luckily this time not too accurate, but Lt. Miller's ship 42-107 did sustain some damage. This ship had made one trip to Ploesti with Lt. Maclin as pilot July 9, 1944. It would make two more flights to Ploesti and then did not appear again in Lt. Miller's flight log. It is interesting to note that in the formations as shown in Ray Miller's log, ships were flown by many different pilots. Occsionally they would fly the same ship two or three times in succession, then other ships. 42-107 went to Ploesti with a different pilot each time, with some damage sustained on each trip. It is tribute to the hard and faithful work done by the ground crews to keep this and the other planes in the air. The ground crews did their job with as much pride and devotion as the flight crews, though they seldom were ever given credit for it in the publicity releases by the public relations division. Granted, it was more thrilling to read about the combat missions. The combat crews did make every effort to show appreciation to their ground crews for a job they felt was very hard, and one their life depended on. 42-107 must have had a great ground crew.

Lt Miller took off at 0555 the morning of August 10, formed up and came into the target area at 26,000 feet. The bomb load was 20 250-lb. G.P. bombs, a full load of gas. The afforementioned "not too accurate" flak hit #107 causing a broken oil line in #2 engine and that engine had to be feathered. The hydraulics were also hit so the bomb bay doors could not be closed. The bombardier tried everything in the world to get those doors closed. He tried manually and hydraulically but they would not come up. That is a real drag, all that air coming up inside and holding the plane back, and it causes the pilot to use more gas to keep up. As luck would have it, when the group was half way home they ran into a storm cloud that went up to 40,000 feet. They couldn't go thru it so they had to go around it and that was more mileage. This was a 1,234 mile trip. With that extra drag the gas was going fast, so fast it "was sickening." Lt. Miller continued on over the Adriatic and the #4 engine ran out of gas. Lt. Miller had used all the fuel from the auxillaries and the dead #2.

Lt. Ray Miller relates the landing events:

I was in the fourth flight with only Lt. Markland behind me. Unless you had wounded aboard you stayed in formation and took your turn to land. I called the tower. They would not let me in. They thought I wanted to get in early so I can have a beer or a drink before the others. I pulled off my earphones so I could not hear the cussing and the stuff going on. We were flying around the base and the first flight was going in. When the first flight peeled off, I left my flight and grabbed the spot right behind the last plane in that flight. Now these proceedings are timed pretty well and precision-like, so that the leader of the second flight was in position to come in and I had just pulled in ahead of him. It would be like a car pulling right in front of you on a hiway.

My co-pilot was repeating what was going on over the radio. "Who is that SOB that got in front of me? Get that plane number, get him on the radio!" He was mad! I had cut him out and he had to pick up and go around and come in later. I landed because I knew I was in trouble and just didn't have time to explain to the tower what was going on and what was wrong with my ship. By then I was scared and had ten men that I was not going to see killed because I might make a Colonel mad or bend "procedure." Before I finished my taxi after landing and before I got to the revetment, my third engine went out — no gas. It went out between the revetment and the middle of the runway, so I would have lost it while waiting my turn to land. Had I not broken the rules it would have been a mess because you don't fly a B-17 on one engine. I parked my plane with just one engine wheeling!

I went to debriefing and they wanted to know everything, but would not take my word for it. They jumped in a jeep, took four men, Sergeant-Engineers, and they checked all my gas tanks. They found I had none, not even enough to measure. I would have been a goner if I had been wrong, but I was out of gas so nothing happened to me. I hated to think of making a mission and then crashing on the home field.

The oil refineries and storage yards at Ploesti, Romania were for many months a primary target of the heavy bombers of the 15th Air Force. Lt. Ray Miller completed five missions to Ploesti and recalls his feeling about these missions:

Flying over Ploesti was one you didn't relish. Our particular group of planes, as you will, had a certain target to hit. We did not drop in trail or use intervelometer. We hit the refineries and oil storage fields. The Germans would stick those things up so fast it was unbelievable. They would repair them and we would come back and knock them out again. The oil complex was so big you wouldn't get them all knocked out to begin with. You'd have to come back next day or twice a week to get what you didn't get before. It amazed our people the way they got those refineries and storage facilities back together after we bombed them.

I got to thinking they were dummy refineries etc., they stuck them up so fast. They made us think they were real so we would lay off other plants that were in fact the real thing. It was unbelievable to most Americans, we had to go back and go back again. We weren't the only groups hitting it, there were B-24 groups and British groups hitting it too. Bomber Command was after that oil first and then the marshalling yards. If we could knock out the supplies and transportation it would weaken their ability to wage war.

Not known at this time, however, was one source the Germans used by the thousands to rebuild Ploesti — slave laborers. Before the bombers were out of sight they were at work. But under continual bombings even this huge labor force could not keep Ploesti alive. Bomber Command had decided to put Ploesti off the map and the months of July and August 1944 were devoted to this end.

Ray Miller made one more Ploesti mission on August 18, 1944 in ship #317 with ship #107 on his left wing, it had been repaired and was flown this day by Lt. Rackely. The flight log shows the flak again was heavy, accurate and intense. Ship #317 was hit six times, but nothing serious, though it shook the ship several times. His group lost two B-17s and one ditched in the Adriatic, blew up and burned. All of the crew had bailed out. Two ships of the group went down and dropped life rafts. The next day the Exenia Oil Refinery in Ploesti was the target. Four of the group planes could not make it to 30,000 feet so returned to base. The others made the mission. This time though flak was heavy and intense, it was below them.

For the third day in a row the 483rd hit oil refineries. The 20th of August the objective was the Oswiecim, Poland Oil and Aluminum plant. Lt. Wood was being checked out as first pilot and so flew the left seat. The enlisted crew was that of Lt. MacSparran. The ever-present flak, heavy, intense but not too accurate. The fighters came in greater numbers and made many close passes at the group. Plane #332 flown by Lt. Wood was hit on successive passes by Me109 aircraft, no serious damage was done and there were no injuries to crew members. The fighters made such close-in attacks that some of their ejected shell casings entered the B-17. The attacks were made head on and the gunners in the #332 ship made no hits on the enemy aircraft.

It was getting close to the finish of Lt. Miller's 35 mission mark and the war on oil and aircraft continued with his remaining missions taking him to the Weiner Neudorf engine factory at Vienna, the Pardurice, Czechoslovakia airdrome and factory, followed by a milk run to the Prostonov Airdrome and Brno, Czechoslavakia. He again had Lt. MacSparran's enlisted crew of which Sgt. Black, Waters, Jackson and Shortridge completed 49 sorties. The day after Brno, August 26, an important bridge at Borovnica, Yugoslavia was the target. Described as a milk run, two runs were made on the target with the results unknown. Lt. Griffith, co-pilot; Lt. Ninfo, navigator; Lt. Conaughton, bombardier. Lt. Ninfo and Sgt. Winters finished 50 sorties this day. For the fifth straight day Lt. Miller was in the air and again it was an oil target, the very well defended oil target at one of the German oil centers, Blechhammer, Germany. The flak this time was intense, heavy and accurate. Ray Miller described this mission as, "A pretty rough mission."

Lt. Ray Miller finished out his 35th mission at the synthetic oil plant at Moosebierbaum, Austria. The mission summary states: "Really plastered target, flak was heavy, intense and accurate, received a few hits in wing. Lt. Bloom, my bombardier and I finished 51 sorties — Hurray!!"

The last two missions flown by Ray Miller were in plane #42-102922. It is of interest to note a few remarks in the diary for the last two missions. These have to do with engine and aircraft malfunctions, no doubt a list for the line chief to look at after the mission. "August 27, 1944, Blechammer; Artificial horizon-out; #4 cylinder head temp-low-140-15 and #4 carb air temp gauge out when filter is on, OK when off." The next day, which was his last mission the #4 cyl temp was still bad and #4 temp gauge still bad, but the artificial horizon was repaired. In addition the elevator trim tabs creep and the flaps creep. Getting war weary, but old 42-102922 was still able to get to the target and back.

Ray Miller, civilian, mentioned some things in retrospect:

Some odd things happened on missions. One mission, I was flying, all of a sudden the taxi window just shattered and disappeared, I started to feel where I was hit, as sometimes when you are hit you feel numb. I knew there had to be blood, but I could not see blood, wasn't numb. pretty soon my good senses came back, and I looked at the taxi window. It had vibrated loose with the top turret funs firing right above me and I hadn't tightened the lock too secure, and the wind had carried off that window. I thought the fighter attack had caused it.

We had planes going into Rumania and Germany at night to pick up Evaders. The Underground set up night pick up spots and my group went on several of these. It was ultra hush-hush. The underground would bring bunches of these Evaders to these out-of-the-way places with these guys they had successfully filtered through the German lines.

Ray was asked the question of whether the German fighters or the flak bothered him most. His reply:

With the flak and fighters it seemed to depend on the situation. If you had fighter escort you didn't worry too much about the fighters, but if you had none or if you were too far out, you did worry a little. Still when you have a group of 17s flying tight, 28 in a group, you have a lot of fire power. I can't say I worried as much about the fighters as I did the flak, however, on one occasion this was not so.

I was on an off day and we were not scheduled to fly. My flight went out but was recalled due to bad weather. The Group flight leader did not hear the recall and went on. The Germans had enough fighters to take on the whole group because the Germans knew they were coming. They only had to take care of a flight of 28 B-17s. If there was ever a slaughter, this was it. I'm glad it was my day off.

This incident is detailed by clippings and documents from the 483rd as well as information from one of the men who was in the ground crew, but who also had flown some missions, had been wounded by flak but desired to remain with the group after he was released from the hospital.

Sgt. Everett S. Allen, of Bellvue, Colorado was in the ground echelon of the 483rd Bomb Group, 816th Squadron. Once again this group of dedicated men should be given a well done for their efforts to keep the planes in the air, as they had a lot of pride in keeping "their" airplane in the air and like all the other ground and flying personnel, sweated out each mission. They waited near the tower if at all possible. If other duties would allow it they stood waiting as if they had sent a part of themselves along with the combat crews and were waiting for it to come back to them.

This day Sgt. Allen would wait a long time as the mission described by Lt. Miller was the disaster of Memmingen, Germany.

Lt. Col. Cyril Carmichael, of Pelham, N.Y. and Lt. Col. Willard S. Perry flew as observers, Col. Perry as a tail gunner. Major Louis Seith of San Diego, California, flew as lead pilot in the lead plane. For his bravery and tenacity in pressing home the attack, despite the overwhelming odds, he was awarded the Distinguished Service Cross.

As the wing formed over the Adriatic Sea it encountered very bad weather and the groups became separated. Two groups were unable to penetrate the weather front and returned to base. One other group swung off to bomb an alternate target. Even the expected rendezvous with the P-38 fighter escort was thrown off schedule. To foul matters up even worse was the reception of fake messages from the German radio directing the 483rd to bomb alternate targets. Major Seith challenged the radio messages and when he got no answer to his recognition signals he pressed on to Memmingen.

As they closed on the target, Col. Carmicheal saw 75 enemy fighters, Me109s and FW190s forming up for an attack from the rear. At the same time, Col. Perry called in from his tail gun position 100 more single engine fighters, then still another formation of enemy fighters. The Germans were in no hurry, they knew they had the 483rd cold turkey and planned on methodically shooting the group right out of the sky. There were an estimated 200 fighters to annihilate the 483rd. The Germans, however, did not count on the tenacity and bravery of the men in the bombers. The German fighters came in waves of five and six from the rear, one wave after another.

Col. Carmicheal stated:

The last box of our formation composing seven Fortresses was destroyed in the first attack. Three had blown up immediately, three others went down slowly on fire, but still firing their fifties as they went down. The seventh aircraft went down out of control and broke apart as it descended. The enemy fighters swept around again and practically destroyed another box of seven B-17s using the same tactics as in the initial attack.

From his tail gun position Col. Perry saw Fortresses exploding around him, burning, with their metal skin peeling off. Men were falling to the earth with their parachutes on fire. Enemy fighters were shooting at others as they drifted helplessly toward the ground.

During this time Major Seith was desperately calling for fighter escort, knowing that unless they had fighter protection they just might not make it back to base. When the bombers got to the target they found it well protected by flak batteries. They continued with the bomb run just as they would have on any other mission. Though lacking in numbers, the bombers were able to destroy at least part of the original target area. As the Fortresses turned off the target, a fighter group of a dozen P-38s arrived and began to pitch into the German fighters.

Of the 26 planes that started into Memmingen with the 483rd, 14 were lost to enemy. One hundred and forty-three brave young men were lost inside burning bombers, or plummeted to earth in parachutes that were on fire. Others that did reach the ground safely became guests of the Third Reich as kriegsgefangenen. Other were wounded and would survive and still others would not. It was a costly day for the 483rd and one they would never forget.

The German fighters did not escape the fight unscathed. The B-17 gunners took a toll also, they were given credit for destroying 53 enemy fighters and probably destroying eight others. In the bombing of the airdrome the Germans lost an additional 35 aircraft and three large hangars were destroyed, others damaged.

It was a sorrowfull several hours back at the base when Sgt. Allen and the others watched the small remnant of the group return to base, many crippled and damaged, others unscathed, but whole squadrons had been completely destroyed. This would not have been considered a great loss had the attacking force been of several hundred bombers, but 14 of 26 was a loss of staggering consequences. It was hoped some of the planes had landed at other friendly bases, but this was not to be. This day would set a tradition for the 483rd, they had not turned back, and would not in the future no matter how great the odds. Lt. Miller continued this tradition in the remainder of his missions, but was very glad and very lucky he was not on this one.

Again relating incidents Ray goes on:

Other things that happened to most flight crews was the hang up of bombs in the bomb bay — bombs that would not drop. When you're up there twenty or thirty thousand feet with a bomb hung up in the bomb bay, it is cold. If the bomb has a vane and it is spinning, it is armed and you don't have a lot of time to get rid of it. I think this happened too frequently as far as I was concerned. One time our bombardier, Clarence Stone, had only from his knees to his feet in the plane, he was hanging down in the bomb bay, two guys were sitting on the calves of his legs to keep him from falling out and he was working trying to release the jam. If you don't think that isn't thrilling and a frightening experience just waiting for this guy. Does he know his job well enough to clear the jam? This is what makes a crew close, you have to depend on each other. He's hanging down there with the temperature 20 or 30 below zero, you've got to depend on him and he knows it — it's a thrill. There were bombs set to detonate before impacting, maybe set for 500 ft. for whatever reason, for the spread effect I assume. You can't know if you have bombs that detonate above ground or on impact, you just know — get it out, get it out. I definitely remember two hang ups and probably three. Who is to blame? Who is at fault — the armorer, the bombardier or the outfit that manufactured the bomb racks? One day they work, the next day they don't, it's hard to say. It seems to me if they are hung in balance they would come out OK, but if hung not in balance they won't fall just right, so it is the ground crews fault. Well too, maybe you hit a bump or bounced the plane when taking off, so it's the pilot — so it is everybody's fault or nobody's. Everybody has to take responsibility, this goes for many things.

When we turn onto our initial turning point onto our bomb run, it is the pilots responsibility to check all positions in the plane — tail gunner, top turret, ball turret and so on until all positions answer. They were all to be ready for whatever they were supposed to be doing at that particular time. One time everybody checked in but the right waist gunner. I called twice and no answer. There is only three feet between the two waist gunners. The left waist gunner turned around and here is the other gunner flat on his back, unconscious. He had put on his flak suit, this again was one of the many green crews I flew with, the flak suit is heavy and when he put it on the top part pinched his oxygen hose. Thank goodness for these procedures we had — they happened to save his life. This waist gunner could have been dead in a couple of minutes. We always checked each position to see if they were alert and ready for battle. (Note: Checking Miller's flight log it shows this mission was on August 19, 1944 on a raid to the Exenia oil refinery at Ploesti.)

Just to keep sharp we would take six planes up and practice formation flying if we were weathered out of combat for a few days. When we got done we would go down to the next field and give them a class buzz job, pull up tent pegs and things like that. The next day here would come some B-24s or some P-38s and do us a number one buzz job. The P-38s would go low enough to go between the rows of tents. One time a 38 hooked a tent or two with his wing tips. The base C.O.s got together and said no more! It was bad enough with the enemy killing our men let alone killing them ourselves. It was fun though, and I enjoyed it and in fact I enjoyed the job the other fellows did on us at our place.

When we were getting mustered out the airline companies were trying to recruit pilots. They wanted the "recruits" to go thru six months of extensive training as co-pilots before turning the ships over to them. As it was put by these reps, we had gotten a little careless. We had all been over flying four engines. Some of the guys were instructors. The rep maybe got two guys out of a hundred — we were insulted.

I still have two pennies and a pocket knife I carried on my first mission. I just kept them as lucky pieces. Everytime I went on a mission I had those lucky pieces. They are old and beat up but I still have them. I still have that little piece of flak too.

It wasn't an easy life flying in the war, but you had to make the best of it. I think we enjoyed it as much as it was possible to enjoy and still be sensible about it.

Lt. Farrar, 2nd Bomb Group pilot, flew four missions to Ploesti in the month of July, 1944. With a vast resource of slave labor the Germans were able to do amazing rebuilding jobs on the bombed refineries. The August 1, 1943 mission to Ploesti had done a great deal of damage that was repaired and the refineries were in full production shortly, with one exception. So the following raids were made to really knock them out and keep them out.

Lt. Farrar tells of his missions:

Our missions were very routine, went in the same way every time in that we would proceed up the north end of the valley, make our bomb run north to south right down the marshalling yards. They had flak guns set up on flat cars and it was a turkey shoot — they would shoot the b-jabbers out of us every time. But we did it that way every time to take advantage of the wind. So we started down the marshalling yards dropping bombs intrail and walked our way across the refineries and by this late in the war, they were so well bombed out all we were doing was to make sure they would not rebuild them. They did some amazing things to get those refineries back in operation. And if we hadn't been doing these harassment-type bombings they would have done a lot more. But it was probably just as important to hit the marshalling yards as it was the refineries, so that's what we'd do — just start dropping intrail every second or two, whatever the intervelometer was set at. Just kick out a 500 lb. bomb in mass with the whole Air Force bombing. Walk down the yards across the refineries, maybe a right turn, and go back to Italy. We were putting up 500 to 600 B-17s and B-24s.

I got shot up pretty bad once on one of the Ploesti missions, the July 15th mission. Got hit in the vertical stabilizer and chewed up bad. I really could not tell how bad it was. I looked out the top turret and could see stuff flapping around, but still could not see how much was missing. I stayed with the Group during the bomb run and until we got out of the combat zone and halfway home, then broke away because it was just too difficult to fly formation. A couple of fighters from the 325th Fighter Group peeled off and escorted me in to the first available base which happened to be their base. We left the B-17 there and a plane was sent from our base to pick up the crew and to leave some maintenance people to change the tail.

Kaz was born in Syracuse, New York, July 5, 1920. His family moved to Denver, Colorado in 1923 where he attended Denver Public Schools until graduation, at which time he apprenticed in cabinet making and became a journeyman.

He enlisted in the Army Air Corps Reserve in July, 1941, and was taking flight training at a civilian flight school in preparation for being a glider pilot when the Japanese bombed Pearl Harbor, December 7, 1941. His class was immediately called into active duty as Staff Sergeants, sent to Lubbock Field, Texas for further physical examinations and training. At this point Sgt. Rachak was washed out because of partial color blindness in spite of being told before enlistment that he would be given a waiver. Kaz had been sent to flight school and trained in small Pipers and Aronicas. He completed all but four hours in the first phase of flight training. At this time new orders were issued and he was no longer in the glider program. His new orders sent him to Aircraft Mechanics School at Shepherd Field, Texas. From there he was sent to Tyndall Field, Florida for Gunnery School. His next assignment was to Ellsworth Air Force Base in Rapid City, South Dakota, where he was to be assigned as a combat crew member on a B-17 bomber. He waited over two months there to be assigned to a crew — a typical Army 'Snafu.'

Kaz and his friend Walt spent most of this time on the flight line assisting the maintenance crews and learning as much as they could about the B-17, even reading manuals on the engine systems, etc. They had decided that if they were to be on an aircrew they wanted to know as much as possible about the planes that would carry them over enemy territory and would want to keep them in the very best working and flying condition that they could. This group of eager Sergeants were still in training when the invasion took place on June 6, 1944.

From here on will be the words of Sgt. Rachak relating the remainder of his story:

When we did get assigned to flight crews and got some flying time in B-17s, we went down to Kearney, Nebraska and picked up a brand new shiny plane. We would go out and get flight experience — not the full crew but the pilot, co-pilot, navigator, radio operator and myself — the engineer, and of course the bombardier. Everyone made certain his part of the plane was checked out.

From here we went up to Grenier Field, New Hampshire, stayed several days, then on to Gander, Newfoundland, for two weeks before we got orders to fly to England. There were as many as fifty planes making these trips. We were to be replacement crews. The enlisted men always spent a lot of time checking the plane out since there was little else to do.

The radio operator would tune in all the intercoms to the radio (commercial stations) and if you wanted music you could get it on the intercom, most of it from eastern U.S.

I had the other crew members go with me on my check-out to show them what I did so they could familiarize themselves with the plane and the functions of the power plants. At least enough so they could tell if things were functioning properly, and we did this for something to do. We would preflight the plane nearly every day. I would find a fault now and then — nothing big — lack of coolant and things like that. I felt pretty good about the fact that the officers of my plane allowed me to preflight the plane when they were not present. I felt this was a compliment. A lot of the officers of other planes would not let their engineers start their plane's engines if they were not present. I started our plane up every day and our pilot, Lt. Walthall, was never around. The day we left for England I was preflighting the plane when Lt. Walthall got there. I glanced back and he was standing in the radio compartment. He waved at me and came up and asked, 'How does it check?' I said, 'Everything checks OK.' He said, 'Are we ready to go?' I said, 'Yes Sir!' He got into his seat, the co-pilot, Lt. Myers, got into his seat and we started to taxi. I felt that was a compliment. We were on our way to Wales, England, over water.

Our navigator, Lt. Ingerson, predicted our arrival time to the very minute. It was just a long boring trip — 13 hours from Gander to Wales, England.

When we got to Wales we could not get clearance to land, so we had to fly around above the clouds. Lt. Walthall got tired of that so he called the tower and told them we were low on gas, which we were by then, and they cleared us to land. There were a lot of planes in the air circling around. We came in on a radio beam through a dense overcast until we got down to 200 feet altitude and broke out over the water and then spotted the field.

We stayed at this English field for a short time. The accommodations were somewhat primitive compared to our American style. The plumbing and electricity was what we called antique. The pilot, co-pilot, radio operator and engineer made a lot of training flights, formation flights, just to get familiar with the procedures we would use in England.

For the short time I was with the 486th Bomb Group, I felt the flight crews were treated well. You never knew when you went on a mission if you were going to come back, so they made an attempt to give you the best conditions possible. As engineer, I was issued a bicycle. The co-pilot did not rate a bicycle, and Lt. Myers was a little sore about that and he had to buy one. You had a lot of territory to cover around those fields.

As for missions, my first mission was to France. It was called a no-ball mission — to bomb a missle site — very uneventful. We went in, bombed and came out — no flak and no fighters.

Then my number two mission was on August 4, 1944. It was just thirty days after I had landed in England from the U.S. till I was a POW.

It was a mission to Germany and it was near Bremen where we went down, but I don't recall exactly what the mission was, where it was, or where we were going, other than knowing that it was in Germany. We were flying Tail-End Charlie, which is the lowest echelon, and we were on our way into Germany.

We were near Bremen, which is a seaport. We had checked our guns and then we started seeing flak. We'd see these black puffs of smoke where they were exploding and started seeing it up around the planes. Then we actually saw some fighters, but they hadn't made any attacks or anything. We did have some escort at that time — P-47s that were escorting. The P-47 fighters would pick you up after you got over there since their range was so much shorter than the bombers. They'd just come in and pick you up and try to escort you in what they considered the critical areas if you were to be attcked by fighters. I was in the upper turret and I remember swinging, turning around, trying to look for any enemy attack. Just as I brought it around and was facing forward, I realized there was a B-17 with its tail directly over our 3 and 4 engines and we were coming together. Our 3 and 4 engines were coming in directly underneath the tail of the plane above us. They were either coming down or we were going up — I don't know exactly how. Apparently we had gotten some propwash. If you are flying directly behind a plane, you start catching all of his propwash. Then it's almost impossible for you to control the airplane. We were flying the lowest echelon and were flying right wing to the plane that we ended up crashing into. It wasn't until afterwards that I heard that the plane that we crashed into was actually the plane on whose right wing we had been flying. This means that some way or another they either had to come up and over and above our right wing, or we went down, moved over and our 3 and 4 engines came up underneath the tail of the other ship. I think about that poor tail gunner on that other plane — he didn't have a prayer to survive that at all. There was no way because the 3 and 4 engines came right up into the tail of that ship. When that happened, I remember saying, 'Oh, God!'

298

I don't know whether it was a maneuver or what, but I know that I felt like I was slammed down into a sitting position on my gun turret where I'd normally stand. I was aware of the turret bubble breaking up and the debris flying around my head, and also of electrical flashes. The plane had a feeling of being uncontrollable. We were in a spin or something and the pilot had hit the bail-out buzzer. I was wearing a chest pack harness and I didn't have my parachute on. Strangely enough, I had put it in a certain place by my turret and I reached for it and it was there. I snapped my chute on and realized when I put it on, that the "D" ring was on the left side instead of the right side. In my own mind I said that doesn't make any difference to me whether I pull this with my left hand or my right hand. I wasn't going to stop and try to unhook it and turn it over since it was a chest pack.

There is a tunnel underneath the pilot and co-pilot up into the nose section, and I dropped down into that hold section. Our altitude was over 20,000 feet but we didn't have oxygen masks on by that time, or they were disconnected. Quentin was motioning towards the escape hatch. I opened the escape hatch which was directly in that tunnel as you go up in the nose. I motioned for Lt. Quentin Ingerson to jump. He bailed out and Graham, the bombardier, was right behind him. He motioned me to bail out, so I went ahead. From that point on I don't know what happened to the rest of the crew. I don't know why more guys didn't get out.

At the time you bail out, all you are aware of is that you are going down awfully fast, and of course, in training they told us to make sure that you drop out of the area (freefall) long enough to get you out of the formation. We were Tail-end Charlie, so that wasn't a problem, although I probably did drop over 10,000 feet. I had my shoes tied onto my pack — all I had on was the flying boots. One flying boot was pulled off by the jolt as I came down, and that made me mad, so I kicked the other one off. I kept looking over my shoulder because it seemed like I was on my back in a reclining position as if I was in a Lazy Boy. I was coming down in that position. I remember I put my hand out, thinking that maybe I could control the descent just a little bit in order to see what I could do. When I did that it was like being completely out of control. I started tumbling all over, so I stopped that in a hurry. Finally, when I started breaking down through some of the clouds, I could get a pretty good view of the countryside. I pulled the chute and it was like a snap of the fingers, and there you were just floating along. It was really a beautiful day. The freefall had been pretty fast. It didn't seem like it took much time for that. Once the chute is open and you were just floating around, you start looking around trying to orientate yourself — figure out where you are and your direction. I was coming down in the countryside and I could see all these farms — a beautiful part of Germany. I could see a forest of trees. I thought if I get down what I'll try to do is to get over to that forest. Of course I had the regular escape packets (maps, money, compass, etc.) It was American money, I don't recall how much money was in there but it was considerable. There were some candy bars and other things to help you.

I could hear the dogs barking. It was a beautiful, peaceful day, and we were floating down, and of course I knew that I was in Germany. I landed in an open field. The ground was kind of soft as the cows had walked all over the field and there were holes all over it. When I hit, I just had socks on and I dislocated my right ankle. I stood up and I shook my foot and it popped back into position. It's a wonder that I didn't break it because of the way that my foot went sideways. It immediately started swelling and I had to spill my chute. By the time the chute spilled and I sat down to put my shoes on, my right ankle had swollen so much that I almost had to take the laces completely out in order to get my shoe on. I grabbed my chute and took it over to a little stream at the edge of the field. I hadn't seen anybody but I realized now that I was being watched. They had watched me coming down, that would be the Home Guard, which they call the Volksturm. I had gone over to the stream and I had the chute all bundled up in my arms. I stepped into the stream. It wasn't a very deep one, maybe six or eight inches deep. There was an overhang where a tree had been growing out close to the bank. I stuffed the chute back underneath this overhang. Then I started upstream in the direction of the forest that I had seen. I realized how sore my ankle was. It was absolutely killing me — I could hardly walk. I did manage to go up that stream a ways, and then I got out of the stream and started across a field. I was staying down low on my hands and knees going in the direction of the woods. I heard somebody hollering something like "Hello." I realized I was not going to go anyplace with my ankle the way it was, so I stood up and looked around. I saw some guys that turned out to be French prisoners. The Germans used a lot of the French prisoners on farms as laborers. One of the prisoners had been the one saying hello to me. Then I started to see other people with shotguns walking toward me in the field. These were the Home Guard. When they came up, one guy grabbed me by the arm which made me kind of mad and I jerked away from him. He kept indicating to inquire where my gun was and I tried to tell him I did not have a gun. That was one thing they had stopped issuing us in England. We had been issued them in the states but they had taken them away from us in England which made sense. You don't go down in enemy territory with a forty-five on your hip. You're not a one-man army and you're not going to do any good with that gun. Then he wanted to know where my chute was. He kept saying something like 'balloona' which I thought might mean parachute. I finally pointed in the direction where I had hidden it, but from there you could not see it, so he made me go get it. Of course, I had to step into the water again to get it. The one German pointed to his eyes as if to say, "You did a good job of hiding it."

I had to carry that wet parachute and I could hardly walk with that bad

300

ankle, but you walked whether you wanted to or not. We walked toward some other Germans. There was a ditch which we had to cross — it was dry, no water in it. A German was standing on the other side of the ditch and he said something to the guys that were with me. There were two of them and there were four on the otherside. After the one spoke, the two with me stepped aside, and I saw that one German across the ditch had a shotgun levelled at me and at the time I thought, "Boy, this is it! This guy is going to blast me." That shotgun looked like a cannon, especially when you knew it was pointed at you and you wondered if he was going to shoot you or what. He lowered the gun and indicated with his gun to cross the ditch. So I went across the ditch and went down a little trail. It was very beautiful — it was picturesque countryside — but at the time that was not uppermost in my mind, just my misery.

We started down toward a little village. By the time we got there, there were quite a few people milling around. The word had spread so we stopped at a place and they allowed me to sit down and rest. I really needed to wrap my ankle but did not have my wits about me to cut a piece of that huge parachute for a bandage. The German women would come over and feel that parachute cloth. It was made of nylon and I was thinking how they would really like to have that material. I had some gum in my pocket and there were some German kids standing there looking at me, so I took out the gum and tossed it over to them. It landed near them and an adult German came over and was real angry and mashed it into the ground with his foot. So, I thought, he thinks that is some kind of poison. I took a piece of the gum and put it into my mouth and showed them that it was good gum. Those kids really wanted that gum. The Home Guard had taken my survival packet and they had gone through it.

Shortly after this, here came Quentin, the navigator. They had picked him up also. I asked him about the rest of the crew, but he said he did not know anything about them. They took us to a house — sort of a jail house. When we got there, there were two other guys that turned out to be the pilot and co-pilot of the plane we had collided with. According to what they said, they could not tell us much about what caused the crash or just what happened. But with the tail of their plane cut off it was completely out of control. They said they did not even know how they got out. They thought the plane might have broken up and they were thrown free, but they were the only survivors. There were just two survivors out of their plane and two survivors out of our plane. That meant fourteen men lost their lives when those two planes met at 20,000 feet for just a few brief seconds of time.

The Home Guard turned us over to the military and we were taken to an unused airfield. I had complained about my ankle so they took me to a doctor. When I got there, there was a little kid talking to the doctor. They were having a nice conversation. When the conversation was over and the

301

kid was getting ready to leave, he stepped back, clicked his heels together, threw up his right hand and yelled, 'Heil Hitler!' I thought, boy there isn't any question — I'm in Germany.

The treatment the doctor gave me for my ankle was very simple. He took some paper similar to crepe paper, wet it with water, and applied that to my ankle. There was no cloth or any kind of support for the ankle and believe me it was killing me — I could not rest or anything. I was really in pain, but that is all the aid I ever got for that ankle.

The military then decided to move us to Oberusel, but on the way they took us through Bremen during blackout conditions. We rode on an old streetcar. We got on that streetcar — four of us Americans and two German army guards. We were getting dirty looks from the civilians. They knew we were Americans but they called us "Terrifliegers," which means terrorist flyers. They were completely ignoring what Germany was doing to the civilian populations of England and the other Allied countries.

Riding in the trolley made me nervous as it was dark and I did not know what was going on, or if one of the civilians was liable to try and blow our brains out.

While we were in Bremen they had an alert and they found a bomb shelter to take us into. This was a night raid by the English and we could hear the bombs. While we were in there, we had the company of some German civilians. We did not care for some of the threatening looks and sounds from them, so we were moved to another room in the bomb shelter. The guards could speak English and one asked us, "Do you know what they want to do in there?" We said, "No." He answered, "They want to hang you guys." That is why they moved us.

From Bremen to Oberusel to the interrogation center by car. If you have seen movies of the Germans speeding down country roads with chickens and geese scattering, that is what they were doing on this drive to Oberusel.

For interrogation purposes they had the camp divided into separate sections for officers and for enlisted men; consequently, this was the last time I saw Quentin and the other two officers. It was now a single "I" rather than "we."

I remained in the center for about a week — in solitary confinement. They wanted to know all about my Group, my crew, and that sort of information. It was mostly of no significance at all, but they did already have a lot of information. They knew our Bomb Group and many names. They gave out more information than they received as all they got from me was name, rank and serial number. After they made it miserable for me for three or four days, they received a new bunch of prisoners so they sent me off. They sent me to Wetzlar Dulag Luft.

As Air Corps noncommisioned officers, the Germans did not work us as they did the regular enlisted men and they sent those men to a different camp.

Our transportation to Wetzler was in a box car on a train, much like the ones they transported the Jews in enroute to the extermination camps. The only facilities they provided was a bucket. There were so many of us in a car that not all of us could sit down at the same time. We would sit down for awhile and then stand up and let someone else sit down in the place where you had been sitting. With only the one bucket for relieving yourself, most of the time you just held it, especially if you had to defecate. But it got to be a stinking mess. I was in three different camps and between each I was transported in these boxcars.

One time we were in a railyard and were trapped during a bombing. It was daylight and the Americans were working over that railyard. The German guards just took off and left the train and headed for the ditches and whatever they could find for shelter and left us in the boxcars. We watched the bombing and strafing. What else could we do? There were no visible marks to identify our boxcars as POW cars and we were locked in. Railroad tracks were flying in the air like spaghetti. Railroad ties and other debris was flying around and making a terrible noise. Luckily we didn't get hit by a bomb nor were we strafed.

We got to St. Wendel Stalag Luft VI but it did not make an impression on me that it was different than the other two camps that I had been in. It, too, was a family-type camp. The barracks were just long wood buildings with a crawl space underneath them. The idea was that it would keep the guys from digging tunnels. We had mattresses filled with excelsior and in no time at all that was like sleeping on a board, but even at that you got used to it. The blankets were not much to talk about either. If they got wet they felt like a soggy piece of leather. They were pretty bad. The food was nothing great. After eating in a U. S. military camp and then in a German POW camp, there was quite a difference. The U. S. food was gourmet — the German was a one dish meal. It might be potatoes or barley soup or a soup with cabbage or turnips. Meat was very scarce, and on those occasions you did not know what kind it was. We had two meals a day. The first was practically nothing — issued around noon, and the main meal was at night. It was better when things were better for the Germans. We also had our Red Cross parcels which were really a Godsend. They had cigarettes, candy, meat (Spam), crackers and jelly. You might also find a deck of cards once in awhile or a chess board or checkers, etc. A real break for me at the time was that I did not smoke and cigarettes became like money so you could bargain with them. It was a means of getting extras. For instance, a half a pack of cigarettes would get you a couple of rations of bread. As a result, my good POW buddy, Leon Peragallo, who also did not smoke, and I had the opportunity to get extra food. It was hard to believe that some guys would trade food for cigarettes.

There was not a lot to do in the camp. They had a few instruments and some of the guys could play them and would give a concert. We'd have football games, volleyball games, and we did a lot of walking. People would just walk around constantly. They were pretty good sized compounds and arranged in sections that were square, and divided like a cross with the main gate at the intersection. Barbed wire was strung along the top of a wire fence. About twenty feet in from the wire fence was a single strand of wire. That was to designate no-man's-land. To go beyond that was strictly a no-no — you could be shot.

The barracks were broken up into rooms, and you had cold running water. At the end of the barracks there was a wash room with no toilet. Our toilet was an enclosed pit toilet which had to be pumped out when full. Twenty guys to a room. One guy in each room was the room leader. I was the leader in our room. That meant that you were the arbitrator if there were problems between the Americans or problems with the Germans. You would see to it that the food was distributed evenly because when things got real tough some guys can be real horses asses. You can't believe the pettiness and crappy little things that go on in a prisoner of war camp. You would think that everybody would pull together to make it as easy as possible on each other, but that was not always the case.

In the POW camp there was a marked tendency to "live by the cards." Everything was divided or distributed by chance or "by the cards" — that was the way. Some of the men wanted to live that way because they felt that it would be like fate — if the cards indicated they got that portion of food, that would satisfy them and they could accept that. I thought it was ridiculous and I did not go along with their game, and I told them so. I would not live by the cards. I wasn't trying to be a goody-goody or a martyr. For instance, I was the official bread cutter and I cut the bread into six equal portions. I would cut the bread and I would say, "Here, you guys take your piece of bread and just leave me one piece of it. I don't care if it is the end or the middle or where, just leave me one piece." I had it cut equally and there was no reason to portion out the bread in any special way — such as dividing it up by the cards. But we did play regular card games as well — hearts, poker and games like that.

I spent a lot of time embroidering. I used a handkerchief and a hoop that I made from a coffee can lid. I traded good socks for a pair of worn-out argyle socks so that I could unravel them for the different colors of thread. The silver in the wings and the USAAF was made out of thread from parachute silk. It turned out to be a good way to use my time and also to record my story. I really protected that handkerchief, and I now have it framed.

While in camp at Stettin-Stalag Luft IV C, I saw about 50 crews that had gone over as replacements and had gone down. At that time I was under the impression that the "luck" part of this flying was over, because it can't be nearly as bad as when the air force first started flying missions over Germany. At that time the German had plenty of planes, men to fly them, fuel as well, and also plenty of anti-aircraft guns. It was unusual for an original crew to finish a tour. I thought that after being at war that many years we were going to have it pretty good, but that proved to be very wrong. After meeting some members of the replacement crews, I found what had happened to some of my buddies in my group. One was Walter Midget, who was married with a family, and he had bailed out on a mission. He came down in a village and was hung up on a house with his parachute — he was up off the ground just hanging there when a German civilian came up and shot him in the head. He was probably one of the best friends that I had while I was in the service. It was tragic.

At Stalag Luft IV C we were close to the Russian front, so we were moved when Germany began to be overrun. The last two months in Germany we were moved out and did not know what they were doing, but we found out later that had we been left there we would have been freed by the Russians within a week. The Germans did not want this to happen so we went on what I call a 'walking tour of Germany.' All we did was walk and walk, sometimes as many as twenty miles a day, other times just ten or fifteen miles a day. We did this for two months, rain or shine, it made no difference. We would stop in bigger farms where they had huge barns and we would bed down in these barns. They cooked the same potatoes for us that they fed to the hogs. There was nothing really wrong with it — they just had a lot of potatoes. The people in the farmhouse also ate the same potatoes.

I remember one farmer who had chickens, and, as he didn't trust the prisoners, he kept the chickens penned separately. We were nosing around and I decided that I could crawl over a partition into the chicken pen and get some eggs — which I had not had in a long time. As soon as I got them, Leon let me out through a side door. I no sooner got out of there when I saw the farmer coming with a bucket to gather eggs — but I had gotten all of them. When he went into the pen and found no eggs, he came out just a storming. He knew darn well some of the prisoners had gotten his eggs. He raised hell with the guards, shaking his fist at them and pointing to the prisoners. We later boiled the eggs and had ourselves a feast.

When traveling we had to rig up some type of cooking pot. I had a little pot and a little stove which we had made from a small can and a larger can. We would collect grain and cook it into cereal. We always managed to find the farmer's grain storage. I had found a coffee grinder in an abandoned German farm with which we could grind the grain. I went into the business of grinding wheat for the rest of the guys. I let them use the grinder in my sight or Leon's — we never let them use it out of our sight. The fee was twenty-five percent of the grain. There were a few die-hards who were not going to pay 25% for the use of the grinder. But they came around when they

305

saw the other guys cooking up the ground wheat. Soon I had them all, so I did not have to scrounge for grain.

We tried all kinds of concoctions — mixing up ground crackers with chololate bars and then try to make a cake out of it. We tried to scrounge salt for the potatoes, and onions were a real treat with them. Just anything to get a little flavor into the potatoes.

If we found vegetables, we would make a stew out of them. We would take some of our cereal and put some of our chocolate bar in there and have chocolate cereal. Anything to get a little flavor. We had tea in the Red Cross parcels and, of course, we used that tea bag until there was absolutely no sign of color in the water before you disposed of it. Some guys would even go so far as to dry the tea leaves and smoke them. You had to try to utilize everything.

One time we stayed in a factory — a dish factory. We were on the second floor and on the main floor. On the third and fourth floor was where the dishes were stored. For a while we all ate off fine china dishes and even set tables with full china service. One day while we were outside of this factory we heard some planes come over. They were A-26 bombers and they were flying low — so low that we thought we could hear the bomb bay doors open. They were after the railroad station and yards about a block way. They leveled that railroad station — and it was a big one. While we were out there away from the factory, as we thought that they might hit it also, a single P-47 fighter came by very low and as slow as he could and he waved to us.

Our walking tour was about to come to an end as Germany was getting smaller and smaller. The Russians were closing in from the east and the Americans and British from the west. They were keeping us in between.

In one town we saw a lot of people — Germans as well as French ex-prisoners that had been set free. Their German guards had simply said, "Go." The Germans knew that this war was over. There were thousands of Germans who did not want to be taken by the Russians as they would just kill them. All of the freed French prisoners and the Germans were clogging the roads headed for the American lines.

We got to the edge of a town where there was a fork in the road. At this time I had lost track of my pal Leon Peragallo. He had received some flak wounds in his legs when he had been shot down and his legs were not in good shape. The Germans had said that they were taking some of the wounded men out of the march and Leon was one of them. I had now palled up with Gus Gustoffson from San Francisco. I told Gus that the bunch taking the left fork were headed for the American lines while our group was taking the right fork. I didn't see any point in staying with our group any longer, so let's head for the American lines. We started right on down that fork, right past the German guards, and I know that they looked us over and realized that we were American prisoners, but they could care less. They probably thought that we were just two less prisoners that they would have to worry about. We kept walking and reached a point where the number of people really thinned out so that we were almost by ourselves except for a couple of Frenchmen who had indicated that they wanted to go with us simply because we could speak English. We had no objection to that and they came along with us.

On our march we had seen many towns that were burning, and we saw military equipment burning along the way. I started to pick up one of the German helmets when one of the Frenchmen tore it out of my hand and threw it down. He was trying to tell me that I was asking for trouble as they would take me for a German. About eleven or twelve at night we reached a town where we could see a lot of fighting. We could see fires burning, and the houses that were intact had white flags in the windows, but there was no one around. The Frenchmen were pulling little carts and wagons filled with their possessions and clattering down the cobblestone streets. We kept on moving down to what appeared to be a barricade. We got to within a hundred yards of that barricade, which seemed to be in the middle of the town, when someone yelled, "Halt!" That was music to our ears as it had to be Americans, so I yelled back,"Amerian and French ex-prisoners of war HF we'd like to come through." The GI hollered to us, "Americans come forward, the French stay behind." Gus and I went up to the barricade where we were asked for identification. All we had was our dog tags. They were very good to us and invited us to stay with them. Then they had the French come up and they grabbed the Americans and were kissing them. The GIs didn't go for that and pushed them away. They sent the French on through. We stayed.

They took us to a German house which they had taken over and one GI asked us if we wanted to eat. We said that we would like to eat, and he said, "How about some ham and eggs?" "Sure." So these two GIs fried up a batch of ham and eggs. We could not eat much, however, as our stomachs had shrunk from the small rations that we had been living on. They found us some beds and we stayed that night.

The next day they took us back by jeep to an Eighth Air Force camp as we had been in the Eighth Air Force. The Air Force had taken over a field where there were some ME 262 jet fighters. Earlier in our march we had gone by a German airfield where we had seen some of these new jets. As we walked by the airfield we saw one of these fighters lift off the ground. It was as if he turned the nose of that plane straight up, and he shot straight up in the air with a roar. It was a frightening sound as we didn't know what it was the first time. We just couldn't believe that there was such a plane around. I had heard of the jets before and had seen one crash. At that time there didn't seem to be any other plane around when the jet went straight down and hit the ground at a terrific speed and exploded into a ball of flame.

307

When we got to the Eighth Air Force base, they had some ME 262 jets there, most of them intact, but inoperable due to damage by our fighters from strafing. This was my first glimpse of the jet up close. I have been told that with the V-1 rocket and that 262 jet, Hitler could have won the war had he not been so stubborn. He wanted to make the 262 as a bomber rather than as what it was designed for HF a bomber interceptor. There was nothing in the sky at the time that could stay with that plane. I dread to think of the great and terrible losses our bomber crews would have sustained had the Germans used that plane. I guess there were some bomb groups that did come in contact with it. With its four thirty-millimeter cannon, it could tear a B-17 apart.

After staying at this base awhile is when we first heard about the extermination camps and the atrocities that the Germans had committed. One officer asked me if I wanted to see one of the camps, but I declined. Sometimes I wonder if I should have gone or not. Perhaps I should have, but I didn't go because at the time my only thought was to get the h--- out of that country and get home.

After staying there several days getting cleaned up and getting used to being free again, a Captain said that he was taking us to LeHavre, France. We went by car to another airfield. At this field the Air Force was flying DC-3s into Paris, and we were told that we would get priority seating over the many officers who were trying to get into Paris. We were being treated very well all this time. We boarded first and I sat next to a one-star General, but when I tried to carry on a conversation with him he was not talkative so we made the trip in silence.

In Paris they put us up in a hotel and we got to do a little touring around for a couple of days. We then went to LeHarve where we were processed. We had no gear of any kind because we just had the clothes on our backs. The only thing I had was my rolled-up embroidery work. We were issued more clothes in LeHarve, and then we boarded an Italian liner. After two weeks of rough water and what seemed a very slow trip, we landed in New York. When you see the Statue of Liberty, you know you are home.

The next portion of the trip was by train to Denver where I was given a 90-day leave after which I reported to Santa Monica and was asked where I wanted to be transferred to. I said, "As close to Denver as I can get." I was dispatched to the 2nd Air Force in Colorado Springs where I was discharged after several more months of duty.

Thinking back over things gone by: I had several POW pals, one of which was George McCrary, who wanted to be a doctor. He was from Georgia. I tried to find him after the war, but never did. I often wondered if he ever became a doctor. On our march through Germany, George had a bad case of cracked lips. As we were marching down one road, I said, "George, you just don't know how lucky you really are."

He said, "What do you mean, Rachak?"

I said, "'Well, did you ever think that you were going to get a tour like this through Germany? Now this is the greatest thing that ever happened to you."

George looked at me and with puckered lips said, "Damn it, Rachak, I don't want to laugh." His lips were so cracked that they would have split open. I thought that if I ever found George and he was a doctor, I would ask to see him and then ask his nurse to ask him if he would treat someone with cracked lips. George would have been out in a second, but I am sorry that I have never located George again.

I met Melvin Stark in mechanics school. He lives in Denver. We went to gunnery school, and then he went to another training school when I went to Rapid City. I had been in POW camp about two months when I saw Mel walk in. I found out later that he had been wounded by 20mm flak in his legs and he had been in a hospital. When I saw him walk in, I walked toward him and when I got about ten feet from him, he looked at me and yelled, "Rachak, what the hell are you doing here?" I said, "The same damn thing you are."

Joseph Melnyk was from New Jersey, I believe. A nice guy, though I did not get to know him well, but I tried to keep in touch with him. He had always talked about becoming a priest.

Leon Peragallo and I have kept in contact since the war and have visited back and forth. He is married and his son went through the Air Force Academy. Leon and I keep in touch, but I wish I knew where the other guys ended up.

Tour Summary

Narrator: James Abrams, Ball Turret Gunner
Group: 390th Bomb Group, 568th Squadron

Jim Abrams was a small, wirey, very rugged man who had worked at ranching in Wyoming and then in Colorado before entering the Air Corps from Fort Collins, Colorado, his present home. After making all of the training tours, as had his predecessors, in the gunnery schools, Jim, because of his size was assigned to the ball turret — not to his liking. He had the feeling of being penned in — something that he had no relish for. As a true westerner he loved the wide open spaces and the ball did not allow that.

In the ball turret you were 100% isolated, unable to wear a parachute. The harness was strapped on and there was also a safety belt that hooked onto the side of the ball so you would not be sucked out if the door came off while you were in flight in the ball. This same strap also prevented you from being able to turn around far enough to see if the door of the ball was properly latched. This became the job of the waist gunner. He was responsible for latching and hooking this door. There were two pins that went through the two latches and these rolled out of the way so the ball could rotate 180 degrees and turn 360 degrees. With a heated flying suit, oxygen mask and the harness, there's not much room to move around. To add to the discomfort, the electric wires in the suit ran across your kidneys and put a lot of pressure on them. As Jim described it, "Your kidneys literally kill you — bad." There was a relief tube in there but that too, was nearly impossible to use because of all the flight gear you had on.

The parachute was just laid on the floor of the ship near the ball turret. When forced to exit the ball, the gunner rotated the ball so that the guns were pointed straight down and the door was up. He unhooked his safety strap, pulled the two pins, came out of the ball, snapped on the chest pack chute and went out the waist window or the bomb bay.

One of the first things that the ball turret gunner did after snapping himself in, was to hook up the intercom and call in to the pilot that he was in his position. All pilots drilled this procedure into their

310

crews. It was also standard procedure to call in once the ship was in formation. In training on one occasion Jim Abrams was chewed out for not following this procedure. He recalled:

We were up and formed and I crawled into the ball, got plugged in, got my safety strap on, and wham! That damn door came off. It had not been properly latched. Had I not had my safety strap hooked on, I would have been sucked right out of that ball. Needless to say, when I came out of there I was scared and mad enough to kill that waist gunner on the spot. The pilot chewed me out for not calling in. There was no way that I could have called into anyone on anything — I was speechless. I had a bad feeling for that waist gunner from then on. That is the most lonesome place in the world down there.

Before I got to England the crew that I had trained with had gone ahead of me and I was assigned to a different Group. I was put in Lt. Dinwoodies crew. It was a good crew, but I always made the rounds on my days off to see if I could get a ride on some other crew in order to get my missions finished. I wanted to get back to my wife, Jo, as fast as I could.

When we were alerted for a mission, someone would wake us up maybe three hours before. We would go to the chow hall for breakfast and then to briefings — the officers to theirs and the enlisted men to ours. There we would get an idea as to what to expect as escort and how far they would go with us. Most of the time we had P-51 Mustangs for escort, especially on our missions to Big "B," though on others we had P-47 Thunderbolts. At the plane, the crew would meet under a wing and the pilot would tell us the things he had been briefed on — how many flak guns to expect, enemy fighters and their type. Our target was given to us when we were formed up. We had a primary, alternate and a target-of-opportunity. If weather kept us out of one we would go to the other.

One strange thing that happened to us now and then was when we were headed for the continent over the channel, we would run into some of the British returning from their night missions. They never did learn how to fly formation and looked like a bunch of mosquitoes. There had even been some head-on collisions with them. The 43rd Combat Wing — the 390th, 95th and 100th Bomb Groups — flew at designated altitudes going over and different altitudes coming back. Very strict discipline about this and very precise. Our C. O., Col. Moller, even had us up flying practice formations in bad weather when we could not go on our missions. One time we got out toward the channel and were picked up by British radar and they began shooting at us. We had wandered too close to the coast where we were not supposed to be flying.

It gave you a kind of spooky feeling when you were running down that runway with a full load of gas and bombs. On the Berlin raids we would

311

warm the engines up and then top off the tanks again. We wanted every drop of gas we could get for that trip. On those long missions we would just get to the coast and the German flak guns would start shooting at us. Old "One Gun Charlie" would invariably get an airplane or two — not knock them down, but damage them. We tried to knock those guns out several times — even used liquid nitro, or maybe it was napalm. The flames from those bombs would reach right up to you. They were literally burning the ground up. Over other targets the Germans would use a lot of colored flak from time to time — yellow, purple and red bursting all around you like a fireworks display. Maybe they were trying to cause our pilots to be fascinated by it and to fly into it.

The chaff ship usually flew in the lead to drop the chaff. He was in a vulnerable spot. We had flown that slot a few times and it seemed that we always got some flak holes. I never was worried with the flak as much as I was with high altitude frostbite. It is down as cold as fifty below zero up there. It was hard to impress on some gunners not to take their gloves off when they had a gun malfunction. If one took any time at all he could get frostbite, and in a few days his flesh would just begin to fall off. Gangrene would set is and it was a hell of a mess.

Asked if he gave his guns any special treatment, Jim said:

No I just kept them as dry as I possibly could. I never did use anti-freeze like some other gunners. We did have a dry lubricant though, and we always fired a few rounds before we got to the enemy coast to be sure they were working.

We did see some of the German jet fighters late in the war. I'm glad they did not use them until late. If they would have, it might have been a horse of a different color. We would have lost a lot of planes and crews. They had four 30mm cannon, and when they dove down through a squadron they took someone with them. When someone would call "Bandits at 12 o'clock," they went "pppssssssssssshhhhh," and they were gone. You just got a glimpse of them. I always said that no gun could ever keep up with them.

The Germans were still sending over those buzz bombs toward London, and once in awhile we could see them and hear them. We had seen some of the buildings they had hit, and they were pretty well demolished. We had our base bombed a few times too. I don't know how they sneaked in, but they did. They never did much damage, though, and one time we found five un-exploded bombs.

One of our waist gunners liked to hunt pheasants and so do I. In this part of England there was good quail and pheasant hunting. We all had to take gunnery training, officers and men, at the skeet range. The waist gunner and I got in good with the range people and when they were not too busy we would sneak off with a shotgun and some shells and go bird hunting. Jack got caught one day by one of the Parham town magistrates, and we were fined 25 English pounds. That was a lot of money in those days as the pound was worth $4.16 American. It cost us that much for shooting one of the King's pheasants.

The assault before the invasion of Europe was a sight to see. Everything that could fly was in the air. Any place you looked you could see airplanes. We also had a lot of gliders flying, and the ground was littered with them. It looked like match sticks had been thrown up and scattered as they fell. That was a sight that you only see once and will never see again.

When I was in Scotland later on my way home in a B-17, we had to wait for weather and I met a glider pilot who was from Longmont, Colorado. In visiting with him I found that I had played with his two younger brothers. That is the closest I ever came to finding anyone from home. I also met a gunner from the original crew that I had trained with. I inquired about the crew, and it was bad news for them. He had been sick the day of their first mission, so he had to stay behind. The plane went roaring down the runway on take-off for that mission, but never got off the ground. It crashed and everyone on board was killed. Just one of those things you have to think about — you can call it whatever you like.

When I first went over, there was an option that I heard you had on your 35th mission. You could bail out of your plane just to say that you had in case you had wanted to but had not. When I reached my 35th mission, I had no desire to do that. I had had all of the war that I wanted.

Tour Summary

Narrators: **Fred McCullough, Billy Bittle,**
Doug West, Merle Hess
Groups: **385th and 100th Bomb Groups**

We used to get a bucket of coal a day in the winter in England. The type of stoves we had were the English style with a chunk of concrete in the middle to act as a firebrick, I guess, but the stove would never heat up. We never could get that stove to warm up, so we would take the concrete, bust it up and take it out. The stove was so flimsy that it would soon burn out. We lived in Butler huts. When our coal was gone we would just go to where it was stored and steal some more. There was a guard there at the coal pile and we would go up to him and say, "We are going to steal some coal. Would you go to the other side?" He would and we would proceed with the theft. The doors on those huts would often bang at night, but no one would ever get up to shut them — it was too cold to get up.

Spam and cabbage are the two things that will never be received with relish by Fred McCullough. I have never had any of it in my whole married life. Corned beef and cabbage — we used to call the corned beef "buzzard guts." You could have all you wanted from the mess hall. The crew chief of our plane had a labrador dog and she had eight pups. We'd go up to that mess hall with a sack and fill it up with that stuff and feed it to the dog and her pups. She had the nicest set of pups you ever saw — raised on corned beef.

We got a lot of gin, and with every bottle of gin we got a gallon of grapefruit juice. We had one guy that was a librarian in civilian life and a real prissy sort of guy. He got into the Army and started to drinking and became an alcoholic. He was in charge of the liquor room and sometimes four of us would go up there and one of us would keep him busy while the others would fill their pockets with anything we could find.

One day he went to town with his jeep and trailer to get our allotment of booze. Somewhere in London he stopped to see his girl friend on his way home. When he got back to the jeep to leave for the base, it had been stolen — jeep, trailer and booze. This type of thing happened.

When we first got to the base and with the 549th Squadron, we were briefed by a Captain who gave us a talk. He said, "Take a look at the guy next to you — in two weeks one of you is not going to be here." By golly he was right. They didn't paint any rosy picture of what it would be like. For a period of time I might be the only survivor of the bunch that came with me into the squadron. At one time my co-pilot and I were the only ones left in camp while we had one crew at the rest home. Later they got shot down. I don't recall the pilot's name, but I had flown with him once or twice.

When I enlisted from my folks home town, which at that time was Lance Creek, Wyoming, I was Assistant County Agent at Sundance, Wyoming. I was sent to Jefferson Barracks, Missouri for a time, then sent to Coe College in 1943 from February till July. From there to Santa Ana, California, and then to good old Victorville, California — class of '44. I enlisted and I didn't get into bombardier school as a pilot wash-out, rather, I went right into bombardier school. After our training at Victorville, we were shipped to Yuma, Arizona for three weeks. We were to be shipped out on B-25s as cannoneers, but the Army changed its mind and sent us to Lincoln, Nebraska where we were assigned to crews and sent to Rapid City, South Dakota where we trained as a crew. Then it was back south to Kearney, Nebraska to pick up a brand new B-17. We flew it to Ireland via Bangor, Maine; Goose Bay, Labrador; and Iceland. Our radio man had been called home for an emergency so we had to wait for another one to replace him, so we did not get to go over with our own Group, but went later with others also flying over.

Our base was number 155 at Elmswell near Ipswich. We joined the 385th Bomb Group, 349th Squadron. The ship which we tried to call our own was named "Nan" — no reason other than its call letter was "N" for Nan. That is what we called it although we had nothing painted on it. The set-up in the 385th at that time was two crews for every position. One day when our "B" crew was flying, our ship got shot up so that we had to fly whatever came along, or whatever was flyable when it was our turn to fly.

Of the crew that I went over with, only the tail gunner was left when I completed my tour and he had 18 missions. I had been put on another crew as the others had been shot down. We had lost three men on our fifth mission to Berlin. My co-pilot on his 31st mission landed in France. He called our base and told them that he was coming back. Supposedly he took off, but he never did show up. Three days later Air Sea Rescue found two of the gunners floating in the English Channel.

As bombardiers we were given a briefing on all the targets. We went over the map, and were given all of the information on the flight. We then went out and checked the bombs, put the bomb sight in and checked it out. Usually the gunners on the crew put my guns in for me. I did load all my own bombs. They were not loaded until I got there to be sure that they were in right. I usually went to briefing about 0100 and took off about daylight — 0530 or 0600. My chin turret had a K-14 computing sight on the guns, one of the best sights of any gun on the ship. It just had two handles and the guns were motor driven. The navigator had a gun on either side of me — the cheek guns. I never had too much chance to use the guns. I had a few shots, but the bandits never seemed to hit our squadron. The best fighter protection we could have was a couple squadrons of B-24s with us in the B-17s.

The fighters would go through us to get to the 24s.

Our tail gunner got credit for shooting down an Me-262 jet fighter. We saw those all the time, but mostly just the vapor trails in the air. I am sure they were 262s. Also we saw a 163 Comet now and then, but at a distance. One time we were going over the Zuider Zee and the Germans launched a V-2 rocket. We got the position and our navigator plotted it and the next day a strike was made against that launch pad which knocked it out. That was about the time of the end of the V-2s.

We bombardiers were supposed to destroy the Norden bombsight with a few slugs from our .45s, but I never even took mine along. It was still in cosmoline and was hanging on my bunk when I left. I thought you would not be treated as badly by the Germans if you were unarmed.

When the campaign to knock out the German oil refineries began, we went to Ludwigshaven. Our Group was flying deputy lead on this mission and we lost two wingmen due to flak on this one. Magdeburg on 14 January 1945 was different. Our fighters hit the German fighters above our formation and it literally rained fighters right down through our formation. It was really a slaughter of Germans. We went in as if we were going to Berlin, then just before we got there we turned to Magdeburg.

The 390th Bomb Group was among 841 aircraft the Eighth Air Force sent out that day to deal with Hitler's oil supply. General Spaatz underwrote the importance of even hitting the less important oil targets. In a message to his command he wired: "The output of oil products has been reduced to the point where the German reserves are now critical. Your task is to defeat his desperate attempts to rebuild the industry and renew his reserves. Your success will limit Germany's offensive strength on every front, both on the ground and in the air, and contribute immeasurably to ultimate victory."

The 14 January mission by the 390th to Derben like that of the 385th was a diversion from Berlin. That is, the Group made the Germans believe Berlin was the target but turned off to the oil targets. Where Lt. McCullough mentions Magdeburg as their target, there were others. The 390th report states:

After numerous missions in which no enemy fighters were seen, on this date 100 single-engine fighters attacked.

At the time of the attack, "A" and "B" squadrons were in good formation; "C" squadron was minus a low element, being composed of eight aircraft. One of the superchargers of the lead ship of "C" squadron went out, and the squadron fell behind and about two thousand feet below the rest of the Group.

Using no apparent plan of attack, a hundred Fock-Wulffs and Messerschmitts concentrated on "C" Squadron. In the fighting, which lasted over thirty minutes, all eight B-17s were shot down. Thirty of the fighters attacked "A" Squadron, while 25 hit "B" Squadron and added a ninth B-17 to their score. It was the Group's greatest casualty figure, but all of the fighting was not one-sided.

Twenty-four fighters were destroyed, two probably destroyed, and four damaged. Like Munster, the toll would have been much greater had the crews of the shot down planes been able to add their combat victories.

Bombing results were difficult to access as most of the bursts landed in smoke of preceding Group's bombs. However, some were plotted in the southern portion of the target area.

The Group's efforts against Derben are best shown in a comparison against the background of 841 planes which the 8th Air Force sent out. The Air Force lost 20 planes and claimed 31-9-7 enemy fighters.

Lt. Billy Bittle, navigator in the famed 100th (Bloody Hundredth) Bomb Group, 350th Squadron, on this date was flying the second of his 23 combat missions over enemy targets. He also flew three "Food Missions" and one mission to pick up French prisoners of war and take them back to Charteaux, near Paris.

His diary of this January 15th mission to Derben, as with many diaries of veterans of combat missions, was very short and to the point. There were no flowing lines of descriptive prose nor reflections of innermost feeling shown, just the bare facts. On this, his second trip, Lt. Fowler was the pilot with whom he was flying.

"Deep penetration into Germany, hit by fighters just after crossing the coast of northern Germany." This fits in with the entry in Lt. McCullough's diary in which he described the dogfights:

The fighters hit the Group in front of us and the one behind us and planes were blowing up. Our fighter cover of P-47s came in and chased them away. We alerted damn near all of Germany — went by way of Bremen, Hamburg, Berlin, Magdeburg, etc. Our target was an underground storage tank farm, but they were empty. We had no battle damage, but other Groups lost plenty of planes.

No doubt Lt. Bittle had heard of the fight the 390th Group had had and of the losses they took. Visibility was good at the high altitude the bombers had to fly at and so the crews could see a long way and make out air battles as they were going on and progressing through the bomber stream.

Lt. McCullough did make it through 35 missions and was the recipient of a "Lucky Bastard" award. He and his crew dropped bombs on 35 targets, and brought bombs back a few times and received no credit for those missions. Fred has a few things he recalls of the missions:

I recall the mission to Kaiserlautern on January 2, 1945. It seemed as the fronts moved in, the Germans were able to concentrate more flak guns and we got hit pretty bad on this mission. No injuries to any of the crew, but the plane had some damage. The pilot took it to a field at Rheims, France where we landed and had it repaired. Then we flew it back to the base. I can't recall what the problem was or what was damaged. We came home so many times all shot up by flak that it is hard to keep the times straight. It was an engine, I think.

On February 3, 1945 we went into Berlin. We were the 18th or 19th Group over the target so that when we got there all you could see was smoke.

Berlin was getting a lot of traffic as the German General Staff juggled its reserves from the Western Front to the Eastern Front and back again. Most of this transport came through Berlin, which had lost its strategic bombing importance but was now a tactical target. So on this date well over 1,000 bombers were dispatched to Berlin. Lt. McCullough dropped his bombs on what he lined up as the target through the smoke. The target was the Tempelhof marshalling yards.

The 390th Bomb Group, not wanting to drop on a well-plastered target, went on from their briefed target and dropped on a canal bridge and barracks area in a built-up part of the city which had not been bombed before. Results were good.

The Bloody 100th Bomb Group went into Berlin this date also and one of the legends of the 100th (Robert Rosenthal) came close to going down but did not. Lt. Billy Bittle was an eye witness to the flak burst that hit Lt. Rosenthal's ship in the right wing and caught it on fire. In his diary of that date Lt. Bittle wrote of his fifth combat mission:

Lt. Wilson, pilot. Visual run. We are 3rd element, lead squadron. Plenty of accurate flak. On first burst the plane at 2 o'clock blew up and just missed us. The lead ship (Rosenthal) got a direct hit in the right wing and was on fire near the fuselage. We saw six chutes come out. The plane headed for the Russian lines 30 miles away. We had a strong tail wind. We got four flak holes — very lucky. Got north of our course coming home and over another flak area. We took over lead of low squadron. Bandits in the area but we didn't see any. We hit communications, roads, etc. Great success.

Sgt. Doug West was top turret gunner and engineer on the plane

318

piloted by Lt. Robert Rosenthal on this February 3, 1945 mission to Berlin. Sgt. West was in the plane and indeed was one of the six parachutes that Lt. Billy Bittle saw come out of the flak damaged B-17 that was leading the Squadron. His words as he recalled this mission on July 3, 1976 at the 100th Bomb Group Reunion at Colorado Springs:

We were flying lead squadron and when the first flak came up, we got hit. I think it was a 115 millimeter shell — it was a white burst — that got us. It wasn't an 88 as that is black. It could have been a 105 mm. I was told later that our target was Gestapo headquarters. I was with Rosie (Lt. Rosenthal.) His aircraft was named *Rosie's Riveters*. On several missions we were PFF Lead Group, Lead aircraft. That flak set us on fire in the right wing. Rosie and one other landed in Russian territory. Winters landed in German territory, but he did not get picked up and managed to walk all of the way back to our lines. This was a bad time to be walking out as things were so disorganized you didn't know which way to go and you had no food. Evading was better organized earlier. My bombardier was killed on the ground by German soldiers. We landed near an artillery base. I was brought back through Berlin after my capture, just a couple of days after the raid. They were still digging out people and the sirens were still going. What a mess. We were brought back to one of their airfields. I think it was Templehoff, but it could have been another. In a room in the building where we were taken there was an RAF enlisted man being questioned by the Gestapo agents. He was being questioned at Gestapo headquarters on the day of the raid. When we came over the Germans all headed for the bomb shelters and left him in the Gestapo building. When I told him that that was our target, he said, "I'm glad you missed."

I was taken to Stalag Luft 7-A. It was similar to the one portrayed in "Hogan's Heroes." To me all the German guards appeared to be like Sergeant Shultz of the show. Real nice guys.

When we were on the march from Nurenburg, we asked the guard what would happed if we tried to escape. He brought up his gun, opened the breech, looked in, and there was nothing in it. The guards were old guys in their 60s. I was in the Nurenburg-to-Mooseburg march. On that march we found where the Germans kept the rutabagas, squash, etc., so we stole that to eat and got probably more to eat on the march than we did in the camp, which was just adequate. On the march some of the guys snuck around the farms and stole eggs.

Sergeant West was liberated just three months later. Lt. Rosenthal refuses to take credit for anything special. As he puts it: "This is my co-pilot Ronald Bailey and my navigator 'Pappy' Lewis. They deserve any credit."

Sergeant West described Lt. Rosenthal as "The Legal Eagle and the Bald Eagle. He looked so unlike what you expect of a hot pilot. He is a unique person."

The B-24s were out on February 3, 1945 also, not as a diversion or bait for the Luftwaffe, but to obliterate the huge oil refinery at Magdeburg. Sgt. Merle Hess flew in his position as tail turret gunner on this mission and reports:

Departed Rackheath at 0830. Landed back at base at 1507. Temperature in the plane was 37 degrees centigrade. We flew at 22,500 feet, had a full load of gas, 2700 gallons. We bombed our target visually. We had ten 500 lb. GP bombs. Flak was moderate, but accurate from coast going in and coming out. Secondary target was Berlin. We got flak from all the big places like Hannover. Flak cut some of our control cables and wires. Very good predicted concentration.

Sergeant Hess said that his pilot was one of the six best pilots in the Eighth Air Force. In his words:

He (Lt. Phillip Reed) was a long, lanky guy and an all-around good fellow. When the flak cut the controls to the tail of the plane, he did things to kick that plane around and do things with it so we could stay with the Group. When we got back the cables and wires to the tail were all completely severed.

The Eighth Air Force was busy in many areas of the continent and many people were affected in many different ways, good and bad.

The Combined Bomber Offensive
Narrators: J.C. Ramsdell and Merle Hess
Group: 467th Bomb Group

When the Combined Bomber Offensive from the United Kingdom was adopted under the code name "Pointblank," it was to be the guideline for many months for the whole U.S. Air Force and the RAF.

In writing up the missions performed by the bomber of the 467th Bomb Group, *Everythin's Jake,* it is noted that all the missions were top priority as to that CBO guideline. Of the 34 missions flown, fourteen were to marshalling yards. This offensive began in October 1944 and continued on to March 9, 1945. This was the last mission to a marshalling yard. The land war was going hot and heavy. The Allies were moving and it was urgent that any German traffic be kept to a minimum, or better yet, eliminated completely. With a huge source of slave labor the Germans in many cases were able to rebuild in a matter of days some of the damage, which it was thought, could never be repaired. However, with bomber strength growing every day and with the fighter escort not only growing in strength but also in the ability to stay with the bombers for the whole trip in and out, it permitted a bit of fun for the fighters by being turned loose on tactical targets on the ground. The trains, airfields, and truck traffic all got a good going over by the P-47s, P-51s and P-38s. All this added up to a huge mess for the Germans and their transportation system. What the bombers did not get, the single engine fighters went after, blowing up ammo trains and supply trains and just about anything that moved including some war machines that were hidden in barns and in groves of trees.

The heavy bombers went with the plan. One of the strategic targets, of course, was oil. The 467th went to oil targets four times. They went after aircraft factories and supply points for aircraft industries on five missions. Munitions factories, rubber plants and ordinance plants found themselves targets on seven of the missions. Last, but not strategically least, there were three bridges the ground pounders needed to have wiped out and the 467th was successful on two of these missions. The other was not so good because of heavy cloud cover over the target.

Some of the missions were milk runs and some were not. In almost every mission, however, *Everythin's Jake* came back with more than a few flak holes. In one case Lt. Ramsdell, with a feeling of wonder, said that daylight could be seen right through the ship where there were so many flak holes.

The Combined Bomber Offensive very logically and methodically destroyed the production of weapons for war. Many people did not think it a good plan at the time and do not to this day. The crews who flew the missions to do the job were in both camps, but never strayed from doing the best job they could, with the hope of coming back alive.

The 467th Bomb Group planes with the bright red tail and diagonal white bar was, according to Sgt. Merle Hess, avoided by the Luftwaffe because the 467th gunners were too good and always on the ball. Sgt. Hess was told by his skipper, Lt. Phil Reed, to "keep those turrets moving — let them know we are not asleep." The other crew members also were showing any enemy aircraft the muzzles of their guns. Sgt. Hess was told when he was first assigned to the 467th he was lucky because of the good gunners that kept the enemy away. They started out with vigor to pound the German war machine.

The mission on August 15, 1944 was the 100th mission to be flown by the 467th. It was just 140 days after the 467th became operational. P-38 and P-51 fighters were the escort for this trip, though a lone Me-109 made a pass at the Group close enough for Sgt. Berry to get a few rounds off at him.

On August 24 the crew was after oil storage at Hannover, described elsewhere. The crew laid down for the whole month of September and the next mission they went on was October 7 to the munitions storage area at Magdeburg.

The *Jake* crew were off again on October 15 to hit the synthetic rubber works at Monheim, Germany. They were met by "meager flak at target and at the lines going in and coming out." To make things more exciting one of the 250 pound bombs hung up in the bomb bay and had to be chopped out.

The Ordinance depot at Mainz, Germany was the target on October 19. *Jake* carried twelve 250 pound G.P. bombs and six 500 pound M-17 incendiaries. "There was moderate flak for 30 minutes.

A 15 minute bomb run and as a rusult *Jake* got six flak holes." The 8th lost eleven bombers and eleven fighters due to flak this day. "The tail guns went out and the nose turret froze up."

Again the 467th hit marshalling yards October 22 at Hamm, Germany and November 5 at Karlsruhe, Germany; followed by the airfield at Hanau, Germany on November 10. This was a real "milk run" and no comments from the crew. The mission eleven days later to the oil refinery at Hamburg was not a milk run. Anything but that. "Flak was accurate and too darn accurate, but was moderate — holes in nose and tail turret and the Martin-elevators and waist."

Lt. J.C. Ramsdell recalls this mission as it was the last one he wrote about in his diary:

This mission to Hamburg was against one of the big five cities in the Fatherland. I have seen some flak before, but today took the cake. As the British would say, "It (flak) was so thick you could let your gear down and taxi across it." Many times in the seemingly endless minutes of flak, I uttered a prayer and closed my eyes for what I expected to be the last time, yet for some reason it was not. Seventeen out of the 29 ships were pretty badly damaged, and we had some nice holes ourselves.

This was the mission where Sgt. Hess was trapped in his tail turret and could not get out until we were on the ground at home. He was secured in the turret by a jammed door with one gun inoperative and bent and the other gun operable only by manual control. He could operate the turret only manually and thru just a few degrees. Part of the turret was gone and the temperature outside was minus 54 degrees. Neither the pilot, Phil Reed, nor myself were aware that he was in that kind of trouble until they got his radio working just before we entered the traffic pattern. It was my duty to call each member of the crew to see if they were clear for landing, particularly the turrets as they were very vulnerable in crash landings. As I called in from nose to tail, everyone cleared except for Hess and he said he was not clear. I told him to get the H--- out of there, and he said, "Tex," I can't get out of here," so we landed with him in the turret.

Sgt. Hess remembered that trip also:

Flak had taken part of my turret away and I thought my radio was out too. I kept calling into the radio and got no response from anyone and for a while I thought my tail position had been severed by the flak and I was sailing along all by myself like I had heard other tail turrets had done. In fact one in our own squadron had been shot away and the turret gunner went down with it and had landed on a sandy beach without injury. I was yelling and trying to get out. I laid my hand on my lap once and I could not feel anything

323

and I thought I had been shot in two. But then I remembered the training we had gotten on what to expect at high altitude as to the cold and what effect it has and effect that a lack of oxygen would have on you.

I was trying to get out of the turret and Sgt. Pulcinella came up and said, "Hess, what the hell you trying to do?" I said I wanted to get out of the turret. We could not get it open so I landed while still in the turret.

The marshalling yards at Offenburg, Germany were hit by 2nd Division B-24s on November 27, 1944. The bombing altitude had been raised up to 25,000 feet. The bomb load was eight 500 pound G.P. with two 500 pound incendiary bombs. Bombing was again visual with some inaccurate flak.

December 10, 1944 found the 467th Bomb Group over the marshalling yards at Bingen, Germany in support of our troops. This trip the target was covered by clouds, so bombing was by PFF. P-51 and P-47 fighters were the escort.

Date: 16 August 1944
Target: Magdeburg, Germany
Narrators: J.C. "Tex" Ramsdell and Merle Hess
Group: 467th Bomb Group, 788th Bomb Squadron

Magdeburg, Germany produced a great quantity of oil for the German war machine and was a primary target of the 8th Air Force right up to the end of the war. Lt. J.C. Ramsdell, better known to his crew mates as "Tex," made four missions to Magdeburg. His first combat mission was to Magdeburg on August 16, 1944. "Tex" flew as co-pilot on this mission as he did on most of his remaining 34 missions. He flew as first pilot on his last mission, which was to Berlin, March 18, 1945, described later in this book.

For a number of missions J.C. "Tex" Ramsdell kept a diary of his missions. He had little to say about this first mission:

Magdegurg, Germany, August 16, 1944, mission #1. This was the first mission! Seems queer even yet to think we got through all that flak with no major damage. We only had one flak hole and it darn near took the wing. One of the planes whose pilot was named Miller got it directly over the target, right in front of us. He simply disintegrated in flame and smoke, only one chute was seen to open.

The photo of the plane piloted by Lt. Miller was taken from one of the planes in the squadron.

Lt. Ramsdell and the regular crew were back at Magdeburg again on October 7, 1944 and as usual were flying through intense and accurate flak. It was always the case at Magdeburg. The only difference in this mission was that it was to knock out munition storage depots and facilities. The B-24 carried ten 500 pound GP bombs and two 500 pound incendiaries. The Group was escorted by P-51s, P-38s and P-47s. Sgt. Hess, tail turret gunner, mentioned in his diary of flak damage "above my head on the tail and the wing — really hit the target."

Up front in the cockpit it was a bit different. "Tex" still has in his possession a piece of flak he recovered from the magneto box. To quote "Tex":

Never in my trips to Germany have I seen so many planes, and everyone with a specific target. Germany was a flaming smoking ruin at every town.

325

Again today our lead ship was badly damaged, the pilot almost lost his left leg — flak above the knee. There was a burst of flak near my side of the cockpit and a piece of flak entered just above my right knee and expended itself in the magneto control box. The impact shattered the plexiglas handle or safety cover on the box, and at the same instant my electric suit shorted out. I felt as if I was on fire on the whole right side. The pilot ripped off his oxygen mask and asked if I was hit. I nodded "Yes," and he wanted to know where. I could smell cloth burning and plexiglas fragments were everywhere, and I was afraid to move. I finally could not stand the heat anymore and managed to move my right arm, leg, etc., and everything seemed to work, so I unplugged my suit. Nothing had happened, but the suit had shorted out and as it happened at the precise instant of the flak's impact, I just knew I had been shot half in two. The piece of flak was still in the magneto box when we got home and had not shorted out any of the magnetos!

The February 3, 1945 mission to Magdeburg has been reported. The next mission to Magdeburg came just twelve days later, on February 15, 1945. Once again the target was oil refineries as well as "support for the Russians" as Sgt. Hess related in his diary. And as usual the flak was in the moderate-to-intense zone with no damage to the plane or crew.

Date: 24 August 1944
Target: Hannover, Germany
Narrator: J.C. Ramsdell
Group: 467th Bomb Group

Hannover, Germany had a number of prime war industries located there and at this time period the 8th Air Force was into the campaign to eliminate German oil from going to the planes, tanks, trucks and other war machines of the German Armies. The 467th Bomb Group with Lt. J.C. Ramsdell, co-pilot, and Sgt. Merle Hess, tail turret gunner, flying with their crew went to Hannover on August 24, 1944. The Hess diary gives the target as "oil refinery, with flak from I.P. to target. It really gave the groups behind us heck. We had holes in nose and Martin turret, two scarecrows came up on tail turret — really thick flak.." (The scarecrows, according to Hess, were rockets sent up by the Germans more as a frightening measure than a kill rocket, thus the name scarecrow.)

Lt Ramsdell wrote in his diary about this mission:

Hannover, Germany, 24 August 1944. Well the third one is over and God am I glad. I could write a book on five minutes of hell. The flak was not intense, but so accurate. We had several holes in the ship. One explosion blew us about 100 feet up in altitude, tore holes in the upper turret and almost blew the nose gunner out of his turret. Not one of us were scratched.

What made this one exciting at the time was the fact that Sgt. Reid, the top turret (Martin turret) gunner and engineer, was in his turret when the flak burst hit as the ship was on the bomb run. The flak burst almost removed his turret, blew plexiglas all over the compartment. Reid had his hands gripped on the handles and controls of his twin .50 caliber machine guns. At the instant of the burst, and through reflex, he gripped the fire buttons and loosed a few hundred rounds of .50 caliber ammo, and what with all the smoke, guns firing, empty shell casings falling into the lower compartment, the crew just knew they had been hit by fighters. After the mission Sgt. Reid got a lot of ribbing about using the grips to hang on with.

Lt. Ramsdell described another incident on the same mission and caused by another near burst of flak:

The burst of flak that got the nose turret put a piece of flak about 1H pounds into the plexiglas turret, right in front of the gunner's eyes. The flak was spent enough that it penetrated the plexiglas, but did not enter the turret, it just stuck right there, completely embedded through 3 inches of material. After we returned home, the ground crew chief took a bar and hammer and removed the piece of flak, about the size of a fist and very jagged. The crew chief very proudly presented it to Zigler, the bombardier and nose gunner. It was meant to be a souvenir. "Ziggy" looked at it as if it were going to blow up and instantly gave it back to the crew chief and yelled, "Get that damn thing away from me. I have stared at it for three hours."

As the Allies compressed the German Armies into a smaller and smaller area from the West and the East, the Germans had to move great quantities of men and material back from the lines to get critical war material to the forces at the fronts. Transportation became a strategic target for the 8th Air Force heavy bomber groups which we are following. The 467th was to finish the air war over Germany with the best record for bombing accuracy in the 8th Air Force. They proved they earned this by many very successful missions to the strategic targets. Beginning in October 1944 the targets picked for them were to be marshalling yards and bridges.

The program against the German transportation system had a threefold objective: to interrupt, in so far as possible, the movement of troops and supplies to the western front; to cause the maximum possible disruption to the German economy; and, by striking at some communication centers and leaving other lines alone, to channelize traffic along fewer lines, thus offering more targets for our fighters and fighter bombers.

Second Air Division bombers began with an October 22, 1944 raid on the marshalling yards at Hamm, Germany. The bomb run was made at 23,000 feet, finding meager flak at the target. The next yard trip was to Karlsruhe with a P-51 escort. Bombing again from 23,000 feet altitude. The Sgt. Hess diary indicates plenty of flak but not too accurate. Thirty bombers and seventeen fighters in all.

The marshalling yards at Offenburg, Germany were hit by 2nd Division B-24s on November 27th, 1944. The bombing altitude had been raised up to 25,000 feet. The bomb load was eight 500 pound G.P. with two 500 pound incendiary bombs. Bombing was again visual with some inaccurate flak, 18 minute I.P.

December 10, 1944 found the 467th Bomb Group over the marshalling yards at Bingen, Germany in support of our troops. On this trip the target was covered by cloud so bombing was by PFF. P-51 and P-47 fighters were the escort, totalling six groups. The bad weather caused several near collisions for Phil Reed, pilot of *Everythin's Jake*.

Hanau, Germany was hit by 8th Air Force bombers on December 11, 1944. The marshalling yards were hit by 36 squadrons of bombers. The following day the crew of *Everythin's Jake* was over Hanau to,"...get the workers who could get the rail yards repaired within forty-eight hours." The bomb run was made from 22,000 feet, visual. Meager flak at target. Twenty-five squadrons flew this mission.

The marshalling yards at Nuenkirchen, Germany were hit on December 28, 1944 at an altitude of 23,500 feet. A mixed load of twenty 250 pound G.P. bombs and two 500 pound M-17 incendiaries. This mission was much the same as the other marshalling yard missions except for the fact that the meager flak this time was accurate and the ship got six flak holes.

Beginning in late December the targets were changed to include the strategic bridges. The Rhine River bridge at Coblenz, Germany was the target on December 31, 1944. Four one-ton G.P. bombs were carried by the 467th *Everythin's Jake*. Moderate, but accurate flak met the group who had to fly a 200 mile, 52 minute bomb run. This mission was a bad one for Sgt. Hess as he got sick. After this one he took advantage of the rye whiskey libation offered after each mission.

The 5th of January 1945 the group flew to Kochem, Germany to get a bridge 25 miles southwest of Coblenz on the Moselle river. Bombing was through cloud by use of PFF. The results of this bombing were not stated in Sgt. Hess' diary, but he did say: "Really a cold old day."

Everythin's Jake made only two more missions in January, going to Hallendorf, Germany on the 14th and to Dresden on the 16th. The Hermann Goering steelworks in the Brunswick area was the first of these targets with bombing under visual conditions. The flak here was "intense and accurate. A dozen holes were received in the Martin turret and tail turret, and the nose gunner passed out from lack of oxygen. The 8th Air Force got 180 German fighters today."

Two days later on the 16th of January the marshalling yards at Dresden were the target. Lt. J.C. "Tex" Ramsdell was in the right hand seat in the cockpit, and Sgt. Merle Hess in the tail turret. *Everythin's Jake*. had a nominal load of two 500 pound G.P. bombs and a nickel load, which is the chaff, or as the British called it "window." The other ships of the bomber force carried ten 500 pound

330

G.P. and some incendiary bombs. The groups encountered flak from the enemy lines going in and coming out. Some of it was intense and accurate. *Everythin's Jake.* had to make a landing at Merville, France on the trip home, and most of the crew returned to England on the 19th.

"Tex" Ramsdell recounts events from the front of the plane on this mission!

Our primary target was to be Dresden, which we eventually hit. We were briefed that due to devious routes that we were to take and the length of the mission, many of the ships would be low or out of fuel. They were expected to land at fields in Allied Occupied France, or other "friendly" areas. We went over the North Sea, north of Holland. It was a long sweep. We encountered flak (heavy) along the way. Over the target we caught a shell just under the bomb bay, almost a direct hit. After we had dropped our pair of bombs, we discovered that our bomb bay doors had been partly shot away and the main longeron in the bottom of the ship was almost cut in two. Since the doors would not close, this created excessive drag and wind resistance, causing us to use excessive fuel. By reducing power and "nursing" it, we managed to get back to occupied France, and as we were approaching what we had hoped were friendly lines, we started losing engines — no fuel. We radioed a May Day, and our navigator had us pin pointed (Mike Burns was GOOD). We were given a heading for an emergency field and cleared for a straight in approach. The code name of the field was "Martini" and the little town there was Merville, France.

"Martini" was a fighter strip and we are flying a B-24. We were told there were burning aircraft on the field and there were three inches of ice on the runway. We knew our brakes would do no good on that ice, and we needed all the drag we could get to stop that 24 on a fighter field. We locked our brakes before we touched down and we lost another engine. Lt. Phil Reed, the pilot, made a spot landing that would have done credit to a carrier pilot. We used every available inch of the runway and a little mud and ice at the end of it, but she finally stopped just shy of a gun emplacement and a hedgerow.

After we were safely out of the aircraft, we found that a piece of flak had sliced the right front tire for about 8 inches, but had not deflated it since the slice was on the top side of the tire when we locked the brakes, otherwise we would have been one of the crashed aircraft on and around that field. Later it was determined that at the time we landed, there were 26 crashed and/or burning aircraft on the field.

After reporting our landing and condition of the plane, we were informed to wait and that repair parts for the plane would be sent, which in time they were. The pilot, myself and the engineer, Sgt. Reid, stayed with the plane.

331

The other crew members returned home in a C-47 three days later, as we did with the 24, less all the guns and armament. We made a Doolittle-type carrier take-off and arrived home three days late.

The first two weeks in February were devoted to raids in support of the Russians in the area near Rhiney, Germany, followed by marshalling yards, oil refineries, machine ships and aircraft factories. Then the first mission in March was on the 3rd. The 2nd Division commanders gave the 467th Group strict orders to "get that bridge." The Germans were retreating and the Allies needed that bridge knocked out. The importance of knocking it out was stressed many times. "Tex" Ramsdell said: "That day we were a lone group, no fighters for cover, a perfect set up for any enemy fighter groups." No fighters were seen, however, and the mission had no interference from enemy action. The weather did raise hell with the raid in that clouds would drift over the target just as the group was on the bomb run and they would have to circle around and set up for one more run. This exercise went on four times, in an elapsed time of one-and-a-half hours. Picture eighteen B-24s going around in circles at 23,500 feet for an hour and a half trying to line up on a bridge. It was nerve wracking to the bitter end. But the words of the brass kept cropping up in the minds of the crews, "get that bridge." Finally they got a good visual run at 18,000 feet, the strike pattern was good and the Bielefeld-Nieburg rail bridge was knocked out. The Bielefeld-Herford bridge was also taken out. Photographs by a P-38 recon plane showed complete destruction.

J.C. Ramsdell was to stay on for seven more combat missions over Germany. Then, in the position he had flown 34 times over enemy territory, he flew as co-pilot when the 467th Bomb Group led the 8th Air Force in the victory salute to the Allied Command on May 13, 1945 at High Wycombe, England. "Tex" was in the #2 ship.

After the March 3rd mission, Merle Hess went on for six more missions. This final one was the March 18th mission to Berlin, of which we have written about elsewhere in this book. He returned to his home at Waverly, Iowa and now resides in Denver, Iowa.

Date: 18 March 1945
Target: Berlin, Germany
Narrators: J.C. Ramsdell and Merle Hess
Group: 467th Bomb Group

Berlin was always a tough mission right up to the end of the war. It was true on B-24 J-737 *Everythin's Jake.* with Sgt. Merle Hess riding as tail turret gunner on his last mission. In his diary he wrote down some highlights:

March 18, 1945 0830 to 1245 P.M. 32 degrees centigrade. BERLIN target AA guns, armament of tanks, etc, 2700 gallons gas. 5-1,000 G.P. I, Berry, Pulcinella, Reed finish today. Reid three more Rhodes five, "Tex" two. Flak accurate and level and intense. Chapman and Schin both had direct hits in bomb bays, saw four chutes. We took the lead in Wing and Group; we all prayed like never before.

Both Sgt. Hess and Lt. J.C. "Tex" Ramsdell recall this mission "all too vividly" as "Tex" wrote. In their words:

We were flying #3 position on the lead ship of the lead Group of the lead Wing. In other words we were leading the 8th Air Force that day. Lt. Chapman was Lead, Lt. Schin was #2 and we were #3. I don't know who was in the slot or bucket. We had been briefed for heavy flak approximately fifteen minutes before the target, and from seven to fifteen minutes after, with fighters anywhere before and after. Up until we were almost on the actual bomb run, not one burst of flak or fighter had been called. We were really sweating.

Sgt. Merle Hess remarked in his recollection:

I did not really have to go on this mission, but I was sort of a lucky charm to the guys. They tended to be a bit wild when not flying and I always tried to be pretty religious and they respected that and considered me as a lucky charm. I went on this mission because of that. But we got the heck shot out of us that last mission. I knew that we were not coming back. In fact I was so scared I was crying. We were the third ship over the target.

The crew knew the flak would be coming, but did not know when or where. The first burst of flak hit the Lead ship directly in the bomb bay. They did not realize for a fraction of second what had happened. The Lead ship jumped straight up in the air; smoke poured out all over.

Sgt. Hess observed the bomber as it was hit and saw a big red-headed Irishman, who must have been standing in the catwalk to release the bombs. When the flak shell burst in the plane it threw him out of there. He pulled his rip cord right away instead of dropping through the formation first, as had been taught in flight school. He did not have his helmet on and he was crying, while sailing down through the bomber stream. Hess said:

The last I saw of him he was floating down in his chute. I thought sure one or more of the bombers would run into him or somehow he would be killed. However, some months later the other guys said that he was able to get back to our lines safe and sound.

"Tex" goes on:

The lead plane then nosed down with a gradual turn to the left. The other two bursts came between us and the box ship and probably some of it got the box ship. The Germans were using the tracking type flak. Guns electronically, three bursts at a time. One out in front then two and three in a row come back to you. Lt. Schin in the #2 slot was then the lead ship and we slid over to take #3 position on him, and as we were sliding over to join up with him, he took a direct hit in the bomb bay and acted very similar to the #1 ship. Thank goodness neither of them blew or they would have wiped out the whole combat box. He nosed down slightly and started a gradual turn to the right and passed from sight.

Lt. "Tex" Ramsdell was at the controls, as the pilot was on his last mission and was flying as co-pilot. "Tex" started to slide over to take the lead of the whole shebang. Seven thirty-seven was just minutes away from bombs away, and "Tex" had to get the bombardier in line to take his bomb run. There was another three bursts of flak dead ahead and level. Realizing the next three would be theirs, "Tex" hit the controls hard left and stood on a wing tip. As he looked through the pilot's window,

All I could see was the open bomb bay doors of a B-24. I had not thought about the slot ship coming up to fly our wing, which was totally my fault and could have gotten all of us killed, but fortunately, whoever was flying that ship was watching close and banked as soon as I did. As soon as I saw the underside of that ship, I hit opposite controls and went back to a semblance of level flight.

As was his usual pattern, Tail gunner Hess called in the three bursts of flak as being right where they had been. Sgt. Hess would call in the flak bursts when he would see them, as soon as he would see them. He would tell the pilot where they were and to kick her to the right or kick her to the left. As usual the bursts were behind the ship, "Why, I don't know," he said, as accurate as the German gunners were at times.

The box ship was losing power and smoking, but did manage to stay with them until the load was dropped. Then the pilot further reduced power and began to fall back. This plane did make it back to base, but of the four ships that went into the target, *Everythin's Jake.* was the only one to come out. They had a good bomb run on the target and got a good strike.

The return to base from this mission was a tense ride until the plane was secured at its tarmack. Then for the second time in his flying career Sgt. Merle Hess got drunk. As was the custom after a rough mission, a full bottle of brandy or rye whiskey and a large glass was set in front of the crew. As Hess mused: "It would be nothing to drink that whole tumbler full of rye whiskey." On his 35th and last mission Merle took that full tumbler a couple of times. He went to the Colonel and said, "You old S.O.B., you won't have to look at me anymore!" Pilot Reed quickly went over to Colonel Albert J. Shower and said, "Take it easy Colonel. This is his last mission." Colonel Shower replied: "Sure, I know how these fellows feel." That was the end of Hess' flying career and his sinus problem.

The Day That Sgt. Hess Cured
His Sinus Problem

Narrators: J.C. Ramsdell and Merle Hess

Lt. J.C. Ramsdell, co-pilot with the 467th Bomb Group, 788th Bomb Squadron, became a "Lucky Bastard" by completing 35 missions. The crew that he started with all ended in that club, not a single drop of blood was shed due to enemy action on the aircraft this crew flew. Sgt. Merle Hess did get a very bad nose bleed due to some foul weather flying.

I had met Merle Hess in 1958 when we both were employed by a firm in Waverly, Iowa, Hess' home town. I had complained of a sinus problem and Merle said he used to have a sinus problem when he was in the Air Force, but that he had gotten rid of it. I asked him how and he related this story to me. I have also spoken to J.C. Ramsdell about it and he was able to fill in a few details. With the aid of Merle's diary we can establish the date.

On January 3, 1945 the 788th Bomb Squadron was on a mission to Zweibrucken, Germany. The target for the day was a marshalling yard near Saarbrucken. The weather was not good so bombing was accomplished by the use of PFF. There was no flak, but bad weather, and, as Sgt. Hess wrote in his diary, "sinus hit me." This alone doesn't mean much, however, by digging out the details I learned that this was the day Sgt. Merle Hess lost his sinus problem. The Hess and Ramsdell stories match almost word for word except for the quotes of the comments made by Lt. Zigler. Ramsdell writes:

This was one of the many times we returned to England to find the country socked in. It was solid up to about 15,000 feet. You could not even see your wing tip. A let-down to base was virtually impossible, but we had to get down. There were literally hundreds of ships up there and they were colliding in mid air; chutes, debris, wrecked aircraft were everywhere. Our navigator told us we were over England, and everyone was trying to find a hole to get down. We were on course and letting down gradually, hoping not to get hit, when I happened to see off to our right a partial clearing, enough that I could see fields below. I stuck the nose of that B-24 down like a fighter plane, and prayed that someone else would not try to use the same hole. I brought that thing down like a 24 should never be treated. Then someone on the interphone yelled that Hess had a nose bleed. About that time I was breaking into the clear at about 2,000 feet, so I had to level out and go back up until he got it cleared. Then he said he was O.K. and we went on home.

Sgt. Hess at the time said that when "Tex" Ramsdell put that plane on its nose and started down through that hole he could see the rivets on the wing panels standing right out and could not understand how a plane could take that strain. He then felt like someone had hit him in the back of the head hard and his nose started to bleed.

"Tex" Ramsdell (yes, he was from Texas) went on to say:

After we had leveled out for home, gunners were cussing me and everyone else was too, because I had stood that B-24 on end and threw everyone all over the place. Lt. Zigler yelled over the intercome, " 'Tex' you S.O.B. I am going to put a bubble canopy on #4 engine so you can fly it like a fighter plane, because a 24 sure ain't a fighter plane."

Merle Hess was glad that that mission was over and he has had no more sinus problem. Not a recommended procedure for a cure, but you take what you get.

On March 24th, 1945 the last great airborne assault of the war began when 14,000 airborne troops went in by parachute and glider near Wesel, Germany. This would be known as "Rhine Day," and the last great push of the war against the Germans. The crossing of the Rhine river at Wesel would literally break the back of the Germans. The crossing of the Rhine was a combined operation of all forces.

The 44th was one of the Groups elected to supply the spearhead. Following the troops in two hours after the landing at Wesel, the Group ran into terrific ground fire just after releasing supplies from 150 feet altitude. Flying within rifle range to supply glider and paratroops is always a dangerous mission for aircraft as large as a Liberator bomber. The dropping zone was near the point where the gliders had set down beyond the Rhine, a few miles east of the river, within sight of the enemy lines. The supplies were necessary to the success of the airborne troops that went in three hours earlier and were battling with light equipment to establish a bridgehead for the crossing in force by the ground forces. The drop had to be low level to assure accuracy and minimize the effect of enemy ack-ack — preferring to run the gauntlet of machine gun and small arms fire to the heavier German anti-aircraft guns. Supplying the ground forces proved to be a very costly operation for the American bombers; however, the final defeat of Germany began when the Rhine was crossed, supplied, and the bridgehead secured.

Two of the 44th Group's bombers were shot down and many others damaged. All together the effort cost the Air Force twenty-two bombers, which placed the mission second to the Ploesti mission in percentage of loss for a low level operation.

Captain Ursel P. Harvell, 44th bomb Group photographer went on this mission as he did on many other of the 44th's missions to film the history that was being made on that particular day. Now deceased, Mr. Harvell went on to become a Lt. Col. and left behind a treasure of films of the episodes of the 2nd bomb Division and especially the

44th. Prior to his death Col. Harvell allowed me to use the information he gathered on the two men who did survive the crash of one of the two 44th planes that went down that March day at Wesel. The Story:

The 44th Bomb Group dispatched twenty seven B-24 s, loaded with 60 tons of critically needed supplies for the airborne troops, who had gone in earlier that day (March 24, 1945). The crews were carefully briefed to drop supplies on previously pinpointed positions from 100-200 feet above the tree tops. The turn from the drop zone was to begin immediately after the drop, to minimize the time over the enemy lines. The turn was estimated to take about fifteen minutes. The mission on the board looked like a milk run. However, almost immediately after the drop the B-24s began to sustain hits from every type of weapon the Germans had in the field, especially when the bellies of their ships were exposed to the enemy as they were making the tight turns to get back to the Rhine.

The first B-24 to be seriously damaged was AC# 42-100314, piloted by 2nd Lt. Max E. Chandler. The left wing was seen to drop down and the ship began to lose altitude. The wing tip touched the ground and the plane bounced back into the air momentarily and then nosed into the field and exploded. The camera film does not show any of the crew surviving this crash. However a few days after the crash the advancing American forces overran the area and liberated two airmen from AC# 314 who somehow escaped the firery crash and explosion. One was tail gunner Sgt. Robert D. Vance and the other was Sgt. Louis J. DeBlasio, waist gunner. Neither men could remember how they got out of the aircraft.

A second ship, AC# 50896, piloted by 1st Lt. Leonard J. Crandell, was picked up by the camera of Captain Harvell, in a vertical dive and exploded near the spot of the first ship. None of the crew escaped from that aircraft. Due to the low altitude of this mission and fact that a cameraman was on the mission, the scene of two bombers being shot down in close range of the camera is a very unique film record.

The official report from the Liberator base in England states:

Reports of fellow Liberator airmen who saw a 44th Bombardment Group bomber crash during the low level delivery of supplies on 3/24/45 to the armies under Field Marshall Montgomery immediately after their spectacular crossing of the Rhine, gave little hope that any of the crewmen could have survived the crash. Sgt. Robert D. Vance, a 21-year-old tail gunner from Empire, Ohio, returned, however, to prove that appearances are deceiving. He also reported that waist gunner Sgt. Louis J. DeBlasio, wounded but alive, had lived to tell the tale. Vance, after a harrowing escape from the ship that had hit the earth once to rise and fly for fifty seconds before crashing and exploding, had been a prisoner of the Germans for eight days and finally liberated by advancing troops of the 2nd Armored Division.

Sgt. Vance stated: "I don't remember much about the crash, all I do remember is flames coming from the bomb bay and a heavy blow which must have been when we hit the ground the first time. The next thing I knew I was crawling from the plane as fast as I could and was telling the waist gunner who was with me, 'Pray; pray now as you never prayed before.'

We crawled away from the wreckage of the ship, there was practically nothing left of it. I don't understand how we got out. We crawled under a wagon and some German civilians came and treated our wounds. I vaguely remember riding somewhere in a haywagon. The next thing I recall is being in a place that was apparently a dance hall. The floor was covered with straw. British, American and German wounded were crowded in there." Asked if the treatment he received was any different from the Germans, he reported that it was not. "We were all treated the same. I have to give them credit for that."

Sgt. Vance was later transferred to a hospital staffed by nuns where he was also treated well. "Easter Sunday was our big day," he reported. "The nuns gave us each three eggs which were really something after nothing but black bread and coffee. We went to both Catholic and Protestant church services although I couldn't understand either of them. In the afternoon, the 2nd Armored Division tanks came into town and we went outside to see them. They threw us K-rations and cigarettes. They were certainly a welcome sight." They returned to the hospital, and soon an American ambulance arrived and started them on their journey to allied territory.

Sgt. DeBlasio remained in a hospital on the Continent for treatment but Sgt. Vance, who had received a slight head wound and a fractured arm, was soon returned to his base in England.

Battle casualties, mission to Wesel, Germany. 24 March 1945:

A/C B24J 42-50896

Crandell, Leonard J.	1st Lt.	Pilot	Peoria, IL
Croll, William B.	2nd Lt.	Co-pilot	Larchmont, NY
Hummer, William H.	2nd Lt.	Navigator	Dover, NJ
Ogilvie, Robert B.	T/Sgt.	Engineer	Auburn, NY
Feeney, Larry L.	T/Sgt.	Radio Optr.	Spokane, WA
Battenburg, Walter R.	S/Sgt.	LW Gunner	Milwaukee, WI
Brown, James M. Jr.	S/Sgt.	Tail Gunner	Rosehill, NC
Germolus, Irvine E.	S/Sgt.	RW Gunner	Albany, NY
Roach, James E.	S/Sgt.	Nose Gunner	Denver, CO

A/C B24J 42-100314

Chandler, Max E.	2nd Lt.	Pilot	Monticello, IN
O' Connel, Hugh X.	F/O	Co-pilot	Brooklyn, NY
Dantzler, Robert T.	2nd Lt.	Navigator	Birimingham, AL
Cordes, Thomas H.	Sgt.	Bombardier	Oradell, NJ
Hedder, Sarkice T.	Sgt.	Engineer	Hyde Park, MA
Elliot, Eugene L.	Sgt.	Radio Optr.	Hartford, CT
Clark, Thomas W.	Sgt.	LW Gunner	Hutley, NJ
DeBlasio, Louis J.	Sgt.	RW Gunner	Brooklyn, NY
Vance, Robert D.	Sgt.	Tail Gunner	Empire, OH

A/C B24J 42-50539

Diaz, Anibal C.*	Sgt.	LW Gunner	Tampa, FL

*This man was pulled out of his plane by his parachute at extremely low altitude 2½ miles WNW of Wesel, Germany. Enlisted man was dropping supplies.

Date: 1, 2 & 3 May 1945
Target: Food Drops to Holland
Narrator: Billy M. Bittle
Group: 100th Bomb Group

The last missions flown by the 8th Air Force into Holland were the well known "food drops." The people in Holland had withstood the occupation by the Germans for many years, had been stripped of their food to feed the German army, and had been kept under the heel of oppression for too long. They were short of food of all kinds. They had helped Allied airmen evade the Germans whenever they could, and now it was time for us to repay them. The drops were organized in late April and early May 1945.

Lt. Billy M. Bittle, navigator in the 100th Bomb Group was a participant in these early food drops. His records give some of the details of his three flights:

We were alerted to be ready to make the food runs to Holland as soon as a truce could be arranged with the Greman forces, who would designate a definite corridor for the flight route. On April 25, 1945, our group had fully loaded bomb bays of C-type rations and other supplies, and the crews were standing by our planes waiting for the word that the Germans would honor the truce. Our destination was Amsterdam.

As no satisfactory truce could be resolved, the drop was cancelled. We again were alerted for a drop over Amsterdam on April 28, 1945, which also was cancelled.

My vague recollection is that for the Germans to agree on a short truce for the food drops, there had to be a definite, precise route flown, at a maximum altitude of 350 to 400 feet, during a definite time schedule over the occupied areas. It was my understanding that this was to prevent the Allies from photographing any military installations at low level. We were to cross the English Channel at 1500 feet, and drop down to 400 feet before flying over Holland on the predesignated route.

Agreement was finally reached, and on May 1, 1945, we made our first food drop at the Hague, from 400 feet.

Our second drop was at 300 feet, over Amsterdam, on May 2, 1945. I vividly remember this drop, as we were literally skimming the terrain, and pulling up to miss buildings, smokestacks, etc. I'm sure there were a lot of broken window panes that day from the continuous prop changes to maintain airspeed.

On that morning of May 2, 1945, we had the first fresh fruit we'd seen in months — oranges! Thinking about the Dutch people and their austerity diets, I filled my flight jacket with oranges. I dropped them over Amsterdam to the people who filled the roofs, waving American and Dutch flags. I will always regret not having a camera on that trip, because we could clearly see the faces, reflecting the happiness of the people and see them waving. We could see the German troops standing in formation in the street.

We were flying single file, and the drop zone was an open field outside Amsterdam. The area was lined with people who began running onto the field after the first plane had dropped its cargo, ignoring the following planes who were dropping boxes in the same area.

I have been to Holland many times on business since the war, and have wondered and asked whether anyone recalls finding squashed oranges, but have not found anyone.

My third, and last, food drop was on May 3, 1945, to Alkmaar. We were not to drop after 11:55, which would indicate that the truce ended at 12:00 noon.

It was a very satisfying end to Lt. Bittle's flying in World War II. He and the hundreds of other bomber crewmen of the 8th Air Force were about to experience the expected joy of the end of the war. They had survived, and they were giving an Ally a helping hand.

Mr. Billy M. Bittle was kind enough to furnish us a copy of a navigators flight log.

TIME	COURSE	W/V USED &/OR DRIFT	TRUE HDNC.	MAC. HDNC.	NAVICATIONAL OBSERVATION	GENERAL OBSERVATION	I.A.S. MPH K	HEIGHT & AIR TEMP.	T.A.S.	RUN DIST.	RUN TIME	G.S.	TO RUN DIST.	TO RUN TIME	E.T.A.
1126	282	104	85	90	Bomb Away	B17 Blew up	7x44					MAR			
1130					FA on fire										
1170					Cosie - B-17 blew up	No chutes			252	1339					
1148	242	-4	234	240	5320 1241	PP		26000		128	40	49	1207		
1207	273	250/63	272	276	5307 1128						108			
1215		70/90	266	271				183		108				
1239	273	70/90	267	274	5307 1116			-		108				
1246		-	255	260	5305 10x5 PP			-		101	25	+14	1300	
1258	303	-22	281	286	5316 0943	DR				122	52	26		
1258	303	+8	295	300	5316 0948	DR					26		1324	
1327		265/75		270	5400 0800E	DR	20000		188	127	101	+53	1420	
1425		270/75	V5V	260	30x530d 0345					135	87	39	1504	
1610					Landed									

PILOT WILSON CW 1ST LT   NAVIGATOR BITTLE BMJR 1ST LT   #4A PLANE 975   DATE 3 FEB 1945

STATIONS	ENGINES 0700 TAXI 0710 T.O. 0725
LEAVE BASE	
COAST OUT	
ENEMY COAST	
I.P.	1108
TARGET	1118
ENEMY COAST	1520
BASE	1530
	LTO 0730

10x500

	MORNING TWILIGHT	SUN Rises	SUN Sets	EVENING TWILIGHT	MOON Rises	MOON Sets

WATCH .... Fast / Slow   RATE .... secs/hour Losing
At .... G.M.T.

FROM TO	W/V USED	HEIGHT Temp.	I.A.S. MPH /K	T.A.S. (K)	COURSE	DRIFT	TRUE HDNC.	VAR.	MAC. HDNC.	G.S.	DIST.	TIME	E.T.A.	TIME CONTROL POINTS & Rendezvous
B428 5213 0133 IPSWICH	322 34	-9 9000	110 130										NE 0845	A ZWOLLE E SUMMERLAND
	-	9000		147	235	+13	248	+9	257	141	18	+8	0854	L HANNOVER
B4 14 5217 0046	-	-		-	301	+5	306	+10	316	115	17	+9	0903	D STENDAL I BERLIN
B4 9 5228 0058	-	-		-	24	-12	12	+10	22	129	17	+8	0909	N WHITTENBURG O LUNEBURG
5005 NIELE 5240 0438	37/1 36	-12 12000		157	107	-7	100	+9	109	180	28	+9	0918	✓
5240 0700	200 45	-22 19000		163	80	-10	70	+8	78	196	110	+33	0950	✓
FUER PLAN BMR 7-12 5240 0256	268 46	23000 -34		178	90	+1	91	+7	98	224	86	+23	1014	✓
	261 50	26000 -4V		189	90	+3	93	+6	99	238	36	+9	1023	✓
5223 0826	260 50	26000 -45		193	132	+12	144	+6	150	220	25	+7	1030	V
5238 0918	-	26000 -45		-	62	-5	57	+5	62	240	32	+8	1038	✓
5233 1135	252 68	26000 -45		-	93	+8	101	+4	105	258	87	+20	1059	✓
5213 1270 IP DFV	248 77	26000 -45		-	126	+20	146	+4	150	224	34	+9	1108	V
5231 1373 TBT PR B	248 77	26000 -45		-	65	-1	64	+3	67	272	43	+9	1118	IP 5313 1319
5245 1348 RP	250 65	26000 -43	180 134	204	47	-8	39	+3	42	272	21	+5	1123	45313 1245E RP 5318 1214E
5255 1340	250 73	26000 -41	110 120	187	331	-24	307	+3	310	160	12	+4½	1126	
5244 1552	-	-		-	28	-11	267	+4	271	118	145	1+14	1261	FORECAST WINDS
5244 0820 ST DESCENT	262 74	-		187	303	-10	243	+6	299	147	52	+21	1302	Alt 340 Temp
5400 0250	V65 48	21000 -37	104 134	195	303	-9	294	+6	300	155	29	+11	1312	Sert 350 25
5345 0500	270 42	2000 -15		165	261	+3	264	+7	271	173	101	+50	1403	
SPOOLSWOLD	270	2000		141	235	+6	241	+9	250	123	147	1+12	1520	
BASE	-	130		132	276	0	+22	+10	286	180	19	+10	1530	

Appendix I

Flak? Or Fighters? Which Is Worse?

Many of the bomber crewmen were asked the question: Was the flak or the fighters more apprehensive to you in your combat flying? Almost to a man they replied — flak!

Sgt. Dean Sommers, ball turret gunner 92nd Bomb Group, 407th Squadron stated:

The flak was worse than the fighters. I was more apprehensive of the flak. The fighters would make a pass and go on until another bunch came along, but the flak was popping and rattling all the time. We were in the Ruhr Valley one mission and had to go to an alternate target. We were flying around with our bomb bay doors open for thirty minutes and the flak was popping all the time. Talk about quiet on the intercom, it was then. You were supposed to keep chatter to a minimum, but several times it had been completely quiet as if it was dead.

Lt. A.O. "Jack" Farrar, pilot, 381st Bomb Group and 2nd Bomb Group:

Flak was a very terrifying thing, you would get those great big puffs of black smoke and if it was close you could see the orange explosion in the center, if you were closer yet, you began to get hits from the flak and you could actually hear it hit the airplane. There is nothing you can do, you stay where you are and fly the best formation you can. The difference with the fighters, you could fight back. Because the number of guns we had in a bomber stream we could give them a pretty good fight, from almost any angle.

Lt. Farrar flew 25 missions with the 381st BG in the 8th Air Force, then he and his whole crew volunteered to go down to the 15th Air Force, where they flew 26 more missions, all without injury to any of them.

1st Lt. Earl Hurd, pilot, 93rd Bomb Group:

Flak? nothing you could do about flak, it comes up and its there, you duck it. I supposed it would take 35 seconds to load, sight and prepare an 88 or 105mm gun to shoot, so we would adjust our course every twenty five seconds. That system made for fewer hits from flak but poorer bombing accuracy. When we got more planes, we quit this. I don't know if it did any good but you got the idea that it worked.

Fighters you could fight with and most of the damage to my plane was from flak, never enough to keep us from getting home. You could see the efficiency of the German fighters decrease as the war went on. At first you could see one in four was a good one, then one in six, then only one in ten, could be considered a good fighter pilot and you could see this as they lost pilots. We shot some down, usually when they were going away or pulling up.

When we first went overseas in the B-24D it lacked the nose turret. It just had a single gun in front and that caused a blind spot that you could not cover with a gun, and if the German fighter came in on that blind spot you could not hit him as you could not bring a gun to bear on him. Then we took the planes over to Ireland and had twin guns put in the nose and that was better but we still had a little blind spot. The Germans found this out and would come in head on, turn on their belly, shoot their guns and pull out.

At altitude you had some fluctuations as you could not fly as good a formation at 20,000 feet as you could down low, so we had some latitude up and down. I would be down, off the wing, I'd see the fighter and when I figured he was coming in I would pull up, or if I was up I would drop down. I don't know if it did any good, but we came through it, so I guess it did.

The B-24 H and J had no blind spots, but the D was a better plane to fly. Attacks from the side or tail made them vulnerable, that is why we flew close formation. That was the best protection we had (next to escorts). If they came from the front, our air speed was 150 to 160 mph and with their 350 to 400 mph it took a sharp pilot to hit you and after the quality of the enemy pilots went down, it was just luck if they did hit you from the front. The first ones were sharp but they got worse as these were killed off.

I think the German pilots claimed more of our planes shot down than we actually had over there. We did not have a lot of planes over there to begin with. So we could not furnish them with enough planes to total up to the kills they claimed.

Other crewmen were pretty well in agreement on the flak vs fighter issue. One 445th Bomb Group gunner, William Brewster, felt the flak was not as apprehensive as the fighters.

At this point the writer would like to state that no effort has been made to edit or change in any way the statements made by all the airmen he has interviewed for this book other than to correct grammatical errors made in speaking. The statements are theirs alone and if they said they shot down x number of E/A that is what is written. Only mission dates have been checked out for accuracy. As in most cases the airmen had diaries written at the time to refresh their memories.

346

Appendix II

The "Prominente" at Coblitz Prison

In Colditz Prison a gradually increasing number of prisoners were gathered into what was called the Prominente — prominent because of personal connections.

One of the members of this group was Lt. John C. Winant, pilot of a 390th Bomb Group B-17 that went down over Munster, Germany, October 10, 1943, who had been brought from an ordinary POW camp in Bavaria. Lt. Winant's father was the American Ambassador to London. Others in this group were a nephew of the Queen of England; a son of British Field Marshall Haig; a son of the Viceroy of India, Michael Alexander; to list a few. When Lt. Winant arrived at the camp he was dressed in light trousers and a loose flying jacket. His hair was close cropped, he was in face, figure and in all else, the Englishman's idea of an American college boy.

At a later time when Germany held less and less control of their own territory, an escape plan was devised with John Winant and four other men being enclosed inside a thick stone wall inside the grounds of Colditz Prison. Stones from an 8-foot thick wall had been removed to permit passage into a tiny chamber about three feet high and six feet long. One small dim light bulb gave them some light.

The arrangement was for one person to sit on a stool provided at the bottom of the shaft, while another sat above him on a wooden plank that had been fixed, not too firmly, athwart the shaft. Two people could lie in the tunnel side by side, while the remaining person sat with head bowed on a lavatory pail that had been installed near the point of entry. It was with misgiving that they listened to the scraping sound of the stone being cemented back by their Dutch cohorts. Positions in this tiny cubby hole were changed at intervals: 1. First recumbent man stood up in shaft. 2. Man on bucket took his place. 3. Second recumbent man sat on bucket. 4. Man on stool in shaft lay down. 5. First recumbent man (now standing in shaft) climbed to shelf in shaft. 6. Man on shelf got down on stool. Repeat this sequence every two hours unless, as often and exasperatingly often occurred, the bucket was wanted out of turn.

Food was slipped to them by the Dutch officer the second night. On the fourth day tapping noises from a distance sounded in the small hole, gradually getting stronger as though someone was pounding on the walls. Very methodically getting closer, suddenly the wall caved in! Machine guns were poked into the hole. The prisoners exited to light amidst a group of

347

grim S.S. troopers.

It was thought a certain Dutchman, who was known to be a German stool pigeon had got wind of the plot and had betrayed it.

The group was transferred to a different POW camp, then was put under the command of Obercruppen Fuhrer Gotlieb Berger. With an S.S. Doctor and several troopers they were driven in a large Buick car to the American headquarters at Innsbruck, thence to freedom once again.

SONG OF THE COTTONTAIL'S
Author Unknown

NOTE: Baksheesh (pronounced "Buckcheese") means EASY.

A mission tomorrow at dawn for us, hurray, hurray
they'll notify next of kin for us, hurray, hurray
With the fifty missions we have to fly,
And odds that we shall bail out or die,
So we'll drink to the baksheesh missions we'll never fly.

A mixture of concrete should never grow wings, hurray, hurray
A B-24 is one of those things, hurray, hurray
It floats through the air with the greatest of ease,
Just like an eggbeater batting the breeze,
So we'll drink to the baksheesh missions we'll never fly.

Our number three prop has run away, hurray, hurray
and our number one turbo has gone to stay, hurray, hurray
With a short in the ball and the nose gun out,
The top turret's jammed and just spinning about,
So we'll drink to the baksheesh missions we'll never fly.

The target's protected by trainer planes, Mc Kamy says,
The flak is feeble and poorly aimed, Mc Kamy says,
But the trainers are Messerschmitt 109's
And the feeble flak holed us three hundred times,
So we'll drink to the baksheesh missions we'll never fly.

And stormy tells us it's clear and blue, hurray, hurray
We find it ten tenths and can't get through, hurray, hurray
What a funny statement the Colonel makes
He's greasing our way to those pearly gates
So we'll drink to the baksheesh missions we'll never fly.

Precision bombing at noon for us, its Kaecker's Day
With a ten second nose and a forty-five tail delay, hurray
We aimed at the harbor, we hit all around
Survivors are feasting on the fish that they found?
So we'll drink to the baksheesh missions we'll never fly.

Our bomb bay doors are gone again, hurray, hurray
The Bombardier toggled them out in the train, hurray, hurray
At twenty four thousand it's forty below,
My A-10 is frozen, my gas is low,
So we'll drink to the baksheesh missions we'll never fly.

We circled the target to steady Jerry's aim hurray, hurray
And when we get back, Major Orris, we'll blame, hurray, hurray
We pick all the towns that have most of the flak
We circle them all on our way coming back,
So we'll drink to the baksheesh missions we'll never fly.

We return to our base and we think we are through, hurray, hurray
But we circle the field for an hour or two, hurray, hurray
You're so damn tired but hell you're alive,
And next morning's mission is scheduled at five,
So we'll drink to the baksheesh missions we'll never fly.

For us next comes the interview list, hurray, hurray
You tell them about the targets you missed, hurray, hurray
You say that you hit it and set it on fire,
The next man says different and makes you a liar,
So we'll drink to the baksheesh missions we'll never fly.

You go to the mess and you're hungry as sin, hurray, hurray
The food is all gone and they won't let you in, hurray, hurray
The ground grippers ate it all up that day,
While you were out there with your hair turning gray,
So we'll drink to the baksheesh missions we'll never fly.

You crawl into your sack to get some rest, hurray, hurray
You can't get to sleep though you try your best, hurray, hurray
The alarm is sounded — the air raid is on,
You have to get up and put on your gun,
So we'll drink to the baksheesh missions we'll never fly.

The 50th mission's the final one, they say, hurray,
They let you go home to catch up with your fun, they say, hurray,
Instead they give you an M.P. tour,
But, take it from me. That's a pile of manure,
So we'll drink to the baksheesh missions we'll never fly.

The B-24's are here to stay, hurray, hurray
They'll plaster them in the 450th way, hurray, hurray
She's short and she's chunky, a queer looking hack,
But she'll take you out there and she'll bring you back,
So we'll drink to the baksheesh missions we'll never fly.

The B-24 rules the land and sea, hurray, hurray
They look like squatting ducks to me, hurray, hurray
But the cotton tail's will have to stay,
And finish the job the 450th way,
So we'll drink to the baksheesh missions we'll never fly.

350

Index of Names

Index of Bomb Groups